STRANGE VERNACULARS

Strange Vernaculars

HOW EIGHTEENTH-CENTURY
SLANG, CANT, PROVINCIAL
LANGUAGES, AND NAUTICAL
JARGON BECAME ENGLISH

Janet Sorensen

PRINCETON UNIVERSITY PRESS
PRINCETON & OXFORD

Copyright © 2017 by Princeton University Press

Published by Princeton University Press,
41 William Street, Princeton, New Jersey 08540

In the United Kingdom: Princeton University Press,
6 Oxford Street, Woodstock, Oxfordshire OX20 1TR

press.princeton.edu

All Rights Reserved

First paperback printing, 2020
Paperback ISBN 978-0-691-21074-2
Cloth ISBN 978-0-691-16902-6

Library of Congress Control Number: 2016955222

British Library Cataloging-in-Publication Data is available

This book has been composed in Miller.

Printed in the United States of America

For Benjamin and Mattias Hoz

CONTENTS

Acknowledgments · ix

INTRODUCTION 1

PART I WANDERING LANGUAGES:
    FROM CANT TO SLANG 25

CHAPTER 1 Reappraising Cant: "Caterpillars" and Slaves 27

CHAPTER 2 Daniel Defoe's Novel Languages 57

CHAPTER 3 John Gay's Overloaded Languages 86

CHAPTER 4 The Gendered Slang of Century's End 106

PART II THE LANGUAGE OF PLACE:
    FROM "LIVING" PROVINCIAL
    LANGUAGES TO THE LANGUAGE
    OF THE DEAD 129

CHAPTER 5 Provincial Languages out of Place 133

CHAPTER 6 "I Do Not Like London or Anything That Is in It": The Provincial Offensive 167

CHAPTER 7 Provincial Languages and a Vernacular out of Time 192

PART III WANDERING IN PLACE:
    MARITIME LANGUAGE 231

CHAPTER 8 Our Tars: Making Maritime Language English 234

Notes · 273
Index · 321

ACKNOWLEDGMENTS

IN THE TOO MANY YEARS it has taken me to complete this book, I have been the fortunate recipient of all manner of support. My editor at Princeton University Press, Anne Savarese, has been steadfastly in my court, at all points both judicious and kind. I thank my lucky stars for her. Katherine Harper provided meticulous and persevering copyediting, for which I am grateful. Ellen Foos and her team at the Press have shepherded the project through production with care and good cheer. To my anonymous Press readers—I wish you could know fully how much your generosity meant to me. To Ian Duncan, Steve Goldsmith, and Roxann Wheeler, who gave me the gift of reading so much of this manuscript and counsel to see it through, I hope you do know.

Institutional assistance allowed me time in the archives and space, figurative and literal, to think and write. I am beholden to the National Endowment for the Humanities, the Indiana University Arts and Humanities Initiative, the University of California at Berkeley Division of Arts and Humanities, the University of California at Berkeley Townsend Center for the Humanities, the Andrew Mellon Foundation, and the Newberry Library for crucial funding. The Departments of English at the University of California at Berkeley and Indiana University and a series of charitable chairs of those departments helped negotiate the time I needed for research.

Whether with provocative questions or insights offered after careful reading of a chapter or chapters of the manuscript, an invitation to share work in a variety of forums or a home shared for thinking, particularly in the frantic period near this book's completion, or even an encouraging word when the too many years were adding up, the following friends and colleagues have helped me in ways they do and perhaps do not know: Srinivas Aravamudan, Oliver Arnold, Frank Banta, Stephen Best, Purnima Bose, Patrick Brantlinger, Marshall Brown, James Bunn, Miranda Burgess, Shannon Chamberlain, Adriana Craciun, Nigel Davey, James Davies, Sheila Davies, Leith Davis, JoEllen Delucia, Daniel Dewispelare, Jonathan Elmer, Mary Favret, Stephanie Foote, Lynn Festa, Penny Fielding, Anne-Lise François, Kevis Goodman, Marjorie Goodman, Kristin Hanson, Simon Joyce, Valerie Kratzer, Celeste Langan, Nigel Leask, David Lieberman, Jessica Ling, Deidre Lynch, Ruth Mack, Susan Manning, Michael McKeon, Richard Nash, Daniel O'Quinn, Joanna Picciotto, Gary Pool, John Richetti, Elisa Salasin, Clifford Siskin, Katie Snyder, Daniel Soto, Susan Walker, William Warner, Nicholas Williams, and Eric Weiner. Whatever contributions this book makes are largely due to their critical acumen and warm encouragement. Any errors and missteps, of course, remain my own.

The staff of the following libraries were enormously helpful: the Lilly Library at Indiana University; the Bancroft Library at the University of California, Berkeley; the Lewis Walpole Library; Newcastle City Library; Newcastle University Philip Robinson Library; the University of Manchester Library; the University of Glasgow University; the National Library of Scotland; National Archives of the United Kingdom; Caird Library and Archive at the National Maritime Museum; the British Library; the University of Chicago Library; and the Newberry Library.

My father, the child of immigrants, was my first introduction to those odd terms in English that seemed both inside and outside of the language. He passed away before seeing this book. Here's my two bits, Dad. My sister, Susan Holt, did some mighty heavy lifting with family duties in Chicago in the final hours of this book, for which I am forever in her debt. My family—mother, aunts, uncles, nieces, and cousins—have always made Chicago a sweet home, my work there, pleasure. My final words, for now, are for my husband and son, Benjamin and Mattias Hoz, who have not only put up patiently with my passion for words, even when it took me away from them, but have provided the physical and emotional sustenance—and comic relief—that allowed me to keep at it.

STRANGE VERNACULARS

Introduction

EIGHTEENTH-CENTURY BRITISH READERS were anxious to learn and master the English that was being standardized throughout the century—so much so that they made grammar books bestsellers and, when they could not afford Samuel Johnson's famous *Dictionary of the English Language* (1755) in its entirety, bought it in serial form, week by week.[1] As deportment and manners, often most immediately discernable in one's language practices, played an increasing role in establishing class status, knowing, speaking, and writing a standard English mattered more.[2] Yet eighteenth-century men and women also exhibited a fascination with words and phrases that fell well outside of polite, improving texts. They thumbed through Francis Grose's popular *Classical Dictionary of the Vulgar Tongue*, where they found words such as "IDIOT POT, the knowledge box, the head" and "RANTIPOLE, a rude, romping boy or girl, also a gadabout dissipated woman."[3] They collected provincial terms, as Joseph Banks's sister did in her neatly written list that includes the entry "Coggle, pebble," and read dialect dialogues in which provincials shouted insults such as "ya blow-monger baarge!"[4] They scooped up William Falconer's dictionary of nautical language and eagerly struggled through his poem *The Shipwreck*, with its many technical terms, such as "topping-lift" and "nittles."[5] If the naughty words excluded from proper print seem far afield from harmless regionalisms and technological jargon, what they share in eighteenth-century print collections and representations is a tantalizing obscurity and an association with the "common people," an intersection *Strange Vernaculars* explores.

Scholars have long discussed the printed texts that helped standardize English, and the relation of these texts to the formation of a British national identity.[6] Less studied have been print representations of languages attributed to the "common people," variously defined—of the street, of dialect-speaking regions, of the workplace—representations that traded in opacity and puzzlement, yet also developed the notion of a national vernacular, adjacent to the developing standard.[7] *Strange Vernaculars* examines the glossaries, novels, poems, plays, and songs that represent often-baffling terms shunned by representations of a standard English—terms that complicate the story we have come to tell about the rise of English and the British nation it helped underwrite.[8] These works, which I call print institutions of the vernacular, reveal how strange and estranged languages, even or especially in their obscurity, came to be claimed as British, making for complex notions of the nation and the strangers who composed it.

That the vernacular is in many ways strange is a less-surprising notion when we remind ourselves that, as Michael Warner has observed, nations are a way of "organizing strangers."[9] The strangers of modernity are not foreign outsiders but, necessarily, those within one's national midst, compatriots. Britain, as James Vernon writes, was "the first to experience the new social condition of modernity, namely living in a society of strangers."[10] While much of the material discussed here falls before what has been called the "great transformation," the free market's erosion of social ties and conversion of society into an assemblage of strangers, and it often takes forms different from those of the Romantic "stranger syndrome" David Simpson has analyzed, it attests to an awareness—and sometimes creation—of strangeness within Britain throughout the eighteenth century.[11] In the Preface to his *Dictionary*, for instance, Samuel Johnson's characterization of the "strangers" responsible for the "transformations"—and estranging—"of a language" shifts, in a few sentences, from foreign merchants to anyone who invades the seclusion of an uncivilized, illiterate tribe: any member, that is, of a modern nation. The reckoning with—and sometimes construction of—diversity in eighteenth-century representations of language allow us to observe the "sense of otherness far more profound and more unsettling than has been previously allowed" within Britain itself, upon which Saree Makdisi has remarked.[12] That sense of otherness, in the form of linguistic obscurity, permeates the printed works instituting a national vernacular in the eighteenth century.

That linguistic otherness can be disquieting, literally so in the printing of strange languages that attempt to reproduce the audible difference of odd words through phonetic intonation, as in the cant phrase "rumbo ken" (a pawn shop) or the provincial scolding expression "'chell baste tha'."[13] Such representations of "noise" make apparent the extent to which language is not a two-way system; there is a third element, the interference or static that must be cancelled out.[14] Indeed, the establishment and exclusion of such noise is the dynamic underwriting one model of communication. The representations of language under study here, however, suggest a model that moves between exclusions and inclusions, with the excluded "noise," sometimes defining community by way of contrast, but those same strange sounds also sometimes seen as making up separate languages and communities that must in turn themselves be incorporated within the nation.

The audible and visual otherness in these texts, then, is also disquieting in the sense of being disturbing, as it represents strange languages increasingly not those of the "outsider" but those of the "common people." While Britons were strangers to each other in many senses—including as immigrants, practitioners of different faiths, followers of divisive political parties, gendered beings—the strangeness I pursue in this book is the strangeness troublingly pressed by the very concept of the "common people." Strange languages, whether those that simply varied from an emerging standard English or those of particular occupations or even those of criminals, came to be ascribed to the "common people" in a kind of vernacularization of these languages. To put this differently, print institutions of the vernacular made room for the "common people" within national culture, but only after representing their language as strange. Criminal cant, a coded language imputed to scheming thieves that slowly transmuted into something akin to our idea of slang in the course of the eighteenth century, is perhaps the best example of this process of vernacularization, making strange terms stranger—and British. The 1725 *New Canting Dictionary* heaps scorn on cant terms such as "BUGHER, a dog," or "FLEECE, to rob," castigating them as particularly pernicious because they are the words of dangerous foreigners, "Gypsies from Bohemia."[15] By 1785, however, Grose's *Classical Dictionary of the Vulgar Tongue* reveled in the strangeness of these terms, yet lauded them as national, a sign of "British freedom of thought and speech, arriving from and privileged by our constitution."[16] Tying languages that defy the norms of standard English—strange languages—to a rhetoric of English liberty, Grose and others make curious, sometimes even inscrutable, words into signs not of underworlds or amusing outliers but of Britishness itself. Today's sense of slang—a lingo trafficked in by inventive, streetwise strangers, but also, intriguingly, part of "our" free, living language—emerges in this period and is in part shaped by this refiguring of criminal cant.

Provincial languages, too (perhaps surprisingly, given their seeming connection to the places of Britain), were presented as strange, outsider tongues, yet on those terms also reclaimed as British. A sixteenth-century commentator described the languages of different regions as those of the "stranger . . . worthie to be derided, and scorned." In the early eighteenth century an instructor in English language was typical in his description of provincial language as "jargon . . . almost unintelligible."[17] Yet by the end of the century Samuel Pegge would esteem provincial words as "free-born," and critics writing on dialect poetry endowed its strangeness with a purity now lost to standard English and with a deep connection to place.[18] The very strangeness of provincial languages also came to seem a guarantor of their historical value, a sign of connection to national ancestors, forebears who had established British liberty. This historicizing basis of revaluation was to make depictions of provincial languages especially important to later national tales and historical fictions as they worked the terrain between the familiar—a wooden spoon, a cup—and the strange provincial terms that named them.

Even the technical speech of mariners, such as "tackle yards" and "bowsprits" (described in one early account as "Greek to a cobbler") shifts in valence over the eighteenth century to become the oddly sentimental language of "our tars" fighting for British freedoms.[19] The texts instituting the vernacular continuously turn strangers into familiars, even as they charge familiars with an enticing strangeness. In his study of lyric obscurity, Daniel Tiffany has pursued "the pleasure of cruising the unknown in a text" that is inherent not simply in elite literary but also in vernacular poetry, in "slang, jargon, or dialect."[20] For Tiffany, the communities such obscurity helps form are "subcultures," some version of "canting crews" (underground bands of criminals), their "canting songs" appearing from the sixteenth century through the present like a "verbal spring ... passing through literary history" (156). *Strange Vernaculars*, alternatively, traces the structures by which eighteenth-century print representations of odd, enigmatic languages tie them not only to "infidels" but to emerging conceptions of the "common people." While this book considers curatorial representations of strange languages—Daniel Defoe representing criminal catchphrases or antiquaries collating provincial terms—it also takes up the writings of provincials who were themselves deploying what they called "dialect," and of mariners salting their poetry and novels with dense sea jargon. Yet it raises skepticism at claims that this writing was that of active subcultures. Instead, it traces how such writers responded to a dominant, vernacularizing discourse that had already positioned them as strange and placed them nationally.

In making them British, many print representations of the obscure languages that came to be associated with various sectors of the "common people" could not be said to be simply moments of clandestine resistance, Tiffany's "infidel" languages. Nor, however, are these print representations only part of a process of homogenizing the strange, what Makdisi calls a "domestic Occidentalism": an ordered, British uniformity that works in tandem with the production (and disciplining) of the strange in colonial Orientalism (10). The print dialogues of provincial languages, published depictions of sailors' jargon, and dictionaries of cant and slang that appeared, as Makdisi notes, alongside dictionaries of Arabic, Persian, and Sanskrit did not merely translate these languages into English but imbued them with a compelling sense of foreignness, even while claiming them as British.

To be sure, readers brought their own proficiency and ignorance regarding diverse languages to the texts representing them, but these texts, especially imaginative works that put these languages in the mouths of narrators and characters, also gave readers cues for how to think about those languages, inviting puzzle-solving pleasure, comic amusement, aesthetic delight, and sentimental affect. Makdisi explores how, in the nineteenth century, "the weaving of more and more people and ultimately the national population into a putatively homogeneous 'we'" took place through translating social difference into universal, recognizable terms (ix). The "we" of eighteenth-century Britain, however, is predicated in part on vernacular languages that are made strange and often remain so, oscillating in their print representations between British and quasi-foreign.[21] The legacy of these representations might be found in the criminal language in *Oliver Twist*, spoken in domestic settings but also starkly dangerous—for the domestic settings are those of criminal gangs. We find it, too, in the sentimental and vaguely sinister quality of provincial language as depicted in such works as Emily Brontë's *Wuthering Heights*, in which the provincial is part of the British landscape, but a troubled part: "'Wuthering,'" Brontë's narrator explains, "being a significant provincial adjective, descriptive of the atmospheric tumult to which its station is exposed in stormy weather."[22]

Such representations are as much about estranging the domestic as they are about representing the strange. They bestow upon the familiar and the low enchanting and sometimes frightening qualities. Crucially, eighteenth-century writing initiated and developed a vision of a porous relationship between the merely "common" and what we might designate as "deviant." Ned Ward's tellingly titled *The London Spy* (1698), for instance, casts familiar London scenes, including coffee houses and taverns and their languages, as secretive sites, available only through furtive peering into strange worlds. Its descriptions of the least-glamorous pockets of London make them shimmer with quasi-gothic mystery, even if only for a moment in an otherwise ribald and humorous text. The "spy" fascinates readers with an illumination of the threshold to Billingsgate—"a gloomy cavern; where, at a distance we saw Lights burning like candles in a Haunted Cave, where Ghosts and Goblins keep their Midnight revels."[23]

This surveillance fiction, observing unfamiliar or defamiliarized worlds, is, as Srinivas Aravamudan has shown, a mode of Enlightenment Orientalism. It is a mode that modulates not only representations of the foreign but also of the domestic, but when directed toward the domestic, it does not always, as Aravamudan argues "collaps[e] into innocuous voyeurism."[24] Instead, British writing about the domestic at times adopts modes that, like Enlightenment Orientalism's treatment of the foreign other, strategically preserve a sense of "contrasting and essential cultural attributes" in their depictions of the common people (64). Captain Bland's *York Spy* offers another compelling image of this startling sense of the strange difference of the otherwise common: "[P]eeping in at a Key-hole, we saw Book-keepers, Journey-men, and Apprentices, and their Taudry Margaretts kicking up their Heels to a Scotch Trump, and looking as . . . Wild, as so many Tarpaulins just Landed from Barbadoes or China."[25] Tinged with the foreign, these "common people" take on otherworldly qualities, a pattern continued throughout the century, perhaps most famously when Robert Burns in "Tam o' Shanter" conferred upon Scots farm-women the supernatural qualities of witches at an unholy Sabbath.

Strange Vernaculars demonstrates that much of the work of estranging and translating the "common" happens at the level of language. Ward's Spy's encounters with common yet odd figures, such as tarpaulins (sailors) and fishwives, are marked by obscure, riddlelike language—various low groups, it seems, are knowable, but also known as different, by the very strangeness of their language. The spy explains how street "Tatterdemalions" he encounters offer to "say the Lords-Prayer backwards, Swear the Compass round, give a new curse to every step in the Monument" (37). A "Drunken Tar" calls out to an inn owner, "you horse tardly spawn of a fresh-water lubber, why don't you . . . induct me to my cabbin that I may belay myself. . . . the devil damn the ratlins" (43). Watermen on the Thames cry out what sounds to the spy like a bemusing question—"Scholars, Scholars, will you have any Whores?"—when they are only asking about "scullers" and "oars" (49). Sometimes the very sounds of the vernacular—the languages of fishmongers, sailors, street musicians, night watchmen—are reduced to mere noise, no longer recognizable as English or even human language but "croaking" (32), "squalling" (33), "bawling" (40) racket in an association of the obscurity of the vernacular with the sounding body that I track across this book.

The Spy, like glossary compilers and dialect poets, authors of criminal fiction and maritime writers, indulges in the pleasure of odd language. He slings his words and phrases like pay-for-view freakish displays—slanglike, then, as the origin of the word "slang" was, at least as George Parker claims, "to exhibit any thing in a fair or market, such as a tall man, or a cow with two heads."[26] In making a novelty of language in order to sell it, commercial print representations of "common language" alienate it in ways not so far removed, perhaps, from the hawkers Ward describes, peddlers who isolate and sing strings of language—as in "Hot Bak'd Wardens" (pears)—to move their wares.[27] On the pages of his book Ward himself represents with italics the sound of the cries: "My ears were so serenaded on every side with . . . the melancholy Ditties of *Hot Bak'd Wardens* and *Pippins*, that had I had as many . . . Ears as Fame, they would have been all confounded, for . . . nothing could I hear but noise."[28] Ward enlists classical allusions to position jocularly those recurring fragments of everyday life embodied in the sounds of hawkers, but that is only one of a series of estrangements. Print mediates voice, which the Spy then recasts as "noise." Crucially, in Ward's description these snippets of peddlers' cries oscillate between "melancholy" and mere "noise," between sentiment and nonmeaning, inclusion and exclusion, in a dynamic that informs institutions of the vernacular throughout the eighteenth century.

The images that comprise the London Cries, of course, singled out sounded language as the distinguishing trait of the hawkers whose images they sold.

Interestingly, it is at the turn of the seventeenth century that particular series of "Cries of London" that featured individual hawkers and their cries began to appear. These "underscored but also promoted . . . the new visibility of commoners," as Sean Shesgreen has shown, and, we might add, audibility, as their cries become their metonyms.[29] In a complex vernacularization of the languages of the street, the prints made "commoners" and their sounded language visible, alluring, and claimable as British in a graphic, reified version of their "cries" available for purchase, and they remain ubiquitous to this day in guesthouses hoping to convey a sense of Britishness. Throughout the century the "Cries" became "increasingly identified as an indigenous genre about a British city and its British inhabitants" (90), in a process that both estranged and familiarized British "commoners" and their languages—and that might serve as a template for the vernacularization of various languages I am describing.

This dual estrangement and familiarization takes place at the level of represented sound: the Cries emphasize the auditory in the captions that reproduce the calls of the peddlers announcing their wares, such as "Ripe Strawberries" or "Golden Pippins." Some Cries were even printed with musical notes.[30] In his adaptation of Jacob Amigoni's print *Golden Pippins*, G. Child amplifies the distinct sound of the apple seller in captioning the image "M'st ye ha some Golden Pippins" in a font as outsized as the shouted call.

Markers of speech—phonetic representations of sound, contractions, apostrophes—take on an unusually formal character here, as both title and caption of the engraving, in an expensive graphic image that also, nonetheless, gestures toward the lowly print ballad form. While, as Sean Shesgreen has noted, Amigone's image suggested a sentimental relationship between viewer and the "commoner," Child's more linguistically based image elicits an erotic one, particularly a low erotics of the street. "She'd Education in the Mint, / When Whores and Thieves did most live in't," the verse lines beneath the image explain, and tell us that Nell "hopes to have . . . her Lilly Breast . . . prest." Significantly, her voice is the charged site of these erotics: "Her trill Voice, we'll think we hear, / Tells you the soundess of her ware"—less pippins in this account than her sexualized body. The voice reveals what the straw cap, barrow of fresh apples, and simple nosegay belie—that the seeming innocent rustic is not what she appears, but is rather shot through with criminal history and illicit sexuality. Like the familiar empty Southwark field on which she stands, which routinely transformed into the site of riotous festivals and a lively September market, the common Nell has a charged other side.

That strange and estranging sense of the language of the "common people" informed the period's generic experimentations, such as its mock pastorals, ballad operas, and early fiction, in ways that we have not yet fully estimated. Consider John Gay's mock-georgic *Trivia*, with its surveying vision of London that nonetheless dramatically defamiliarizes language that is unmistakably English. Both insider and outsider himself, commentator and the object of his

FIGURE 1: Jacob Amigoni, "Golden Pippins," 1739.
Courtesy of the Lewis Walpole Library, Yale University.

commentary, the speaker claims that his wide-ranging depiction of a free "Britannia" is inspired by a nationalist impulse: "My country's love demands the lays" (2). *Trivia*'s peripatetic speaker walks a cityscape that reveals strange scenes, yet promises "not to wander from my native Home" and to avoid the "tempting perils of foreign cities," such as "Paris . . . Where slavery treads the streets in wooden shoes."[31] The speaker is on national turf, yet the cries in particular that make up the poem's vernacular soundscape are alien and alienating, sometimes menacingly so, in part because of a slippage between their singers' shifting identities, sometimes merely common and sometimes criminal. The familiar if unpleasant "shrilling strain" of the ballad singer, for instance, turns out to be a diversion "to aid the labours of the diving Hand," or pickpocket (58); daylight "begging tones" (62), the counterfeit cries of the nighttime thief. In other cases, the cry is infused with the uncanny. A mock epic story within the poem describes an underworld goddess's supernatural aid for an orphan, the gift of a shoeblack's gear, which precipitates as it estranges familiar sound: "His treble voice resounds along the *Meuse* / And *White-hall* echoes, *Clean your Honour's shoes*."[32] A sound naming a service or item for sale shifts from its status as direct object to become the subject, as when the coal-seller disappears in the line "*Small-coal* murmurs in the hoarser throat."[33] The sounded fragment, "small-coal," severed from and supplanting its speaker, takes on a life of its own.

The peculiar disembodiment of the decidedly embodied speech of the cry takes a horrifically literal form in the mock elegy for Doll the apple peddler. She falls through the ice of a frozen Thames, "her Head, chopt off, from her lost shoulders flies: / Pippins she cry'd, but Death her Voice confounds, / And Pip-Pip-Pip along the Ice resounds" (38). To institute the vernacular—established here as recognizable cries connected to the speaking bodies of the "common people"—is also to estrange it, to decouple it from those speaking bodies, to make it obscure or without meaning at all ("pip-pip-pip"), to reduce it to pure, repetitive, but also highly charged sound, even to to confound the human and the inhuman, as indeed all dolls do. Such print evocations of haunting lifelike sound give the lie to the notion that enlightened modernity suffered "hearing loss" and an accompanying disenchantment.[34] Gay's ocular—print—display of acoustic phenomena is characteristic of some institutions of the vernacular, beguiling in its entwinement of odd sight and sound but also unnerving in the brutality associated with their imbrication.

The gruesome violence of Doll's decapitation is matched in its comparison in the next lines to Orpheus's beheading—"So when the *Thracian* Furies *Orpheus* tore, / And left his bleeding Trunk deform'd with Gore / His sever'd head floats down the silver Tide" (38). The voices of the disarticulated Orpheus and Doll continue from beyond death, and yet are transformed and transforming in that crossing: "His yet warm Tongue for his lost consort cry'd; / Eurydice with quiv'ring Voice, he mourn'd / And Heber's Banks Eurydice return'd" (38).

If from that liminal space between two worlds, life and death, Orpheus's voice, ambiguously, causes Heber's Banks to return Eurydice, recalling the former powers of his voice, Doll's voice, while comic in comparison, has its own mesmerizing powers.[35] The resounding "pip-pip-pip" breaks through the barriers between visual print and sound, between low and high or general, between death and life, moving readers as the cry moves between the familiar and the terrifically strange.[36]

Gay was not the only poet to figure the poetic institution of the vernacular as Orphic in its challenge of transforming low, particular language into language that might travel between irreconcilable worlds. In *The Shipwreck*, Falconer describes his efforts to make poetry of the technical argot of the sailor:

> Not more advent'rous was th'attempt to move
> Th'infernal Pow'rs with strains of heavenly love,
> When faithful Orpheus, on the Stygian coast,
> In sacred notes implor'd his consort lost;
> . . .
> Than mine, in ornamental verse to dress
> The harshest sounds mechanic Arts express.[37]

By the time Falconer was writing, in 1762, the comic implications of the comparison had dropped away. There is no humor, only pathos and violence, in his claim that bringing sea language into the mix of British poetry—and into the national vernacular—was an effort as profound and with a result potentially as moving as Orpheus's imploring song.

Similarly, poet Josiah Relph, who also attempted to call up sound on the page through phonetic representation of Cumberland dialect, compares the effect of his provincial spinster's singing to that of Orpheus striking his lyre.[38] The motif of the voice that sounds from beyond the grave is especially apposite when provincial languages of the present were said to be the English of the departed—of long-dead national ancestors. Figuring as Orphic the transmutation of various languages—cries of street hawkers, mariners' shipboard talk, provincial "dialects"—into the vernacular grants those languages an otherworldly quality, their movement to a "general" print space nearly impossible, but the necessity and power of that movement inarguable.

Why necessity? In part because an inclusive model of the polity demands representation of the whole range of society, even the "low" and "mean." This reevaluation of the low was part of a long transition from an aristocratic, exclusive understanding of the body politic to a British national polity based on rhetorics of inclusion and liberty. Moreover, as contemporary political rhetoric heralded Britain as "the most tenacious of liberty among all the civilized nations," the English language itself was viewed as both sign and product of that liberty.[39] John Barrell writes that "continuously related to the idea of the characteristic freedom of the English people is a notion of the 'freedom' of the

English language," a formulation John Locke helped usher in with his theory of both political society and language as contractually based.[40] Barrell and Olivia Smith document the ongoing hostility to vulgar languages—those of trades, of provincial speakers—despite notions of a contractually based English. Nonetheless, representations of such "vulgar" languages did make their way into the press, and occasionally writers linked such appearances to English liberty. Grose, as we have seen, tied the inventiveness of English slang to British freedom. And even before Locke, James Howell had invoked the rhetoric of liberty to describe proverbs as "the peeples [sic] voice / ... Coin'd first, and current made by common choice ... / ... Free-Denisons ... / They can Prescription plead 'gainst King and Crown."[41] The strangeness of the languages of the "common people," foregrounded or even instituted in many texts, was recontained in these claims regarding the inherent British liberty that these languages supposedly indexed. Sometimes this structure of recontainment was significantly supplemented by contrasting free Britons and their language to the unfree: not only continental Europeans, with their dictatorial language academies, but, notably, increasingly racialized Africans, with their even lower pidgin languages, who appeared as slaves owned by those liberty-loving Britons. At other times speakers of the vernacular were themselves figured as beggars and slaves, posing a distinct model of liberty altogether.

The paradoxical representations of outsider languages that are also English might be related to the double duty of the words "common" or "vulgar," which in the eighteenth century shared an overlap in meanings, shuttling between the sense of general and of low, even as both were being defined and codified.[42] Thus, in his *Dictionarium Britannicum* Nathan Bailey defines the term "vulgar" as "common, ordinary, general; also low, base, mean, vile."[43] It is precisely that movement between general and low language that *Strange Vernaculars* investigates, specifically the ways in which readers were invited to think of various strange and low languages as "vernacular," meaning as Bailey defined it "peculiar to the country one lives in or was born in" even as the term could also mean "proper" to that country.[44] Institutions of the vernacular position speakers of "low, base" language among the strangers of the nation, but the notion of the vernacular also makes them familiars, so much so that their low language is the property of the whole country.

The vernacular, then, was the language one possessed by dint of living in a particular place, even if it was at times low. That low element could be alienating—"base" and "vile"—and tantalizingly obscure, making the vernacular at times strange even if it was also one's own. To put this slightly differently, estrangement is inevitable when, as John Guillory puts it, " 'common' language seems to efface social stratification by making language itself the vehicle of a common national identity."[45] While Guillory traces the "literary" language that reinstalls difference at one end of the social spectrum, this book tracks representations of "common" and "low" language that make it a site of common national identity but also differentiate the other end of the social spectrum.

The status of the "low" and its relation to the "general" took various forms in eighteenth-century Britain. During the Civil War, Cavaliers had rallied around traditional, if lowly, popular rites, songs, and other cultural practices as part of their campaign against Puritanism in a political association that lasted into the eighteenth century.[46] Yet by the beginning of the eighteenth century, Joseph Addison's Mr. Spectator repositioned the low as worthy of general appreciation outside of such party political terms. He remarks on his "Delight in hearing the Songs and Fables . . . most in Vogue among the common People" and justifies his pleasure in this demotic fare through an aesthetic capacity shared by all, high and low alike:

> [I]t is impossible that any thing should be universally tasted and approved by a Multitude, tho' they are only the Rabble of a Nation, which hath not in it some peculiar Aptness to please and gratify the Mind of Man. Human Nature is the same in all reasonable Creatures; and whatever falls in with it, will meet with Admirers amongst Readers of all Qualities and Conditions.[47]

Mr. Spectator views approval by the common people as a yardstick for what would—and should—"please and gratify" everyone; only the affected would miss the enjoyment of songs beloved by the "rabble." Addison's is a democratizing vision—it is because "human nature is the same in all reasonable creatures" that the rabble can serve as a gauge.

That the low are close to "nature" is a commonplace of the period, a commonplace not always accompanied by Addison's democratic turn of linking nature to a common "human nature." Instead, the low could also be viewed as rough-natured, deprived of interaction in polite society in which, as Lord Shaftesbury had written, "We polish one another, and rub off our Corners and rough Sides by a sort of *amicable Collision*."[48] For Horace Walpole, their unrefined proximity to nature was what distinguished low domestics from "princes and heroes."[49] For Walpole and others, the low, as "nature," might not have shared a sensibility with the high, yet they were worth representing as part of a social whole. In the second preface to *The Castle of Otranto*, he legitimates his inclusion of the low language of his servant characters: "My rule was nature. However grave, important, or even melancholy, the sensations of the princes and heroes may be, they do not stamp the same affections on their domestics: at least the latter do not, or should not be made to, express their passions in the same dignified tone" (10). Shakespeare, himself undergoing canonization in the period as national "bard," provided one important basis for Walpole's and other British writers' inclusion of low language. Walpole wrote, "The great master of nature, SHAKESPEARE, was the model I copied. Let me ask, if his tragedies of *Hamlet* and *Julius Caesar* would not lose a considerable share of their spirit and wonderful beauties, if the humour of the gravediggers, the fooleries of Polonius, and the clumsy jests of the Roman citizens, were omitted, or vested in heroics? Is not the eloquence of Antony... artificially exalted by the rude bursts of nature from the mouths of their auditors?" (11).

As we see with the turn to Shakespeare, the value of representing the low was increasingly couched in nationalist rhetoric. For Walpole, the British willingness to represent such "nature" distinguished Britons, pitting them against the French and the neoclassical principles they espoused, most notably in Voltaire's attack on Shakespeare. And Addison's more general "human nature" was actually, it turns out, something closer to English nature. One of the "darling songs of the common People," the ballad "Two Children in the Wood," he wrote, is "the delight of most Englishmen."[50] As Bailey's definition of "vernacular," with its sense of a proprietary relation, suggests, it was not so much all of human nature as the "peculiar" character of one's own country that low and general populations might share. Addison's own use of the term (the one Johnson cites in his *Dictionary*) appears in a plea that war reportage draw its military terms not from a foreign, primarily French, lexicon, but from an "English vernacular," making salient the national stakes of the concept.[51]

Oliver Goldsmith went so far as to declare the low the true representative of the particular "genius" of a nation, writing that "in an estimate of the genius of the people, we must look among the sons of unpolished rusticity."[52] This rethinking of the "unpolished" low was to some extent a function of contemporary political economy and its understandings of the "improvements" fostered by commerce, among them a cosmopolitan politeness that effaced national borders with a universal set of refined manners. The belief was that when the market "polished away the barbarism, rudeness, superstition, and enthusiasm of premodern societies," it polished away, too, the very particulars that constitute what writers were coming to understand as a national culture.[53] At that point, as Goldsmith writes, "the polite of every country pretty nearly resemble each other."[54] The impolite, the low, alternatively, retain the "genius of the people," enabling a perception of national culture. As Natalie Zemon Davis has argued, an emerging theory of "primitivism" characterized "the people's customs and speech [as] old, naïve," offering "an ordering principle, and thus a small step toward an anthropological concept of culture."[55]

If all nations flourishing in an age of commerce were subject to polishing homogenization, attention to the low was particularly pressing in Britain because of a political discourse that identified its model of mixed government as distinct from that of other nations. The British polity, according to some, was unique, a model nation that produced a wide range of "manners." As David Hume wrote:

> [T]he ENGLISH government is a mixture of monarchy, aristocracy, and democracy. The people in authority are composed of gentry and merchants. All sects of religion are to be found among them. And the great liberty and independency, which every man enjoys, allows him to dis-

play the manners peculiar to him. Hence the ENGLISH, of any people in the universe, have the least of a national character; unless this very singularity may pass for such.[56]

English national character is to be found in the singularities its mixture produces. An English diversity in manners was understood in some circles to be a source of national strength, as Wolfram Schmidgen has illuminated, explaining that "mixture could explain how the many generated the one and how the one depended on the active and continuous involvement of the many."[57] This revaluation of the many has implications for thinking about the low, for comprehending Britain would mean knowing its breadth of manners, including low languages. George Parker's glossary of "low" terms, the one in which he introduced the word "slang," invokes this model of a mixed nation to legitimate his attentions to the low. He insists that "general discoveries ... with regard to English men go a very little way toward an explanation of a people so various in temper, manners, and behavior as the English," and that studying "low" society and its language is necessary for a full "knowledge of his country."[58]

If, for Hume and others, the "liberty" of the English generated the diverse manners that compose their national character, eighteenth-century nationalist rhetoric increasingly saw liberty itself as the product of a constitution that foregrounded the role of the people.[59] For this reason, as Kathleen Wilson has argued, "populist beliefs and discourses were a crucial plank in the construction of national identities and consciousness," even if most of "the people," of course, did not yet have any real political voice.[60] Within certain political rhetorics, representing "the people" honored both the origins and consequences of British liberty. It is, perhaps, from both of these angles that Britain, as John Barrell writes, saw itself as "a form of polity which enable[d] and demand[ed] consideration of the whole of society," and this led to "a progressive relaxation of the embarrassment at writing or reading about objects, occupations and people regarded at the start of the century as too 'low,' 'minute' or 'mean' to be worthy of literary attention."[61] This might help explain why eighteenth-century imaginative writing was, as Margaret Doody has noted, distinctive in "reproducing colloquial speech," in "catch[ing] verbal manners, the tones and habits of speech appropriate to the character's rank [and] background."[62]

Writing and reading about the "low" and "mean"—be they the "rabble of the nation" or "unpolished rusticity"—are, however, as we have noted, continuously accompanied by a sense of distance and obscurity, vernacular languages as much an alienation as a production of "knowledge of one's country."[63] There is a sense in which movement, travel to remote places to discover the low and common, is crucial to its production. Mr. Spectator, already distanced in the very position of "spectator," arrives at his recognition of the value of the songs of the "common people" through a process of spatial estrangement. He begins his passage on their delighting value by positioning himself as a stranger in a strange land—that it was, "When I travelled" that "I took a particular Delight in hearing the Songs and Fables ... among the common People of the Countries through which I passed."⁶⁴ The songs of the "common people" must be made strange, must be encountered from outside and as foreign, to be revalued and to revalue the "common people" themselves. Similarly, in a separate recounting, it is when Mr. Spectator leaves his urban haunts for "any house in the country" and "pr[ies] into all sorts of writing," that he meets with the "song of the common people" that gives him so much pleasure.⁶⁵

It might be literal outward travels or figurative downward descent into the nefarious underworlds of London, but some form of alienating expanse divides the writer and reader from the vernacular in order to institute it. Parker, for instance, introduces and explains the term "crap-merchant" (meaning hangman) as he regales readers with tales of his daring sojourns to "night-houses" with "doctor Goldsmith," where he heard the term.⁶⁶ Jacques Rancière gets at this sense that the "discovery" of the common people is always a function of establishing distance, of a definitive estrangement. It is a "traveler" who is able to "recognize, in its very foreignness ... the proletariat in person."⁶⁷ Think, too, of eighteenth-century writings' use of the convention of the observing foreigner—Lien Chi Altangi, the Chinese philosopher of Goldsmith's *The Citizen of the World*, or the Indian of Tom Brown's *Amusements Serious and Comical Calculated for the Meridian of London*—to present back to a reading public some version of itself, including vernacular English.⁶⁸

Positioning the diverse, low, and common as "otherworldly" imparts a compelling draw. If language could be a means of attaching readers to the nation, the seeming transparency of an authoritative "official" English, in contrast, might fall short of such affective pull. Standard English might instead be counted among the technologies of abstraction—technologies needed to negotiate a nation of strangers—that might also dialectically produce and revalue the idea of "local" cultures and their concomitant languages.⁶⁹ While cultural nationalism is predicated on the idea and language of the (constructed) particulars of daily life, on the details of customs, on local things found within the horizons of the nation, that language must also possess an esoteric quality. As Viktor Shklovsky has suggestively argued, the alternative, clear prose, "eats away at things, at clothing, at furniture."⁷⁰ One might say the very stuff of life, the very stuff offered up as signs of everyday culture, disappears in the supposedly neutral objectivity of any standard language. Alternatively, strange and estranged languages precipitate those particularities; they "make perception long and 'laborious'" (5). Drawing attention to and reflecting on the strangeness of language and the particulars it names helps crystallize—or, more accurately, produces the sense of—details of life, evoking feelings, perhaps of affiliation, perhaps of desire for the thrillingly proximal but also provocatively obscure.

For Shklovsky, such estrangement is the condition of poetry, which he defines as "impeded, distorted speech." He sees dialect language as a crucial device of that distortion.[71] But the language of English poetry—which, as Guillory points out, did not develop a *Hochsprache*—had little distinction from that found in fiction. And fiction, of course, represents dialect, too: the "coom, coom" (come, come) of *Roderick Random*'s Northern coach driver, or a farmer's use of "nerst" (next) in *Pamela* slow down the reading just as they articulate linguistic particulars of British life (a coach driver telling passengers to get in, a farmer too humble to stand near a fine lady).[72] Eighteenth-century fiction also estranges language in other ways, including the display and explanation of words attributed to the vulgar. Defoe's *Colonel Jack*, for instance, describes the punishment of Jacobite rebels, briefly interrupting the narrative to explain: "transported, *as 'tis vulgarly Express'd*, to the Plantations, *that is to say*, sent to Virginia."[73] Later in the century, Frances Burney's *Evelina*, while clearly warning readers off the ungrammatical English of characters such as the Braughtons, also introduces and explains vernacular terms and phrases. The title character writes, "we have been *a shopping*, as Mrs. Mirvan calls it . . . to buy silks, caps, gauzes" and notes that after the trip, "my hair is so much entangled, *frizzled* they call it."[74] Such moments incorporate and mimic the logic of the period's new vernacular dictionaries and glossaries, isolating and explaining English words, both difficult and common, in a kind of forensic display that draws attention to, slows down, and partly estranges language.

Often the strange languages incorporated into early realist fiction also manage to have an affecting tug. Richardson's *Pamela* conveys the commonness of and readerly accessibility to that most British of heroines in her use of unusual provincialisms, such as "a mort of good things" or "their Clacks run for half an hour."[75] Tobias Smollett's Tom Bowling is "an utter stranger" to the "ways of men in general," and his nautical jargon is utterly strange as well. He comments, unselfconsciously, of his nephew, Roderick Random, "He's new-rigged, i' faith; his cloth don't shake in the wind so much as it wont to do."[76] The peculiarity of these characters' languages, however, is part of what ties readers to them and what registers them as common Britons, an invocation of Britishness via eccentric speech. Roman Jakobson describes the paradoxical sense of this vernacular language, at work, too, in those vernacular aphorisms, proverbs. What supposedly belongs to everyone in the nation, what is common, is also often opaque—considered "personal property," they are, he writes, also "endow[ed] . . . with puzzling vocables, recondite motifs, and inscrutable, challenging allusions."[77]

Although the use of the term "novel" to name the works of fiction in which these words appear might be premature—few authors would embrace the term for their own writing in eighteenth-century Britain—its application in the sense of "novelization" is helpful. Sarah Kareem has discussed the novelization that took place as eighteenth-century fiction adopted techniques to "make the familiar seem strange ... observing common phenomena as if they were rare phenomena," and I would add that such defamiliarization also occurs at the level of language.[78] Kareem sees this fiction as "employ[ing] defamiliarizing devices to produce hyper-attention to the ordinary for aesthetic ... ends," but this concentration on low languages—to common sayings, to argots, to colloquialisms, to provincial speech—can work to different ends, from empirical to erotic. And the aesthetic itself might not be an end so much as a means to institute a vernacular and its attendant cultural politics.

The realist novel's depiction of odd language that is nonetheless English reveals its complex work of imagining the nation not through establishing sameness but by displaying, producing, and consolidating diversity. Eighteenth-century realist fiction renders suggestively unusual an array of vernacular languages that also represent Britishness, assisting readers in their imagining of strangers as familiars, but also of familiars as strangers. Paying attention to representations of strange language that are part and parcel of these works' "realism" might help us answer Srinivas Aravamudan's question, "What if a theory of realism were founded on the pursuit of dissimilitudes rather than the recognition of sameness?" (21). Aravamudan contends that "the *English* novel ideologically recuperates fiction for the nation, thereby becoming the monolingual opposite of what [Mikhail] Bakhtin means by novelistic heteroglossia" (68).[79] As I have been arguing, however, that is only part of the story. When it puts fiction to work to represent the nation, the realist novel must also activate a sense of linguistic difference that it by turns flaunts and assimilates. The novel might not so much "expel" foreignness as redefine and reposition it, highlighting and sometimes producing, if only briefly, a sense of what is strange within the domestic itself. James Buzard phrases this dynamic in particularly helpful terms, writing, "To make the novel's one-making labors *visible*, we have to emphasize the domestic diversities with which it had to contend but also which it had to mobilize—the internal differences that ... had to remain active in any convincing and culturally 'thick' evocation of national unity."[80]

It is tempting to characterize the production and representation of the foreign within the nation as an internalization of colonial otherness, but such a move threatens to diminish the real otherness that also characterizes fellow "nationals." To designate domestic difference as a mere internalization of some truly foreign difference "out there" leaves intact the idea that all Britons, prior to such internalization of the foreign, share a common culture, including a linguistic one. This, of course, is exactly how the myth of nationalism works. Instead, what are internalized, or, more likely, move back and forth between colonial and national locations, are the strategies for representing (and emphasizing) otherness.[81] Taking to heart Aravamudan's caution that there has been too much focus on "the novel's novelty," we might consider the implications of the fact that the English realist novel's representations of domestic otherness are not new but instead borrow from pseudoethnography, that key device of the Oriental Tale.

One result is the complex form of self-representation of diversity that Buzard names "metropolitan autoethnography" (7). He sees this writing as emerging in fiction only in the nineteenth century, yet its "determinedly self-interrupting form" (7) is in evidence in the narrative structure of the presentation of strange language in some eighteenth-century works. These at least anticipate that self-interrupting "pattern of narrative + digression + narrative + digression" (40). This can take the form of narrative asides that pause to offer an odd word and then explain it, dictionary-like. They may be more lengthy digressions, as in the perplexing phonetically spelled epistles meant to convey the dialects of Win Jenkins or Tabitha Bramble in *Humphry Clinker*, passages that slow down the reading as they turn the common language of these letter-writers into riddles. While the other letter writers of *Humphry Clinker*'s epistolary fiction offer straightforward description of the places and manners of Britain, these pose a troubling digression. In one missive Win writes of how "a mischievous mob of colliers, and such promiscuous ribble rabble, that could bare no smut but their own, attacked us ... and called me *hoar* and *painted Issabel*."[82] Buzard argues that in nineteenth-century narrative, "self-interruption" is a means of "safeguarding, salvaging, and recovering cultural territories" (40), the origins of the notion of culture itself. That notion might be emergent in the eighteenth century, however, with the interruptions and slowing down around language in some English novels suggesting an incipient formal strategy of national cultural writing. In its oddness, its wandering in meaning, this style affirms Ian Duncan's identification of "the linguistic homelessness that lies at culture's origins," perhaps especially at those moments attempting to establish "cultural territories."[83]

We might consider, too, the narrator's lexical digressions in *Tom Jones*, as when he interrupts the narrative to explain the phrase "Preservers of the Game":

> This Species of Men, from the great Severity with which they revenge the Death of a Hare ... might be thought to cultivate the same Superstition with the Bannians in India; many of whom, we are told, dedicate their whole Lives to the Preservation and Protection of certain Animals, was it not that our *English* Bannian, while they preserve them from other Enemies, will most unmercifully slaughter whole Horse-loads themselves."[84]

Fielding's quintessentially English novels pause frequently to explain such common English terms. His satirical humor, however, already exposes the linguistic homelessness of the culture. Explaining an English phrase through comparison to "Bannians of India" not only turns to the foreign and imperial but returns to English distinctiveness, the domestic preservers of game far worse than the "Bannians" in their indiscriminate and selfish slaughter of animals. In characteristic fashion, Fielding overloads and complicates any straightforward definition, already suspicious of the claim that the strange—or the nation—might be made fully knowable to all on the same terms. He is one of several writers skeptical, as we shall see, of institutions of the vernacular.

In these and other works of fiction of the period, italics suggest both that the term or phrase is somehow odd, not general, and also often invoke the sense of a spoken voice, the narrator or character quoting another's speech. Such representations, I want to emphasize, are not Bakhtin's heteroglossia, suggesting "a struggle among socio-linguistic points of view."[85] Rather, they are instances of novels' tendency to "organiz[e] heteroglossia", to place, in the sense both of locating and hierarchizing, diverse languages (315). Thus, while eighteenth-century fiction, as Bakhtin notes, "is an encyclopedia of all strata and forms of literary language," more important is its "highly specific treatment of 'common language' . . . the verbal approach to people and things normal for a given sphere of society, as the *going point of view* and the going *value*" (301, italics in original). Bakhtin argues that the fiction writer "objectifies" this common language, and that this objectification is also an instituting of common language, fitting "social diversity of speech types" into specific relations to the "going point of view." We might refer to this process as the institutionalizing of the vernacular. Crucially, this institutionalization does not allow diverse language to remain diverse—they are continuously positioned as they are brought into the fold of a national "common" language through a variety of means that *Strange Vernaculars* analyzes.

As he describes how readers are invited to a sense of distance from or proximity to the languages represented on the page, Bakhtin characterizes this relation not as static but as "to and fro . . . sometimes distant . . . sometimes not" (302). This movement was less a liability and more a part of the mystique and allure of institutions of the vernacular. Even when words underwent intralinguistic translation, either with narrative asides or footnotes or even dictionary definitions, the charm of difference did not always dissipate. As Margaret Doody observes of this period, "the notion of words so unfamiliar as to need explanation had its own appeal. Words were allowed their alien presence, and were not to be simplified back into familiar language."[86] Although Ward's Spy positions himself as illuminating the multiple strange worlds that make up Britain's capital, for instance, he explains those worlds in a language that is itself loaded with distracting, obfuscating language, as when he describes people drinking "sott colored ninny broth" (15). Later in the century, provincial print "dialogues," although they offered glossaries, left some words, such as "whau," undefined.[87] At such moments, many readers were left in the dark, a darkness that continued to inform eighteenth-century representations of vernacular languages, whether in the multimeaning criminal jargon of Gay's *The Beggar's Opera*, Thomas Chatterton's antiquated parlance, or Burns's synthetic thicket of dialect.

Allowing words their alien presence sometimes generates sublime effects. Edmund Burke argued that words, unlike painting, do not raise clear images in the mind, which is what makes them a fitting medium for the sublime, for "In reality, a great clearness helps but little towards affecting the passions."[88] If this is true of language in general, it takes an exaggerated form in obscure language, whether in the crowded figures of Milton's poetry or the opacity of the unfamiliar "low" languages imputed to the vulgar that were becoming part of the vernacular.

Indeed, Burke positions the vulgar as sublime object in his *Philosophical Enquiry*, a text in which, on occasion, as Karen Swann notes, "the vulgar have charisma."[89] For Burke, even those "songs of the common people" that Addison had revalued are a testament to the sublime powers of language and obscurity: "Among the common sort of people . . . their passions are very strongly roused by a fanatic preacher, or by the ballads of Chevy-chase, or the Children in the Wood, and by other little popular poems and tales that are current in that rank of life. . . . poetry, with all its obscurity, has a more general, as well as a more powerful, dominion over the passions, than the other art" (56–57). Such moments of vulgar obscurity make the languages of the vernacular not objects of mastery, to be clarified and familiarized, but sites of seduction. For Burke, however, this is a seduction to be avoided. In his discussion of the songs in which the "common sort of people" take pleasure, their response serves not as Addison's indicator of universal (or national) appreciation but as an elucidating but distancing analogy: as Chevy-chase is to the common people, so elevated poetry is to the elite. In tracing how Burke attempts to ward off the threat of the "vulgar sublime" by insisting on associating the sublime with elevated experience, Swann writes, "if all men are as the vulgar in preferring obscurity to clarity—the implied advice is attach yourself upward" (19).

Institutions of the vernacular, however, invite readers to attach themselves downward, and one of the ways they do so is through generating sublime effects from moments of incomprehension. As Tiffany writes, the sublime might just as plausibly be grounded in "the social misunderstanding of demotic speech" (8), at which point, "instead of reinforcing the traditional association of sublimity and elevation, lyric obscurity may trigger a variation of the sublime associated with the abject: a vernacular sublime" (45). Such an aesthetic experience is another means of negotiating the low-as-strange within national imagining. Burke recognized that obscurity lent itself to certain suspect forms of power, a means of duping the credulous, usually the lower classes who were taken in by, for instance, figures such as the "fanatical preachers" in the quotation above. And these dangers worked in both directions. He had also argued that "all men are as the vulgar in what they do not understand" (57)—that some readers' incomprehension of certain low languages put them into the position of the unknowing vulgar. That relation of unknowing, as I have been arguing, was part of the draw.

Strange Vernaculars also considers how some writers deploy obscurity strategically to exploit those relations of knowingness and credulity at work in the vernacular sublime. Authors from John Collier to Robert Burns use provincial languages in this way. They resist a vernacularization of languages that would locate them in stable geographies of place and class. At their most radical, these writers stage-manage obscurity as a mark of authenticity in order to undermine the very connections between specific place or class and the idea of a language of the "common people" altogether. They expose the idea of a "common people" who make up the nation by detonating the strange, making it multiply meaning, and sometimes just making it up.[90] Their heirs are figures such as John Clare and James Hogg.

The writers under study, whether instituting or questioning the idea of a national vernacular, engage what Ann Wierda Rowland refers to as "strategies of dislocation to locate a culture."[91] Some of this was literal in the dislocations of oceanic maritime empire that brought new ways of valuing and imagining the local. The most dramatic contemplation of the dynamics at the heart of the idea of the vernacular might be William Falconer's *The Shipwreck*. Falconer packs his georgic/epic poem with the technical terms of naval workers, explaining them comprehensively in diagrams and footnotes. The mariners and their material technical world, however, are violently destroyed in a storm at sea, becoming literally subliminal. Just as it seems a specific argot might become the property of all readers, the particulars it calls up disappear in unnavigable depths, reiterating the impossibility of knowing the whole, the enticing promise of the idea of a national vernacular culture. The raging ocean into which they disappear is an apt image for the violent erasure of actual language practices and particular relations involved in instituting the vernacular.[92] It reminds us that if there is anything like vernacular language, its obscurity belies the notion of the common. And it remains unknowable in its sheer multiplicity.

Although not a linguistic study, but rather a study of the cultural work of print representations of "vernacular" language, *Strange Vernaculars* has benefited immensely from a range of historical linguistic studies of the period.[93] From Martyn Wakelin's enumeration of the three main categories of what he calls English "dialect production"—social, regional, and occupational—I take the structural organization of the book.[94] Part One explores the wide body of print representations of language supposedly produced by what Wakelin would call the "social" category—not only subcultures and underground criminal societies, but also merely "low" and "vulgar" social groups. In the eighteenth century, languages once attributed to organized illicit subgroups—"cant"— began to appear in unprecedented collections of vulgar and slang terms, and were even celebrated as a sign of British liberty. I ask how cant, long a symbol of a fallen post-Babel linguistic diversity, its speakers a deep-seated threat to the nation, came to symbolize, in some circles, British freedom. What change in thinking allowed cant and merely vulgar languages to be grouped together? What role did that shift play in the institutionalization of vernacular English? I examine how myths of cant's origins—as the double-tongued language of canny migratory slaves, as a language wandering not only in space but also in meaning—came to figure the mobility and shape-shifting associated with a new modern British subject, for better or worse. Early realist fiction featuring cant-speaking, polyglot protagonists who continuously encounter and explain strange language helped to institute the vernacular through a repeated initiation of its readers into the strange. The shifting narrative point of view in relation to those who speak these languages models fluid readerly attachments. The one site of disattachment, however, is the racialized slave, a disassociation that makes cant-speakers, increasingly conflated with merely vulgar speakers, fully British, free speakers of a national vernacular safely distanced from its imputed origins in slavery and criminality.

There were, of course, skeptics of the idea of a vernacular language that might consolidate the nation through a revaluation of the low and common. I track some of those responses, particularly in the writing of John Gay and Henry Fielding, which burlesques claims of language's ability to organize meaning, structure class, or consolidate the nation. For them, cant undermines British liberty by violating the ancient (linguistic) contract on which liberty is based. And if part of the allure of the new print representations of vernacular was its sometimes riddlelike locutions—both cant and colloquialisms, sometimes represented together, could, after all, be opaque in meaning—these writers seized on that opacity and its tendency to divide rather than consolidate readers and speakers. Cant's proliferative figurative qualities, its innovativeness, might more accurately represent the world than does the contractual standard language—and that is a problem, a point Gay and Fielding emphasize through their texts' linguistic and stylistic layers, which mix folk ballads and high opera, criminal biographies and classical allusions to generate endless and centrifugal meanings. Late-century compilations of slangy vernacular drew from the humor of these burlesque writings but defused the complexity of their language, facetiously tying the inventive wit of the "common people" to the gendered liberties of the freeborn Englishman. In these works, a place is made for vulgar language in the vernacular but only after being firmly located as the language of the low taken up by their well-heeled male counterparts.

Part Two of this book considers shifting representations of "regional" languages, from the foreign-sounding patois of hostile neighbors to the homey terms of sentimentalized compatriots. In this move to characterize provincial languages as quintessentially British, they, unlike ceaselessly adaptable and wandering cant, seem fixed to particular places and past times. Poems, songs, and a new genre, the print dialogue, represent provincial languages as the peculiar tongues of remote rural regions, yet also as part of a composite Britain and its verbal lore. At once designating intimate and mundane particulars of rural life, but also appearing as strange ciphers, provincial languages in these works are filled with outré terms naming humble particulars, technicalities of labor, and crude aspects of the body. The grotesque bodies and oral (mis)pronunciations inhabiting these texts counter a developing understanding of English as a rational, disembodied medium. Naming local particulars, the obscurity of these languages is the guarantee of their authenticity, which also makes for uncanny and gothic effects. As I show, provincial writers themselves, from John Gay to Josiah Relph, Andrew Brice, John Collier, and Ann Wheeler, playfully engaged this poetics of opacity in their representations of supposedly sentimental and familiar, yet also strange, tongues. They assert provincial political virtue but use a concocted, synthetic language to do so, undoing the reassuring ties of place and language even as they seem to reinforce them.

The strangeness of provincial languages derived not only from their distance in space but their remoteness in time. They were also prized—and made part of the vernacular—as the remaining fragments of the language of national forefathers, connected to the liberties they established, and living connections to the now-strange language of such national writers as Chaucer, Spenser, and Shakespeare. Provincial languages thus sometimes became available for sentimental attachment through what I call the anachronization of the vernacular. In this reckoning with estrangement over time, images of spectrality emerge. Provincial writers responded to this anachronization, Burns by offering parodic responses to gothic figurations and Chatterton by producing the effects of anachronism through artificially antiqued language.

Part Three turns to representations of "occupational" language through a consideration of mariners' jargon, tracing how it became part of the British vernacular. I argue throughout the book that mobility, across Britain and further, helped produce and shape notions of the local and the vernacular. In the maritime language of poems, accounts of voyages, seafaring novels, nautical glossaries, and popular naval songs, the locale that oceanic itinerancy generates is that of the ship and its seamen. Works such as William Falconer's hugely popular poem *The Shipwreck* or Tobias Smollett's *Roderick Random* invite sentimental relations between readers and liberty-loving (and liberty-defending) sailors through their technical language. The things they name, however, are often absent or disposed of. Just as low and cant terms become vernacular when their speakers are figured as orphic, and provincialisms become vernacular in their association with the nation's dead, maritime language becomes vernacular when its objects and its speakers are consigned to oblivion. Strange not only in their captivating opacity, the vernaculars instituted in eighteenth-century print were perhaps most strange in the elegiac dynamics upon which they depended, the real and imagined loss they seemed to document.

PART ONE

Wandering Languages

FROM CANT TO SLANG

CANT WAS A WANDERING LANGUAGE. It drifted along with the vagrant crews who supposedly spoke it. It made figurative flights from commonly accepted terms or meanings in English. The 1699 *New Dictionary of the Terms . . . of the Canting Crew* records the departure of the word "Academy," for example, from its original meaning to "a bawdy house" and "Joseph" to "a coat or cloak."[1] Cant even wandered away from itself, its lexicon constantly renewed with the addition of terms. The 1725 *New Canting Academy* adds "Bingo-Mort, a female drunkard" and "Black Mouth, foul malicious railing" to the cant vocabulary, while Francis Grose's 1785 collection inserts "Black Art, The art of picking a lock."[2] Sometimes this strange language lost its verbal meaning altogether. In the early seventeenth century Thomas Dekker described its status as pure sound: "the language of *canting* is a kinde of musicke, and he that in such assemblies can *cant* best, is counted the best Musitian [*sic*]."[3] In the course of the eighteenth century, it wandered in its social meaning, too. At the beginning of the century, lexicographers and writers warned against cant as a coded thieves' language. They drew from publications nearly as old as English print itself that had depicted it as an alien argot shrouding the criminal activities of itinerant hostile bands targeting the good people of England.[4] By 1785, however, alongside these dictionaries appeared Grose's endlessly reproduced *A Classical Dictionary of the Vulgar Tongue*, which classifies cant with the homegrown "vulgar" language of the "common people," representative of Britain's demotic and lively—because uniquely free—national tongue.[5] A wandering language comes to form one basis of the "vulgar" tongue, a strange vernacular of a nation composed (as they all are, after all) of strangers.

The following four chapters track the eighteenth-century's startling reclamation of cant: of terms such as "dudds" (clothes), "pinch" (steal), and "clodhopper" (a ploughman), once believed to be the exclusive and secret language of criminals, as part of the furtively prized vernacular of the British "common people."[6] While Julie Coleman has described the process by which slang words are sometimes incorporated into standard English, the interest in these chapters is specifically representations of the cant language associated with criminals and its odd metamorphosis, in those representations, into a sign of Britishness itself.[7] Why, for instance, do print collections come to situate colloquial terms and proverbs alongside cant terms? What ideas about language and "the people"—particularly notions of a freeborn English people—allowed the wandering language of cant to make itself a home of sorts in the English lexicon? What role did emerging genres, from novels and vernacular dictionaries to comic operas, play in ushering in new ways of imagining a national language? And how did the lingering residue of wandering criminality, of an alien presence in the nation's midst, taint notions of "common" language and the people who spoke it? The following chapters will show cant to be a strange double for a national vernacular more generally, especially in its continuous movement, its wandering between strangeness and familiarity, between opacity and transparency, between being readers' own and not. If, as a number of critics have recently noted, the modern nation demands negotiations with strangers, considering those negotiations at the level of language reveals just how early, and how complex, they were.

CHAPTER ONE

Reappraising Cant

"CATERPILLARS" AND SLAVES

"Caterpillars": Cant and the Threat to the Commonwealth

In the eighteenth century, as realist fiction, vernacular dictionaries, and other print institutions that helped establish a national language took shape, criminal cant terms began to appear alongside a more quotidian if lowly set of terms associated with a common English vernacular. Before examining that shift, it is worth considering pre-eighteenth-century depictions of cant to understand just how unusual that coappearance was and what associations cant brought with it in its eighteenth-century representations. Here I should say that I limit discussion primarily to print representations and the work they do, rather than attempting to make claims about an actual cant language and its speakers. These early works, with their depictions of nefarious, incomprehensible criminals, have much more to tell us about the society that produced those works than about some vague, largely invented criminal element that might or might not have spoken it.[1] Eighteenth-century representations of cant, as we shall see, retained that sense of the language's waywardness, its exciting danger, while folding it into the idea of a vernacular that could familiarize strangers.

The authors of many fifteenth- through seventeenth-century booklets claimed to have discovered a secret language that named the various orders of clandestine miscreants, their crimes, and their methods of "conny-catching" (cheating the unwary, figured as hapless rabbits, or coneys).[2] According to these works, as marginal figures such as rogues, vagabonds, thieves, and prostitutes ranged through the British Isles, they spoke to each other in cant, which one writer referred to as "their native language."[3] In print representations, this imputed language served as their distinguishing trait, and these groups were known as "canting crews."[4] According to Robert Greene's 1592 *Groundworke of Conny-Catching*, their neologisms named not only the illicit, such as "stauling ken," meaning "a house that will receive stolen wares," but also the licit, such as "autem," meaning church, and "nab," meaning head.[5] Similarly, nearly one hundred years later, the list of cant terms included in Richard Head's 1673 *Canting Academy* features not only words related to crime (such as "bite" for "to cheat or cozen" and "fencing cully" for "receiver of stolen goods") but also strange-sounding words for the most common of things and qualities, such as "fambles," meaning "hands," "cove," meaning "a man," and "dimber," meaning "pretty."[6] Print representations depicted this coded language and its unintelligibility to others as the property of a discrete, wandering community with a wholly separate way of life. In such depictions, cant is conditionally intelligible, traded between canters, and strategically excludes "upstanding" Britons.

While terms such as "dimber" and "fambles" pose an alien language, other cant terms such as "bite" (cheat) and "fence" ("a receiver . . . of stolen goods") innovate on English itself, giving new meanings that any speaker willing to think metaphorically might follow ("bite" and the aggression of and pain in being cheated; "fence" in "legitimate" English at this time also meaning to evade a question or to screen or shield). The movement back and forth between alien, unrecognizable words and familiar (if somewhat also defamiliarized) English provides glimmering recognition of the fact that cant and the vernacular might be secret sharers, their proximity increasingly visible in eighteenth-century glossaries that combine riddlelike proverbs and cant terms. The wavering between unknown and familiar language, between non-meaning and meaning, was part of the draw for contemporary readers and would come to characterize, too, vernacular language as at once strange and one's own.

Many sixteenth and seventeenth-century depictions of cant, however, represent it as primarily a strange tongue spoken by isolated, suspect "tribes," its wandering, essentially foreign nature marked by one of its earliest names—"peddlers' French"—its speakers sometimes designated as foreigners—Egyptians.[7] Thomas Dekker holds that "as these people are strange both in names and in their condition, so doe they speake a language called canting which is more strange."[8] Early writers, moreover, believed strict borders between cant and English could and should be maintained. In his print lists of terms, rural sheriff Thomas Harman, who collected, translated, and published cant in the sixteenth century, insists he is "not meaning to English the same" (although that was exactly what he was doing, for "to English" also meant, suggestively, to translate).[9] Decidedly moralistic in his approach, Harman reviles the "unlawful language" of cant and couples it with immoral criminal roving as the language of "pilfering, wiley wandering and . . . lechery."[10] Thomas Dekker calls canters "wild men" and "savages."[11] Canters, these works resolutely declare, are not us, their wandering language not ours. This, despite the fact that, as Jeffrey Knapp has argued, many had seen the Reformation as having made the English themselves wanderers from the unity and stability of the Catholic Church. In this scenario, rogue cant speakers were both a sign and a displacement of England's own disruptions of "traditional notions of community."[12]

For Dekker, however, cant's apparent incoherence is also a lingering reminder of the confusion of Babel and the fallen status of all humans and all languages, a metonym of failure and pernicious linguistic difference that has become part of the condition of language across space. A world in which cant is spoken contrasts the pre-Babel time Dekker describes:

> When all the World was but one Kingdome, all the People in that Kingdome spake but one Language. A man could travel in those dayes neyther by Sea nor land, but he met his Countreymen & none others. Two could not then stand gabling with strange tongues, and conspire together (to his owne face) how to cut a third mans throate[13]

This time offered an ontologically distinct sense of language, for in a post-Babel state, as Daniel Heller-Roazen has put it, "speaking subjects speak only languages, and their basic element is opacity."[14] Post-Babel unintelligibility is a reminder of the history of human sinfulness, pride, and consequent fall. Whether due to national linguistic difference or the difference within a national language between cant and "legitimate" language, it also contains within it the potential for violence. If, in some accounts, writing and the difference between literate and illiterate suggests this—recall the illiterate messenger who unknowingly carries the written orders for his own execution—for Dekker that potential is relocated to linguistic difference itself, in people "gabling with strange tongues" who are conspiring "how to cut a third mans throate." Dekker uses cant as a figure for the violence he sees in a fallen world of linguistic difference. And wandering poses dangerous encounters with strangers and their strange languages.

Dekker and others believed that cant, despite its efficacy for conspiratorial use, was also disordered, a reflection of the chaos of Babel itself. Of the latter, he writes, "Their tongues went . . . yet neyther words nor action were understood. It was a noise of a thousand sounds, and yet the sound of the noise was nothing." This description is resonant with his characterization of cant-speakers, among whom "confusion never dwelt more amongst any creatures," and of their language: "I see not that it is grounded on any certaine rules." (He added that it was marked by "irregularity. . . . [and] within less then foure-scoure yeares not a word of this language was knowen."[15]) Cant was a return to—or reemergence of—the sound without meaning—noise—that was Babel, a language in which tongues go, but "neyther words nor action [are] understood." Richard Head, a hack writing many decades after Harman and Dekker, and less morally outraged by canters than were his predecessors, nonetheless also describes canters' delinquent language as a "speech as confused as the professors thereof are disorderly disposed."[16] In these descriptions, cant is mere "noise," its non-meaning suggesting violence and lawlessness. Such characterizations remind us that language might constitute community through two models, one of similitude and inclusion, in which two speakers share a language, but another of difference and exclusion, in which an excluded third and his or her noise, in this case cant, must exist and must be canceled out (52).[17]

Cant's break between sound and meaning was, in Harman's, Dekker's, and Head's texts, at once morally objectionable and also the basis of its allure. Their works promised revelations, no doubt beguiling readers with the hopes of disclosure of the unknown—seemingly unknowable—and forbidden. Head entices with the pledge of his *Canting Academy, or, the Devils Cabinet Broke Open* to expose "the mysterious and villainous practices of that wicked crew."[18] Here the lingo of these sneaking aliens, rather than conveying no sense, bespeaks edgy lives and outlaw acts hidden in stubbornly locked cabinets and the dark spaces into which a lantern might cast a brief illumination, as described in the quasi-gothic title (and preface) of Dekker's *Lanthorne and Candle-light*. The rhetoric of inscrutability transforms into that of partial revelation in these works, as they hold out the prospect that in their pages lurid and chaotic cant terms, generally hidden from daily life, might be flickeringly exposed. The noise on occasion might be rendered meaningful—but that meaning signals danger.

Like later gothic literature, these early print representations of cant often played on aural sensation and its occulted meaning. Print on the page conjures the aural, either the unclear meaning of strange sounds or possibly malevolent unknown words producing sensation. Dekker's printed cant conjures sound in the reduction of words on the page to acoustic experience, their meaning unknown. The author provides an untranslated list of terms early in his book:

Rufflers.
...
Hookers, *alias* Anglers.
...
Priggers of Prancers.
Palliards.
Fraters.
...
Prigges.
Swadders.[19]

Any English reader could pronounce these sequences of phonemes, but the sounds, for most, would be empty of meaning, though saturated with the ominous connection to conspiring criminals. In Dekker's book these terms then appear in printed rhyme and song lines, where sound—in acoustic patterns—is further emphasized above meaning. Dekker urges his reader to "stay and *heare* a Canter in his owne language" (my emphasis) and offers what he calls "Canting Rithmes": "Enough—with bowsy Cove maund Nace, / Tour the Pa-

> And thefe are their Rankes as they
> ftand in order. *viz.*
>
> Rufflers,
> Vpright-men.
> Hookers, *alias* Anglers,
> Rcagues.
> Wilde Roagues,
> Priggers of Prancers.
> Paillards,
> Fraters,
>
> Prigges.
> Swadders,
> Curtalls.
> Irifh Toyles.
> Swigmen.
> Iarkmen.
> Patricoes,
> Kinchin-Coes.
>
> Abra:

FIGURE 2: From Thomas Dekker, *Lanthorne and Candle-Light* (London, 1608). C.27.b.27, folio 7, verso. The British Library Board.

tring Cove in the Darkeman Case."[20] The lines had appeared years earlier in Robert Copland's *The Hye Way to the Spittal Hous*.[21] Dekker's sense of mystery, however, was not yet a part of that earlier representation. Copland's verse dialogue between a traveler and the porter of a charity house enumerated the various deserving and undeserving poor who sought shelter at the "Spittal Hous," among them the peddler whose language the porter briefly imitates. The language of this supplicant is not especially dangerous or mysterious. And, while Dekker and Harman would later suggest that cant-speakers were so alien as to be from beyond the shores of England, none of the petitioners in Copland's work, worthy and unworthy, are from outside England. His peddler, although a wanderer, poses no threat.[22]

While Copland's porter's surprising ventriloquy of the peddler's cant passes without comment, remaining noise, Dekker's later representation moves into interpretation, challenging readers to construe meaning by consulting his attached glossary. With a disarmingly pedagogic tone he instructs, "now turn to your dictionary"; the meaning of the lines, he notes, "I leave to be construed by him that is desirous to try his skill in the language, which he may use by helpe of the following Dictionary."[23] However, many of the words from the canting rhyme he cites ("maund," "Nace," "Patring") are not to be found there. The fourteen lines of verse offer a tantalizing possibility of meaning, with a few common English words and a couple of inexact matches in the glossary (we find there that "bowse" means "drink" and "Darkeman" "the night"), but the lines hover more in the realm of incomprehensibility. The glossary will not help a reader gloss the phrase "Enough with bowsy Cove maund Nace."

Cant language in this representation functions as a kind of glossolalia, as Michel de Certeau has described it, "a semblance of language" in which "the decomposition of syllables and the combination of elementary sounds ... create an *indefinite* space outside of the jurisdiction of a language."[24] Glossolalia, he writes, occupies a "threshold between muteness and speaking," the coming into being of sound (38); it is a "simulacrum of language ... [that] allows speakers to play out at a distance the real passage from muteness ... to speech" (39). When Dekker discusses Babel and the emergence of linguistic difference and unintelligibility alongside depictions of a meaningless cant, he lingers on this threshold. Cant, seemingly separate from openly meaningful speech, occupies in Dekker's representation dangerous sound that has not yet arrived—and perhaps never will arrive—at meaning. Here, again, is noise that threatens violence.

If such representations of cant emphasize (initially) meaningless sound, highlighting the intermediary space between silence and meaningful speech, they also activate, indeed might be the very condition for the possibility of, interpretation, inciting the assumption, as Certeau puts it, that "*somewhere there must be meaning*" (34, italics in original). These representations of cant, like glossolalia, "excite an unwearying impulse to decrypt" and instigate "efforts to restore vocal delinquency to an order of signifieds" (33). Dekker moves progressively toward a deciphering of cant, a bringing of sound into meaning. In a subsequent section entitled "A Canter in Prose," he eliminates rhymes and verse line breaks, removing the aural component. This, however, is of little help to the modern reader, as the Darkeman couplet cited above now appears as the no-more-meaningful "Stowe you beene cove; and cut benar whiddes." Dekker then half-decrypts this "broken French" in yet a third rendition: "Thus in English"—"Stowe you been cove: hold your peace good fellow, / And cut bena whiddes: and speake better words."[25] He gives the gist of the sentence, a seeming equivalence in the line-by-line breakdown, but does not actually provide a word-by-word translation, even as sounds ("whiddes" for "words") start to take on a recognizable relationship to English. For readers there is a movement, then, back and forth between the promise of intelligibility and ongoing unintelligibility, between dissimilarity and similarity to their own language, between meaningless sound and meaningful word, an enactment of what Certeau refers to as the "reciprocity" that links glossolalia and interpretation, but "in the mode of equivocation" (36).[26] The movement between sound that is not (yet) meaningful and inexact explanation is constantly in play in sixteenth- and seventeenth-century representations of cant language, from songs and poems to dialogues and glossaries. While, as we shall see, eighteenth-century representations aim for fuller explanation, these earlier examples, in their equivocality, stage the unfamiliarity of cant as mysterious and not fully knowable, alerting readers to a fearful strangeness—if also tantalizing erotics—in their midst, where the hovering between meaning and non-meaning poses the possibility of violence.

Critics have commented on how cant's lingering in unmeaning raises not only the specter of danger but also the possibility of aesthetic pleasure. Indeed,

> Lanthorne and candle-light.
> *Canting rithmes.*
>
> ENough--with bowsy Coue maund Nace,
> Tour the Patring Coue in the Darkeman Cafe,
> Docked the Dell, for a Coper meke,
> His wach shall feng a Prounces Nab-chete,
> Cyarum, by Salmon, and thou shalt pek my Iere
> In thy Gan, for my watch it is nace gere,
> For the bene bowse my watch hath a win &c.
>
> This short Lesson I leaue to be construed by him that is desirous to try his skill in the language, which he may do by helpe of the following Dictionary; into which way that he may more redily come, I will translate into English, this broken French that followes in Prose. Two Canters hauing wrangled a while about some idle quarrell, at length growing friends, thus one of them speakes to the other. viz.
>
> *A Canter in prose.*
>
> STowe you beene Cofe: and cut benar whiddes and bing we to Rome vile, to nip a boung: so shall wee haue lowre for the bowsing ken, & when we beng back to the Dewse a vile, we will filch some Duddes off the Ruffmans, or mill the Ken for a lagge of Dudes.
>
> *Thus in English*
>
> Stowe you, beene cofe: hold your peace good fellow,
> And cut benar whiddes: and speake better words.
> And bing we to Rome vile: and goe we to London.
> To nip a boung: to cut a purse.
> So shall we haue lowre: so shall we haue mony.
> For the bowsing Ken, for the Ale-house.
> And when we bing backe: and when we come backe.
> To the Dewse-a-vile: into the Country.
> We will filch some duddes: we will filch some clothes,
> Off the Ruffmans: from the hedges,
> Or mill the Ken: or rob the house,
> For a lagge of Duddes: for a bucke of clothes.
>
> Now

FIGURE 3: From Thomas Dekker, *Lanthorne and Candle-Light* (London, 1608). C.27.b.27, folio 9, verso. The British Library Board.

as Daniel Heller-Roazen notes, the emphasis in print representations of cant on sound and the pause and movement between sound and meaning are shared by poetry.[27] Dekker even describes the "rithmes" canters make as "charmes of Poesie."[28] Daniel Tiffany has analyzed "the phenomenology of lyric obscurity" that both cant and poetry share, describing the person experiencing Copeland's cant as "a sentimental reader who, though unfamiliar with the 'thieves' latin' in which these lines were composed, nevertheless found pleasure in 'reading' such lyrics—without understanding them."[29] The dependence of the aesthetic power on *not understanding* is anti-Orphic, a dynamic that would shift in the eighteenth century, as understanding became the point, even as the toggle between strange and familiar continued to inform the sense of vernacular language itself.

Making use of Friedrich Schiller's description of sentimental poetry, Tiffany has referred to readers' "unavoidably *sentimental*" relation to cant and characterized printed cant song, like sentimental poetry, as "always abstracted, or infused, by its own reflections."[30] He does not consider, however—while I want to insist on—the social and historical specificities of that sentimental relation. Crucially, as Tiffany notes, it is made possible by cant's—and poetry's—obscurity. What obscurity figures, however—who supposedly knows and who does not—and how obscurity might function in shifting understandings of cant (and, in the eighteenth century, of the vernacular, as we shall see) are historically specific, undergoing continual reorganization. Thus, even as its early recorders described cant's "charmes," those charms were unavailable to all. Dekker bestows charming sound, sound without or before meaning of both "poesie" and cant, with "civilizing powers." Canters, however, remain immune to their language's aesthetic affects, untouched by the refining force of the charms of their own poetry: "rithmes . . . those charmes of Poesie which (at the first) made the barbarous tame, and brought them civility, can (upon these savage Monsters) worke no such wonder."[31] Sound fails to tame these "others"— they are so monstrous as to be beyond the powers of poetry's charms, unlike non-canters, who can hear the music of cant and are civilized by its "rithmes."

Incapable of a sentimental relation to cant, canters themselves are positioned as outsiders in many sixteenth- and seventeenth-century texts, without civility, without laws, without aesthetic capacity, beyond society. Speaking a purposefully unintelligible language and unable to access its charms, canters are, in these earlier works, not only beyond the pale of English society, but enemies bent on its destruction. "Rogues and cunning canting gypsies," Dekker writes, "hurt the peace of the kingdom" and are "up in armes against the tranquilitie of the Weale-publicke . . . [with] stratagems."[32] These representations of cant portray it as unlike other linguistic subcultures, its obscurity associated with sheer foreignness and aggression against its host society.[33] This vision extended into the eighteenth century in some works. The 1725 *New Canting Dictionary*'s anonymous compiler attributed the language's introduction to interlopers, "gypsies from Bohemia," who were "nourishers of disorder."[34] In these works, cant and its speakers had a violently antagonistic relationship to "the people" of England.

Cant sounded horrifyingly enthralling, in part because writers portrayed this intriguing, noisy form of communication between moral and geographical outsiders, with its hidden malignant threat, as the language of aliens dangerously near, lodged within the nation. Dekker's cant-speaking "savages" coexist with English readers, "living in an island very temperate, fruitfull, full of a noble nation."[35] In this sense, they might stand in for the figure Michel Serres describes when he writes that "to hold a dialogue is to suppose a third man and to seek to exclude him."[36] This third man is a noisy disruptor, suggestively named in the French phrase *bruites parasites*, meaning both parasite and noise or interference. And so it is, perhaps, less surprising than it might be that canters were figured as parasites, "caterpillars," according to Head; Dekker sternly notes that their "petty enormities are diseases and grand impieties . . . the stabs that go deep into the commonwealth's body."[37] Their use of English, in terms such as "bite" and "fence," could itself be seen as a kind of parasitic poaching, an inhabiting of the native tongue and running interference, making it obscure, as they repurposed it for criminal ends.

These representations of cant as the language used by and comprehensible only to ever-present but largely invisible, parasitic foreign gangs moving within and destroying the nation circumscribed an "outlawed, deviant population, delimit[ing] those who spoke nonstandard English into a distinct and hostile subculture."[38] In these terms, cant and its speakers became the target of exclusion, the "third man" against whom violence is sanctioned to maintain social order.[39] And yet, of course, who or what constitutes that "third man," that noise, fluctuates. Canters, for instance, are understood by each other; in their exchanges it is noncriminal Britons who are the excluded third parties, the "noise" in Serres's formulation.[40] Similarly, distinctions between law-abider and outlaw and between indigenous and alien language were not and could not always be clear in the transforming society of early modern Britain. With mobile populations searching for work, what might constitute familiar Englishness and English language was in a state of constant flux. Vagrancy had long been criminal: from at least the fourteenth century, the state "sought to compel service by the idle, curb movement by agricultural servants and artisanal and manufacturing workers . . . and tie workers to their employers for the duration of their contracts and to their social status for the duration of their lives."[41] The danger of forced itinerancy, however, loomed for many Britons with the enclosure of arable lands. Such conditions foregrounded the sense of England as a nation of strangers, the language of those strangers designated as noise, their relationship to the nation disparaged as parasitic. Denied access to a commons, however, a settled worker might become a vagrant tomorrow, her status changing from law-follower to lawbreaker—just as the laws against vagrancy were becoming stricter.[42]

The third man, the noisy disrupter—and what constituted noise—then, was not stable. For, as dispossessed subjects traversed Britain, their language, transposed into print, might well have wandered into incomprehensibility, imputed with alien, interfering, criminal meaning as it was in Dekker's and Harman's collections. Thus the idea of cant and its hostile speakers worked to demarcate as outsiders men and women who were actually British. In this case, obscurity, arising from forced mobility, was strategically deployed to make alien and criminalize a vagrant population. Thomas Harman, in particular, attempting to order the vagrant languages he encountered, reinscribed words and phrases unusual to him as cant. Julie Coleman has noted that of the 114 cant terms in Harman's glossary, "twenty may be related to terms listed in the *English Dialect Dictionary*" and "around the same number are found in either the *Dictionary of the Older Scottish Tongue* or the *Scottish National Dictionary*."[43] Harman explained that the source of his words was the vagrant population seeking charity from him on his Kent estate, and Coleman points out that "if Harman did compile his list by asking the wandering vagrants who came to his door for unusual words, it is likely that they would sometimes have produced dialect terms and that he would have been most likely to record those that he did not know."[44] Displaced from their homes, people who found themselves outside of the laws of service—the vagrant, the masterless, the idle— were recast as innately and morally adrift, as parasitic, their (newly) mobile language a sign of sheer otherness and even criminality, a vestigial reminder of Babel and the threat of violence in a world of diverse languages.[45]

Contemporary writers characterized cant as a wandering language, meaningless noise in need of ordering, but it seems that what produced or reinforced this idea of cant was imposed wandering and the inevitable moments of incomprehension it engendered. Cant might be a making strange of English itself. Composed of unmeaning sounds at times, and yet at other times drawing from recognizable English terms, if not their meanings, and dependent on the language's grammatical forms, cant underscored the ways in which what was supposedly alien was also, in some strange ways, English. That which seemed alien in print representations of cant language and its speakers, then, might actually be the uncomfortably familiar, redefined as obscure. As Patricia Fumerton has persuasively argued, in this early period cant functioned as a wishful displacement onto a disreputable separate cohort what was in fact an increasingly common experience of imposed movement, of a requisite adaptability, and of encounters with strangeness.

"Having All Things in Common": Early Articulations of Cant and Freedom

At the level of language, this vagrancy-borne obscurity did not always signal threat. As Serres notes, "positions change," and a noise-making stranger might become an "interlocutor" (53). Noise "interrupts at first glance, consolidates when you look again" (14), which suggests that the noise of cant could even help to consolidate the vernacular, in ways we shall now begin to explore. Some early representations of cant, particularly songs and plays, rewrote the new demands to transform oneself as enabling freedom, cant even offering a liberty to defy what Certeau has seen as a "constraint" or "obligation" to make publicly recognizable meaning (31). Such appeals to freedom, linguistic and otherwise, drew from a nationalist rhetoric of England's unique liberty. This rhetoric and its odd link to cant would grow in importance in the eighteenth century, but it is important to first explore its early articulations in the seventeenth.[46]

The songs and plays that celebrate canters and their freedoms mark a shift in tone from the dangerous and mysterious, as seen in Dekker's work, to the comedic. This shift might be related to an ongoing tension David Kazanjian has identified between general notions of "freedom," of British subjects enjoying an "abstract equality"—manifested in descriptions of laborers' freedom from serfdom, from life fixed in one place, from "particular political agricultural and familial identities"—and specific "discursive and material practices of subjection," a reparticularization of those abstractly free figures as "lazy, dirty, undisciplined criminals by draconian legal discursive practices."[47] It is, perhaps, a reflection of this tension when depictions in printed dramas of the period emphasize canters' comedic and low qualities, yet locate and tenuously redeem them within an innovative genre of comic pastoral, with its abstractly free wandering subjects.[48] Cant appeared in these terms in seventeenth-century comic plays as well as in jest books, the stuff of lowbrow amusement. John Fletcher's 1622 *Beggars Bush* and Richard Brome's 1641 *The Jovial Crew* situate the triumphs and defeats of the canting life as the backdrop of their plays—a life of group roving, of scraping by while facing physical duress—depicted with much of the boisterous humor and inconsequence of a drinking song.[49] In these works, cant-speakers are merry-making, itinerant outsiders, as in *The Jovial Crew*, in which a band of vagrants finds temporary accommodation in the barn of the protagonist.

Brome's beggars, enjoyers of "absolute freedom" (I.ii), revel in their own freely created language, which appears in their rowdy songs. Filled with unfamiliar words, these airs, such as one sung by an unnamed beggar, are meant to amuse:

> Here safe in our skipper, let's cly off our Peck,
> And bowse in defiance o' th' Harmanbeck.
> Here's Pannum and Lap, and good Poplars of Yarrum,
> To fill up the Crib and to comfort the Quarron. (II.I.ii)[50]

Later printed editions of the play provide footnotes to translate words, such as "pannum," meaning bread. Sometimes context helps fill in meaning—"defiance" suggests that "Harmanbeck" must be a figure of authority (and means, in fact, a constable). But for most listeners, the cant in this song reduces language to pure sound, the effects of rhyme or assonance trumping verbal meaning. In a kind of verbal liberation for the uninitiated hearer, perhaps akin to the cant-speaking protagonists' freedoms, language ceases to mean—becomes meaningless, pleasurable rhyming sound. And the few words that are clear—"safe," "good," "fill up," as well as the inviting first-person plural—"let's"—connote not danger but good cheer. Here, as Certeau would describe it, cant is not speech but a "fiction of speech," a kind of glossolalia that "plays a role . . . akin to that of laughter" (33).

The transient—and secondary—characters who speak the lines of cant or sing its ditties do not ask to be taken seriously. Rather, they are ciphers—known only by their canting language and footloose ways, inhabiting a comic pastoral idyll. That world is so attractive that in *The Jovial Crew* a responsible steward abandons his staid life for carousing in the countryside with the canting crew every summer. Even the estate-owner's daughters briefly join their ranks (discovering, however, that they are not suited to the rude comforts of this traveling life). In comic pastoral William Empson has found a "double attitude . . . of the complex man to the simple one ('I am in one way better, in another not so good')."[51] If the "complex man" is "better" in terms of an elevated social position, he is "not so good" in his ability to partake in the freedom seemingly available to the vagrant.[52] A blithe and carefree bunch, the jovial crew, while clearly outside of stable, upstanding English social life, present a mythic, if lowly, alternative world of play and freedom.[53] In drawing from pastoral, these plays bequeath to their cant-speakers the sanctioned and harmless wandering of the shepherd and the freedom of those who have nothing to lose. As one cant-speaker in *Beggars Bush* puts it, "Where the Nation live so free, and so merry as do we? / . . . here at liberty we are, / . . . To the fields we are not prest."[54] The canter sings in English, but like their labor-free and unmoored lives, the tribe's private language exhibits a linguistic freedom to stray from the strictures of sanctioned language.[55]

For a small segment of the newly itinerant population, the claims to freedom—at least to a legally sanctioned ability to move—were true. The settlement acts of 1662 and 1697, saw, as Patricia Fumerton notes, "some acceptance of mobility for working men," the legal status of these newly mobile laborers shifting, because of labor needs, to a legitimate one.[56] Even for those newly free to move, however, the emancipatory quality was illusive. As Karl Marx observed, "the historical movement which changes the producers into wage-labourers appears, on the one hand, as their emancipation from serfdom . . . but on the other hand, these newly freed men became sellers of themselves only after they had been robbed of all their own means of production."[57] Their "emancipation" coincided with their loss of property, with their "freedom," their alienation from the means of production.

In many early works, however, propertyless cant-speaking vagrants become a projection of other possible free English selves, posing that seductive movement between alien and familiar increasingly important to representations of cant and its speakers. They are intoxicatingly unrestricted partakers in alternative forms of liberty, in this case one predicated on the complete absence of private property within their community.[58] In *The Jovial Crew*, Hilliard, a young gentleman, says of cant-speaking beggars, "They are the only People, can boast the Benefit of a Free State, in the Full Enjoyment of Liberty, Mirth and Ease; having all things in common" (I.ii). Here, it is those who recognize no private property who enjoy the liberties usually ascribed to the English freeholder. These outsider cant-speakers might be commoners of a sort—but the commons they enjoy are predicated not on a benevolent estate-owner but on the absence of any property-owners among them. Readers, in turn, might enjoy the same liberty by making cant a property held in common. In these plays, cant remains the language of outsiders, yet the rhetoric of freedom and liberty attached to it transforms it into a valuable property in which all English readers might share ownership. What is emerging here is a sense of cant, on the one hand, as representative of alien forces, as *bruit parasite*, and, on the other, as deeply linked to England and to shared claims of language and liberty as a national patrimony.[59]

If, however, as Bryan Reynolds and Lincoln Faller have argued, contemporary readers sometimes identified surreptitiously with the imagined freedoms of the criminal cant-speakers who were the heroes and heroines of these early printed works, this identification was based on characterizations of them as daring, but also scandalous, audacious others located in a realm of pure fantasy.[60] Thus, these works did not position the criminal languages they revealed and reveled in as "of the people," did not yet illuminate parallels between the position of cant and that of vernacular language. This was a movement that would take place tentatively and incompletely in the eighteenth century, to which we shall now turn.

Englishing Cant in the Eighteenth Century

It was, in part, through an appeal to the nation's theatrical history that writers began to consolidate cant with notions of Britishness. Both Alexander Smith's *The History of the Lives of the Most Noted Highway-Men, Foot-Pads, House-Breakers, Shop-Lifts, and Cheats of Both Sexes* (1719), which begins with a canting glossary, and Charles Johnson's derivative *A General History of the Lives and Adventures of the Most Famous Highwaymen, Murderers and Street Robbers* (1734) open with the life of William Shakespeare's Falstaff—no foreign interloper.[61] Commencing their volumes with this erring yet good-spirited character (who resembles, in this regard, the canters of *The Jovial Crew* and *Beggars Bush*) and grounding their histories in a Shakespearean character, just as Shakespeare himself was being enshrined as the nation's "bard," Smith and Johnson bestowed a British genealogy on the generations of criminals they memorialized.[62] While both filled their volumes with, for the most part, profiles of actual men and women, those criminals, often traceable in historical records, exist on a par with this British dramatic character, and, like him, act out a performative fantasy of large living. The cant-speaking criminals found in these pages, it would seem, were not strangers to Britain, not purely malevolent beings speaking an unintelligible language, but a kind of national property.

Criminals, whether real (Jack Sheppard) or imaginary (Macheath), continued to appear as characters on stage in the eighteenth century, most notoriously and popularly, of course, in John Gay's *The Beggar's Opera* (1719), the complex relations to an English vernacular of which I explore in Chapter Three. The eighteenth century, however, saw fewer representations of cant language on the British stage in general. When *The Jovial Crew* and *Beggars Bush* made their way back to the boards as comic operas and in new printed editions, almost all of the cant was deleted.[63] Cant continued to appear in some printed songs in the eighteenth century (including a few in new editions of *The Triumph of Wit*, a collection of entertaining jokes and tales),[64] as well as in novels and glossaries.[65] When we do find dramatic representations, as in Frisky Moll's "Canting Song" in *Harlequin Sheppard* (1724)—a fascinating pantomime that stages repeated escapes from the law by the title character (modeled on Jack Sheppard)—the terms are explained in footnotes. The printed text describes Harlequin's silent gestures, but both play and text end with sound, as it were, in the form of Moll's cant song, the opening lines of which read:

> From Priggs that snaffle the Prancers strong, (1)
>   To you of the *Peter* Lay, (2)
> I Pray now listen a while to my Song,
>   How my *Boman* he hick'd away. (3)
>
> He broke thro' all Rubbs in the Whitt, (4)
>   And chiv'd his Darbies in twain; (5)
> But filing of a Rumbo Ken, (6)
>   My *Boman* is snabbled again. (7)

Footnotes appear at the bottom of the page:

> (1) Gentlemen of the Pad. (2) Those that break Shop-Glasses, or cut Portmanteaus behind Coaches. (3) Her Rogue had got away. (4) *Newgate*, or any other Prison. (5) Saw'd his Chains in two. (6) Robbing a Pawn-broaker's Shop. (7) Taken again.[66]

In its reproduction of odd terms, the song conveys an aural sense (with Moll's added imperative—"listen"), the reader initially confronting a mix of known English and unknown terms, mere sounds. This printed work moves toward the codified translations of the eighteenth century, offering a hybrid of older cant song, printed as broadsheet, and comprehensive cant glossary, with its footnotes. It is the oscillation between that sometimes-threatening,

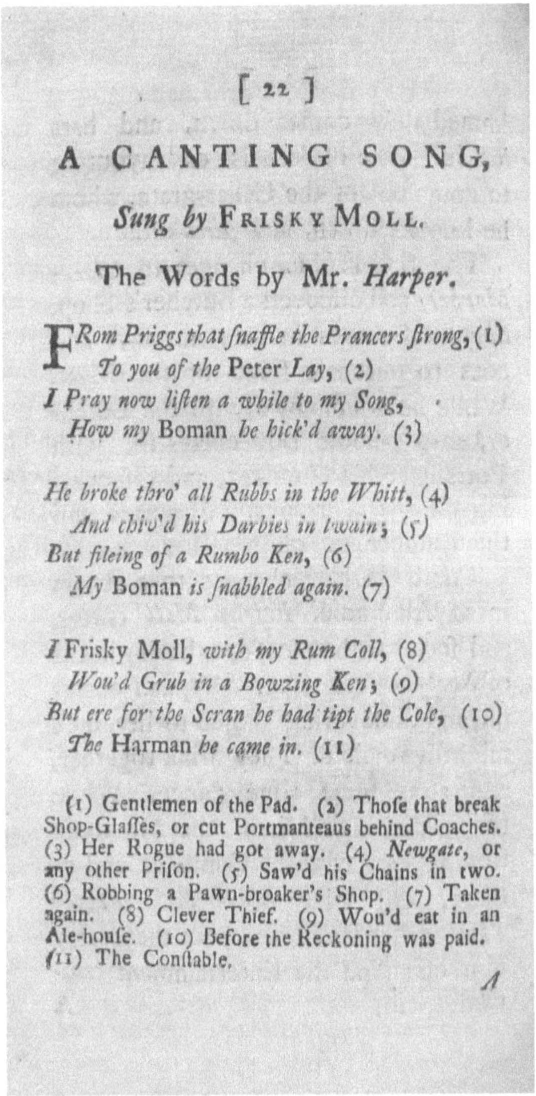

> [22]
>
> ## A CANTING SONG,
>
> Sung by FRISKY MOLL.
>
> The Words by Mr. *Harper.*
>
> FRom *Priggs that snaffle the Prancers strong,* (1)
>   *To you of the* Peter *Lay,* (2)
> *I Pray now listen a while to my Song,*
>   *How my* Boman *be hick'd away.* (3)
>
> *He broke thro' all Rubbs in the Whitt,* (4)
>   *And chiv'd his Darbies in twain;* (5)
> *But fileing of a Rumbo Ken,* (6)
>   *My* Boman *is snabbled again.* (7)
>
> *I* Frisky Moll, *with my Rum Coll,* (8)
>   *Wou'd Grub in a Bowzing Ken;* (9)
> *But ere for the Scran he had tipt the Cole,* (10)
>   *The* Harman *he came in.* (11)
>
> (1) Gentlemen of the Pad. (2) Those that break Shop-Glasses, or cut Portmanteaus behind Coaches. (3) Her Rogue had got away. (4) *Newgate,* or any other Prison. (5) Saw'd his Chains in two. (6) Robbing a Pawn-broaker's Shop. (7) Taken again. (8) Clever Thief. (9) Wou'd eat in an Ale-house. (10) Before the Reckoning was paid. (11) The Constable.

FIGURE 4: From John Thurmond, *Harlequin Sheppard* (1724). Case Y 195.T43. Photo courtesy of the Newberry Library, Chicago.

sometimes-aesthetic quality, between total incomprehensibility and the promise of definition that is key to both representations of cant and, as we shall see, of the vernacular in the eighteenth century.

Sound without meaning, foreignness, wild lawlessness—these aspects of cant recede in the eighteenth century, although they still lurk behind the alphabetized columns and discursive paraphrases that attempt to render cant legible. Sixteenth- and seventeenth-century representations of cant have received a fair amount of scholarly attention, but their eighteenth-century heirs remarkably little, despite the attention that has been paid to criminal literature of the period, including criminal biographies, the Ordinary's Accounts, Sessions notes, plays and novels depicting criminals. Eighteenth-century representations of cant and its important move from song, performance, and only partially explained textual representations to more comprehensive print glossaries and prose fiction that sought to bring meaninglessness to meaning have gone largely unremarked. Perhaps this is because the period's familiar characterization as the "Age of Johnson" has emphasized the language standardization that took place in its dictionaries, grammars, elocution lectures, and polite writing more generally. From that angle, the language of Britain appears to have settled. If men and women still found themselves on the road and using language at a distance from the standard, the meanings of words still taking flight, ongoing vagrancy laws and widespread interest in and publications of "proper" English attempted to keep such movement within increasingly tighter bounds, disavowing the basis of the common tongue in wandering languages.[67] And yet, in the eighteenth century cant itself came to be seen as English, both in the national and linguistic sense. As I explore in the following sections, the declining fortunes of certain once-common English words, the increasing acknowledgment of the obscurity of colloquialisms, and the link of cant to a rhetoric of English freedom helped make cant English in the minds of writers and readers.

"The Dregs of the People": Cant and the Common Tongue in the Eighteenth Century

Popular glossaries and other print representations of cant abounded in the eighteenth century.[68] Cant continued to fascinate the reading public as scintillatingly other, but was also becoming, as Alexander Smith's British pedigree of cant-speakers suggests, more closely associated with the national vernacular language that was itself being institutionalized at this time. The popularity of cant dictionaries is somewhat surprising given the century's alignment of linguistic standardization with both moral probity and national cohesion. Strangely enough, cant's wandering into a sense of Englishness as the century moved on might well have had something to do with the period's well-known obsession with linguistic propriety and its attempts to weed out even colloquial terms and phrases. Familiar words, turns of phrase, and even grammatical structures often found themselves, with cant, on the wrong side of what constituted proper English—all becoming the languages of strangers within the paradigm of that standard.

The institutionalization of a standard English relegated once-acceptable terms to a degraded status not far removed from the "unlawful language" of cant, a policing that sometimes had the odd effect of making colloquial terms and phrases strange.[69] It was not always so. Joan Platt writes of the "much simpler" language system of the early eighteenth century, when "the most selective form of speech was that used by scholars; most other urban speakers used a less fastidious type of speech, although a class of criminals and vagabonds existed in London who spoke a slang idiom of their own."[70] In other words, as late as the early eighteenth century, a scholarly refined speech existed at one pole and cant at the opposite, presenting two reified languages of high and low, but most people spoke a not especially refined language somewhere in the middle, and their relatively coarse speech was not particularly marked as low.

For this reason Jonathan Swift, in his 1719 recommendations on sermon style, could write dismissively of "Young divines" who, when they wanted to distance themselves from university learning, did not turn to a less-refined English, for that language was not recognized as the polar opposite of scholarly speech. Instead, they turned to cant. He notes that "to shew that their studies have not been confined to sciences, or ancient authors, [they] will talk in the style of a gaming ordinary, and White Friars, when I suppose the hearers can be little edified by the terms palming, shuffling, biting, bamboozling and the like, if they have not been sometimes conversant among pick-pockets and sharpers."[71] Crucial here is the fact that merely colloquial or even indelicate language does not yet seem capable of announcing nonelevated status, low obscurity, or reprehensibility. Cant, with its patently low status, its association with the desperate debtors of White Friars and "bamboozling" criminals of gaming houses, must do that work. And yet, the unlearned with whom the young divines attempt to communicate have little hopes of being "edified," as cant is not their language—it is simply the type of speech the latter use to try to distinguish themselves from the "sciences or ancient authors."[72] They trade the obscurity of learning for the obscurity of criminal language in their attempt to invoke an idiom that would indicate movement down the social scale.

Conversely, as the eighteenth century progressed, and as men and women aiming for refinement became more cautious about their language, the texts they followed began to relegate an increasing number of once-acceptable terms and grammatical forms to the status of a reprobate language, oddly akin, at least rhetorically, to that of criminals and vagabonds.[73] The condemnation of once-common language as "specific and subordinate" is a linguistic version of something that Raymond Williams noted: that the senses of "common" and "vulgar" shifted and shrank, over the seventeenth and eighteenth centuries, from applying to the more capacious "a whole group" to the quite restricted "a specific and subordinate group."[74] We can track this shift in the term "vulgarism," which in the seventeenth century had simply meant "common or ordinary expressions" but by the eighteenth was defined as "colloquialism(s) of low or unrefined character," terms to be avoided.[75] In this linguistic scenario, impolite and even merely "common" language of the whole group began to take on a marked quality that distinguished it, like cant, as low in relation to a new distinctive standard. By the second half of the century Swift's young divines would no longer have to speak cant to distance themselves from elevated academic language: many once-"common" language forms, in the sense of common to all, were now common, in the sense of low, and characterized as linguistic infractions.

Eighteenth-century critics, then, recategorized myriad terms and proverbial phrases as low and vulgar. Susie Tucker has tracked how *The Critical Review* consigned once-acceptable terms to the rubbish heap of low language, even if those terms had appeared in the works of respected authors. As early as Volume 3 (1756) its writers claimed that only the vulgar used the term "dumbfound." More than twenty years later, proverbial phrases such as "death is hard by" and "O that I should come to this" came in for similar attack.[76] *The Critical Review* also deemed vulgar the expression "Undo this button," despite its being uttered by Shakespeare's King Lear.[77] Bishop Robert Lowth's influential *Introduction to Grammar* was characteristic of this new approach to language, as it criticized some language of even the "best authors" as "irregular . . . capricious," referring to certain grammatical constructions as "hazardous and hardly justifiable," and condemning once-acceptable forms as "inexcusable."[78] Lowth equated "vulgar" with "improper" language, locating common terms and forms outside of proper English and low on the social scale.[79]

Samuel Johnson, too, had participated in this reallocation of once-"common" words to low "common" status: in his final *Rambler* he identified as one of its lofty endeavors "to refine our language to grammatical purity and to clear it from colloquial barbarisms."[80] Terms such as "to bill . . . to publish by advertisement," "bishop . . . a mixture of wine, oranges and sugar," and "brogue . . . a kind of shoe" are labeled pejoratively in his 1755 *Dictionary* as "cant"; the entry for "cant" lists not only "a corrupt dialect used by beggars and vagabonds" but also "a particular form of speaking peculiar to some certain class or body of men."[81] Johnson did end up including a good number of "particular forms of speaking" in his *Dictionary*, colloquialisms such as names for varieties of produce ("sea pea," "pig pea"), and the terms "pawed" for "broad footed," "penny, Proverbially a small sum," and "piping [this word is only used in low language], Hot. Boiling." Indeed, without such particular terms and colloquialisms, it is difficult to imagine what is left of, what gives texture to, a national language. And yet, including them was more concession than aim, for such terms, in their particularity, worked against a polite "general" diction. This censure suggests that in one way "irregular" language—especially language deemed "low"—was coming to occupy the symbolic linguistic space that cant once did, as a language within, and not entirely welcome within, English.

The Lure of the Obscure: Print Collections of Cant, Colloquialisms, and Proverbs

Low or vulgar expressions sometimes, too, share cant's sense of fascinating opacity. The invitation to imagine these terms as infused with the allure of cant was formalized in part through their surprising coappearance in eighteenth-century cant dictionaries. At the same time that standard grammars and dictionaries were excluding once-acceptable terms, works such as the 1725 *New Canting Dictionary* began to include some of those now-low terms, cataloguing not simply coded cant words such as "bite" or "dimber" but vulgar and colloquial expressions such as "fat" to mean "rich," or "*feather-bed-lane*," to mean "any bad road, but particularly that betwixt Dunchurch and Daintry," or "*To feather his nest*, to inrich [sic] himself by indirect means, or at the expense of others."[82] If cant had been a strange, at-once threatening and yet also "charming" language circulating in readers' midst, then estranged colloquial and proverbial languages, their defamiliarization drawing attention to their figurative and riddlelike aspects, might answer to the same characterizations. Such mingling of the colloquial and proverbial with cant on the printed page alerted contemporary readers to the captivating strangeness of their own language. "Feather-bed-lane" was a term at once odd and wittily figurative, familiar.

As early as B. E.'s 1699 *A New Dictionary of the Terms Ancient and Modern of the Canting Crew in its Several Tribes of Gypsies, Beggers* [sic], *Thieves, Cheats &C, with an Addition of some Proverbs, Phrases, Figurative Speeches &C*, there was a shift to viewing cant and colloquial language as suggestively proximal, even in its title, which mixes cant terms and proverbs in one list. A significant work both because it was the first alphabetical freestanding dictionary of cant—unlike its predecessors, it was not a brief appendix to a larger work on the "canting crews"—and because it formed the basis for subsequent cant dictionaries of the eighteenth century, the *New Dictionary* is remarkable in its promiscuous combination of cant and colloquial terms. Allon White notes that "many of the dictionaries of cant are notable for their strange mishmash of contents and this is not surprising given the radical heterogeneity and elusiveness of the low language," but, as I am arguing, the idea of "low language" itself is a moving target, undergoing important transformations at the beginning of the eighteenth century.[83] B. E.'s collection contains a range of terms earlier cant glossaries had considered to be criminal, including the entire contents of Head's *The Canting Academy*, such as "*Anglers*, cheats, petty thieves, who have a stick with a hook at the end, with which they pluck things out of windows, grates." It lists alongside such cant terms, however, colloquial names for aspects of everyday life, such as "*Dead-men*, empty Pots or bottles on a Tavern table," or "*Chuck farthing*, a Parish-Clerk (in the Satyr against Hypocrites) also a Play among Boies [*sic*]" (one recalls the game stopped mid-play as Yorick appears in an early episode of *Tristram Shandy*), or "*Damask the Claret*, Put a roasted Orange slasht smoking hot in it." "Trumpery," too, appears, defined as "old Ware, old Stuff, as old Hatts [*sic*], Boots, Shoes" and illustrated by a rhyming proverb: "For want of good Company, welcome Trumpery." The term returned, in some sense, to strange sound in the rhythm of the spoken adage that includes it.

This intermingling of cant, colloquial terms, and proverbs continues in later publications. Cant and vernacular forms began to merge in other print compendia as an increasing number of books included glossaries of cant alongside collections of jokes, popular tales, proverbs, and sayings. The *New Canting Dictionary* of 1725 includes colloquialisms and proverbs, and *Bacchus and Venus*, published in 1737 and often reprinted, includes a collection of cant songs and a cant glossary "Intersper'd with Proverbs, Sayings, Figurative Speeches, &c.," as the title page promises.[84] Policed out of acceptable polite English, colloquial words and phrases dropped downwards in social status, accounting in part, perhaps, for their appearance at this time alongside cant terms. That juxtaposition, however, makes the captivating strangeness of proverbs and colloquialisms more apparent. Although it is intuitive to think of cant as divided from colloquial language, not least in cant's pointed obscurity, the colloquial terms in these dictionaries remind readers of their often esoteric qualities. Some colloquialisms, like cant, might hover for many a reader between the etymological sense of cant as song, pure sound (perhaps familiar sound, without signification), and their "Englished" sense, deciphered into surprisingly familiar meanings. The *New Dictionary* notes that the term "keffal" (a likely mistranscription of the French *cheval*) means simply "a horse." Other familiar terms can be defamiliarized: the combination "Pea-goose," for example, is defined in B. E.'s collection as "a silly creature."

The movement between familiarity and obscurity is less surprising when we consider phrases such as "another kettle of fish," familiar and repeated, yet not clear in literal meaning. Roman Jakobson has described the paradox of proverbs and colloquial language: that users of proverbs and colloquialisms "deal with [them] ... as personal property," yet these terms and phrases keep their users under a "spell, Endow[ed] ... with puzzling vocables, recondite motifs, and inscrutable, challenging allusions."[85] Terms opaque to readers, terms that might cast readers under a spell—such had been the understanding of cant. In locating cant terms alongside colloquialisms, however, B. E.'s and later expansive collections foreground these surprising parallels. Both cant and the colloquial are obscure languages in need of ordering and explanation, charming in their opacity, a reader's property and not. Thus terms found in B. E.'s *New Dictionary* such as "*chittiface*, a little puny child," or "*chounter*, to talk pertly and sometimes angrily," or "*Pateepan*, a little pye or small pasty," at once name aspects of everyday life and yet appear in a glossary of unusual words.

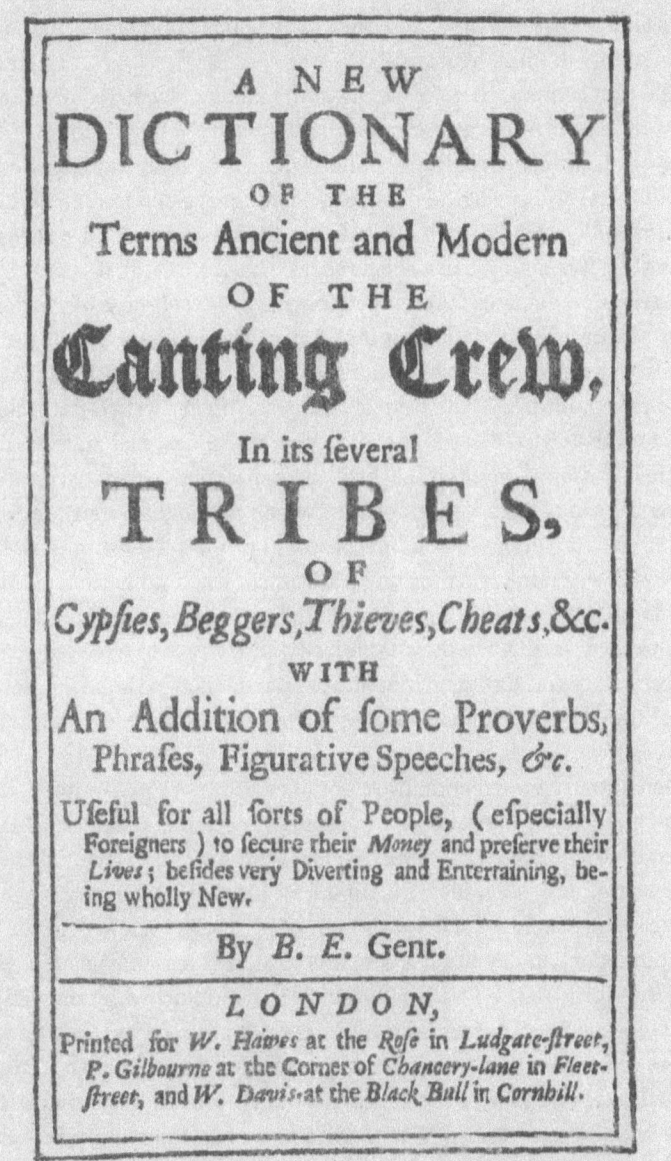

FIGURE 5: Title page, B.E., *New Dictionary* (London, 1699). PE3726.B21699. Courtesy of the Bancroft Library, University of California, Berkeley.

For whom were these known and meaningful terms? For whom were they unfamiliar and odd, only to become homey when explained and recognized? Some of B. E.'s terms are figurative riddles, not unlike those found in cant expressions, such as "batchelor's son," meaning bastard, and "cow-hearted," meaning fearful. These share the wit of cant terms such as "bite" (cheat), noted earlier. They are the language not only of others but also of English, strange expressions whose meaning, nonetheless, depends upon knowledge of English and an ability to think figuratively.

Like cant terms such as "prog," meaning meat, or "scowre," meaning to run away, familiar proverbs also shimmer with opacity.[86] On his tours of England the seventeenth-century scholar of natural history John Ray collected, alongside botanical and geological data, English language and lore. In his *Compleat Collection of English Proverbs*, he includes findings such as "After cheese comes nothing" or "Six awls make a shoemaker."[87] Lest we think it is only historical or geographical distance that renders some proverbs obscure for readers in our own moment, it is worth noting that Ray himself frequently felt the need to "translate" expressions for his readers, as in "every cake hath its make, but a scrape cake hath two," which he explains as: "Every wench hath her sweetheart, and the dirtiest commonly the most: make, i.e., match, fellow."[88] Here we find Jakobson's "puzzling vocables, recondite motifs, and inscrutable, challenging allusions" in a verbal form of which all English-speakers were also being invited to think as a kind of "personal property"—Ray and B. E. designate their collections of words and phrases as "English" in their titles. Oddly, it might be their very inscrutability that allows proverbs to function as common property. Reified by their familiarity, they cease to have connections to their referents, and this detachment from particulars in time and space is also what allows them to circulate on a wide scale, not claimable by any one era or region.

Even authoritative dictionaries, not of cant but of English itself, work this tension between opacity and clarity, strange and familiar. Nathan Bailey's *An Universal Etymological Dictionary* (1721) addresses "persons of a small share of literature," but includes colloquial and proverbial language, words that might have been among the few those readers already knew.[89] In the subtitle of his dictionary, Bailey situates cant amongst or at least adjacent to "the Generality of Words in the English Tongue."[90] Distinguished by the designation "C" (and sequestered in later editions in a separate appendix), cant nonetheless appears alongside the rest of his comprehensive list of English terms in this best-selling dictionary of the century. Bailey's broadly inclusive lexicon includes with its cant terms, "Words and Phrases us'd in our Ancient Statutes, Charters, Writs, Old Records . . . and the proper names of Men, Women, and Remarkable Places in Great Britain: Also the Dialects of our different Counties" and "our most Common Proverbs." The repeated proprietary "our" suggests an attitude toward cant that is again different from the disavowal of the earlier cant lexicons. Like B. E., Bailey puts what was once the language of "outsiders" in a volume that also collects "our common proverbs," those verbal adages that represent a repository of, critically, "common" wisdom. The diverse languages of this collection comprise a vernacular that includes cant and proverbs, official English and colloquialisms, all complexly making up the "English tongue." If the "our" makes this language a kind of property—not only intimate vernacular but also strange cant as a shared patrimony—then it changes the status of both as they appear alongside each other as the readers' own—but oddly in need of collection and explanation.

What is especially interesting about the dictionary format is its moving back and forth, presenting to readers what they thought intimate ("our ancient statutes," "our different counties") as alien, and rendering the unfamiliar known. To read B. E.'s *New Dictionary* or Bailey's *Dictionary* is to move through a gallimaufry of terms from different regions, occupations, and domestic customs that are at once quotidian and peculiar. One finds in Bailey, for instance, particular and sometimes humble terms such as "Baufrey, a beam or foist," "Stag-Evil, a disease. A palsey in the jaws," "Thirdendeal, a liquid measure containing three pints," and "Thokes, fish with broken bellies." Dictionaries of "our" language, as well as collections of "English proverbs," however, also present as intimate language that could be, in fact, strange and unknown.[91] When Ray included "English" sayings, such as "As tender as a parson's leman (or sweetheart)," he felt he must translate for his readers not only the word "leman," but also the expression "a parson's leman" as "i.e. a whore."[92]

The proverbs and colloquial expressions collected in these dictionaries are "English" in their titles (and in the imaginations of many), but like cant, they can also be opaque in meaning, encryptions that depend upon obscure meanings or the poetic techniques of metonymy and metaphor. Cant, then, shares something of the semiotic logic of the proverb and the colloquial and vernacular more generally—a surprising sense of opacity, sounds or written signs without clear meaning, a kind of glossolalia that incites questions about meaning, and, in the case of some colloquialisms and proverbs, a presenting back to readers what they thought intimate and familiar as new and puzzling. Both cant and colloquial languages draw from and depend upon a familiar native language but also estrange it or illuminate its points of strangeness. If this is a strangeness buried within the common language, it is also a reminder that all nations and national languages necessarily harbor strangers not unlike the cant-speakers with whom we opened the chapter. This figure of the mysterious outsider continues to haunt the sense of vernacular language, even as various texts come to represent strange languages as English.

In eighteenth-century Britain language was becoming critical to the imagining of strangers—whether by way of class, education, region, or religion—as national compatriots via standardized dictionaries, grammars, even poems and fiction that invited readers to think of themselves as part of a shared language community.[93] As we are seeing, however, print representations of cant and colloquial languages were also often poignant reminders that, as Michael Warner has put it, "in modern forms strangerhood is the necessary medium of commonality."[94] Strangers and strangeness are givens in the equation of nation-making, and these textual encounters with language, in which one encounters strangeness and overcomes it, only to be reminded of linguistic strangeness all over again, mimic and dramatize, even as they attempt to facilitate, that process of national imagining.

Both cant and colloquial/proverbial languages moved between familiar and alien, yet I do not want to overstate the extent to which eighteenth-century cant dictionaries invited a proprietary sense of familiarity with their lexicon. Some of them, not surprisingly, continued to adopt the same distancing relationship to the languages within their pages as had earlier cant dictionaries, even if they now included the occasional colloquialism and proverb. Some maintained a moral tone, such as the 1725 *New Canting Dictionary*, which impugned cant, as well as the colloquialisms that appeared alongside it in its pages, as "confused jargon, [its] practitioners the chief fathers and nourishers of disorder."[95] This work, as well as word-for-word reproductions of the lexicons of Harman and Head in collections of light literature such as *Bacchus and Venus* (1737), and glossaries appended to criminal biographies and accounts of street robberies, continued to juxtapose cant and its users against the stable and worthy people of Britain.[96] Some even turned the screw in their depictions of the moral turpitude of cant-speakers depicting them as irrevocably, brazenly criminal. While B. E.'s *New Dictionary* had defined "Alsatians," for instance, as simply "the inhabitants, such as, broken gentlemen, tradesmen, &c, lurking there" (that is, in debtors in "White Friers" [*sic*] or "the mint in Southwark"), the *New Canting Dictionary* adds the judgmental observation that they are "extravagant spendthrifts . . . in defiance to their creditors and the laws."[97] To "Abram-men," which B. E. defines as "the seventeenth order of the canting-crew. Beggers antickly trick'd up with ribbands, red tape, foxtails, rags, &c pretending madness to palliate their thefts of poultrey, linnen, &c," the *New Canting Dictionary* adds "shabby beggars" and "itinerant hedge robbers and strippers of children"—making them much more unquestionably reprehensible."[98] The term "fambles," which Head's *Canting Academy* defines as "hands," appears in the *New Canting Dictionary* as ill-gotten lucre, goods likely to be stolen—"Famble cheats, gold rings or gloves: and Fambles, rings; the hands are also called fambles."

Such representations might well have contributed to a sense of a stable national identity by making visible, by contrast, the "confused" and depraved language of its putative outsiders—the "noise" that must be cancelled out for meaning-making in English. Yet as we are beginning to see, cant collections, as they swept up common terms into their dragnet—"bilk," a term from the game of cribbage that now also meant "to cheat," appears in the *New Canting Dictionary* (*NCD*), as do "booty" and "bauble," not particularly criminal words of at least Middle English origins—blurred the boundaries of what was outside and what inside of English, what comfortingly familiar and what menacingly alien. The preface claims that older English words and even terms of "scholarship" have made their way into the cant lexicon, and *NCD* itself is responsible for reassigning recognizably English terms, such as "din" and "doltish," to its cant lexicon. What is more, there is a movement in both directions, as the book's compiler laments: "even unknown to ourselves, we have insensibly adopted some of their terms into our Vulgar Tongue, as 'Bite,'... 'filch,' and 'flog.'"[99] Words of the "vulgar tongue," of the common people, are transformed into cant and then readopted back into the vulgar tongue in a repeated movement of defamilarization and refamiliarization.

Eighteenth-century representations of cant suggest its wandering status between insider and outsider language and its social meaning in literal terms of geography. Are its speakers, as the *NCD* claims, "gypsies... from Bohemia" who emigrated to those perennial sites of internal outsiderness, "Ireland and the Highlands of Scotland," and thence to England?[100] If so, why does *NCD* attribute good old English words such as "bawd" to them? Or are cant-speakers a section—if the lowest—of the British people themselves, as is also suggested by that text's characterization of cant-speakers as "the dregs of the people, who have not virtue and industry without compulsion, to maintain themselves and their families by labour"? If cant is part of English, its speakers English (or, after 1707, British), what, besides its distance from a refined, proper language and its opacity and strangeness, might link it to a specifically vernacular Englishness?

From the Mouth of the Beggar: Cant, Proverbs, and British Freedom

We saw depictions of cant as the language of the free in early modern plays such as *The Jovial Crew*. These reemerge in odd ways in cant dictionary prefaces of the eighteenth century. In their speculations on cant's origins, these introductory texts placed proverbs and cant in the mouths of slaves and then beggars. These figures, however, functioned as bizarre signs of freedom, a freedom that supposedly distinguished Britain from other nations, for Britain's contemporary beggars were the descendants of the slaves it had long ago freed. In some ways, as we have seen, cant was a product of new mobilities and social relationships, but these prefaces located its origins in a remote English past.[101] The *NCD*, for instance, claims that cant-speakers, the "dregs of the people," are the legacy of a past act of liberation in England. The preface describes how "The publick... freeing [slaves] from bondage... has intailed a perpetual rent-charge," for that emancipation has "given rise to the numerous bands of pilferers and robbers."[102] In this narrative, speakers of cant might be the "dregs," the undeserving poor, but they are, nonetheless, "of the people," specifically a group of the once-enslaved, now "freed" by "the Publick," figures to whom the latter has some affiliation, even responsibility.

In the preface to the earlier *New Dictionary*—from which *NCD* draws its surprising rhetoric of freedom—B. E. had offered a similar "historical account" of cant-speakers, the "beggars" of England. Insisting on an even tighter connection among England, its common tongue, and beggars, B. E. states that beggars were the first speakers not only of cant but also of proverbs, and were also linked to "our" Christian freedoms. "Christianity," he writes, "ransom'd no less than all at once from pagan Slavery, at no dearer a rate, than the rent-charge of maintaining the beggars, as the price and purchase of our Freedoms" (n.p.). The beggars of B. E.'s time are licensed to move about the country freely, existing outside the bonds of servitude and immobility, but they are also the incarnate sign of former enslavement and the freeing of slaves that was supposedly part of the distinguishing history of B. E.'s English Christian readers.[103] In these accounts, beggars are not simply separately existing free spirits, like the gypsies of *The Jovial Crew*, but also the lingering evidence of a past slavery ended by their countrymen. They are the continuing price—and embodied reminder—of "our" collective freedoms.

As the author of the *New Dictionary* interweaves national and religious narratives, he aligns the beggars' freedom allegorically with freedom from the bondage of sin. Beggars and their language might be a reminder of fallen man and his fallen language, but their liberated status also betokens Christian redemption. Dekker's incoherent post-Babel speakers, we might say, have been saved—and are now a sign of freedom. Waxing patriotic, B. E. connects this history to what he sees as a present-day liberating and, preposterously enough, non-slave-owning England, when he describes another kind of wandering Englishmen, the Christian armies who "daily . . . redeem[ed] slaves from the Turks."[104] Thus, in B. E.'s estimation, readers should cherish rather than rebuke beggars—now members of "canting crews"—as symbols both of religious salvation and of England's uniquely free and slave-freeing society.[105]

In his history of beggars, B. E. specifies freedom as an English Protestant phenomenon, facetiously revising the religious distinction between Christian and pagan, freeman and slave, as a distinction between Protestant and Catholic, claiming that beggars appeared "upon the Dissolution of the Abbeys" in England—an allusion to the "slavishness" of Catholicism over which English Protestantism had triumphed. Such characterizations had powerful resonance, for, as Roxann Wheeler observes, "Britons in general could, at times, laud their freedom in comparison with Catholic, Islamic, or pagan countries. Parliament, a limited monarchy, and the constitution were widely believed to make Britons peculiarly free, even in comparison with fellow Europeans."[106] Whether invoked to describe the unnatural "bondage" of Englishmen under Cromwell, the rightful freedom Charles II bestowed on his countrymen, or the perversion of British freedom under the "slave driver" Robert Walpole, a rhetoric of English liberty punctuated political debates of the seventeenth and eighteenth centuries.[107] This drew from Biblical mythology and also from the myth of an "'ancient constitution,' an order based on law holding since time out of mind, in which Parliament had its rightful place beside the King."[108] Further, in their formative writings on English law, Edward Coke and, later, William Blackstone, common law, the law of precedent, and customary law, based on ages-old oral practices, had greater authority than written statute law.[109] In its strongest iterations, neither monarch nor written rules could override the ancient unwritten constitution and customary practices of a free people.

In the eighteenth century, cant's and colloquial language's social meaning wandered tortuously alongside this political rhetoric of English freedom. Conceptions of a unique national liberty saturated discussions of what we might call linguistic sovereignty and contemporary debates about who had the power to determine linguistic usage.[110] As John Barrell has noted, "writers on language practice exploited comparisons between laws of England and the rules of good English" and believed that "the language, like the constitution, had its theoretical origins in contract"; both "breathed a spirit of liberty."[111] John Locke writes of the contractual origins of signification that "words ... come to be made use of by men, as the signs of their Ideas; not by any natural connexion that there is between particular articulate sounds and certain ideas, for then there would be but one language amongst all men; but by a voluntary Imposition."[112] According to this logic, the contractually agreed-upon linguistic practices of a free English people rightfully determined their language (as opposed to a universal language that might someday be recovered or a language that operated along principles of analogy or dictates from a language academy, something like statute law). Even Samuel Johnson allowed custom the "sovereignty of words," although how custom had acquired that authority was, for him, an open question. In his *Plan of an English Dictionary*, he promises, "I shall ... since the rules of style, like those of law, arise from precedents often repeated, collect the testimonies on both sides, and endeavour to discover and promulgate the decrees of custom, who has so long possessed, whether by right or by usurpation, the sovereignty of words."[113]

As Barrell and William Keach have pointed out, just whose "custom" underwrote its decree was a key question. As well, the "imposition" of this now-ossified custom on contemporary Britons might belie the claims that it was a sign of British liberty.[114] The works that imperiously defined the terms of this "customary" English, often tyrannical in tone, seemed to veer from the freedom upon which England and then Britain prided itself. B. E.'s vision of cant's and proverbs' origins posed a different model of linguistic sovereignty, one in which freewheeling vagrants had created and traded in the common language of the land. James Howell's characterization of proverbs as "the truest Franklins [freemen] or Freeholders of the country" gets at this sense of common English, its colloquialisms and proverbs, as the most valid incarnations of British freedom.[115] The odd characterizations of beggars as generators and carriers of proverbs and common language—and cant—poses an alternative to the "freedom" of a contractually based standard English. Landless, these beggars were nonetheless freeholders of a sort, with a freedom not of the possessive individual subject but of those who held all property—especially the linguistic variety—in common.

We might say that beggars, with their inscrutable, mysterious origins, had connections to the unknown and the unknowable of time-immemorial events and clandestine oral language associated with the idea of the Ancient Constitution.[116] As one-time pagan/Islamic/Catholic slaves, however, that is, as putative others, they also implanted a strangeness in the heart of common language. Underscoring that strangeness, B. E. explicitly situates proverbs (the "philosophy of the common people," as one seventeenth-century lexicographer had called them) in the mouths not only of beggars but also of the distinctly unfree—slaves.[117] In describing the origins of proverbs, B. E. notes, "Nor is it also new to meet the beggers [sic] and the Proverbs together, for the fashion is as old as Plautus, who puts the Proverbs and the jests in the Mouth of his Slaves."[118] More recently, he points out, Shakespeare had followed the same fashion. For B. E., beggars, the "rent-charge" of freedom, remained nearly identical to—significantly, unracialized—slaves, the difference "not greater than between Fathers and their Heirs." His choice of the term "heirs," and not simply "children," suggests a legacy, an inheritance of slavery, in the figure of contemporary beggars. Beggars and slaves, speakers of both cant and proverbs, are weirdly woven into the fabric of B. E.'s sense of national vernacular linguistic culture.

To invoke Plautus, the playwright known for his witty house-slave characters, is to cause a frisson of the familiar and strange in the vernacular, for these verbally astute characters, enslaved though they were, were also masters of their masters' colloquial tongue, fluent in proverbs and colloquial language.[119] In fact, in the allusion to Plautus, cant itself temporarily disappears, for there is nothing like criminal cant in classical writing.[120] In this reference, cant gives way to vernacular language, and slaves are its speakers well before beggars. This proximity of the slave to the vernacular is not as extraordinary as it might initially seem, for the term "vernacular" itself, as Daniel Tiffany helpfully alerts us, derives from "verna," Latin for "house slave," a lowly, dominated outsider who is also, however, included within, an inhabitant of, the master's domestic space.[121] It is the "house" aspect of the term "vernacular" that is connected to its "native" and "indigenous" senses, definitions that the *Oxford English Dictionary* cites from sources as early as the seventeenth century. Similarly, in Johnson's 1755 and revised 1774 *Dictionary*, vernacular is defined as "native, of one's own idiom or country." (His first of two illustrative quotations, however, is of Gideon Harvey's describing consumption as a "vernacular" disease—not an especially positive connotation for the term.[122]) While the term only came to signify expressly "of a slave: that is born on his master's estate; home born" in 1804, the ambivalence between subordination and intimate attachment is embedded in its etymology, in "verna," and, I would argue, in the specter of strangeness that hovers around the eighteenth-century conception of the vernacular.[123]

In the proverb-speaking slave, the vernacular English of freeborn Englishmen is accompanied, even supplemented and haunted by "social particularities" of the low—slaves and their heirs, beggars and criminals, and their surprisingly related cant languages. B. E.'s discussion of those "freeholders," proverbs, and of cant is itself caught up in the entanglements of freedom and slavery. Freedom, as Aristotle had argued, depended upon the ability of "slaves and common laborers to liberate the citizen for political life."[124] B. E. also acknowledges that the citizen's sense of living in a free state depended on beggars, the "heirs" of slaves and uncanny reminders of past enslavement. These distinct beings, nonetheless, also spoke and were a source of vernacular language. Here is a moment where, as Michel Serres puts it, noise "consolidates when you look again" (14). For what was once noise is becoming part of the vernacular—and the very terms of inclusion are refigured, as the parasite is no longer the cant or vernacular speaker, but rather those who live off the vernacular speaker's—the slave's—labor.

Other entanglements between slavery and freedom haunt the vernacular. The ongoing wanderings imputed to beggars and canters subtended particular freedoms and linguistic mastery. Significantly, it was the wandering or, more accurately, the compulsory movement of Plautus's at once marginal and central clever slaves that put them in a position to master many tongues, not only of their own countries but also of their conquerors. These characters were polyglots because they had been captured and transported in the course of Rome's imperial expansion. Although nonnative subjects, slaves were fluent in the vernacular, and the vernacular itself was, in odd ways, nonnative. Similarly, in *ND* the internally and externally alien, the experience of wandering and of change, are folded back into the notion of the language of "the common people." Wandering, not just domestic but international, finds its way into B. E.'s glossary, with foreign terms such as "Florentine," "Cacafuego," and "Banditti." Other terms in his collection suggestively tie together native and foreign, as in the English "*Buccaneers*, West Indian Pirates ... also the rude rabble in Jamaica."[125] As Coleman notes, B. E.'s far-flung lexicon includes etymologies pointing to Dutch, French, Indian, Middle Eastern, American, and West Indian origins.[126] And collections of proverbs often included "foreign" examples, which, in their folksiness, come to sound local, as in "he that makes a basket may make an hundred" or "a black hen will lay a white egg."[127] Wandering, it seems, is what not only cant but also vernacular languages and speakers do.

This, of course, is a rewriting of the linguistic diversity that Dekker had seen as a sign of human culpability and its punishment. He believed that cant resonated with the sin against God that took place at Babel—a rejection of God's law forcefully echoed in cant's lawlessness, but evident in all languages and their (fallen) diversity. An emerging understanding of signification, however, viewed the connection between words and ideas as never having been imposed by God, never adhering to universal, if now lost, rules or "statutes," but instead adopted in voluntary multiple, if remote and wandering, circumstances. The resulting diversity was a sign of human freedom. James Bono has described the early modern shift in attitudes toward language diversity's origins at Babel as a sign not merely of human failings but of intriguing multiplicity and particular histories: "If the event at Babel figured a descent into history, with humans now divided into separate linguistic communities whose very modes of communication were subject to growth, [and] variation ... then the study of language might acquire a historical and contextually specific coloration.... the languages of man could become the object of intense critical, textual, contextual, and, in short, historical scrutiny."[128] Diversity and particularity here present not evidence of man's irretrievably fallen status but are revalued as material for study.

In citing Plautus, B. E. suggests that low figures, especially the wandering slave and then beggar, boast the greatest linguistic freedom and ingenuity, in part because of their movement through and familiarity with a range of languages. Eighteenth-century representations of cant depicted mobility as critical to new ways of knowing, ways that emphasized familiarity with a full range of particulars. B. E., credited as "Gent." on *New Dictionary*'s title page, indexed the social movement downward that was necessary to procure the language of the low—a language, nonetheless, that writers increasingly saw as worth collecting and printing. To know Englishness was to know its particular customs and practices, including, for better or worse, its seamy underside and its myriad languages. This perspective helped to underwrite the complex shift in attitudes toward cant language, from a constricted sense as the language of criminal aliens to something closer to our own sense of slang. To learn these specific languages, one needs to get one's hands dirty, becoming familiar with the intimate details of mundane, humble practices of all corners of the country, including the most base and disreputable. The "slumming" narrators who witness and are party to stealthy scenes of low debauchery in such works as *The London Spy* early in the century or, later, George Parker's *View of Society and Manners*, adopt this position, as we shall explore further in Chapter Four. These works present the strange languages of those worlds back to readers, as it were, rendering them as vernacular—at once strange but also British. The techniques of fiction, to which we shall now turn, helped make English readers truly intimate with those worlds and their languages.

CHAPTER TWO

Daniel Defoe's Novel Languages

ARRAYING PARTICULAR LANGUAGES, including cant, was the business of offbeat popular glossaries and dictionaries.¹ It was also, increasingly, the business of fiction. Both the realist novel and the vernacular dictionary began to take shape as genres in the eighteenth century. In obvious ways distinct, they shared, as a condition of their formalization as genres, an orientation toward comprehensive knowledge, especially of empirical particulars that would ground, but claim to be grounded in, common national experience. As lexicographers transformed dictionaries, once repositories of "foreign and hard words," into collections of sometimes well-known, sometimes obscure English words, writers attempted to establish the legitimacy of a particular type of prose fiction. They did this, in part, as William Warner has argued, through warding off the taint of the foreign, focusing frequently on the quotidian experiences of British men and women.² Both presented back to readers what were often familiar and sometimes low terms, objects, places, practices, experiences—ways of life, supposedly, of English-speakers. To read early realist fictions alongside the popular English language lexicons of their day is to be reminded of their shared generic work in producing the very idea of the nation, of their shared history in a mutual articulation of national imagining.

In this chapter I situate the emergence of realist, nationally focused fiction alongside vernacular English and cant dictionaries in order to illuminate the complex ways they position readers in relation to vernacular languages. While it is tempting to view these genres as merely assembling, codifying, and making accessible to readers the diverse languages, places, and practices of the British nation—addressing English readers as English, and making them so, by positioning them as possessors of a comprehensive and transparent knowledge of all things English—they are working along far more interesting lines. These genres of the vernacular, as we might call them, present back to readers the familiar in print forms, yet do so in terms that render it unfamiliar—at once a reader's own and yet also strange. Or, they present the actually unfamil-

[57]

iar as, nonetheless, part of the reader's national world—what should be, but, alas, is not familiar. English dictionaries and realist fiction of the eighteenth century create readerly expectations of discovering in a new print form what is already one's own, but also prompt a realization of the strangeness of what one might have thought was one's own. They address readers as familiar with English language and culture, but also as strangers in need of introduction to and explanation of both the mundane and the unusual.

That this should be the case is less peculiar when we remind ourselves that, as Michael Warner has observed, nations are a way of "organizing strangers" and are predicated on "stranger relationality."[3] The strangers of modernity are no longer simply foreign outsiders but, necessarily, people within one's national midst, compatriots. Foreign outsiders wandering one's own town and country in canting crews, as we noted in Chapter One, are only an extreme figure for the many instances of strangers put into relation under the national rubric—strangers no longer from "outside" but now coexisting "inside," from different and sometimes opposing classes, regions, religions, political allegiances, lines of work. English dictionaries and realist novels both stage and attempt to negotiate that stranger relationality, a dynamic particularly apparent at the level of language. To draw from Michel Serres's model, as discussed in the previous chapter, the space of the third man, that excluded presence who would make communication between two people possible, grows increasingly noisy in genres of the vernacular. Those same genres, as we shall see, engage in a kind of noise reduction, as they continuously transform just who or what might constitute that space of the third man.

From its inception, a time of "unifying, centralizing, centripetal forces of verbal ideological life," Mikhail Bakhtin argues, "the novel . . . was being historically shaped by the current of decentralizing, centrifugal forces."[4] In other words, in the face of the standardization of national languages, the early realist novel emerged as a site that instead acknowledged and sometimes highlighted the counterposing languages of strangers. Even when it took a national form, shunning the explicitly foreign and attempting to occlude its deep and ongoing roots in other places and languages altogether, the novel, in its generic heterogeneity, necessarily brought together a "diversity of speech."[5] Thus, if and when the novel was national, it "mimick[ed] the structure of the nation, a clearly bordered jumble of languages and styles."[6] The "clearly bordered" quality of the nation might be mere wishful thinking; the languages circulating within the geographic territory, variously familiar to some readers and not to others, threatened to unravel from within the very unification nations claimed. When realist novels such as those of Defoe dramatize linguistic stranger relationality, they seem to work in the realm of heteroglossia and thus might seem to endanger the very concept of a unitary language that nations must posit.[7] As Allon White notes, "heteroglossia not only foregrounds the words of people normally excluded from the realm of the 'norm' and the 'standard,' it also relativizes the norm itself, subverting its claim to universalism."[8] In this chapter, however, I argue that Defoe's novels organize heteroglossia, structuring it through cues of narrative and voice. These signal both the strangeness of various languages and the terms upon which they might be made English, made unitary.

To read eighteenth-century English vernacular dictionaries alongside realist fiction of the time is to be introduced to humble practices and the sometimes-obscure words naming them, both the intimately familiar and the unusual made familiar in lists of definitions and prosaic writing, and unfamiliar in the staged translation in the pages of dictionaries and early realist prose. Works of fiction by Daniel Defoe, William Chetwood, Samuel Richardson, Henry Fielding, and Tobias Smollett, writers who have come to define Britishness, not least through their use of language, include a variety of linguistic registers and lexicons with cant terms (e.g., "divers" for pickpockets and "rapping" for perjury), within their movement through unmistakably British landscapes and alongside their "Anglo-Saxon" prose.[9] At the same time, they pause to explain, dictionarylike, the most prosaic of terms. In *Joseph Andrews*, Fielding's narrator describes how Joseph and Parson Adams "agreed to ride and tie" and halts the characters' literal progress and the text's narrative movement to define the expression: "a method of travelling much used by Persons who have but one Horse between them," going on to expand further on the term's meaning.[10] Smollett's *Roderick Random* describes Mr. Launcelot Crab "drinking a liquor called *pop-in*, composed by tossing a quartern of brandy into a quart of smallbeer" and also explains to readers that "carriers . . . transport goods from one place to another on horseback."[11] A mundane act in simple language is made strange in the dictionarylike descriptions the narrator provides.

Similarly, however exotic the name of Samuel Richardson's eponymous heroine *Pamela*, she and her language are recognizably common and British, perhaps most evocatively so in the strange Bedfordshire dialect terms Thomas Keymer has detailed.[12] While I shall have more to say about Pamela's pointedly odd provincialisms in relation to an English vernacular in Chapters Five and Six, here I want to contemplate briefly what it might mean that consciously British works invite readers to imagine the nation, in part, by imagining a national language, but often invoke that national language, that vernacular, through unusual and low terms. The correspondent whose letter to its editor prefaces *Pamela* rails against efforts to "*frenchify* our *English* Solidity into Froth and Whip-syllabub" by appealing to language, imploring, "let us have *Pamela* as *Pamela* wrote it, in her own words."[13] The plea for "native simplicity," "her own words," against a "multiplicity of fine idle words," is, of course, notoriously complex, the confusion between person, character, and book in evidence even in the italicized "*Pamela*" of this brief quotation. The "neat Country Apparel" that figures Pamela's language associates it with the simple and rural. Troping language as "Apparel," however, also acknowledges that words, however simple, are a put-on, and sometimes endowed with the charged erotics of Pamela's outfit.

In her "neat Country Apparel" Pamela famously and approvingly gazes at herself in a mirror, an apt image, it would seem, for Srinivas Aravamudan's description of the objective of a national canon-making that prioritizes realist fiction: "the consolidation of citizen subjects in full narcissistic contemplation of their own idealized images."[14] What might it mean, though, that this image itself emphasizes native dress as a costume, to be put on or taken off? More to the point of this chapter, what might it mean that the linguistic "native simplicity" the garb figures is often in need of translation, odd (or presumed to be odd) to readers, not a singular language but multiple ones marking the strangeness and conflicted differences of others? Aravamudan has written that "resistance to cultural foreignness and genre variety" was internalized in a "stranger intimacy" that took place at the level of individual subjects.[15] My point is that those dynamics of "stranger intimacy" were also internalized within realist fiction itself, which borrows from the generic techniques of the Oriental tale Aravamudan tracks so effectively, particularly a "pseudoethnography" that translates for readers what they might or might not already know.[16]

Defoe and Obscur(ing) English

For Daniel Defoe, whose novels *Moll Flanders* and *Colonel Jack* I examine in this chapter, cant, that strangest of all languages within Britain, is, for better or worse, a part of the British landscape, one of a series of languages adopted now and then by the struggling protagonists on the move, geographically and socially, throughout his novels. Explanations of cant appear alongside explanations of mundane linguistic practices, as in Jack's description of how "near Goodman's fields, the Johns are generally call'd Jack."[17] Such practices are odd enough to need explanation, like cant, and yet are lowly and English enough to merit representation in Defoe's realist fiction. In his novelistic technique, we find the realism Erich Auerbach analyzed, a realism paraphrased by Terry Eagleton as "tak[ing] the life of the common people with supreme seriousness, in contrast to an ancient or neoclassical art which is static, hierarchical, dehistoricized, elevated, idealist, and socially exclusive."[18] Defoe's novels are about common people who elude the comic antics to which so much writing had limited them. They are "relevant to an Auerbachian approach," too, as John Richetti has noted, in their "erosion of stylistic division and rhetorical hierarchy so essential to classical literature."[19] Defoe's novels pose the question of just what readers' attitudes toward the lower styles and speakers in his works should be, in part through his varying characterizations of cant. The author's complex use of narrative voice suggests an ambivalence regarding cant fluency—is it liberatory, a sign of freeing mobility and adaptability with which readers might identify, or is it, once again, a sign of criminal otherness, an especially egregious form of a damning particularity that serves, in fact, as a sign of servitude and an ongoing bondage to sin?[20]

Before exploring the intricacies of Defoe's narratives, intricacies that will return us to questions of freedom and servitude, as part of the process of Englishing cant, I want to pause to consider the diction of these novels, wandering amongst and tying together as it does colloquial, proverbial, regional, trade, and cant languages. Early fiction writing that moved from romance's worlds, unreal and remote—or ungrounded altogether—in time and space, to others more familiar to readers, drew from journalistic techniques in their minute descriptions of a spectrum of British social life. Among these was the representation of empirical particulars and, on occasion, of the low and even criminal, in decidedly unelevated language, including cant. Defoe's prose fictions, while still deeply indebted to conventions of romance plot such as the improbable reunion or mistaken identity, are especially interesting in their concomitant shift in linguistic registers.

The attention to empirical specifics and the sometimes-low language naming them was, in part, a bid for credibility, not just for the emerging form of realist fiction but for the idea of Britain itself. Moll, for instance, refers to "Mr. Henzill's Glass-house," an actual old glassmaking establishment on the River Thames, a culturally specific reference point that helps convey the credibility of both story and location, one of a series of particulars accrued through her travels throughout Britain that fills in the details and attempts to substantiate the idea of a British nation. Not just any details, however, will do. In positioning itself against, or at least as different from, romance, with its dedication to the lives and loves of well-spoken aristocrats, Defoe's fiction delves into the low and commonplace. Cant appears alongside and is of a piece with corroborating banal particulars. In *Moll Flanders*, coexisting in the verbal space of national particulars, such as "Pinnace" (a fine boat with six oars) (115) and "the stage coach to West-Chester" (140), are terms found in contemporary canting dictionaries, such as "Cleave" (94), which Albert Rivero notes is "contemporary slang for 'wanton woman,'" "juggle" (a sleight of hand, a cheat) (117), and the "mint" (the miserable south London neighborhood to which insolvent debtors fled to avoid prosecution) (51).

The social meaning of cant wanders alongside and holds an especially important place amongst other particular and low languages in Defoe's fiction, not simply as a kind of truth-telling, an establishing of credibility, but also as a seemingly transparent rendering of the demotic. In his discussion of glossolalia and the imperative it catalyzes to make unknown phonemes into meaningful speech, to order and to "write" language in moments when confronted with non-meaning, Michel de Certeau asserts that the "voices of the people ... define the places where it becomes necessary to write."[21] We might think of the appearance in Defoe's novels of such cant terms as "Moll" or "Mother Midnight" (128), or "fatal Tree" (215), or colloquialisms such as "wet day" (as in the rainy day for which one saves) (95), or "bag and baggage" (164) (akin to the phrase "lock, stock, and barrel"), as staged moments of encounter with and writing of such voices. Like the cant and vernacular lexicons and the linguistic wandering they betray, these are attempts to make strange diversity somehow familiarly national. Despite Moll's editor's prefatory disavowals of cant and low language, they are not only necessary to the novel's realist representational strategies (and its imagining of the nation) but are also part of a grander claim for the powers of written language to render the multiplicity of confused and rambling verbiage and even incoherent sound into meaning, to make accessible and real the voice of the people itself.

Similarly, like B. E.'s and Bailey's lexicons, Defoe's novels move between cant language and proverbs. *Colonel Jack* (published in the same year as *Moll Flanders*) features proverbs, such as "my Money would be my Crime, *as they say*" (23), and references to common fables, such as "Now were we something like the Cock in the Fable" (47), alongside cant expressions, including, in a description of a criminal outing with a partner, "we walk'd Abroad together" (42), and cant terms such as "peach'd" (72), "blown," (73), and "punk; a whore" (64). If proverbs represented, as we have seen, ancient stock of English language, their meaning often deriving from customary use, Defoe's cant language sometimes exists within a similar dynamic. Moll and Jack repeat terms such as "bargain" and "purchase" enough times to establish them as criminal argot for stolen goods. At points, cant even merges with remote English customary and legal history (as we saw above, a set of laws supposedly established through custom, positioned against more top-down statute law). Colonel Jack's comrade makes casual reference to "handsel" (22) to back his claim to the larger portion of their first ill-gotten booty. The term, which appears in *Sir Gawain and the Green Knight*, refers to the custom of a presentation of a gift early on in a relationship in hopes of lucrative future outcomes. Jack deploys it as a custom shared by criminals.

Sometimes the proverbial and cant even overlap, as in Moll's use of "Leap in the dark" to describe a woman's precipitous and unscrutinized jump into marriage. Putting her own narrative on hold, Moll uses the phrase as she pauses to give advice: "Ladies always gain of the Men, by keeping their Ground" (61). A man might propose marriage unthinkingly, she explains, but he will have little respect for a woman who "having but one Cast for her Life, shall cast that Life away at once, and make Matrimony, like Death, be a Leap in the Dark" (62). The phrase, as Rivero notes, was also both a cant expression for "execution by hanging" and reputed to be Thomas Hobbes's final words about his impending death—in another text Defoe had "cited [the phrase] as such."[22] This layered expression insinuates that, at points, cant does not border English but is a distinct reverberation of it, even in its legitimate and most proverbial forms. In speaking it in the course of her argument about marriage proposals, Moll offers a suggestive model of language use, moving from the highest register (the dying words of a political philosopher) to the lowest (a cant phrase) and to the colloquial in a single phrase whose use is designed for maximum rhetorical impact—it ends the paragraph. Here, as well, both cant and proverb function figuratively, even opaquely, at once familiar but at the same time somewhat obscure—popularly known and oft-repeated, yet with impenetrable, mysterious origins.

Moll's and Jack's knowledge of cant is related to and derived from their wandering familiarity with the intricacies of Britain's geography, both spatial, from intertown coach roads to London streets, and verbal, from English proverbs and fables to dialects and colloquialisms. All are part of the particulars of life newly valued in publications mapping and cataloguing Britain.[23] In the "leap in the dark" instance, Moll's usage goes unremarked: she gives no notice that this circulated as a cant phrase, no translation, as it were, which is also the case with "job" (for a theft) and "hit" (for a successfully executed crime) (164). More often, however, such knowledge about cant—and other particular languages of Britain—is not assumed. Guiding readers through cant is one leg of an ongoing domestic tourism in Defoe's novels, with their sense of negotiating readerly encounters with unfamiliar but also specifically British experiences. Here, the vernacular, like cant, is unfamiliar, strange, and must be translated by a specially positioned (low, itinerant) subject in writing that resembles what James Buzard calls "metropolitan autoethnography," a "determinedly self-interrupting form."[24] Traveling across England, Moll at one point interrupts her narrative to explain, "[I] paid my Reckoning, telling my Landlady I had gotten my passage by Sea in a Wherry. These Wherries are large Vessels, with good Accommodation for carrying Passengers from Harwich to London; and tho' they are call'd Wherries, which is a word us'd in the Thames for a small Boat, Row'd with one or two Men; yet these are Vessels able to carry twenty passengers" (208). Any number of regional and craft terms would be, like cant, unknown to many readers, and Defoe's characters offhandedly stop to translate them. All form the chequered and changing linguistic topography of Britain. To situate cant among them is, in effect, to "English" cant terms while also pointing obliquely to the ongoing strangeness of the national linguistic environment.

In the eighteenth century, with increased movement throughout a transforming country, the Union of England and Scotland, and the concurrent attempt to collect and stabilize a singular English language, many people would have encountered linguistic strangeness and multiplicity in what was supposed to be one linguistically unified nation. In Defoe's novels, Britain is a Babel of regional, trade and craft, foreign, and cant languages. In London, especially, which saw a doubling in size in both the seventeenth and eighteenth centuries, linguistic confusion would have been the norm.[25] Yet there are no aspersions cast on the languages Defoe's narrators translate for readers: Jack makes many off-the-cuff observations about the ones he encounters, noting, for instance, that the people of Edinburgh call those "that take in horses to keep" "stablers" (102), while refraining from any castigating remarks about Scots. Navigating linguistic perplexity without effort, Jack, at the docks of Billingsgate, speaks of "Crimps" (contractors for unloading coal ships) and "the masters of coal ships, who they call Collyer Masters" (42). He even ventriloquizes legalese, referring to "cocquets" (20) and "mittimus" (29), both meaning warrants. A certain level of obscurity becomes part of the experience of the English language itself. And while cant itself might be a figure for this obscurity, there is nothing particularly problematic about this for Defoe's protagonists. Instead, they revel in a condition of linguistic opacity, rapidly invoking strange and unfamiliar terms, but—and this is crucial—just as quickly translating them.

This readerly process, moving between obscurity and transparency, creates an odd sense of belonging and a counterintuitive notion that the vernacular, like, cant, is a language into which readers must be initiated, and that linguistic familiarity must be learned. In Defoe's descriptions of the most ordinary of experiences—checking out of an inn, figuring out how to feed one's horse when money is dwindling—new terms, such as "stabler," continuously appear, igniting curiosity within prosaic scenes with the brief shimmer of the unknown. Yet just as continuously, Defoe's protagonists obligingly explain those terms, putting readers in the know in a kind of linguistic initiation that takes place over and over again. In these novels, a sense of belonging demands an initial sense of incomprehension, of a secret unknown, and a subsequent passage into knowledge of what turns out to be familiar experience. The reader is both estranged from and returned to the familiar.

The dynamic might be illustrated in Jack's description of the sleeping quarters of his early, homeless childhood: "Those who know the position of the glass-houses, and the arches where they neal the bottles after they are made, know that those places where the ashes are cast, and where the poor boys lye, are caveties [sic] in the brick-work, perfectly close except at the entrance, and consequently warm as the dressing-room of a bagnio" (16). The passage starts with an exclusive appeal to "those who know" this scrappy East End locale, marking the redundancy of this information for them with a syntactical repetition, "those who know ... know," but goes on to describe in minute detail what it is they would know to those not in the know. By the completion of the description, the reader knows as much as those who "know the position of the glass-houses" and, moreover, as much as the urchins who secretly find cozy rest in their depths. At the same time, the glass houses are defamiliarized. No longer merely the place where glass is made, they have been revealed to be the clandestine housing of countless desperate children and described with the foreign and somewhat scandalous word "bagnio," which at this time could mean not only a public bath but also a Turkish prison for the detention of slaves or a brothel.[26] Still further, Jack invites readers to imagine this familiar site relocated to "*Greenland* or *Nova Zembla*," where its constant warmth would remain unerring. Specialized knowledge—that of those who know London's geography well or who know first-hand the warmth of sleeping in glass-house ashes—is held out as privileged information, known only to some, but then shared in detail. The strange is made familiar, even as the familiar is made strange.

Defoe's initiations into secret and alluring pockets of society oscillate between familiar and unfamiliar; they are, as well, often contingent on an initial familiarity with English language and landmarks. *Moll Flanders* reproduces a fragment of a canting song, "If I swing by the String, / I shall hear the Bell ring. / And then there's an End of poor Jenny" (216), including, uncharacteristically, a footnote explaining: "The Bell at St. Sepulchre's, which tolls upon Execution Days" (216). A reader needs to know what "string" means metaphorically (a noose) and the significance of St. Sepulchre's (the church next to Newgate prison), for a full appreciation of these lines of song. The positioning of the reader shifts from that of outsider to insider, as it were, not just because one word, "bell," is translated in a footnote but also because his or her comprehension depends upon a preliminary familiarity with the English verbal and cultural landscape. To make sense of this strange riddle is, as it were, to be reminded of what one already knows.

The cant in Defoe's novels—less completely incomprehensible than that of earlier print works because it so often works figuratively (as when a "string" is a recognizable figure for a noose)—also allows for this play between familiar and unfamiliar. Words such as the early cant terms "dimber" and "fambles" do not appear in these novels, but Jack talks of "hankering" (42), and he punctuates the narrative of his introduction to crime with the term "Divers, or pickpockets." The metaphorical character of this language—with its image of furtively plunging hands, of loitering as its own form and time of desire—portrays cant as making its own new language out of defamiliarized standard English words in order to name novel aspects of common life. If the wit that yoked surprising images and terms together had fallen into disrepute in poetic circles, it seems alive and well in the cant that appears in some eighteenth-century printed texts. The cunning new usages attributed to it, born of emerging ways of being in the world, such as the increasing, and increasingly uncomfortable, experience of anonymity in proximity that allows strangers to invade the recesses of another's clothing or the suspicion of idling that causes mere loitering to be suspected as targeted longing, would seem to make cant the language best able to respond to emerging social relations that seemed to throw unlike together, to make the familiar unfamiliar.[27] Cant is an adapting and adaptable language well suited for a mobile population's encounter with the new, just as it is being asked to think of this experience as familiar.

More accessible to readers, these cant terms function as riddles of sorts rather than merely opaque alien terms. They pose a momentary "sudden disruption in the flow of communication," to borrow Carla Mazzio's useful formulation.[28] Mazzio argues that such moments "expose the exclusionary logic integral to established communities of linguistic exchange, revealing the logic of affect—of... awkwardness... alienation—with regard to codes of language and interaction" (9). And yet, in Defoe's works, such moments form part of a sequence: exclusion, awkwardness, and alienation posed briefly but then overcome. Unmeaning passes into meaning; seeming exclusion morphs into inclusion. Resolving riddles and deciphering cant based on what a reader might already know reinforces that reader's membership within an English vernacular community, even as its "exclusionary logic" is briefly revealed. Recognizing the meaning of cant's adaptations of English, and understanding that this depends upon an already existing fluency, makes for an ongoing movement between incomprehension and revelation, strangeness and familiarity. Full apprehension of figurative cant terms is grounded in and articulates novel aspects of a shared modern life, including the repeated experience of needing to learn something new.

Cant and Colloquies with Characters

As in Defoe's novels, in cant dictionaries such as B. E.'s *New Dictionary* readers would find cant terms such as "*Bully-ruffins*, Highway-men, or Padders" listed and explained on the same page as the more familiar "*Bumpkin*, a country Fellow or Clown" and "*Bumper*, a full Glass," a proximity already surprisingly suggestive, I have argued, of a new sense of linguistic common ground between cant and colloquial language. A reader might move into surprised comprehension of a figurative cant term, as in "*Moon-curser*, c. a link-boy, or one that under Colour of lighting Men [home at night], Robs them or leads them to a gang of rogues that will do it for him"—cursing the moon, presumably, for the prohibitive light it shines on such scenes of criminal opportunity.[29] The format of dictionaries, with their columns of words assembled by an offstage collator, however, has limited powers to create a sense of affiliation to this language in its readers. Defoe's innovations in voice in narrating itinerant individuals' life stories, alternatively, invite readerly attachments to mobile, shape-shifting, polyglot characters as they encounter and translate a range of languages, including cant, in their street-level view of life in Britain and beyond. In this way, they invite readers to claim as their own a vernacular marked by diversity and change.

Defoe's texts drew from popular print accounts of descents into the real or imagined underworlds of London, including seventeenth- and eighteenth-century prose narratives of cant-speaking criminals, from the Ordinary's Accounts and Sessions papers to brief biographies of malefactors. In this prose, as Lincoln Faller has noted, a significant shift took place in the representation of criminals, as "writing about actual crimes and criminals began to organize itself around, typically, the life histories, characters, and deeds of specific individuals rather than, say, the stratagems, tricks, and knaveries of criminals in general or their affront to good order."[30] Such writing, with its focus on personal stories, might realign readers' relationship to the world of cant, inviting a sense of attachment to the cant-speaking men and women such works profile. Alexander Smith's *Lives of the Highwaymen*, even, on occasion, depicts the interior thoughts and motivations of individual criminals, providing readers access to the inner lives of characters whose language is thick with cant. In recounting the life of one Arthur Chambers, Smith writes, "having been often punisht at hard labour in Bridewel [*sic*], which beating of Hemp the Thieves call *Mill Dolly*; whipt at the Cart's Arse, which they call *Shove the Tumbler*, or *Crying Carrots*; and burnt in the Hand, or Face, which they call *Glain*, he had an Inclination to leave it off, for fear of the *Nubbing-Chit*, that is to say, the Gallows."[31] Here, readers gain a glimpse of the criminal's thoughts—"he had an inclination to leave off"—in the peculiar cant language that describes events of his life.

Smith's representation of such characters and their language, however, is uneven. Frequently they and their language return to the low as comic, as in his portrait of Moll Raby, who goes "upon the *Buttock and Twang* by Night, which is picking up a *Cull, Cully*, or *Spark* . . . she takes him into some dark Alley so whilst the decoy'd fool is groping her with his Breeches down, she picks his Fob or pocket."[32] After pickpocketing her "cull," Moll must hide under a bed to avoid detection during a "Night sneak" or house burglary. Repeatedly hit by the various heavy metal household objects the unknowing servants toss under the bed, Moll cowers there, "but the dog still growling in the Room the Fear of his betraying her rais'd such a sudden Looseness in her, that she could by no means avoid discharging herself."[33] Such scatological humor sets this Moll up for readerly disidentification, her cant language distant and distancing.

Alternatively, when cant appears in Defoe's novels, it is neither the glossary's list of terms attributed to faceless and nameless outsiders, nor even, as in Smith's biographies, the reported speech of criminals recorded by a third-person narrator, sometimes to low comic effect. In Defoe's first-person narratives, cant emanates from the mouths and immediate perspectives of self-narrating protagonists fluent in and consistently translating cant and common tongues of the land.[34] Defoe's narratives, as Faller has persuasively argued, are "very much concerned with presenting a variousness of consciousness, both in and around the voice of his narrators," and it is that sense of access to a consciousness, all the more believable for its variousness, that is key to transforming readers attitudes toward the cant they speak.[35] The endlessly talking Moll and Jack, the conversational tone of their thoughts, the representations of their dialogue, are all crucial to the making colloquial of what had been thought of as beyond the pale: cant and low languages.

The term "colloquial" was itself newly minted in the eighteenth century, its etymological origins in the Latin term *colloquy*, literally a speaking together, a conversation. For Defoe, the "colloquial," the language produced and learned through a kind of informal "speaking together," is not, as it would be for Johnson, a kind of "barbarism," with that term's sense, from its Greek etymological origins, of linguistic outsiders betrayed by the incomprehensibility of their oral speech, but rather the language of insiders, known precisely through the seeming speaking together of his voluble narrators. In situating cant and low languages within these conversational contexts, Defoe's narratives continue to open their formerly quarantined sense. This structure of a "speaking together" is important from the opening pages of *Colonel Jack*, in which the title character narrates, from a retrospective position, his very young self's induction into criminal society and language. After watching his comrade Major Jack rise in their meager world by joining a gang of pickpockets, the child Colonel Jack yearns to become a member of criminal "society." Jack relates his conversation with an older rogue who recruits him:

> He solicited me earnestly to go and take a Walk with him ... adding that after he had shown me my Trade a little, he would let me be as wicked as I would ... I hesitated at the matter a great while, objecting the Hazard.... Well, Colonel, says he, I find you are faint Hearted, and to be faint Hearted, is indeed to be unfit for our Trade, for nothing but a bold Heart can go Thro' Stitch with this work. (18)

The older rogue speaks with Jack, and Jack, in a sense, speaks with his readers. Jack relates how his comrade casually slings cant—"take a walk" (go out in search of victims to rob)—and proverbial language—"go Thro' stitch" (continue to the end)—in a conversational manner that invites readers in while mingling the two languages.[36]

Jack's unusual openness to conversation is how he acquires his knowledge not only of cant but also of many corners of British society. Even as a ten-year-old boy of the streets, Jack notes that he "had a natural talent of talking" and "many times bought my self off with my tongue" (7). He describes how "the Colonel" (oddly momentarily switching to the third person to describe himself), "always held talk with the better Sort; I mean, the better Sort of those that would Converse with a Beggar-boy; In this way of Talk, I was always upon the Inquiry, asking Questions of things done in Publick as well as in private, particularly, I lov'd to talk with Seamen and Soldiers" (10). Jack's colloquy with the "better sort" (here, humorously, soldiers and sailors) produces knowledge of colloquial language that includes cant—a cant that is then "spoken," as it were, with his readers, of both the better and worse sort. Ronald Paulson has argued that the low and popular are distanced in "the remote simulacrum of the print in a book," but here the narrator's garrulousness works to draw readers closer.[37]

Moll's talk is more limited; she cannot engage in Jack's easy public "conversation," in part because of the sexualized sense of that term.[38] The *Concor-*

dance for *Moll Flanders* reveals that when Moll "talks" it is usually in private conversation and the term "conversation" in that text has mainly sexual meanings.[39] The novel, nonetheless, also offers a narrative "speaking together" that transforms the sense of cant in relation to readers. The narrative opens with the language of cant, as the title character—crucially, a reformed Moll who tells her tale in retrospect—speaks of former "Comrades" who have "gone out of the World by the Steps and the String" (9) (the gallows), and describes her mother's thievery as "borrowing" (10) and how, when caught, her mother "pleaded her belly" (10) (claimed pregnancy for a temporary reprieve of her punishment), but after delivering her child was "call'd Down, as they term it, to her former Judgment" (10). Such criminal turns of phrase speak to a covert world, but Moll just as immediately opens up that world to readers in her personal revelations. "I often expected to go" by those same steps and string, she confesses in the second paragraph of the book, following that sharing of her recurring fear with a description of her earliest memories and hopes (9). Cant here moves beyond establishing a credible representation of the world, or of Britain, to grounding the believability, by way of portraying the interiority, of a character.

This is possible in part because the first-person narrative in Defoe's novels, and the kind of intimate opening-up it makes possible, is considerably more complex than that of earlier criminal biographies. In such seventeenth-century narratives, as Faller has pointed out, one could just as easily substitute third-person for first-person pronouns with little change in meaning. Consider, in contrast, this passage from *Colonel Jack*, in which Jack recalls his childhood witnessing of a comrade being whipped:

> The poor Captain stamp'd, and danc'd, and roar'd out like a mad Boy; and I must confess, I was frighted almost to Death; for tho' I could not come near enough, being but a poor Boy, to see how he was handled, yet I saw him afterwards, with his Back all wheal'd with the Lashes, and in several Places bloody, and thought I should have died with the Sight of it; but I grew better acquainted with those Things afterwards. (12)

Defoe's first-person narrative is here certainly a means of intimate revelation, as Jack divulges, "I must confess, I was frighted almost to death." The author, however, also uses the first person as an instrument for tracking and reassembling the complex accrual of knowledge and the development of consciousness through time. Although Jack begins the description with the incongruously theatrical scene of the torture of an anonymous, almost animal figure—a stamping, dancing, roaring mad boy—and follows that with his confession of heightened fear, he then notes that he (also a "poor boy") was not actually close enough "to see how he was handled." Was his fright based on the dumb show, the distant pantomime of suffering? Or was it from what he witnessed up close, after the fact? Or did his sense of fright come from later, second-hand descriptions of what others, who could see the goings-on, told him of the event? His fright seems chiefly to come from what he saw first-hand afterward, the effects of physical brutality—a "Back all wheal'd with the Lashes, and in several Places bloody." Yet when he narrates the scene, he artfully recomposes it, providing a retroactively constructed spectacle that he himself could not see, eliciting a response in the reader, and compounding that image with what he did later witness, the grotesquely lacerated body of his friend. Adding another layer of temporality, of retrospection, he explains his own transformation over a still-greater length of time. In the course of his life since this early event "I grew better acquainted with those Things," although "those Things" remains unspecified. The narrative of a horrific, potentially estranging event for the reader nonetheless becomes a means of creating a kind of intimacy with Jack.

The availability of Defoe's novelistic criminals for new forms of attachment becomes clear in contrasting them to a slightly later (1728) work, sometimes attributed to Defoe, titled *Street Robberies Consider'd*, which also travels through and exposes poor and criminal parts of Britain, including the cant language spoken there. This first-person account of the life and various ruses of a cant-slinging hero, often written in the same prosaic, matter-of-fact tone as Defoe's fiction, even includes details shared with Moll and Jack. Like Moll's, the protagonist's mother is transported, leaving (like Moll and Jack) a motherless infant to be raised by a sequence of surrogates. Like Jack, the protagonist desires to read and write and learns to do so. This "Converted Thief's" brief autobiography is as outrageous as Moll's or Jack's, perhaps even more so—caught stealing rings, his mother claims to be pregnant in order to avoid execution and then frankly invites sexual partners to impregnate her, at last succeeding with a whole gang of pirates. And this narrator—like Moll and Jack—trades in cant and vulgar language while also speaking in a clear, plain English, using phrases such as "which epithet." As well, his discourse is strewn with English proverbs, such as "Once a thief, always a thief" (95) (not true in his case, he claims) and "There cou'd be no harm done where there's a child got" (7), brushing plain and proverbial English alongside outrageously vulgar and cant terms. The narrator, who regales the readers with stories of his various criminal disguises and plots, speaks a canting language of "nimming" (thieving) and "collaring the coal" (laying hold of money) (31).

Converted Thief, however, is also markedly not like Moll and Jack. He distinguishes himself from Defoe's fictional characters with his foul-mouthed claim that "the first word I could speak plain was Bitch," the term he uses to call his mother (11–12). This use of language thoroughly divides him from Moll and Jack, who never swear. More important, *Street Robberies Consider'd* is a pasted-together generic hybrid of sensational depictions of criminal escapades, a glossary of cant, musings on the causes of crime, and advice for the wary who wish to avoid becoming victims. The text is missing the narrative elements crucial to the period's realist fiction writing, which aims (if it does not always succeed) at seamlessly integrating such diverse generic influences. Unlike Moll and Jack, the protagonist never receives a proper name, going only by "Converted Thief." And rather than offering unreal access to his psyche, the voice in which the short work is written is a return to the criminal biographies, in which the first-person voice might as well be third—there are no moments of reflection, of narrative complexity, of intimate confessions that would provide the unreal sense of access to a subjective interior that fiction of the period was beginning to develop, even in works such as *Moll Flanders* and *Colonel Jack*. Consequently, readers have only two modes of relating to the cant language found in *Street Robberies Consider'd*: they can view the text's cant as either part of the comic entertainment to be had in the converted thief's outrageous stories or as urgent information for their own protection. Converted Thief writes, in a reversion to an older view of cant, "I shall give this by way of Advice... whenever any Person hears such a language, Speech, or Cant; or what you please to call it, let them take Care of the Speaker; for they may depend on't they are certainly of the Nimming Clan, and therefore to be avoided" (29).

Fictions of Attachment

The layers of recollection and narration, the promise of unreal access to characters' interiors, and the suggestion of depth, then, distinguish Defoe's criminal writings from others of the time and contribute to a sense of *Moll Flanders* and *Colonel Jack* as fiction. As Catherine Gallagher has argued, it is precisely an openly fictive quality that enables readers to sympathize with characters. "Characters' peculiar affective force," she states, "is generated by the mutual implication of their unreal knowability and their apparent depth.... Because we know their accessibility means fictionality, we are inclined to surrender to the other side of their double impact: their seductive familiarity, immediacy, and intimacy."[40] This openly fictive element, as opposed to the merely realist, credibility-building sense of Defoe's novels' language, is critical for readers' affiliation with these characters and the languages they speak and, through complex shifts in voice, an ability to understand linguistic attachments as themselves fluid.

For Gallagher, such fictionality is not yet available in Defoe's novels, which instead mark the last moments of the genre of the "true history," in which readers understand the heroes and heroines to be actually existing beings, not fictional nobodies. I want to pause to question that classification. While it is true that the titles of these works style them as "history," and the preface to *Moll Flanders* insists on its difference from "Romances" (3), as instead a "private history," the texts undo these assertions in significant ways, making space for something that is not quite history and not quite—although still indebted to— romance: in a word, fiction. When the editor of *Colonel Jack* avers, "neither is it of the least Moment to enquire whether the Colonel hath told his own Story true or not; If he has made it a History or a Parable" (2), he dispenses with the idea that the text is necessarily a history, a true narrative of an actual life.[41] Whoever the Colonel is, the life history he has produced might well not be "true"—he might be merely the imaginary protagonist of a "parable." Similarly, the editor asserts in the preface that in the telling, the events of Moll's life have been "garbl'd"—meaning at this time to "clear dross out" and "to mutilate" with a view to misrepresentation—to impart a moral "Fundamental" (5).[42] Parts of her story have been "left out" and "shorten'd," and "There is an agreeable turn Artfully given them in the relating" (4). Defoe's preface to *Moll* (and later, *Roxana*) figures the text as a dress, as clothing, which ends up displacing entirely the "true" body; the sense of an actual person behind the story becomes quite beside the point.

It is by attending to the complex representations of language in *Moll Flanders* and *Colonel Jack* that their fictionality—and its stakes—become most clear. The editor opens his preface by distancing his publication from "Novels and Romances" and insisting, "the Author is here suppos'd to be writing her own history" (3). The criminal, low, and ranging language of *Moll* and *Colonel Jack*, as we have noted, helps distinguish these works from romance writing. But the editor quickly admits that at the level of language, this is not "her own history" (3). While he discloses that he has "garbl'd" the story itself, he prioritizes, by discussing first (in the third sentence of the preface) his alterations to its language: "the original of this story is put into new words, and the stile [*sic*] of the famous lady we here speak of, is a little alter'd, particularly she is made to tell her own tale in modester words than she told it at first, the copy which came first to hand, having been written in language more like one still in Newgate than one grown Penitent and Humble, as she afterward pretends to be" (3).

The language itself teeters between a mark of the real and an admitted fabrication. Seemingly nitty-gritty expressions from Moll, such as "he did not keep, as they call it," that is, keep Moll as a mistress; the "fatal tree" (215), meaning the gallows; "the college, as they call'd it" (216), meaning Newgate; and "breaking open the house" (165), meaning burglary, are, as the editor tells us, his own "modester words," and not Moll's. While these revelations of criminal argot seem like conversational intimacies, the direct language of others ("as they call it"), they are actually mediated, despite the narrative techniques that attempt to efface that mediation, from the use of the first person to the reproduction of unfamiliar, coded language. Here, Defoe's work draws from the generic conventions of the Ordinary of Newgate's Accounts, with their invented descriptions of convicted criminals' lives and dying words and contemporary criminal biographies. Like those printed works, Defoe's prose fictions harbor a mediating presence that structures and translates representations of criminals and their language, even as they present the language as unmediated.

It is not only this re-presentation of cant and low language's open variance from some original that makes these characters' language pointedly unreal—it is also their comprehensive mastery of a broad swath of so many languages. It is in their capacity to comprehend different social, regional, and occupational languages, a knowledge crucially obtained by their itinerancy through strange zones, not simply squalid urban places but distinct classes, locations, and trades, that Moll and Jack most clearly exhibit their fictional status. Their effortless movement between lingos offers a most egregious instance of "unreal knowability" in their unreal knowingness.[43] For while, as Adam Hansen writes, following John Barrell, fears abounded in eighteenth-century Britain that "no one person would be able to comprehend the many different dialects and languages, of regions, trades, and immigrant communities, constituting what seemed like an increasingly, and dangerously, polyglot nation," Moll and Jack occupy a clearly fictional rhetorical space of just that comprehensive linguistic knowledge.

Theirs is an unreal position that nonetheless seems to hint at moments of depth. The editor ntoes disapprovingly that Moll wrote in what must have been something like cant, a "language more like one still in Newgate than one grown Penitent" (3). It was the editor who changed it. Much rides on the scandalous terms that he claims to have deleted from the reader's view, for the immodest language in which Moll supposedly recorded her history belies her claims to penitence. The story's concluding ambivalence regarding her repentance might already have been resolved here on the first page, settled by way of her unrepresented—and unrepentant—cant, her finally unsettled language. Moll's own language, too depraved to be represented on the page, suggests the sort of concealment and depth associated with actual people, a sense of depth used at this time to help readers believe in and attach to fictional characters. Here, we find an early, barely visible moment of the erotics of language as disguise, activating notions of surface and depth that would take fuller form in *Pamela*.

Protean Affiliations

Providing unreal access to characters' interior thoughts, pointing to the discrepancy between these stories and "true history," invoking the real through the patently unreal—be it a character's ventriloquized language or unlikely knowledge of a range of tongues—all allow *Moll Flanders* and *Colonel Jack* to approach the fictionality that, as Gallagher astutely shows, seduces readers into feelings of affiliation. These texts, then, through their modes of fictionality, participate in the gradual eclipse of the sense of cant and its speakers as external and separate. But to what, exactly, are readers becoming attached, and how might that affect their views of vernacular language? That Defoe's narrative techniques make that question difficult to answer suggests that the relation of both character and reader to strange and even familiar language is one of fluid attachments.

Even the titles of the works make any readerly affiliation to the eponymous protagonists and their language an attachment to something fluctuating, the foreign made colloquial in an ongoing process. *Colonel Jack*'s title page reads *Colonel Jacque, Commonly Call'd Col Jack*, frenchifying a good old English name, in reflection of Jack's cross-channel migrations. Similarly, the title *Moll Flanders* combines Flanders, with its allusions to Belgium and the Netherlands and the embargoed lace produced there (and making its furtive way to British markets), with "Moll," a name familiar from English criminal biographies, a tentative name bestowed upon her by her envious colleagues—and, of course, readers never learn her actual name.[44] These characters and their names figure an ongoing and necessary shape-shifting, like cant, with its sense of a word's changeable relationship to meaning. All are invented out of particular exigencies, with meanings specific to particular situations and groups.[45]

To what do readers affiliate in these ever-changing characters and their slippery names and languages? Even Moll's and Jack's relationship to different languages and linguistic registers shifts continuously and unpredictably, short circuiting anything like an invitation to identify with a single subject position and any one specific language. Crucially, their mutability often hinges on irregular shifts in voice. When Jack names his partner-in-crime's whipping punishment, for instance, he turns to the third person: "he was called out to be corrected, *as they call'd it*" (12, emphasis in original). Casting those who use the term "corrected" in the third person illuminates the double-voiced meaning of the term here. "They," it would seem, are the officials administering the punishment and those who agree with them. In using the third person, Jack distances himself from but reproduces the dominant contemporary "commonsense" perspective on the value of whipping signaled through the language of reform. Readers might know the term "corrected," but Jack's drawing attention to it as a language of one specific group—"*as they call'd it*"—precipitates a sense of the doubledness or irony in language. This invites readers to ask whose interest is served in describing a vicious, largely punitive act as correction. In these instances, the first-person narrator locates himself within the subculture of the criminal. He offers what Hansen sees as an "oppositional" perspective typical of Defoe's criminal writing, while illuminating how, as Bakhtin had put it, "the seeds of social heteroglossia [are] embedded in words."[46] "Corrected," in this instance, is literally heteroglossia in Bakhtin's sense of "another's speech in another's language," which reveals the social contest at work in language and distances readers from official authority and its vocabulary.

Inversely, as Moll and Jack distance themselves from such upstanding moral colloquialisms, they often adopt cant terms and a criminal worldview as their own. Moll describes a cant phrase for drunkenness in the first person: "what we call being *in drink*" (224). She expresses her frustration at her failure to steal from a stash of "goods that were privately got on shore," her euphemism assimilating the criminal language and worldview that in other words would simply be understood as stolen or smuggled. She complains, "I was not used to come back so often without purchase" to describe her failure on one occasion to procure ill-gotten loot. Jack's similarly unremarked use of the term "purchase" to describe property acquired by a thief—"as fast as they made any purchase, they unloaded themselves" (13)—indicates his own linguistic affiliations with a criminal community.

At still other times, however, and significantly, Defoe's heroes and heroines deploy the distancing third person in regard not to dominant language ("corrected, *as they call'd it*") but to criminal argot. When Colonel Jack intimates in the past tense that his young comrade, Captain Jack "was got among a gang of kidnappers, as they were then call'd, being a sort of wicked fellow that us'd to spirit people's children away" (11), it is not clear who called kidnappers "kidnappers"—criminals or the rest of society. It is only clear that Jack feels he must translate the term, that it is familiar to some but not to others. He knows the term but at the same time knows it to be strange, not exactly his or his readers'. In this world, cant and low language are elements one might both don and doff. Thus, while Defoe's novels present a variety of idiolects and particular languages, they appear neither as unwaveringly belonging to first-person protagonists nor as exclusively the language of others. Rather, they function complexly, indicating social collectives and values variously distinct from and then proximal to the narrating characters'—strange, and then not, their relationship to various languages varying at different points in their lives. If B. E.'s significant shift in attitude toward cant still adhered to what William Empson understood to be pastoral's division between "complex man" and "simple man," such divisions break down in Defoe's treatment of cant.[47]

Defoe's characters' own fluctuating sense of affiliation and disaffiliation to particular groups and their mores opens them to the possibility of their later rather unconvincing moments of social transformation (Colonel Jack becomes a gentleman) and repentance (Moll experiences a conversion). More convincingly, it represents a protean adaptability necessary to succeed, although often at great cost, within the context of new social and geographic mobilities. Their shape-shifting, as well as readers' shifting attachments to such linguistically and socially volatile characters, suggest an emergent structure of feeling of loose, volatile linguistic and other affiliations, a way of being in the world that demands constant movement between detachment and attachment, strange and familiar.[48] Such an attitude toward language—what we might see, even, as an attachment to the protean itself—might anticipate a later nationalist rhetoric of a uniquely English flexibility toward language diversity and even change, said to be evidenced by a rejection of the language academies found in France and Italy. Defoe, even in his early call for an academy to resolve disputes regarding language, celebrates the "comprehensiveness of expression" of English, its "energy," its "wit"—its movement and changeability.[49]

Cant and the Rhetoric of Freedom

Devising narrative voices that invite readerly identification, sometimes with shape-shifting itself, Defoe's texts allow readers to veer between affiliation with and disavowal of cant and colloquial language—imagining them both as their own and not. But what made these languages specifically English? The texts deal in the low to evoke the real and, indeed, the national, but that doesn't tell us how readers might affiliate with those languages as English—or British. The adaptability evidenced in Defoe's characters' relation to languages and their summons of readers to that position of alternating attachment and detachment might return us, in a roundabout way, to B. E.'s connection of cant and proverb to a complex rhetoric of a specifically British freedom—of movement, from servitude. Just as B. E.'s discussion described transformations and reversals—slaves become beggars, signs of freedom—so, too, Defoe's characters' trajectories map a course of transformations. Unregulated movement could represent a kind of freedom but also a new form of entrapment. Servitude, both in the material circumstances of indentured servitude and in the figural motif of Christian redemption, could, surprisingly, lead to freedom.[50] It is in their link to such freedom, finally, that Defoe's characters and their languages become English.

In their mobility, Defoe's characters and their readers participate in what Deidre Lynch has described as an eighteenth-century "to and fro of bodies in motion: modern bodies, unmoored from the traditional corporate identities associated with the Guilds, Church, and Court."[51] As we have seen, such itinerancy itself was undergoing a transformation in relation to ideas of freedom. In his *Second Treatise on Government*, John Locke had already made a surprising connection between disenfranchised mobility, freedom, and membership in the English polity, arguing that mobility itself was one form of evidence of "tacit consent" to submitting to government—and of one's status as a liberal political subject. Locke writes:

> The difficulty is, what ought to be looked upon as a tacit consent, and how far it binds, i.e. how far any one shall be looked on to have consented, and thereby submitted to any government, where he has made no expressions of it at all. And to this I say, that every man, that hath any possessions, or enjoyment, of any part of the dominions of any government, doth thereby give his tacit consent, and is as far forth obliged to obedience to the laws of that government, during such enjoyment, as

any one under it; whether this his possession be of land, to him and his heirs for ever, or a lodging only for a week; or whether it be barely travelling freely on the highway.⁵²

One might read this passage as a description of the veiled workings of power: any number of seemingly independent acts, from owning land to renting a room to travelling, suggest "tacit consent" and "obedience" to the government. However, it also refigures the itinerant as enjoying a slippery kind of freedom, a condition we have already seen in B. E.'s discussion of beggars, who were both akin to slaves and a sign of freedom. If "travelling freely on the highway" had long been a potentially criminal act of vagrancy, here it becomes the opposite of criminal, a sign of agreeing to "obedience to the laws of that government." Even as it means a kind of passive partaking in "the dominions of ... government," traveling freely on the highway is here also analogous to "possessions ... of land ... or a lodging for a week." Mobility becomes a kind of property that, while it subjects one to the government, also underwrites one's status as a consenting and free political subject.

Moll's and Jack's geographic, social, and linguistic wandering represents a kind of freedom, and, as they see it, a legitimate one. While wandering was suspect, even illegal, for members of their class without proper permission from an employer, these characters never betray any sense of their vagrancy being unlawful (although in Jack's case, it does lead to a new form of servitude when he is pressed into military service). As many commentators have emphasized, when Moll and Jack describe criminals and their language in the third person, it is not only to reveal an alternating detachment and attachment but also, at times, to distance themselves decisively from criminals. They claim persistently, if intermittently, that they are better than and not, finally, the rogues of criminal biography who are in bondage and only ever temporarily free from the penitentiary or hanging tree. If, as we saw in Chapter One, being uprooted from particular places and traditional groups, while liberating in one sense, could, in another, project the newly vagrant into the relative unfreedom of criminality, Moll and Jack avoid permanent criminality—that, at least, is what they tell themselves, and their claim is borne out in the denouements of their stories.

We have seen, too, that, in Karl Marx's account, people newly "liberated" from traditional social and economic bonds who rejected criminality faced a new lack of freedom in the wage labor into which they were often forced. Crucially, however, Moll and Jack also avoid such labor and its markedly unfree relations.⁵³ At the tender age of eight Moll learns that the magistrates have ordered her to go to work, but she already has "a thorough Aversion to going to Service, as they call'd it, that is to be a Servant" (12). And indeed, despite being born into poverty, she manages to avoid manual labor for the rest of her life. Likewise Jack, abandoned to poverty by an unknown father, is bid to believe himself a gentleman. But for a brief stint in the fields of Virginia—of which I shall have more to say in a moment—he, too, manages to elude servitude for most of his life.

Moll's and Jack's on-again, off-again relationship to cant outside of any position of servitude is hugely important, for it reveals how as the century moved on, cant, low, and colloquial language came increasingly to be revalued as a sign of British liberty. This revaluation necessarily excluded any links between cant and the specifics of labor, and dramatized the ways in which the relationship between cant, colloquial language, and servitude, like that B. E. had described, was purely rhetorical, relegated to a mythical, superseded past. The erasure of labor took place at the level of cant and colloquial language itself. I have discussed elsewhere the linguistic aftermath of the reconfiguration of formerly legal practices of nonwage compensation—such as the leatherworker taking a bit of leather from his master for himself, a practice known as "clicking"—as criminal.[54] When "to click" appears in B. E.'s *New Dictionary*, it is shorn of that labor context and defined simply as "to snatch." Terms naming such customary labor practices were cast out of official English—none of them, including "click," appears in Nathan Bailey's *An Universal Etymological English Dictionary* of 1721, for instance, although there is evidence that they were still in use at that point.[55] As they appeared in cant and colloquial collections, becoming part of and defining British culture, it was as terms detached from relations of production and labor, hastily invented, supposedly, by free, if ne'er-do-well Britons. When print collections of cant and colloquial languages redefined once-customary labor practices as criminal, and included them in an English vernacular on those terms, they presented back to contemporary readers a transformed, even alien version of their own tongue as a strange moment of freedom. Representations of these argots recuperated them in outlaw terms, as part of an at-once renegade and vernacular language.

Customary labor and production terms disappeared from a print vernacular at the same time as "criminal" cant language was made a part of it. Within this context, Moll's and Jack's constant traveling and dogged avoidance of labor, or at least the formalized labor that would put one into the legal relations of servitude, take on a loaded relationship to their familiarity with cant. Their freedom from servitude and seeming unfamiliarity with labor more generally (for Jack might know labor, but the reader never sees it) detaches the cant they know and sometimes speak from labor altogether. The terms upon which they partake in a freedom from servitude, a freedom of mobility and fluid language use, unmoors cant and vernacular language from any labor contexts. Moll's and Jack's use of cant, however, is tied to their criminal lives, which are in turn a life of bondage to sin. Their freedom remains incomplete, in need of further travel and servitude for full redemption—or at least the fullest redemption Defoe's characters are ever able to achieve.

Cant and Racialized Slavery

In the complex overhaul of conceptualizations of cant, colloquial, and low language, what was once depicted as the language of outsiders becomes more like a vernacular, but only when evacuated of its labor history, separated from explicit servitude. Moll and Jack participate in a variety of language communities, the members of which, it seems, have entered into their own linguistic contracts, freely establishing their own (temporary) language conventions, detached from the servitude of labor or an older model of customary usage. Moll and Jack, whose wide, unhindered travels situate them as adepts and guides to a full range of vernacular English, would seem to inhabit, at least figuratively, the position of the freeborn English man (or, more tentatively, woman). And yet, these characters also have an unstable, hazardous relationship to that most binding form of servitude, slavery, illuminating once again the indeterminacy of the notion of freedom itself in this period.[56] Both Moll and Jack are forced into transatlantic migration, sold into indentured servitude, and violently separated from their natal families, with, for Moll, especially heinous consequences. *Moll Flanders* and *Colonel Jack* stage their protagonists' proximity to slavery only to redeem these cant-speaking figures, finally, as representatives of British freedom. As Dennis Todd has astutely argued, it is servitude that allows these characters—with greater success in the case of Jack—to claim their freedom.[57] Their transport and servitude place their cant-speaking in the past as an overcome, if vestigial, reminder of the slave and the by-turns free and unfree figure of the beggar associated with cant and proverbial language.

We saw earlier B. E.'s odd invocation of slavery in England's remote past in his narrative of cant's origins. While that discussion was almost purely rhetorical, some of the terms of his lexicon stray beyond Britain's shores and perilously close to the materially extant worlds of enslavement under erasure in his preface. The term "*Indulto*, his Catholic Majesty's Permission to the merchants to unlade the Galeons, after his demands are adjusted," for instance, is a rather cryptic description for bribes the British paid to Spanish officials for illegal trading, namely of slaves.[58] Excluded from B. E.'s preface, aspects of a contemporary racialized slave system make their way into the lexicon, even appearing in unusual references to England itself, as in the entry "*Black Indies*," meaning "Newcastle, from whence the coals are brought," in an evocative use of distant, colonized zones of slavery to name English places, specifically introducing connections between blackness and brutal labor into the English language. The connection between the new particularity of racial "blackness" and certain regional British laborers was actually widespread, for, as Gwenda Morgan and Peter Rushton have noted, in the eighteenth century racially charged notions of "dirt and 'blackness' were associated with coal miners and their living conditions—and with whole towns, in fact, in some descriptions of northeast England."⁵⁹

B. E.'s and other early eighteenth-century representations of cant and colloquial language more often offer indirect but suggestive points of contact between English "cant" and Atlantic slavery. Perhaps the most striking of these is the making visible—criminally visible—of bodies. Eighteenth-century print was a textual economy whereby the bodies of the poor were particularized, writ large, and disseminated. Print descriptions of criminal laborers situated them in a position similar to that of the slave in contemporary Britain and North America. Morgan and Rushton have shown how both white criminal laborers and runaway slaves shared an embodied status particularly through the classified ads describing "runaway slaves or servants . . . deserting recruits or . . . stolen goods and their takers" (1). The bodies of both of these groups are described in detail—their birthmarks, gaits, and branded body parts. For Morgan and Rushton, the bodies visibly particularized in certain print forms participate in a textual economy in which criminals, laborers, and slaves share a status as reprehensibly particularized, embodied figures.

Cant dictionaries run rife with terms for bodies. In B. E.'s *New Dictionary* we find "*Leatherhead*, a thick-skull'd, Heavy-headed fellow," "*Long-Meg*, a very tall woman," "*Lord*, a very crooked deformed or ill-shapen person," "*Malmasey-nose*, A jolly red nose," "*Mannikin*, a dwarf or diminuitive fellow," "*Muzzle*, c. a beard (usually) long and nasty"—and we shall continue to track the larger meaning of the many terms of embodiment found in vernacular collections in the following chapters. Here I am interested in the overlap in representations of African, laboring, criminal, and slave bodies. B. E., for instance, offers such expressions as "*Labour in vain*, lost labour, such as washing of Blackamoors" and "*negro-nosed*, flat nosed." In Colonel Jack's early cant-speaking days, he invokes the language of physical blackness to describe himself as a member of "the black crew" and "black wretches," as Dennis Todd notes.⁶⁰ In these instances, "black" is surely overdetermined, Jack and his fellows dirty from sleeping on ashes, but "black crew" long related to crime in the parallel expression "canting crew," "wretches" signaling poor and miserable but also outcast. Alternatively, the white bodies of the criminals are marked—brandishing that criminal embodiment associated with slaves and indentured laborers, Moll's mother reveals to her "a very fine white arm and hand, but branded in the inside of the hand" (71). This physicality, associated with the speakers of cant, would halt circulation and a freedom of movement geographically and socially, at least in Britain.

Cant, then, has a strangely ambivalent relationship to freedom, servitude, and the possibilities of mobility, both literal and figural. If, on the one hand, cant is the language of those freed from slavery and servitude, on the other hand, it is also a language with odd and dangerous proximities to enslavement. I want to trace a few of those intersections marking Moll's and Jack's careers, before turning to the terms upon which Defoe decisively distinguishes cant as English, as a language of a universally free English people, against racially enslaved others. This might help us address the question of how it was that the sense of enslavement faded from, while remaining secretly lodged within, the signification of "vernacular."

Both Moll and Jack come closest to an enslaved status in their transatlantic transport, suffering, at points in their stories, compulsory dislocation, loss of kin, and even, in Moll's case, something like a figurative heritable condition of enslavement, following her mother into indentured servitude.[61] Such state-sanctioned transport, as Peter Okun explains, institutionalized in the year 1718, "mandated banishment of condemned felons to America" and "provided Europe with a repository for criminals," not to mention cheap labor.[62] Jemy, one of Moll's husbands, associates slavery, if only (oddly) the slavery of antiquity, with his impending transport, likening North America to "the plantations, as the Romans sent slaves to work in the mines" and adding "that servitude and hard labour were things gentlemen could never stoop to" (236). Nearing her transport to North America as a convict, Moll finds herself confined to the belly of a ship, "clapt under hatches, and kept so close, that I thought I should have been suffocated for want of air" (240), a description resonant with Middle Passage undertones.[63] Jack describes his sickening realization that he has been tricked into boarding a ship bound for Virginia, and with others must be "hand-cuffed, carried down between the decks, and kept as prisoners" (112), in a scene that repeats the underhanded entrapment, initiated with a feast and seemingly gracious entertainment, of that famous royal slave Oroonoko. In North America, Jack finds himself laboring alongside those other victims of kidnapping, African slaves—fellow "servants," as Jack initially calls them, although Moll refers to both enslaved Africans and indentured "servants" as "slaves" (70).

While scholars have begun to think about Moll and Jack in relation to their transatlantic movement, I want to consider specifically how language operates in that context, for while North American slaves inhabit some positions analogous to Defoe's characters and their languages, language also becomes a key point of their differentiation—the site from which Moll and Jack reestablish their abstract freedom against the particularity of the African slave.[64] As we have seen, *Colonel Jack* features cant as well as English proverbs such as "fire in my flax" (157) and domestic colloquialisms, such as "brick" for a loaf of bread (15). But it also includes the bizarre renderings of the expressions of African slaves, such as "Whipee lashee" (137) and "muchee sorree" (136). Representing what might be either pidgin (a language containing lexical and other features of two or more languages) or, more likely, creole (a pidgin "naturalized" as it is transmitted between generations), such expressions also represent the slaves' speech as heavily embodied, grounding its transcription in mouthed, oral sounds. Their only alterations of the English imposed on them—but the signs, too, of their alienation from it—are their grammatical impropriety and the repeated phonetic suffix of "-ee," a making strange of language, whether reducing it to sound or estranging common words, which parallels, but finally diverges from, the workings of cant.

By this time period, grand oratory from a royal African slave, such as that which emanates from Aphra Behn's Oroonoko, was no longer feasible. As the institution of slavery became fatally entwined with race, people with black bodies became the outsiders, inhabiting an implicitly criminal, embodied, and subordinated status. Depictions of their language helped underwrite this status; as David Kazanjian has noted, representations of black speech (such as Defoe's, I would add) work to represent it as "shattered, rendered inarticulate," and this "embodied speech emerges as an inarticulate, particularized black speech 'void of intellect' so that white speech may emerge as the disembodied, articulate, universal sign of intellect as such."[65] Polyglotism must have been necessary for any slave's survival, but not even an approximation of such African linguistic mastery appears in fictional renderings—only an oral, physically inflected and degraded language, a speech that does not emerge into greater meaning.[66] Defoe's slaves, clearly, are not Plautus's quick-tongued clever slaves. Instead, the white, British Moll and Jack, code-switching between an assortment of languages, come closer to those figures and their surprising freedoms.

Defoe's novels must work to establish a distinction between European and African, for even as their representations of African slaves' creole language debase it, the novels also suggest points of contact between this odd-sounding speech and the cant of the protagonists, itself a particular, embodied language that likewise cannot always function as the "disembodied, articulate, universal sign of intellect." In their moments of cant, low, and colloquial use, Moll's and Jack's language is not unlike that of the African slaves, a denatured, perceived-as-low language generated through forced mobility, sound that makes sense only to initiates, yet that also comes to function as a kind of local vernacular, passed down from generation to generation. As Moll and Jack readily present, translate, and take on a variety of languages, they display the necessary adaptability of displacement figured in creole. If at points their language falls far short of the "universal sign of intellect as such," its contrast to the African slaves' speech is crucial, for the parallels loom dangerously close.

Orphaned, for all intents and purposes, from an early age, and consequently bereft, in some senses, of that "natural" linguistic phenomenon, a mother tongue, these English characters encounter a defamiliarized language from the maternal figures in their lives. In the opening pages of *Colonel Jack*, in Jack's earliest moments of recall, his young nurse, a stand-in for his executed mother, punctuates her sentences with odd and particular terms related to the navy and press gangs, such as "press smack" and "tarpaulin" (4). Jack, as we have seen, learns cant terms such as "divers" as a young child. The earliest moments of Moll's existence are preceded and named, almost called into being, by criminal cant expressions: "My mother pleaded her belly" (10). And on the eve of "disposing" of her own illegitimate infant, Moll recalls that she herself was not "nurs'd by my own mother" (who had been transported) (138). Her own adoption of cant language, occurring later in life when she falls on hard times, is coextensive with and facilitated by another proxy mother figure, the head of the criminal home in which Moll resides, to whom she actually refers as "mother" (137). An inversion of a mother figure, this Mother Midnight runs a "lying-in" house for "ladies of pleasure" in need of ridding themselves of their unwanted children (134). It is this home (and mother) that Moll initially seeks when she aims to erase the traces of her own unwanted pregnancy, and it is in this moment of rejected maternity that she adopts as her own the cant language of women who, like her lost mother, "pleaded their bellies" and "ma[de] their market" (cut a deal in prison by betraying their partners in crime) (161). Like a creole language, Moll's adopted cant at this point in her life is an invented mixture of languages, naturalized as it is passed from generation to generation (from "mother [Midnight]" to "daughter" [Moll]), a perversion of the concept of a mother tongue, or an acknowledgment that a mother tongue is often an adapted and adopted one.

I use the term "creole," with its evocation of imperial domains and colonial submission—and indeed, slavery—advisedly. Moll and Jack are not slaves; the former makes a fortune from slave labor as a prosperous plantation-owner and the latter comes to rest assured of his own identity as a gentleman by way of contrast to the slaves he manages and later trades in. And that is exactly the point. The figure of the inarticulate African slave becomes one critical means by which the mobile, polyglot, low- and cant-speaking Moll and Jack become, in contrast, free Britons. Even from her earliest mysterious origins, Moll insists that she never had her skin "blacken'd," the suggestive common practice of criminal bands feigning to be "Egyptians" or Gypsies," with whom Moll thinks she traveled as an infant and very young child (11). And in both books, the plantations of North America, the places of enslavement for Africans, are not or are not long sites of labor or servitude for their protagonists. For Moll and Jack, the plantations are, rather, transformative in rendering class and even criminality of little significance. In North America, Moll tells Jemy, "nobody could upbraid us with what was past" (238). She invokes a vision of abstract freedom to declare how in North America "we should live as new people in a new world, nobody having anything to say to us, or we to them" (238). Moll and Jemy do, indeed, go on quickly to purchase their freedom along with the slaves who make the fortune upon which their own future freedom from servitude depends. Moll, however, can only tentatively overcome the particularity of her gender—a limiting of the freedoms of cant and the vernacular to male cross-class associations that, we shall see, becomes more explicit by the end of the century in Francis Grose's *A Classical Dictionary of the Vulgar Tongue*

(1785).[67] Jack frees himself from servitude—and from his status as a "black wretch" or a member of a "black crew"—by learning how to manage African slaves, goes on to trade and make alliances with those infamous slave-owners, the Spanish, and concludes his days living in comfort from the returns of his slave-labor plantations. Revealingly, it is in North America, and in relation to slave-driving, that Jack comes himself to use that term "correction"—as a name for "reform," an expression from which he once distanced himself. Reflecting on the whipping his young criminal colleague received, he had underscored that the term was used by a faceless and distant "they." It is now an "I" who "ty'd [a slave] by thumbs for correction" (135).

In both *Colonel Jack* and *Moll Flanders*, it is the notion of race, and the emerging distinction between (white, European) indentured servitude and (black, African) slavery, that provides a conceptual bulwark against which to define a Britishness that could include Britons of all classes, including low cant-speaking ones. As George Boulukos has argued, Defoe "present[s] colonial whiteness as a ready means to, or replacement of gentility."[68] When whiteness replaces gentility, "low" as well as "high" become mere subsets of the determining category of whiteness, itself associated with an abstract freedom. These emerging racial politics had implications for—and helped shape—the understanding of cant and vernacular. As we saw, B. E.'s preface's odd invocation of the slavery of England's remote past fails to mention the slavery of contemporary Britain (despite the terms from the New World that make their way into the lexicon). Yet the racialized slave and the institution of slavery under erasure in that collection must come to the surface in Defoe's texts to make possible the connection between the languages of (free) white beggar, white vulgar, and white Briton more generally. In this light, one wonders if the "discovery of the people" that Peter Burke so thoroughly documents, and which we have been tracking on a linguistic level, might have been related not only to the cultural definition and (largely artificial) cultural distinction of high and low classes but also to distinctions between racial and national subjects. The decoupling of the "vernacular" from the figure of the racialized slave (and from labor altogether) allows cant to represent what Grose would come to deem British "freedom of speech and thought," so that the wanderings of cant and the movement of its speakers are not signs of criminality or compulsion but of a kind of freedom.[69] We might say that in these texts, the particularity of race displaces the particularities of criminality and low and cant languages, making them languages of the house, as it were.

Defoe's works participate in the transition Roxann Wheeler describes, away from religion and toward "national origin, slavery, and skin color" as the means of dividing "Europeans and people of both Native American and African descent."[70] The arresting rhetorical closeness between slave and "free" Briton that we have seen in stories of cant's origins and in Defoe's narratives, however, points to the oscillation between strange and familiar within a consolidating

Britain. Such oscillation between universal freedom and particular forms of servitude, universal freedom and particular race, expansive empire and restrictive national borders, is central to the logic of an emergent modern capitalism, as Kazanjian has argued.[71] The abstraction of the universal freedom of the "free" British subject depends upon particularization, on the development of the notion of nationalized and racialized subjects who form defining counters to that freedom. Estranged from English, these subjects and their languages must remain a defining part of it. In this way, *Moll Flanders* and *Colonel Jack* make once-suspect wandering, linguistic innovation, and the shape-shifting associated with low figures and figured in cant, undeniably British.

CHAPTER THREE

John Gay's Overloaded Languages

WE HAVE BEEN TRACKING A SHIFT in attitudes toward cant, observing its odd commingling with the colloquialisms and proverbs lexicographers collated. In Defoe's criminal fiction, we saw this suggestive blending, along with a recognition of the surprising aptness of an adaptable low language to the modern national experience of mobility, change, and inevitable encounters with strangers. In codifying cant and colloquial languages, these dictionaries and early realist fictions estranged readers from the languages of Britain, but only to invite them to imagine these and a variety of languages as part of their own complex and heterogeneous vernacular tongue. This perhaps-grudging acceptance of the need to display and explain such language as part of a British vernacular, however, was by no means shared by all writers of this time. When John Gay deployed cant language, he returned to its older associations with violation and outsiders in order to represent a Britain in which self-serving cant-speakers were difficult to distinguish from corrupt members of "legitimate" society. The disorienting mixture of respectable and cant languages in *The Beggar's Opera* signals disturbing, if also creatively productive, breakdowns of distinctions between high and low, right and wrong.[1] Although I have been arguing that a shift in thinking about cant was taking place in some quarters in the eighteenth century, Gay makes use of an ongoing understanding of cant as the *sine qua non* of criminals, a language of dangerous outsiders that illegitimately departs from given meaning. The outrageousness of the society *The Beggar's Opera* depicts is matched by an equally outrageous cant language, as characters nonchalantly speak of the "lock" (a warehouse of stolen goods), a "child getter" (one who impregnates imprisoned women so the latter can "plead their belly"), and being "pumped" (the cold-water drenching of a pickpocket). That cant terms are becoming naturalized in Britain is a sign that the nation is fast becoming alien and criminal itself.[2]

Gay draws not from the lexicons of the period that positioned cant as common, but from the many glossaries that would cordon it off from English, continuing to make it an emblem of a menacing delinquency. *The Regulator* of 1718, which includes a glossary, describes a "countryman" surveying a thieves' den and remarking, "with all my heart, this can be no other but an entrance to hell, or the very gate of it ... I was never in such a place before, neither did I believe any such would be suffered in any parts of his majesty's dominion."[3] Cant-speakers here inhabit a distinct place, as marked by the countryman's emphasis on a threshold separating him from them; across it lies alarming difference, and the observer claims to require a translator to explain both the particular crimes and languages of each respective evildoer. A quick glance at other early- to mid-eighteenth-century cant dictionaries confirms some texts' ongoing sense of cant as despicable, its speakers in need of reform to become fully British. For instance, despite borrowing heavily from B. E.'s *New Dictionary*, the 1725 *New Canting Dictionary* responds directly to the former's claims about cant's connections to English freedom. It regards cant-speakers, instead, as immoral "dregs," "pilferers and robbers," not complex avatars of righteous freedom. The anonymous compiler of the *New Cant Dictionary*, after making dismissive reference to B. E.'s claims, quickly proposes the elimination of beggars altogether by putting them into workhouses to serve the burgeoning wool industry. This anonymous author advocates that, in imitation of Holland, Great Britain should force all beggars into relations of servitude, which would both end their status as (free) mendicants and eradicate their specific language, said to be daily and dangerously infiltrating English.[4] In this text, people who initiate and use cant are truculent and suspect enemies of the state in need of the discipline of the workhouse. Their wandering and the wandering of their language must be stopped.

If, in some early dictionaries and in Defoe's novels, colloquialisms and proverbs appear alongside cant, comprising, for better or worse, a demotic, diverse vernacular that toggles between the strange, even foreign, and the homey and intimate, Gay runs interference through this model of a composite, adaptable language. He disrupts important genres in the institutionalization of the vernacular, from the pastoral to realist fiction, and holds in place hostile attitudes toward cant to underscore what is wrong when high and low speak the same language. For the eighteenth-century cant lexicographers and fiction writers we have been examining, cant and colloquial languages pose an obscurity, a strangeness within the common national linguistic culture, which they both highlight and help bring to meaning for readers, inviting attachments, if on complex and shifting terms. In Gay's texts, alternatively, the opacity of the language of others is an end in itself—Doll's language in *Trivia* is an alluring spectacle, not otherness to be explained, not strangeness with which to become affiliated. We might say that Gay restores noisiness, the third man, but the result is not communication between the other two. For Gay, such noisiness is not a function of the language of others, of subordinate groups, but of all languages, even the most "transparent" of them. This is particularly true in the intersections of various languages he likes to set up, where meanings proliferate, making dubious any claims to a comprehensive and consolidating vernacular. Language, hopelessly overloaded, makes meaning only briefly and provisionally for separate, changing groupings—petty criminals, men of business, aristocratic hangers-on, or, indeed, particular groups of readers and viewers capable of grasping various levels of meaning. If some new collections and fictional representations of cant and low speech helped them resonate with a sense of a consolidating vernacular, Gay's representations of language often collapse into no single meaning at all.

"Nothing into All Things"

We might begin where we ended in Chapter Two, noting that in Defoe's *Moll Flanders* and *Colonel Jack*, the institutionalization of an English vernacular, including a reestimation of low and cant languages, was beginning to become possible, in part, by transatlantic movement. In these novels, African slaves become the noisy third. Moll's and Jack's travels across the Atlantic solidify their status as free Britons, despite their also having been criminal cant-speakers when on their home turf. Alternately mastering and disavowing cant, Moll and Jack are shape-shifters whose transatlantic travels whitewash their pasts.

In tracking John Gay's distinct understandings of cant and Britishness, I want to start by showing that in *The Beggar's Opera* and its sequel, *Polly*, transatlantic movement in particular signifies nothing. In "Air XLII" from the former (whose tune is taken from "South Sea Ballad" and punctures the fantasy of easy wealth to be made in the West Indies), jilted Lucy complains that her love affair with Macheath has likewise come to nothing. The original ballad itself offers a jaded take on Defoe's and others' images of the fortunes to be acquired in speculating on maritime trade, with such sarcastic lines as "Our cunning 'South-Sea,' like a God, / Turns nothing into all things" (III.i). Not an actual means to transformation, investment in the South Sea fantasy offers the illusory promise of creating new value from nothing, but more likely, as it was to do for Gay, turns value into nothing, in the great swindle that was the South Sea bubble.

The Beggar's Opera depicts transport across the Atlantic, in particular, as little better than financial ruin or its consequences. The gold-digging Mrs. Vixen brags of "bleeding" apprentices of so much money that she "sent at least two or three dozen of them to the plantations" (II.iv), transport here a punishment, not a merciful promise.[5] Equally empty are the images of life across the sea—they are mere romantic topoi, as when Macheath sings of Polly on Greenland's coast improbably keeping him "warm amidst eternal frost" (I.xiii). Even when that seductive highwayman counsels Polly and Lucy to "ship yourselves off to the West Indies," it is a hollow erotic fantasy, as he jokes that there they will "have a fair chance of getting a husband apiece; or by good luck, two or three" (III.xiii).

In Gay's suppressed sequel, *Polly*, Macheath himself is transported to the West Indies, and Polly follows him. It is far from Moll's and Jack's land of opportunity. While his betters, such as Ducat, make a fortune, as they did in London, Macheath cannot transcend his criminal past, like Moll or Jack, but rather, is at last brought to justice in an offstage hanging, while the "rich men" and "better company" to whom he compares himself evade such a fate (III. xiii). Not an alternative to Britain, the West Indies of *Polly*, as several critics have noted, simply replicates the immoral profiteering that *The Beggar's Opera* depicts at its center, London. Transported figures such as Diana Trapes shift from dealing in the stolen goods of her gang in *The Beggar's Opera* to purveying the stolen flesh of the slave trade in *Polly*.[6]

Further, unlike Defoe's novels, where emerging structures of racial division in the Atlantic are beginning to ground a British vernacular based in part on the idea of British liberty, *Polly* presents race and class as nonnegotiable. Macheath, transported into slavery, "blacks" himself to pass as rebellious African king Morano, inhabiting an in-betweenness, signifying "both blackness and whiteness," as Peter Reed notes.[7] However, while Defoe's Jack shifts from fellow slave of the Africans to slave-owner, Macheath's adoption of an alternative identity is, as Reed also notes, permanent—he never returns to his whiteness, free to don identities and then set them aside as Defoe's protagonists do. As well, while Macheath's band of pirates, also transported, temporarily shed their enslaved status, they return to it after a rebellion and a failed attempt to steal the gold of the indigenous people. Further, when African slaves (improbably) walk away from their enslavement to join forces with Macheath's ill-fated band, they, too, find themselves returned to their former condition by the play's end. Polly, sold as a slave to a wealthy plantation-owner after finding herself impoverished and alone in the wake of her transatlantic travels to find Macheath, disguises herself as a man and is, by the play's conclusion, betrothed to an Indian king. She is not entrenched in her cross-dressing costume, not killed as a "black" as Macheath is nor reenslaved as his band and the Africans are, yet she also does not return to Britain and whiteness as both Moll and Jack do. America in Gay's *Polly*, then, is not, as it was in Defoe's works, a site of ultimately liberating and upwardly mobile transformation, rendering one-time cant-speakers white, free, property-owning, and British. Instead, the cant-speaking Macheath and his band meet their doom in their attempts to elevate their status there.[8] In foreclosing a connection between transatlantic wandering and liberal freedoms or the possibility that enslavement might lead to salvation, possibilities that had been available to B. E.'s beggars or Moll and Jack, *The Beggar's Opera* and *Polly* return cant's own wandering social meaning to irredeemable criminality, low language to mere vulgarity.

The Beggar's Opera's *British Vernacular*

Moll and Jack are both one-time cant-speakers who, as they ascend into comfortable positions as free Britons, also leave their cant behind.[9] Cant might stand as a figure for complex negotiations of foreignness, subordination, and freedom at work in the formation of an English vernacular, but in Defoe's novels it is not, finally, presented as that vernacular. What might it mean that only six years after *Moll Flanders* and *Colonel Jack*, when Gay burlesqued Italian opera, deflating it in part by Englishing it, he turned specifically to the lives of indelibly criminal cant-speakers for his subject matter, made a beggar its writer, and punctuated his newly invented genre, the "ballad opera," with proverbs and with cant?[10] Whatever else we might make of Gay's complex work, this positioning of the low, signaled through criminal subjects, popular songs, proverbial apothegms, and cant phrasings, as British against the high of polished Continental opera, poses a relationship between criminality and Britishness. The association undermines the very possibility of salutary British diversity and a unifying vernacular.

At first blush, Gay's innovative *The Beggar's Opera* might seem a vernacular spectacle par excellence with its popular ballads and colloquial terms and proverbs, those musical and linguistic forms increasingly offered up as signs and means of cultural—and national—belonging. His audacious new genre features humble, familiar English (and Scottish) ballad tunes, such as "An Old Woman Clothèd in Gray" and "A Soldier and a Sailor," and the characters speak folksy adages, as in Peachum's opening observation, "a good sportsman always lets the hen partridges fly, because the breed of the game depends upon them" (I.ii).[11] In its turn to vernacular elements as the basis of its high burlesque of the Continental music, ornate settings, and foreign language of Italian operatic form, however, the play also overwrites the vernacular with criminality. Gay's work, of course, plays that low and criminal for laughs. The laughter owes much to the repositioning of popular culture, be it printed publications of criminal life or street performances and songs, as a kind of insider knowledge that allows audience members in on the play's jokes. Steve Newman describes the circuit between the "commonplace" and criminal when he notes that "inclusion in the club of 'we who know' . . . requires a knowledge of the popular signifiers that refer to the underworld. . . . Gay insistently reroutes those pleasures of distinction bound up in being among the 'we who know' back toward the commonplace."[12] If this sounds a lot like the dynamics of the vernacular traced in the last two chapters, in its toggle between strange and familiar, it is, however, different in that this rerouting precipitates laughter, an approach distinct from that of Defoe and some dictionaries that was, nonetheless, also becoming prevalent in the eighteenth century.

Contemporary reviewers immediately noted the play's unseemly low vernacular elements, one disapproving commentator complaining that the music of *The Beggar's Opera* was that of "the Performers at Pye-corner, Fleet-ditch, Moor-fields (and other Stations of this Metropolis, famed for travelling Sound) of their undoubted Properties . . . what shock'd most Ears, and set most Teeth on edge, at turning the corner of a Street, for half a Moment."[13] Not at all alluring, the "travelling sound" of these street performers is mere unpleasant noise, both familiar and aurally alienating. Sermons denounced *The Beggar's Opera* as a turn to the rude, one cleric protesting "the play's being adapted to the Taste of the Vulgar."[14] The danger, it seems, was precisely that the low, humorous, and illicit—sometimes synecdochically figured through cant—were hailing and forming a version of Britishness itself. The scandalized hero of one novel, published in the same year as the play's initial production, exclaims, "The cant of Newgate [which] . . . was accustome'd to be so shocking to a thinking Soul, when any account happen'd to be given of it by the Ordinary, is now a matter of Mirth, and charms the *British* genius more than *Shakespeare* or than [Thomas] *Otway* ever could."[15]

This character puts his finger on the very problem some glossaries and Defoe's criminal novels presented—making cant English by positioning it as part of vernacular language. Gay pushes this Englishing a step further in deploying pastoral. For when cant "charms the *British* genius," we have the Newgate pastoral Jonathan Swift had suggested to Alexander Pope.[16] In its turn to the low, pastoral mounts a ruse of inclusiveness, presenting what William Empson calls "beautiful relations between rich and poor."[17] *The Beggar's Opera* jokingly poses a specifically British inclusiveness, including elements not only of simple British low but also elegant high linguistic culture. Think, for instance, of Macheath's use of cant terms such as "bit" (to have been bamboozled by criminals) and "the tree" (the huge wooden triangle for hanging prisoners at Tyburn) (I.ii) alongside the language of romance, as he invokes those conventional tropes of the flower and the bee. A highwayman sings the cavalier line "Love with youth flies swift away" (II.iv) and cites Shakespeare's well-known "If music be the food of love, play on" (II.iv). In combining depiction of high and low, pastoral, as Empson explains, aims to "make classes feel part of a larger unity or simply at home with each other."[18]

As I consider *The Beggar's Opera* with an eye toward notions of the vernacular, I want to think with Empson's reading of pastoral and of the play. Empson's work is especially helpful. First, the work of pastoral to depict the friction-free relations between rich and poor that he analyzes (an effort, as it were, to represent the strangers of different classes as at home with each other), is the work, too, of the institutions of the vernacular we have been following. Pastoral texts, most dramatically in the form of the double plot, may seem as if they "deal with the whole of English life," as Empson observes.[19] But they do so by merely conjuring an illusion of the whole in the presentation of stock elements of high and low. In this way, pastoral allows strangers to feel at home with each other, but only once they know their place. In mocking the pastoral with its criminal urban setting, however, Gay's play undermines that work of the pastoral, insisting on the tension between those whom the pastoral would put in "beautiful relation" and highlighting the strangeness of those languages that the conception of a vernacular would make familiar—"ours." Gay's attack, in particular on the pastoral of Ambrose Philips and his supporters, with its aims to incorporate the specifics of British "Proverbial sayings, Dress, Customs," is also an attack on, and achieved through, the undercutting of the notion of a unifying vernacular. Although Empson nods in this direction, noting that the pastoral's sense of representing the "whole of English life . . . is palpable nonsense, but what the device wants to makes you feel," I want to demonstrate how *The Beggar's Opera*, in intermingling cant and colloquialisms as part of a complex satire, makes Britishness and the very idea of a vernacular not just strange but venal. Pitching genres and linguistic registers against each other, Gay's mock pastoral actually emphasizes the "palpable nonsense," the humor, of the pastoral's and the vernacular's claims to cross-class wholeness and homeyness.[20]

Second, I want to pause with Empson to revise the terms of his important observation regarding the "independence" he sees *The Beggar's Opera* as establishing. For Empson, Gay's mock pastoral, with its implicit questioning of the "beautiful relations between rich and poor," ultimately reflects a breakdown of old-order notions of society as a unified whole. "There was a feeling that the unity of society had become somehow fishy," he writes (200). Thus, Empson goes on to argue, the play also harbors heroic elements, and its achievement, in fact, is a resolution of heroic and pastoral into a "cult of independence," figured powerfully in the antihero Macheath (203). Macheath is "not merely an object of satire; he is like the hero because he is strong enough to be independent of society" (200). That idea of independence would have been especially important to an early eighteenth-century political rhetoric that emphasized the threats to British liberty posed by Robert Walpole and his regime, one of the targets of Gay's satire as we know from Peachum's derisive reference to "Robin of Bagshot . . . Bob Booty."[21] Reading the play through the lens of the "cult of independence" might return us to earlier discussions of cant and freedom, for part of the draw of the play is its criminals' freedom to remake the English language itself. But the language of *The Beggar's Opera* affirms the independence of neither the whole of Britain nor of single individuals. If we attend in more detail to the play's languages, we might tell a different story than that of individual independence, one not only about its boisterous exposure of the unifying claims of a vernacular and the ruse of pastoral inclusiveness but also its conceptualization of "independence," one that moves beyond the individual to various temporary, shifting, provisionally independent groupings.

Pastoral, Burlesque, and The Beggar's Opera's *Stereophonic Language*

The Theocritean pastoral promoted by Gay's contemporaries Ambrose Philips, Joseph Addison, and Thomas Tickell advocated the representation of simple, low, and specifically national life. Tickell argued that the pastoral writer should aim for national specificity, "deviating" from the generalities of ancient writers for the particularities of English "Climate, Soil and Theology" and "Proverbial Sayings, Dress, Customs, and Sports."[22] This called for a language closer to a humble English than the "elegant turn on the words, which render the numbers extremely sweet and pleasing" that Pope advocated in pastoral writing.[23] For Addison, elegant language was appropriate for Georgic writing; the pastoral speaker, however, should "speak with the simplicity of a ploughman."[24] The pastoral model of Philips, Tickell, and Addison, with its depiction of the particulars of English culture and simple, unrefined language, provides a platform for claiming "beautiful relations between rich and poor" on a concrete, national level. Pope, Swift, and Gay notoriously derided this vision, and Gay's *reductio ad absurdum* of the formula pursues the simple, particular, low, and English down to the scandalous street life of London criminals.[25] His characters' very names, such as Nimming Ned (described with a cant term for stealing) and Dolly Trull (cant for prostitute) rebuff the model of pastoral that would realistically portray humble English language by presenting a disgraceful version of the English far down the social scale. Such mocking propels viewers and readers out of any sense of pastoral's "beautiful relations between rich and poor."

Gay's descent to low life and language even led to some contemporary efforts to pin down the play to specific events, as some quasi-documentary writing of criminal biography or fictional realism did. In 1729 an edition of *The Flying Post* claimed to provide an "account of the circumstances which gave the first hint to the celebrated *English Opera*." Traveling on the road, "the author [Gay] and a friend of his" found themselves in the company of

> the genuine Peachum (executed a few years ago) who discours'd with great freedom on his profession, and set it in such a light, that the poet imagin'd he might work up the incidents of it for the stage, and in order to make Mr. Peachum reveal the mysteries of his art, he ... pretended that both he and his companion, were upon the same expedition with himself.... The poet, who continued to personate a — had several in-

terviews afterwards with Mr. Peachum, and, as some say brought him some things, which he pretended to have got by slight [*sic*] of hand. By his great familiarity with him, he let him into all the knavish practices and intrigues of the thieving trade[26]

With its reference to "the genuine" and its parenthetical aside—"executed a few years ago"—this article attempts to reframe Gay's work as a mimetic reproduction of a dangerous criminal world. It even casts Gay as a shape-shifting Moll or Jack as he strategically impersonates the distinctive languages and practices of criminals to engage in colloquy that produces deeper knowledge of the illicit. The article positions the play in the mode of the vernacular formations that stage an encounter with and disclosure of some real, hidden criminal world and its language as part of a diverse Britain.

Gay's play, of course, is remote from such texts and the work they do, first, as we have been exploring, because its criminals are humorously exaggerated mockups of one version of pastoral's simple, low English men and women. Significantly, it is the very implausibility of their language that situates them in mock pastoral, as the characters speak cant but not the incorrect "vulgar" language one might find in fictional realism.[27] We need not go as far as John Bender's claim that in *The Beggar's Opera* the "manner of speech ... is that of gentlemanly discourse" to agree with his point that, at least in its grammatical propriety, the language is "far from being modeled on low life."[28] This pretense of politeness ties the work to a pastoral mode that was fading, for as Empson noted, after the Restoration, the old pastoral's ability to make "simple people express strong feelings ... in learned and fashionable language" was increasingly impossible. "A feeling gradually got about that anyone below the upper middles was making himself ridiculous ... if he showed any signs of keeping a sense of beauty at all" (12). The relegation of certain once-common terms and phrases to low status discussed in Chapter One played no small role in that linguistically marked division.

Gay's work is far from a mimetic representation of a criminal underworld, second, because its very generic structures alienate the vernacular diversity that Defoe's realist fictions had dramatized and made inviting for readers.[29] While we have seen how new narrative techniques of fiction might have worked in Defoe's novels to facilitate tentative connections to cant-speaking characters, Gay's play offers neither fiction's unreal access to character depth nor its sense of representational transparency in following the events of an individual protagonist's life.[30] The cant-speaking characters of *The Beggar's Opera* do not float in and out of cant usage and criminal life, explaining new practices and languages in ways that might assist readers in identifying with those characters. They already know all that lingo, and the play offers neither explanatory asides, nor any of Jack's and Moll's distancing "as they term it" phrases, nor guiding footnotes in the printed text for its cant expressions.

Moreover, a halting and sometimes static temporality in Gay's play, as opposed to the sequential narrative, pause, narrative movement of Defoe's realist fiction, is especially important in positioning readers in a different relationship to cant and its speakers. As Moll and Jack wander through different groups, they explain a variety of languages—place names, regionalisms, cant, trade argot. They learn, adopt, and leave behind any number of these, leveling hierarchical distinctions between them. The mythos of national diversity in Defoe's fictions is in part a function of this sequential introducing and leveling of linguistic difference. Rather than emphasizing high and low in language—high language is, for the most part, not represented—these works present diverse languages as moments of difference that characters encounter and assimilate as they assimilate for themselves and their readers different spaces and their language in linear time.[31]

Fredric Jameson has described "two systems of temporality" of fictional realism: "a present of consciousness and a time, if not of succession or of chronology, then at least of the more familiar tripartite system of past-present-future."[32] Defoe's Moll and Jack might be said to occupy both. In their retrospective narratives, they move through a past and present, anticipating a future. They exist, however, in the intersection of that chronology and an ongoing "present of consciousness." As they pause the narrative—the forward movement through time—to explain an odd colloquial or cant word, they occupy something closer to a "present of consciousness." It is the chronological encounter with a series of languages that underwrites a sense of national diversity, while the "present of consciousness"—something close to the open fictionality discussed in Chapter Two in the unrealness of a character's pausing to explain to some unseen listener—enables unlikely access for readers and promotes a concomitant investment in those characters and their diverse languages.

At the most basic of formal levels, as a play, Gay's work refuses the linear forward movement of the life of the protagonist of Defoe's fictions, turning instead to various recognizable generic patterns of drama, such as the known and predictable plots regarding tragic heroes or love's trials. The conventions of the staged play in eighteenth-century London also resist any seeming forward movement of an individual life in the constant "disruptions, and attractions of the audience" that Lisa Freeman has documented.[33] In moments of "pointing," for instance, actors stopped to pitch their performance not to the other characters or events on stage but to the audience, inviting playgoers to assess not meaning but the particular actor's technique, making any sense of continuous action quite beside the point. It is worth noting that this is not a "present of consciousness"; its realm is not access to mental interiors but artifice, as the theatergoer appraises not the consciousness but the acting of the actor on stage. Even more disruptive and discontinuous would be the temporality of "celebrated operas" of the period to which Beggar compares his production in the introduction. The very temporal structure of early eighteenth-century Italian opera, often a mere "concert in costume," nearly foregoes narrative movement altogether for a continual pausing for song. Characters do not move forward in time, confronting and assimilating difference, but rather stop movement. And rather than narrative fiction's pausing for digressions to explain words as discussed in Chapter Two, opera singers pause to display the accomplishments of their voice. The arias that make up so much of these productions, like pointing, are "discrete moments, not part of a whole" (32). Like the narrative forms Jameson distinguishes from realism and calls "closed entities and episodes," these moments exhibit "named emotion": isolated, conventionalized feelings (40). Rather than following a presentness of consciousness at the intersection in which it unfolds through time, viewers and readers confront a variety of static characters, scenarios, and set-piece emotions.

In Gay's innovative ballad opera genre, the terms of ballad transmission resist fictional realism's system of temporality as well in their rearticulation of ages-old elements, either air or event. (Although, as we shall see below, *The Beggar's Opera* also often emphasizes the noisy, altering transmission of ballads.) Whether the invocation of an old song, the tune of which everybody already knows, as in "Grim King of the Ghosts" (Air VIII), or the rehearsal of a well-known tale, such as that of the popular ballad "Chevy Chase" (Air XX), the ballads embody the narrative form Jameson and others have counterposed to the realist novel, the *récit*—the tale that describes the memorable event "worthy of retelling over and over again," sharing in common motifs of death (as they do here) or, in more general terms, a sense of the "irrevocable," which makes a presentness of consciousness impossible.[34] As well, the sense of retelling over and over again is literalized in the repetitive form of the "catch," the form by which, the beggar notes, he earns his living. As their performance as "rounds" in the play suggests, "catches" work in a repeating circle, stopping or halting linear movement, each subsequent singer returning or retelling, as it were, the same words and melody.

At the level of language, rather than moving sequentially through and assimilating new cant terms, argots, and provincial languages, Gay's characters speak or allude to two or more already-known languages at once, one always echoing in the background of another. While Defoe's characters learn to produce different languages in particular scenarios—this is part of their shape-shifting mastery—Gay's characters are themselves produced by the stereophony of languages playing simultaneously. This produces, crucially, not depth, but something closer to a solid (*stereos*, in Greek) surface.[35] If, as Freeman has argued, the eighteenth-century stage "highlighted the multiple, contradictory, and opaque surfaces of character," *The Beggar's Opera*, with its conscious stereophonic playing of genres and languages against each other, stresses and exaggerates those qualities of its characters.[36] The simultaneous play of languages renders pointedly implausible *The Beggar's Opera*'s characters, with their multifaceted surfaces. They offer neither Defoe's relatable probability nor his openly fictive access to a consciousness (subjective depth) in time. To return to the question of pastoral, in highlighting the improbability of its characters and their languages, the play exposes that genre's conventions, making its sense of harmonious inclusiveness equally implausible.[37]

We might test this out with the character of Polly Peachum, the one figure whom some critics identify as singularly good, and thus capable of mobilizing sympathy from the audience—a character with seeming depth enough to allow viewers and readers to feel with her. But even she demonstrates her multiple and contradictory allegiances and radical unknowability, significantly, through divergent languages, including cant. In her sentimental soliloquy, in which she envisions Macheath's hanging, she describes how

> I see him already in the cart, sweeter and more lovely than the nosegay in his hand! I hear the crowd extolling his resolution and intrepidity! What vollies [sic] of sighs are sent from the windows of Holborn, that so comely a youth should be brought to disgrace! I see him at the tree! The whole circle are in tears! Even butchers weep! Jack Ketch himself hesitates to perform his duty, and would be glad to lose his fee, by a reprieve. What then will become of Polly! As yet I may inform him of their design, and aid him in his escape. It shall be so. But then he flies, absents himself, and I bar my self from his dear dear conversation! That too will distract me. (I.xii)

"Jack Ketch," a cant term for the hangman, derails the pathos of Polly's vision, reminding readers and viewers, even as she narrates this heroic scene, inviting sympathy both with the "sweet" and "lovely" young man and his weeping witness—even butchers cannot help themselves—that she is fluent in criminal lingo. In her stereophonic language—"sweeter" and "lovely" mix with "Jack Ketch" and "tree"—Polly remains inscrutable. And if her use of the lexicon of the spectacle of hanging implicates her in that tawdry world, those terms also implicate readers who presumably know them. While they are likely caught up in the sentiment of the images Polly tearfully presents, they are also made to snap out of it, in part with the help of these low terms. Polly's mixed vocabulary echoes alongside her use of the term "conversation," imbuing it, too, with its untoward sense of sexual intercourse. Excessive sentiment tips over into sexual entendre as readers experience unstable movement between sympathy and distance, an unsteady movement toward the risqué enabled in part through the play's multiple registers of language.

Both the narrative structure and linguistic stereophony of Gay's play produce not a knowable diversity but indeterminate, split subjects and languages that work on top of and against each other. Macheath, for instance, is constituted in part from the criminal biographies and pantomimes portraying Jack Sheppard, the famous carpenter turned fugitive burglar. In the final image of this character, he is singing of his life with his many "doxies" (that cant term for "she-beggars") as he functions as a symbol of criminal freedom not unlike the endless images of Sheppard eluding the literal chains that would bind him.[38] Macheath, however, was also composed from the tales and songs of the surreptitiously admired highwaymen of this period, heirs to the aristocratic rogue figure that Erin Mackie has analyzed, and his language and song locate him within a courtly Cavalier tradition, as he sings, "Love with youth flies swift away, / Age is nought but sorrow" (II.iv).[39] It is not without emotion that viewers would hear Macheath sing, "But hark! I hear the toll of the bell" (III.xv), referring to the same bell of St. Sepulchre's that Moll's fellow prisoner sang about (although here the reader gets no footnote to explain it). Is it the laboring-class hero or courtly rogue who elicits such feeling? Echoing behind the elevated "but hark" is the cant language of "doxies" and the bell heard by those within Newgate. Macheath signifies on several contradictory and unresolvable levels, made a seemingly solid set of surfaces, as it were, by this stereophony of high and low that permanently estranges unified meaning.[40]

Amping up this stereophonic quality is the engine of the play's burlesque. It is the confusion of low and high in the layering of Peachum's respective languages, the one of respectable business ("let me see how much the stock owes to his industry" [I/III]), and his proverbial and cant expressions, such as "she may plead her belly" (I.ii) or "the gang take her off" (I.ii), that gives a sense of his fixed—and absurdly multifaceted—character.[41] Over time, Defoe's cant-speakers can move between classes: Moll lives with a genteel family in her youth before becoming a criminal familiar with cant and later ascends to the status of respectable estate-owner in North America, leaving behind her adopted cant language. Gay's characters, on the other hand, inhabit multiple positions and their attendant languages all at once, to ridiculous effect. In mimicking high language, they participate in the ludicrous imitation so central to burlesque, and indeed sharply ridicule the low imitating the high. The members of Macheath's gang speak the elevated, aristocratic language of martial right, declaring with bravado that "what we win . . . is our own by the law of arms, and the right of conquest" and making heroic claims to be "sound men and true. . . . [W]ho is there here that would not die for his friend?" But their criminal lingo and acts deflate that language of martial right, and their self-interest repeatedly trumps any sense of "honor" between friends.

Significant here is the burlesque of the vernacular itself, as the proverb lends itself surprisingly well to the criminal. *The Beggar's Opera*'s various proverbs and adages are repeated with ludicrous and criminal difference, as when Matt of the Mint (a debtor) offers, "One man may steal a horse, better than another look over a hedge" (101)—meaning that some people escape punishment for crimes while others are penalized for merely looking as if they might. This assertion resonates with the Beggar's observation (a truism, really) that people of the "lower sort" are severely punished for crimes of a lesser degree, while the "higher sort" go free (101). And yet, of course, Matt's "truism" is also self-serving: Macheath, to whom the assertion refers, has not merely "looked over a hedge" but stolen a horse, so to speak, and worse. Characters repeatedly engage the form of the proverb as collective, "common," aphoristically presented humble truth—the stuff of which vernacular wisdom is made. Yet the play burlesques these proverbs, remaking them in repeating them to describe and scandalously legitimate various forms of criminality.

These are moments when the play estranges the vernacular and leaves it so. Its meanings multiple and manipulatable, the vernacular here does not unify rich and poor in pastoral's "beautiful relations." Nor does it fill out the bottom section of a representation of the "whole of England." Gay illuminates in powerful ways the extent to which such claims are, in Empson's phrase, "palpable nonsense." Even English itself, and not simply colloquialisms and proverbs but standard terms such as "burnt" (III.i), "bubbles" (III.i), "leaky" (III.ii), and "lock" (III.iii) generate multiple meanings, slipping into sly alternative senses understood by some characters and not by others. Like the signifying systems of the fables Jayne Lewis has analyzed, those of *The Beggar's Opera* are both "plain and devious."[42] Lewis explains how Augustans prized this doubled form in terms that might work as well for the language of Gay's play:

> Fables finally harbor little reverence toward their own pretense that signs naturally point to a single meaning, that there can be pure bonds between words and things, that such bonds would be particularly equitable or reassuring if they did exist.... More than their superficial invocation of the sensible world, it is fables' demonstration of their own contingency—of the ways meaning is made—that in Augustan eyes, invested them with something akin to natural authority.[43]

In Gay's writing, seemingly simple vernacular elements highlight contingency, undoing their own "plain" sense and exposing as an illusion their ability to help different classes and groups feel at home with each other. It is precisely those familiar, homey elements of proverb and ballad that Gay's burlesque alienates and undermines at every step. The stereophony of its languages and its endless generation of meaning position *The Beggar's Opera* in direct opposition to pastoral and vernacular institutions. Its "vernacular" is layered and divisive, its various speakers never at home with each other.

Languages of Independence

As the denizens of Gay's criminal underworld sing songs with familiar phrases that make sense on a variety of levels, with meanings available to some, but not to all, and meanings that change in relation to other languages, playgoers and readers interpret them independently, depending on their familiarity with various languages. The multiple registers, the layered meanings of a single term, and the transformation of languages in relation to each other are also part of what allows individuals such as Macheath to enact their independence, in part by improvising with language for their own ends. In his reading of the play, Empson focuses on what he calls its "cult of independence," but does not take up its cant or colloquial language. Instead, he discusses Macheath's independence just before characterizing developments in style in late seventeenth-century prose, observing that a "feeling for independence comes out in the Restoration development of an analytic prose with short sentences" (203). For Empson, it is this plain style that allows individuals autonomy of reasoning and expression. The linguistic style of *The Beggar's Opera* is not, however, that analytic language "purged of associations of feeling and made to stand on its own," clearly not a "basic English . . . flat plain-man writing . . . with analytic powers of generalization" (203). If we pay attention to the play's complex interplay of languages, we see them forming and formed by neither some unified vernacular nor independent individuals but rather by distinct and shifting groups, often hemmed in by the commercial market, as I shall explore in this section.

In its witty reworking of English, cant often inhabits and explodes "flat plain-man writing," remaking words such as "finger" and "catechism" or expressions such as Filch's reference to shrewd thief Betty as "so good a customer" and his own "education" in the "business" (44). These innovations suggest a kind of independence of thought on the part of the language-user, but, much like the crude witticisms one finds in B. E.'s *New Dictionary* (such as using "academy" to mean "a bawdy house"), it is the independence not of an individual but of a group. The terms represent a kind of code shared between various speakers and readers, Serres's noisy third not an individual but a group. Moreover, the multiple independent groups that Macheath's band and their enemies assemble through figurative, contingent languages are notably temporary and provisional. Peachum and Macheath share the same coded cant, but that is a fleeting basis for allegiance, quickly and profoundly displaced by their differences. Peachum is a vested businessman of sorts, with allegiances closer to the lawyers and politicians he can bribe, and whose language he speaks, while his dangerous opponent Macheath finds temporary solidarity with his caddish fellow highwaymen and the language of romance. The play demonstrates the constantly shifting relations of meaning and noise without resolving them, even temporarily.

As the play assembles groups free to invent and exchange languages, including cant, then, it does so only to disband them or, at times, even reinforce a sense of mutual entrapment. Peachum's power over Macheath, Macheath's power over Peachum, and a looming Newgate and Tyburn put paid to any notions of meaningful criminal independence.[44] Gay's play troubles notions of independence further in the figure of the beggar. Like B. E.'s *New Dictionary*, Gay's work identifies the figure of the Beggar as the source of its playful combination of cant language, colloquialisms, and proverbs. It is, after all, "his" opera. Historically, as we have noted, beggars and slaves were closely aligned. As John Richardson has pointed out, in his other works Gay had even equated the two.[45] In some accounts, as we have seen, the beggar and slave were also vaguely connected with freedom—evidence of English liberties, in the case of beggars, who were said to be the direct scions of freed slaves, or, in the Christian and legal discourses around slavery in Defoe's writing, a symbol of a temporary endurance of bondage leading to freedom. In Gay's play the Beggar's independence, however, is vitiated. If, on the one hand, he is free to combine genres and languages in unorthodox ways, then on the other, he must draw from proverbs and colloquial language to do so, and he is also bound to write his heady mix of colloquial and criminal languages to make money.[46] "If poverty be a title to poetry," Beggar asserts, "I am sure nobody can dispute mine."[47] Moreover, while he seems free to determine Macheath's fate (granting his "reprieve" near the play's end), that freedom is limited by his need to cater to the dictates of the market.[48]

Participating in, while underscoring the venality of the commercial literary market, *The Beggar's Opera*, however, demonstrates that it is not simply cant or specialized languages that disperse groups. More recognizably vernacular elements, such as colloquial phrases and popular songs, presumably unifying in their widespread circulation, also fragment meaning and readers. Air LXVIII, for instance, is called "All you that must take a Leap," the opening words of the English song "A Hymn upon the Execution of Two Criminals," which provides the music for Gay's air. Here, the large group familiar with the popular song is subdivided into those who know the phrase that renames it—"All you who must take a leap in the dark"—and those who do not. Some would have encountered it in *Moll Flanders*, which, as we have seen, described women entering into precipitous and unscrutinized marriages as those who "make Matrimony like Death, be a *Leap in the Dark*."[49] The phrase, as some (but not all) readers and viewers would also know is, in addition, a cant expression for execution by hanging (Macheath's own anticipated hanging forming the backdrop to this scene). Hanging and marriage were often compared in popular sayings and imagery, as Peter Linebaugh has described.[50] The many meanings embedded in this colloquial phrase and popular song instate distinct, independent groups recognizing and not recognizing those separate and multiple meanings.

The Beggar's Opera reminds us that the vernacular might mark an uneasy overlap between that which is familiar to and cherished by many and the commercial market. Not only Beggar's narrative choices but also his use of vernacular elements represent not some range of practices of a widely defined and free people, but the commodification of language and song. Contemporary playgoers might have known these phrases through perusing the glossaries and criminal narratives available for sale. Ballads themselves were akin to other print street fodder—the broadsheets of murderers' dying words, criminal biographies, cant dictionaries—all articles for sale. *The Beggar's Opera* even burlesques a ballad song culture that critics such as Joseph Addison were newly valuing for its historic ties to the nation and the pastoral vision it promised of Britain.[51] Old ballads, Addison's "songs of the people," appear here as the urban and commercial artifacts they so often were, made even more unsavory in their relation to the criminal.[52]

Familiarity with popular songs and even their commercial circulation makes additional contingencies of meaning possible. Air LXVIII is taken from Lewis Ramondon's "A Hymn upon the Execution of Two Criminals," a song about two repentant condemned men advocating a clean life and Christian courage. Knowing its source makes its presentation in *The Beggar's Opera* as a love song sung by doxies Lucy and Polly pining for their criminal rogue especially scandalous. The approaching execution of the speaker no longer supplies the occasion for moral reflection, for the idea of a soon-to-be-executed man instead incites a sexual response, as Lucy swoons, "There is nothing moves one so much as a great man in distress." She sings, "Would I might be hanged!" and Polly follows, "And I would so too!" (III.xv), an allusion to the longstanding erotic visions associated with men at the gallows.[53] The women now desire another "leap in the dark," one that would demand a kind of courage, a meaning brushed obscenely against the Christian mettle advocated in "Hymn." As well, Gay's air cheekily reduces the "courage" of that original song to the contents of a bottle of drink, as Macheath turns his bottle upside-down and observes, "see, my courage is out" (III.xv). The phrase "leap in the dark" bursts with distinct and sometimes opposing meanings, and knowing the original song further disturbs any notion that language, even the vernacular language, might speak to or consolidate a unified group.

The Beggar's Opera imbues common songs and proverbs with alternative meanings or brings to the surface less seemly elements, rendering the low complex and multivalent—neither one part of a mimetic representational field nor, finally, simply one side of a high/low binary deployed for satire. Alternatively, even for those readers or viewers who might feel at a distance from the world invoked by a song titled "All you that must take a leap," its criminal singers, and their sordid perversion of Christian meaning, that distance is overcome—indeed, the independence to choose not to identify with the song is undermined—when the address of the title is considered. The "you" of "All you that must take a leap" refers as well to all mortals—"leap in the dark" meaning also to die, in Thomas Hobbes's famous last words. And Ramondon's "Hymn upon the Execution of Two Criminals" speaks not to criminals exclusively but to all and any hearers, as mortals, with something like the admonishment "look on these damned criminals and repent." Readers and auditors cannot put themselves outside of the song—they are summonsed by their own mortality and sinfulness.[54] Ramondon's song already offered multiple positions for its hearers and singers, distancing them from but also including them with the teary-eyed witness, the sexualized spectator, the soon-to-be dead, and the apostate.

The "Hymn," however, despite its moral platitudes, was not published in devout collections of religious songs but in volumes of demotic "pleasant" songs intended for "diversion."[55] Like many of the ballads to which Gay alludes, it appeared originally in Thomas d'Urfey's *Pills to Purge the Melancholy*. Steve Newman has provided excellent insights into the dense cultural politics of this collection, not the least of which is "an association between the Stuart cause and the beauty, unrestrained sexuality, and timeless rituals attributed to rural England," a politically strategic merging of high and low against a Puritan middle.[56] In this sense, the song suggests still another basis of affiliation. At the level of the popular song, vernacular divides as much as it unifies, its promise of a consolidating symbolic economy of language and song breaking down into particular, tentative groupings, such as Puritans and Cavaliers.

The song appeared as well in an eighteenth-century collection titled *The Merry Musician*, which makes room for less reverent songs such as "Praise of Punch."[57] As we are seeing, Gay's riff on Ramondon's "Hymn" is not simply a play on and a reveling in the multiplicity and fractured meanings of what we would now call vernacular languages and forms, but also a reminder of their location in popular commercial publications.[58] The market-driven mixing of languages and forms undoes and multiplies meanings, a dynamic that Gay's ballad opera burlesques. This mixing, of course, took place not only in collections of songs but also in popular print collections of ephemera, such as *Bacchus and Venus*, which classed proverbs with "Select . . . Songs and Catches in love and gallantry" and a canting dictionary.[59] *The Beggar's Opera* might be as much a commentary on these already-existing print mélanges of proverb and cant as an innovative combination of them.

This suspicious attitude toward the commercial institutions of the vernacular that combined cant and other popular representations of criminals with proverbs and popular songs extended into the middle of the century and beyond.[60] Fielding, too, satirizes these commercial mash-ups, in *Jonathan Wild*. His text combines conventional romance elements—the virtuous persecuted, dastardly villains, well-worn love stories—with components of the criminal biography, proverb anthology, and cant lexicon. The narrator refers to a fictitious *Cant Dictionary* to explain terms in Jonathan's argument:

That the same Capacity, which qualifies a *Millken, a †Bridle-cull or a ‡Buttock and File, to arrive at any Degree of Eminence in his Profess, would likewise raise a Man in what the World esteem a more honourable Calling, I do not deny.

> * A housebreaker
> † A Highwayman
> ‡ A Shoplifter, Terms used in the *Cant Dictionary*.[61]

Here, cant is explained with footnotes in a kind of mock scholarship, and is again an obscure language of outliers. The passage compares the accomplishments of its users to those "of a more honorable calling," but as in Gay's writing, the moments of familiarity between strangers—cant-users and people of an "honorable calling"—are awkward and damning. By association, the popular texts combining criminal and colloquial, gritty realism and romance, are equally suspect. Fielding undoes the promise of fixing cant, of stopping its wandering in the ordering of a dictionary or footnote, by overloading meaning, including the corruption of commercial context. Like Gay, he runs commercially popular genres into each other to multiply and fracture meaning.

Jonathan Wild also includes proverbs, but they are presented as adulterated *bon mots*, registering, too, a dubiousness regarding institutions of the vernacular, such as print proverb collections. For instance, the narrator notes that the title character "was proverbially said, to *play the whole Game*" (16), but here, as in *The Beggar's Opera*, the "proverb" is adapted to criminality, becoming a euphemism for cheating, a cant phrase that, interestingly, had also been used in this way in Defoe's description of a pirate's early illicit adventures.[62] *Wild*'s narrator also adapts and invents proverbs, frequently producing wry and jocular aphoristic remarks, such as "nature is of all other females the most obstinate" (81). As he becomes something of a proverb-spouting machine, the organic production of proverbs and their circulation by the Molls and Jacks of the world dissolves into the cynical commentary and invention of an authoritative, sardonic narrator.

Like *The Beggar's Opera*, *Jonathan Wild* draws from print institutions of the vernacular, again, not as part of a common British culture but as the product of a degraded commercialized print culture. Sections of the novel feature proverbs and their print format with hare-brained commentary, such as: "Proverb I: The greatest Men may sometimes overshoot themselves, but their very mistakes are so many Lessons of Instruction. *To teach others the Art of over-reaching*" and "Proverb IV: Arguments among Men are like Bones among Dogs; they serve to set them together by the Ears. *Ergo, an Argument is called a Bone of Contention*" (79).[63] Fielding here satirizes commercially available modern learning with its valuation and belaboring of national, and not especially elevated, linguistic culture, as found in figures such as John Ray, the compiler of *Compleat English Proverbs*. Ray had not only valued and collected English proverbs but also offered pedantic commentary, as in

> If the grass grow in Janiveer,
> It grows the worse for't all the year.
>   There is no general rule without some exception; for in the year 1667 the winter was so mild that the pastures were very green in January, yet was there scarce ever known a plentifuller crop of hay than the summer following.[64]

The moderns' embrace of diversity and the medium of commercial print turned proverbs into fodder for more print, presenting back to readers in endless verbiage what they should already have known or what was not especially worth knowing. The allure of the unknown, the toggle between obscurity and explanation becomes, in both Fielding and Gay, a jokey dead end. For Fielding, print collections of cant, colloquial language, and proverbs served not to remind readers of the strangeness of their compatriots and to help them overcome it, but to debase learning and lower the tenor of the culture, familiarizing readers with what was valueless and reasserting the social divisions that the idea of a vernacular aimed to paper over.

As we have seen, texts such as B. E.'s *New Dictionary* or Defoe's fictions placed cant alongside colloquialisms, and put cant and proverbs in the mouths of beggars or modern itinerant subjects, broadening the representational field of what might count as British. In making meaning of the seemingly strange, their texts are part of the hermeneutic operations that Certeau has described as "restor[ing] vocal delinquency to an order of signifieds."[65] A series of languages is both presented as strange but is also explained and joins, if uneasily, the fold of English. In *The Beggar's Opera* and *Jonathan Wild*, by contrast, the representation of a diverse range of languages does not fill out a wide-sweeping survey of Britain. These works instead trouble claims regarding language and its ability to organize meaning or articulate something real. This answers at times to Certeau's notion of the "postlinguistic" sense of glossolalia, that moment when meaning falls back into unmeaning, pointing to "the excesses, the overflows, and the wastes of language": a return to opacity.[66] Gay's play reveals that what we might be tempted to think of as "vernacular" is in fact a set of loaded, layered, sometimes interconnected and sometimes distinct languages that are not particularly unifying. In fact, extensive knowledge of the many allusions in these works produces a confusion of affiliations and meanings. The more one knows, the noisier and less decipherable they become. That which might be recruited and instituted as "vernacular" is too layered and self-divided to unify, too noisy in these barbed critiques, to serve any consolidating purpose.

CHAPTER FOUR

The Gendered Slang of Century's End

THE LAUGHTER GAY'S AND FIELDING'S TEXTS EXCITED could be darkly derisive. Using cant in burlesque writing, however, could also temper what was fearful or threatening about it, making it divertingly comic. That mode of the comic known as burlesque was actually deeply associated with language in the eighteenth century, describing not just cant language in unexpected places, of course, but any language that pointed to its own unruliness. Johnson's first definition of the term "burlesque" asserts that it raises laughter "by unnatural or unsuitable language"; in his second definition, it appears first as "ludicrous language," and he defines "ludicrous" as "Burlesque, merry, exciting laughter."[1] Ludicrous language excites laughter not only in moments of stylistic and thematic inappropriateness—the thief speaking hyperbolic rhetoric regarding virtue—but in its own ludic qualities, as in the euphemism, the pun, or wit's playful movement between words and associations. One commentator on ludicrous language of the period, James Beattie, offers an example of it in Filch's move from his description of being "pumpt"—drenched with cold water when discovered to be a pickpocket—to "thoughts of going to sea." Beattie observes that "one sort of water suggests another to the thief's fancy; . . . there is something . . . incongruous, in the thought, and yet, at the same time the appearance of natural connection" as he attempts to track the "opposition of suitableness and unsuitableness" that makes for laughable language.[2]

In Gay's and Fielding's burlesques, the comic strangeness of cant, and of language itself, is made more so, its "unnaturalness" and "ludicrousness" emphasized often in the interest of cutting satire. Cant lexicographers of the later part of the century, however, celebrated cant's amusing figurative uses of language, especially its humor, perhaps along the same lines that rendered *Polly*'s Macheath/Morano a figure of broad comedy at century's end.[3] They took the humor of the burlesque uses of cant and low languages but left the grim vision behind. While readers might be strangers to the world of canters, later collections of cant language often introduced it to elicit laughter—a laughter that depended on and reminded readers of their own wit and their playful intimacy with a shared and expanding English.

Francis Grose's bestselling transformative collection of what he referred to as both "cant" and "burlesque" terms, *A Classical Dictionary of the Vulgar Tongue*, draws from this sense of the "vulgar tongue" as a ludicrous and entertaining language filled with puns, metaphors, and other witticisms.[4] His important text also, however, reflects the "pseudoethnography" of realist depictions of cant found in earlier eighteenth-century lexicons and Defoe's criminal fictions. Grose compiled his guide, he claimed, from fieldwork, and promised a comprehensive revelation of new words continuously generated in unseen but lively pockets of England's rapidly growing urban centers.[5] In this work, constant innovations, even those by criminals and the low, could nonetheless be designated and exchanged as signs of a collective energetic British freedom, even as more material freedoms (such as access to a commons and customary remuneration) disappeared. In combining the burlesque and ethnographic approaches, Grose's catalogue makes "the vulgar tongue" no longer the language of outsiders, of interloping "bohemians," but fundamentally British. And being British becomes, in part, a matter of being able to follow and trade in humorous low language, thereby building imaginary cross-class affiliations—crucially, between men.

Put slightly differently, Grose's foundational work is one of several texts of the period in which the term "cant" gives way to "slang," with its more comprehensive, less singularly criminal sense.[6] In his *Classical Dictionary*, the first to list "slang" as a dictionary entry, Grose defined it simply as "cant language." Yet the languages indexed in his work answer to slang in a more familiar sense, drawing from not only criminal jargon but also inventive "vulgarisms." In fact, this compilation, which includes many a word from older cant dictionaries alongside lewd and mundane terms, is the first to promise readers a dictionary not of "cant" but of "the Vulgar Tongue." Its entries, whether ludicrous witticisms such as "JUNIPER LECTURE a round scolding bout" or "RED RAG the tongue" or humble terms such as "LOBKIN a house to lie in: also a lodging," are vulgarisms: words that were slipping, from the beginning of the eighteenth century, as we remarked in Chapter One, into markedly disreputable status. These words were catalogued alongside explicitly cant terms such as "BENE FEAKERS Counterfeiters of Bills," but in reclassifying the collection not as "cant" but as "vulgar," Grose invites a rethinking of these terms as everyone's, as of "the people"—a vernacular, in a sense—even as he demotes the status of that ersatz language to something vaguely illicit, creating the category we now call slang.

Nearly a decade earlier, James Beattie had similarly lumped cant and vulgar terms together as "mean phraseology." Distinct from either words of "peculiar dignity" or words "always necessary, used by people of all conditions,

[that] find a place in every sort of writing," mean phraseology consists of "trite proverbs, colloquial oaths, ... the ungrammatical phrase of conversation; the dialect peculiar to certain trades, the jargon of beggars, thieves, gamblers, and fops, foreign and provincial barbarisms and the like."[7] In Beattie's "mean phraseology" and in Grose's "vulgar tongue," the foreign, the criminal, and the colloquial occupy a shared space, excluded from "a place in every sort of writing," the noise, perhaps, that helps define, through contrast, what we would now call standard English. In these works, both colloquial and criminal languages encompass an early version of what Pierre Bourdieu has called "popular speech ... defined only in relational terms ... nothing other than the set of words which are excluded from dictionaries of the legitimate language or which only appear in them with negative labels."[8] In Grose's work, however, that language is also proudly, defiantly English.

The Vulgar Tongue and "Real Characters in the Inferior Rank of Life"

The "vulgar tongue" Grose compiles might be illegitimate, its inclusion of cant and bawdy terms besmirching it with a residue of criminality and rank impropriety, yet, in his jocular revaluation, it is also a point of national pride. In printing his "English Dictionary," as he calls it in his preface, Grose hopes to prove "our language ... at least as copious as the French and as capable of witty equivoque." Moreover, this vulgar tongue, generated in London, is worth knowing by all Britons—and is "absolutely necessary to natives at a distance from the metropolis."[9] I shall turn in a moment to that "witty equivoque" by which he establishes the merits of the English vulgar tongue, but I first want to examine why he and others thought the knowledge of such language "absolutely necessary" to English-speakers near and far. In Chapter Two we saw Defoe's Moll and Jack engage in an ongoing process of displaying and translating what were presented as, in some ways, strange languages within the reader's own country, a gesture repeated in Fielding's and Smollett's novels. These works of fiction, set in Britain, present the customs and languages of fellow Britons as strange, as mundane, but also worth knowing and accessible through a narrator implausibly familiar with a wide spectrum of sectors at the low end of society.

Grose's representation of the "vulgar tongue" as ranging through a variety of low worlds with which he is uniquely familiar and willing to explain reprises that narrative position, one also found in George Parker's *A View of Society and Manners in High and Low Life* and *Life's Painter of Variegated Colours*.[10] Parker, a self-styled raconteur, describes his life as an itinerant, an actor (and, suggestively, lecturer in English elocution) and delves into a broad array of British locales and classes. Like a Defoe character (or Defoe himself), he prides himself on his ability to "talk either ethics with a minor canon of St. Paul's or cant and slang with a lumper of St. Giles."[11] Similarly, Grose, an often-itinerant army captain and antiquary, curates the language of those he calls the "common people" from "soldiers on the long march, seamen at the cap-stern, ladies disposing of their fish, and the colloquies of a Gravesend-boat."[12] Here, the lexicographer inserts himself into various scenes to collect language, blithely descending to the low, boasting of his ability to speak to anyone. True knowledge extends throughout a range of social levels, including the low, and depends on first-hand experience with its speakers; it is increasingly knowledge-producers, and not just criminals, who must be wanderers.

This is distinct from Samuel Johnson's model of collecting language from printed texts only, but it is also distinct from the curatorial methods of earlier cant collections, which generally neglected to discuss how the lexicographer found his words, treating their outlying speakers as hostile enemies to be avoided—and often, in fact, merely drawing from previous printed works. Grose and Parker, alternatively, made use of fiction's invitation to inhabit, albeit briefly, the lives of specific types—probable though not specified beings—with whom readers might even feel some affective relation. The Molls and Jacks of the world might have dropped out of the novel by the late eighteenth century, but their languages, and the overture to imagine them through it, lived on in Grose's and Parker's lexicons and their position as mobile, polyglot lexicographers who prided themselves on persuasive imitation of a spectrum of strange languages, not least of all cant and low ones.

Contemporary readers' introduction to these terms was no longer through a character inextricably immersed in those worlds, however. It was now through an outsider briefly inhabiting those realms and allowing them to look in. It was modeling a kind of explicit voyeurism into English cultures not their own, but perhaps made so in the narratives and lexicons that catalogued their words for readers. Popular texts from, Ned Ward's early *The London Spy* and Tom Brown's contemporaneous *Amusements Serious and Comical* to the later *New London Spy* and *Complete Modern London Spy* tempted readers, as earlier eighteenth-century cant lexicons did, with the promise of revealing low and scandalous aspects of life at the center of the nation, tucked alongside more respectable sites and societies.[13] In these works, not just criminal activity but other diverse, sometimes-common cultural practices appear as strange goings-on best discovered by a spy's or, in the case of Brown's *Amusements*, a foreigner's estranging and therefore more penetrating eye. These texts map the unusual underground worlds of criminals and beggars, bawds and prostitutes, and render strange more generally visible and familiar worlds, from the inns of court to the tea table, from a position, however, never quite of those worlds, a model that extends to later works, from William Godwin's *Caleb Williams* to Dickens's *Oliver Twist*.

Although as a traveling actor, Parker's status is not quite socially sanctioned, he is not the first-person narrator of some of Defoe's prose fictions, slipping in and out of actual crime. And Grose's distance from the people he documents is clear. He was a paymaster in the militia, and it was through this post that he became acquainted with the wide body of nonstandard English terms he collected in the *Classical Dictionary*.[14] Both Parker and Grose announced their authorship of their work (unlike the mysterious B. E. or the anonymous author of the *New Canting Dictionary*). And both, as author figures, explicitly modeled their skills at moving through spaces, adapting to the low communities in which they found themselves, and dexterously recording and translating the vulgar languages they encountered. Pierce Egan's brief biography of Grose describes the latter's pride in his rambles into the worlds of the vulgar and criminal, resembling those of such "pioneers" as Ward and Brown, but with the further aim of self-disguise—to appear as, but clearly not to be one of the common people.[15] Similarly, Parker boasted that throughout his travels he was able to keep up appearances as "one of the vulgar."[16]

Like the eponymous hero of the very popular 1745 *The Life and Adventures of Bampfylde-Moore Carew*, the story of a gentleman who descends from university life to travel amongst the gypsies (a text from which Grose drew), these authors derived power from their ability to imitate, specifically linguistically, subgroups, particularly the roving lower classes often characterized as criminal.[17] Thus, while Grose and Parker remained indebted to the realist fiction strategies of Defoe, they innovated on them. Unlike a Moll or Jack, who invite attachment to characters who inhabit and live criminal lives (if only briefly), the figure of the lexicographer in Parker's and Grose's works invites attachment to interlopers who effortlessly descend into local, strange worlds at will, but can and do leave them just as quickly. This ability to move, to adopt and reject class positions and linguistic registers, is only available, these texts insist, by men. The "vulgar tongue" becomes the coin of the realm exclusively for English males who fancy themselves able to speak between classes in a rapidly transforming nation.

Like some realist novelistic depictions of British society, Grose's and Parker's works suggested that society might be best known through its lower ends, where "the real" was more exposed, less hidden by polite manners. Parker followed the logic that national character and manners were to be found below the cosmopolitan elite, that they were most apparent at the very lowest levels. Referring to himself in the third person, he states that in recording the varieties of local life, attitudes, and languages, particularly at the low end of the social spectrum, "the knowledge of his country ... was indeed his chief study."[18] He complains of "something so evidently bordering on disguise, among the great," and explains that, for this reason, "he has given most of his pictures as drawn from real characters in the inferior rank of life" and related "anecdotes which the polished critic may call *d—d* [damned] *low*."[19]

If part of the point of polite language is to hide away the ungenteel aspects of life (and of national character and manners) by not speaking of them, both

Parker's and Grose's print representations of vulgar language revel in the exposure of these elements, their lexicons providing access to intimate aspects of daily living. Vulgar language, however, also sometimes disguises these humble elements so that they become strange. Grose discloses scandalous meanings to terms such as "TO FRIG. to be guilty of the crime of self pollution" and "DRURY LANE AGUE. the venereal disorder." He sets such terms alongside simple ordinary words, such as "BEDFORDSHIRE. I am for Bedfordshire, i.e. for going to bed" or "BEVER. An afternoon's luncheon; also a fine hat, bevers fur making the best hats." This estranges these familiar terms, as they, too, appear as something to be revealed.[20] Parker combines traditional cant terms, such as "queer bit-makers," meaning the makers of counterfeit coins, with terms for Grub Street performers, such as "chaunter-culls," those who will, for pay, sing "a ballad on a treasonable subject."[21] We have seen the mingling of criminal and colloquial in B. E.'s early eighteenth-century cant dictionaries and Defoe's novels. This also takes place in Grose's composite lexicon, which includes "CHAUNTER-CULLS" as well as "NIPPS, The shears used in clipping money" next to "NOB. The head," and the term "FRENCH LEAVE. to take a French leave, to go off without taking leave of the company, a saying frequently applied to persons who have run away from their creditors." But all now signal a "vulgar" and "low" language accessed from an odd, intrusive, and estranging figure who might provide unique access to "the knowledge of his country," revealing the strangeness at the heart of the British nation.

Burlesque and Vulgar Language as a Language of Effect

Some of Grose's entries answer to vulgarity in our sense of the term as lewd or obscene, such as "NIGHTMAN. one whose business it is to empty necessary houses [privies] in London, which is always done in the night." These terms, for all their reference to normally unspoken foulness, however, work through a figurative metonymy, their exposure of the vile and hidden achieved by way of obscuring wit.[22] Grose and Parker hew toward the playful and comic tone of Gay's and Fielding's representations, often cataloguing euphemisms for the unseemly, as in Grose's entry "Gentleman's Companion" for louse. This comic attitude to the vulgar tongue is one made available, in part, from burlesque, particularly that of Gay, where humor, entertainment, and effect might be said to supplant moral outrage at real criminals and their language. Beattie, in his discussion of "Ludicrous Composition," says as much, noting that *Beggar's Opera* might be "dangerous, scandalously immoral, but it is the wit and humor, not the villainy of Macheath, that makes the audience merry."[23]

The effect, the charm and humor of these terms, is a product, in part, of the need for obscurity, the low language's willingness to name, but also to obscure, untoward aspects of life, as in the euphemisms for a venereal disease, "Spanish

Gout," or execution day, "Collar Day."[24] As Beattie had noted, "euphemism partakes of the nature of metaphor."[25] And, as Grose had put it, the English language and its speakers were especially given to such "witty equivoque."[26] This is, supposedly, part of what made the English language "copious," the possible meanings of words proliferating, as in "PERSUADERS. Spurs," or words combined to make new figurative meanings, as in "WOODEN PARENTHESIS. The pillory" or "GAPESEEDS. Sights; anything to feed the eye."[27] This copious language also illuminated ties between its speakers. The surprising connection between term and definition in an unexpected combination of like and unlike would only be available to those able to comprehend the figurative senses of words; even then, such sense would often only be apparent after the fact of explanation. Such terms functioned, perhaps, more like "riddle and answer," as Daniel Heller-Roazen writes, "learnt as a unit, and it is knowledge of the riddle that is more important than the ability to work it out."[28] And yet, more than merely an occluding code, such terms reminded readers of what they might have in common with their users, the recognition of the figurative meanings available in their shared language. Creating or following the wit of such idioms depends on a familiarity, and ludic playfulness, with meaning unavailable and likely puzzling to the outsider. The humor depends on movement beyond the literal to figural, from obscurity to comic and scandalous intimate recognition.

Its surprising witty qualities, its unexpected figurations and disorienting innovations, are key aspects in the revaluation of cant or slang language at the century's end, a recuperation that emphasized this language as diverting and suggestively shared. This reassessment moves beyond the empirical or mimetic claims we have observed to something like poetic qualities. Parker imagines his audience not as a gawping fairground public but as "that species of people, who, at the same time that they can enjoy the flights of fancy on an attic wing, yet, stooping their pinions, feel as much pleasure in the effusions of what is termed *cant, flash, low wit,* and *humour,* which substantially are quickened by the same *orb,* as the witty compositions of a more refined taste."[29] Slang might be low, but to the right audience its appeal is a function of the same capacity to feel pleasure at higher "flights of fancy." For Parker, cant has in common with poetry its "charmes," something like its aesthetic powers. Unlike Dekker and other early cataloguers of cant, Parker believes this is a capacity shared by its purported creators. Grose similarly justifies his publication of cant and "burlesque terms and ... phrases," or vulgarisms—even in the face of accusations of immorality—by claiming that the language is inherently "expressive," its speakers' "only object being effect."[30] These words "compensate by their wit, for the trespass committed on decorum"[31]; that is, what they say is less important than how they say it. There is a detachment of meaning from expression and a privileging of the "poignant," the quality of touching (the etymology of "poignant" suggesting a literal pricking or piercing), over transparent referentiality. Hearing, reading, and learning the "vulgar tongue" offer moments of delightful effect, an aesthetic response that trumps moral or class concerns and from which its vulgar creators are not necessarily divorced.

The term for this language that emerges at the end of the century—"flash"— gets at this quality. As low, obscure language euphemistically hiding something came to be known as "flash," its capacity to be showy in its very obscurity became prominent. Consider the catachresis of a phrase in Parker's lexicon, "to fly the Blue Pigeon" (stealing lead when installing windows), an evocative image far removed from the actual meaning of the term that calls attention to itself even while (supposedly) attempting to conceal criminal meaning. These outlandish images, inventive metaphors, and colorful language make slang a kind of sensational and freakish spectacle. In fact, Parker defines "to slang" as "to exhibit any thing in a fair or market, such as a tall man, or a cow with two heads, that's called slanging, and the exhibited thing a slang cull."[32]

This flash quality is also in evidence in the aural quality of these expressions. We might recall that "euphemism," a term which itself invokes sound, is taken from the Greek *euphemismos*, for speaking fairly or sounding good. Oblique aurality, as we have seen, had been an aspect of cant from its earliest representations, whether in the sounded phonemes that sometimes had no apparent meaning, something like pure sound/noise, or in the rhymes and sound patterns that focused on sound over meaning. Parker's and Grose's collections are filled with such sound-oriented terms as "jibber the kibber," which Parker defines as "a watch-word made use of by the people ... of Cornwall to point out a wreck. ... [T]he inhospitable mob, who were in expectation of this event instantly plunder the ship."[33] Terms in Parker's list such as "lully priggers" (linen stealers) form nonsensical sounds; the rhythmic sound patterns of "Jigger Dubber" (jailors), "Stoop-Napper" (some set in the pillory) and "Kiddy Nippers" (out-of-work tailors who scissors other tailors' wages out of their pockets) insistently raise aural effect before meaning.[34] In both its aural and figurative qualities, this language moves away from a position of merely representing the real into something closer to the "charmes of poesie" Dekker had attributed to it in some of its earliest print representations.[35] Notably, this quality is ascribed not simply to any euphemistic language but particularly to low euphemistic language. While the powerful and fashionable spoke in euphemisms, as Henry Fielding had exposed in his *Jonathan Wild* and *The Covent Garden Journal*'s "Modern Glossary," their proper English terms, such as "beau" and "fool," had little of the intentionally humorous, inventive qualities and none of the aurally compelling sense of the vulgar euphemisms Parker and Grose assembled.[36]

Euphemistic and showy, the force of the vulgar tongue in Parker's and Grose's accounts derives largely from its wit, which John Locke and then Joseph Addison had described as the identifying of "Resemblance and Congruity of Ideas," finding likenesses amongst the unlike that give "surprise."[37] Both writers had derided figurative language altogether; Locke had argued that such manipulations as the "figurative application of words . . . are for nothing else but to insinuate wrong ideas, move the passions, and thereby mislead the judgment; and so indeed are a perfect cheat."[38] Defoe, too, critiqued figurative manipulation of language. Moll resiliently calls people and acts by their true name—referring to herself as "a meer cast off Whore, *for it was no less*" and railing against "all those Women who consent to the disposing their Children out of the way, *as it is call'd . . .* 'tis only a contriv'd Method for Murther."[39] *Jonathan Wild*'s narrator repeatedly suggests that failing to honor the linguistic contract through the use of euphemisms is itself a kind of criminal activity that works against the unity of the nation.

While such dismissal of figurative language might be relegated to the pursuit of philosophical and moral truths, Addison had spoken scathingly of wit in imaginative writing as well, citing French critic Jean Regnault de Segrais in arguing that "the lowest Form" of poetry readers

> like nothing but the Husk and Rind of Wit, prefer a Quibble, a Conceit, an Epigram, before solid Sense and elegant Expression: These are Mob-Readers. . . . But though they make the greatest Appearance in the Field, and cry the loudest, the best on't is they are but a Sort of French Huguenots, or Dutch Boors, brought over in Herds, but not naturalized.[40]

Addison, and others, had associated wit with the "lowest" form of reading, a mere "husk" enjoyed by "mob-readers" who were also outsiders—"French Huguenots, or Dutch Boors." In Grose's estimation, alternatively, such wit was now playfully naturalized, its creative innovations a function of British freedom, and as such, a quality to be celebrated.

"Freedom of Thought and Speech" and the "Ebullitions of Vulgar Wit"

Both the witty putting together of unlike elements to produce unexpected likeness and the scandalous rebelliousness of the expressions Grose includes in his collection bespeak, for him, British freedom. To Grose, the words and phrases he collected (such as "GUTTING A HOUSE. Clearing the furniture out of it," taken from the expression "to gut," once used to mean exclusively the evisceration of a living thing, or "BEARD SPLITTER. A man much given to wenching") yoked unlike notions together through a surprising likeness and enabled a shared moment of laughter that was a sort of freedom from the bounds of both linguistic and moral decorum. He explicitly connected this lively and forceful ingenuity to the freedoms afforded by the superior political structure of the British nation. He jocularly claimed that it was because of the nation's political freedoms that the speech of the "common people" had greater "force and poignancy" than any Continental language. English, he argued, was shaped by the "freedom of thought and speech, arising from, and privileged by our constitution, [which] gives a force and poignancy to the expressions of our common people, not to be found under arbitrary governments, where the ebullitions of vulgar wit are checked by the fear of the bastinado."[41] This was a return to, and an expansion of, the rhetoric of freedom long and complexly attached, as we have seen, to cant and low language. Freedom was explicitly evidenced in "vulgar wit," itself revalued in Grose's evaluation.[42]

In his jocose praise of a linguistic freedom enjoyed by English-speakers, Grose, then, emphasized the "voluntary" aspect of Locke's assertion that "words . . . come to be made use of by men, as the signs of their Ideas . . . by a voluntary Imposition."[43] "Our constitution," as Grose put it, made possible a language free to innovate, free to make witty connections, even—or perhaps especially—in its naming of the lewd. As we saw in Chapter One, B. E., in his 1699 *New Dictionary*, had situated a language that was the sign of freedom in the mouths of beggars, former slaves whose now-free existence proclaimed the freedom of their "rent payers," English society as a whole.[44] Grose, however, identified not beggars but the "common people" themselves and their "freedom of thought and speech, arising from, and privileged by our constitution" directly as the source of this language and the freedom it betokened.[45] In his humorous estimation, the improvisations of the "common people" produced the "poignant" language that stands as proof that Britons, as James Thomson had put it, "never will be slaves."[46]

Seventeen years later, in her *Essay on Irish Bulls*, Maria Edgeworth would make use of similar claims regarding British linguistic freedoms and political history. What are called "Irish bulls," or blunders, are uncomfortably close to the "unexpected assemblage of ideas, apparently discordant, but in which some point of resemblance or aptitude is suddenly discovered" that form the basis of what in England is called wit and figurative language, both poetic (Edgeworth cites Milton) and common.[47] Edgeworth argues that the English enjoy these linguistic freedoms while the Irish do not. She praises the figurative language of a Dublin shoeblack—a language that sounds much like English cant in phrases such as "sky a copper." (Edgeworth translates: "the lofty idea of raising a metal to the skies is substituted for the mean thought of tossing up a halfpenny."[48]) While the Irish were ridiculed for such language, an Englishman was allowed license for ludicrous statements, for "it would, indeed, be an intolerable restraint upon social intercourse . . . if he were compelled to talk, upon all occasions, as if he were amenable to a star-chamber of criticism, and surrounded by informers."[49] Grose's facetious rhetoric had become familiar enough for Edgeworth to draw from it, as she alludes to a repressive linguistic regime that free Britons avoid.

Edgeworth goes on to deploy her analysis of colloquial and figurative language to undo the boundaries between native and foreign, as we shall see in

Chapter Six. Grose, however, drew from that rhetoric of freedom and cant to which B. E.'s preface alluded, to underscore the witty superiority of the English. While B. E.'s work had suggested a convoluted relationship between slave and freeman, this was not so for Grose, who removed actual slaves entirely from white Britain and its language. "NEGROE" is, in his word list, synonymous with "slave," defining the man or woman by color and dismissing the possibility that a white Briton could ever occupy the same position. The collection also redefines "Black Indies" as "Newcastle Upon Tyne, whose rich coal mines prove an Indies to their proprietors." By filling in the ambiguities of B. E.'s entry for Black Indies as "Newcastle, from whence the coals are bought"—making the point of connection merely wealth—Grose removes the implicit connection between black Africans' and English miners' bodies that had been available in B. E.'s open-ended definition.[50] Britain's connection to slavery is fully displaced, relocated either to racialized African slaves seemingly unconnected to Britain or figuratively transferred to a continental population subject to the arbitrary and unbridled rule of the Catholic Church and of monarchs and their language academies, called up in Grose's metonym—"bastinado."

In such rhetoric, cant wanders from a purely burlesque sense back toward its position as a real language spoken by free Britons. Although ostensibly a language of underground London, however, Grose's lexicon, when examined, is actually that of wanderers, who enjoy, at best, very mixed relations to freedom. Grose's "common people," his "authorities" on the vulgar tongue, were soldiers, mariners, and fishwives (v–vi). Literally roving land and sea or in constant contact with those who do, the speakers of the "common terms" as listed in Grose's lexicon often reworked terms encountered in seafaring—into which laborers were often pressed—as in "SPLICED. Married: an allusion to joining two ropes ends by splicing. *Sea Term*" or "BEARINGS. I'll bring him to his bearings; I'll bring him to reason. *Sea Term*." Similarly suggestive of dislocation and the long arm of the state, George Parker recorded slang used by fugitive expatriates in Dunkirk, "abandoned characters whose infamy and villainy has expelled them from their own country."[51] The "vulgar tongue" that functioned as Parker's true evidence of national manners and Grose's sign of British liberty was in many cases, developed outside of Britain or beyond local contexts, by vagrants whose sometimes-criminal status and connection to the forced mobility shared by slaves had to be suppressed.

In addition, many of the terms included in Grose's "vulgar tongue" are those of that reluctantly mobile population, the Irish, from "BUCK . . . To run a buck; to poll a bad vote at an election. (*Irish term*)" and "LEAF to go off with the fall of the leaf, to be hanged; criminals hanged in Dublin, being turned off from the outside of the prison, by the falling of a board, propped up, and moving on a hinge like the leaf of a table. (*Irish*)" to "PILLALOO. The Irish cry or howl at funerals" and

BLARNEY he has licked the Blarney stone; he deals in the wonderful, or tips us the traveler. The Blarney stone is a triangular stone on the very top of an ancient castle of that name, in the county of Cork in Ireland, extremely difficult of access, so that to have ascended to it was considered as a proof of perseverance, courage, and agility, whereof many are supposed to claim the honour, who never atchieved [sic] the adventure; and to tip the Blarney, is figuratively used for telling a marvelous story, or falsity. (*Irish*).

Irish men and women migrated to Britain for both seasonal and permanent employment. As Peter Linebaugh writes of their language, "in hard times it migrated to England and thrived in the boozing kens of London."[52] Once again, the "noise" of Serres's third man oscillates between disruptive opacity and the basis of meaning-making between British subjects.[53]

Grose's lexicon is a rich amalgam formed through movement, his "vulgar tongue" originating within and without Britain, emerging especially in the obscurity of languages circulating out of context and from varying positions of servitude. It is these contexts, of forced migration, servitude, and borderline criminalization, that often created the occasions for the type of "poignant" language he collected—and not, as he would have it, an organic English freedom. Grose's "common people" and Parker's "slang boys" occupy a shifting relation to place and positions of servitude, wavering between legality and criminality. This recalls our discussions of itinerancy in Chapters One and Two, and debates about whether those wandering the nation's roads were shareholders in British freedoms or *de facto* criminals. Sailors and soldiers are, of course, legally mobile, not the illegal vagrants of the canting crews or the migrant Irish laborers subject to endless persecution—but they might well have occupied that position of illegal vagrancy before being pressed into service, or before their penury forced them to enlist, or again after they found themselves demobilized. The mobility of Irish migrants was encouraged, for they provided cheap labor to the British economy. But they were also subject to vagrancy charges, transitioning in and out of "legal" status.

The status of the vernacular, then, continues in the later part of the century to vacillate between criminal and merely common, an instability sometimes in evidence in the terms and definitions themselves. In Parker's entry "jibber the kibber," the "inhospitable mob" is difficult to distinguish from the criminal as they eagerly anticipate plundering a shipwreck—still more so if, as Parker implies, they have caused the wreck by fastening a guiding light to a refractory horse. As well, while Grose sets "common people" against criminals, he also claims that when compiling his *Dictionary*

> many heroic sentences, expressing and inculcating a contempt of death, have been caught from the mouths of the applauding populace, attend-

ing those triumphant processions up Holborn-hill ... and various choice flowers have been collected at executions, as well those authorized by the sentence of the law ... as those inflicted under the authority and inspection of that impartial and summary tribunal, called the Mob, upon the pick-pockets, informers, or other unpopular criminals.[54]

Grose caught some of the vulgar tongue from the mouths of spectators at a hanging—but where were their allegiances in relation to the criminal? Did they applaud his execution or his bravado, expressing "contempt of death"? More to the point, whose "mouths" supplied the "choice flowers" he collected at executions? It is not clear if they were those of criminals or—not much better—the "mob" watching those criminals and sometimes executing them themselves as vigilantes. Significantly, among the mob's most unpopular victims were informers connected to and serving "legitimate" society.

This confusion between "criminal" and "common people" might correspond with the criminalization of the laboring classes discussed in Chapter One and accelerated in the 1780s, the very period in which Grose and Parker produced their glossaries. During this time, the line between workers and criminals dissolved in terms of the state's treatment; Douglas Hay and Nicholas Rogers note that in the 1780s, "penal sanctions were used as often against workers as they were against criminals." At the same time, military demobilization contributed to a "moral panic among the propertied classes," and the 1780s marked the century's highest number of "prosecutions, death sentences, and hangings" as the demobbed incited fear and were often persecuted and criminalized as a result. Wandering and destitute former military men seeking livelihoods led to a buildup of the national militia, "the barracking of large numbers of soldiers, and their much more frequent use to deal with popular disorder."[55] As paymaster for the Hampstead militia, Captain Grose was directly involved in those internally directed military operations. That position, administering the infrastructure formed to respond to the darker effects of industrialization and mobility, is compellingly connected to his ideological role in rhetorically revaluing criminalized culture as "of the people."

As if to belie the more rigorous punishments of wayward servants and laborers being put in place in late eighteenth-century British society, Grose and other writers celebrated the vulgar-talking Briton, criminal or not, pitching him against his figurative other, the continental "slave" subject to, amongst other absolutist impositions, language academies. Grose's assertion that the very existence of a separate, low language was a sign of British freedoms poses a dialectic of social repression and rhetorical rehabilitation of "the common" and of the vernacular itself. Invoking the freeborn Englishman unfettered by the authoritarian laws of Continental language academies, Grose, like his predecessors, draws from what Hay and Rogers call the "constitutional rhetoric of the freeborn Englishman, free from Continental monarchical oppression ...

an established trope in national politics."[56] It is at the moment that Grose and others celebrated British liberty in their representations of vulgar language, however, that a set of material relationships of labor and property, such as customary remuneration and access to a commons, relationships that might arguably mark a deeper sense of liberty, were being legislated out of existence. Grose himself resurrected the characterizations of beggars as able-bodied people faking destitution, their "voluntary austerities" aimed at "excit[ing] compassion."[57] The new appreciation of a defiant, if also playful, "vulgar" language was haunted by the association of the people with the criminal and with the unfree.

In Grose's *Classical Dictionary*, then, an imaginary freedom of language replaced the freedoms of the commons and of customary remuneration that parliamentary statutes were taking away.[58] If parliamentary statutes criminalized certain customary forms of property and labor relations, the rhetoric of custom as a means of social cohesion could no longer be fully available to national discourse, or could only be available in a much-changed form. Instead, a witty burlesque language, detached from particular contexts, became available for play and trade as part of the imagining of shared cultural terrain. As we shall see in a moment, Grose viewed this witty burlesque language as undergoing constant and rapid change, a temporality that might itself be related to—even a function of—the erosion of the legal and social force of custom. These endless new vulgar witticisms become a kind of coin circulated, crucially, between men.

Cant and Slang: Custom and Innovation

Grose's rhetoric, attributing the poignancy of the vulgar tongue to English freedom, is, not surprisingly, confused. As in the contemporary political theory to which they were sometimes indebted, ideas about language often reprised the tensions between custom and innovation in relation to notions of freedom, exposing the paradox of the figure of the freeborn Englishman. His freedom was based on age-old custom, but what of the freedom to make choices and even invent new practices in the present? At some points, Grose turns to the authority of ancient customary usage, including in his lexicon, as he puts it, "those burlesque phrases, quaint allusions, and nick-names for persons, things, and places, which from long uninterrupted usage are made classical by prescription" (iii). And in his preface, he cites as his authorities a number of by-then antique books of cant language, such as *The Bellman of London* (1608) and Thomas Dekker's 1638 *English Villainies* (iv). Here, Grose the antiquary, who was, after all, best known for his antiquarian publications, is in evidence, his job the preservation of old words, which "on falling into disuse, or being superseded by new ones, vanish without leaving a trace behind, such were the late fashionable words, a bore and a twaddle... these are here carefully registered."[59] Whether or not we have Grose to thank for our continuing use of "BORE, a tedious troublesome man or woman, one who bores the ears of his hearers with an uninteresting tale, a term much in fashion about the years 1780 and 1781," his imperative in reviving a term in circulation five years earlier, already fallen into disuse, was to preserve it.

This honoring of linguistic practices of the past, or thinking about terms of the present as antiquarian items of the future, gestures toward a political rhetoric of British custom. Like the ancient constitution itself, which might also decay in the process of time, this language, Grose believed, must be protected, an odd echo of Johnson's admonition, "we have long preserved our constitution, let us make some struggles for our language."[60] Despite his turn to the past and the value of preservation, Grose was clearly at odds with Johnson, who detested vulgar language precisely because of what he saw as its ephemerality, a quality that made it, in his tautological argument, not worth preserving. It is, we will recall, precisely this imputed innovative quality of certain words that led Johnson to exclude them from his *Dictionary*, suggestively dismissing them as "fugitive cant." He had written, "Of the laborious and mercantile part of the people, the diction is in a great measure casual and mutable; many of their terms are formed for some temporary or local convenience, and though current at certain times and places are in others utterly unknown. This fugitive cant . . . always in a state of increase or decay, cannot be regarded as any of the durable materials of a language."[61] Strikingly, Johnson, like Grose and a number of other writers we have explored, situated cant and merely "vulgar" language together. For both of these men, what tied together the language of "the laborious and mercantile part of the people" and cant was their status as "particular language," one of Johnson's definitions of "cant," and their innovative "mutable" quality. Unlike Johnson, however, Grose and his fellows saw that language was worth preserving, worth reinscribing as a kind of customary English, worth instituting as "vernacular."

Like Grose, George Parker, too, depicted slang-speakers in an ambiguous relationship to custom, at once preserving it and, at the same time, innovating. One song he printed describes in cant language the practice of "rough music" that E. P. Thompson has analyzed.[62] Parker's character Joe sings:

> Ye slang boys all, since wedlock's noose,
>   Together fast has tied
> Moll Blubbermuns and rowling Joe,
>   Each other's joy and pride;—
> Your broom sticks and tin kettles bring
>   With canisters and stones.
> Ye butchers bring your cleavers too,
>   *Likewise your marrow bones.*[63]

This song features longstanding cant terms ("Moll") alongside newer terms ("Blubbermuns," a combination of the cant words "blubber," meaning fat, and "muns," meaning mouth), and enduring cant wit, as in the old comparison of a wedding to a hanging that we saw in *Moll Flanders* and *Beggar's Opera*. The song integrates these terms into a description of the ages-old custom of a crowd's noisemaking on a wedding night, even if the "moral economy" it traditionally invoked is not clearly at work here.[64] In another passage, Joe even refers to "handsel," that customary practice of distribution that Colonel Jack, too, had innovatively mapped onto the world of criminals.[65]

More often, however, Grose's "freedom of thought and speech" and Parker's liberating shape-shifting are evidenced not in recording and honoring past customary practices but in the freedom to invent new terms and expressions. While Grose's lexicon includes a fair share of older cant terms, such as "LAP, butter milk, or whey" or "CLEAR, very drunk," the preponderance of both authors' entries were new. Parker includes "Slang boys. Boys of the slang; fellows who speak the slang language" and "Mizzle. Is sneaking, or running away" and Grose's "LAID ON THE SHELF, OR LAID UP IN LAVENDER. pawned" or "CLAPPER. the tongue of a bell, and figuratively of a man or woman."[66] These neologisms made even the familiar novel and obscure. For Grose, it was this very mutability that must be embraced.

To be full participants in the language and print culture of the nation, Grose avers, readers needed to learn the new words constantly generated and printed in a commercial urban print center. He writes,

> The many ... cant expressions that so frequently occur in our common conversation and periodical publications, make a work of this kind extremely useful, if not absolutely necessary, not only to foreigners, but even to natives resident at a distance from the metropolis, or who do not mix in the busy world; without some such help, they might hunt through all the ordinary Dictionaries ... in search of the words, 'black legs, lame duck, a plumb, malingeror, nip cheese, darbies, and the new drop.'[67]

In this model of social affiliation, as in Defoe's novels, the true national insider must perpetually keep up with phrases that might pop up at any trivial circumstance; as Grose says "these fashionable words, or favourite expressions of the day ... generally originate from some trifling event, or temporary circumstance."[68] What he offers is a kind of ethnography of the ludicrous, the odd and entertaining language continuously reinventing itself. He shares with Johnson the (problematic) sense that the language of the common people is a "fugitive cant," a strange, ephemeral language, but unlike Johnson, he values that language, seeing it as worthy of preservation.

Strangeness here is displaced, becoming a function of time and fashion—of the new—and not of the coexistence of strangers in one's midst. Grose heralded the dazzling and fleeting—with the appositely named "flash"—as the new values of a language he would make available for sharing between English readers. His aim to circulate new terms supplanted custom but also relocated the inevitable strangeness between groups—class, gender, regional, trade, and labor—onto a temporal axis. He thereby remapped that once-threatening strangeness onto a rhetoric of freedom—to make new words, new witticisms continuously—that supposedly characterizes the British common people and their endless linguistic shape-shifting.[69] Britons could innovate these new terms, after all, because, unlike people on the continent, they did not live under "arbitrary governments, where the ebullitions of vulgar wit are checked by the fear of the bastinado" (i). Grose and Parker, then, rewrote the strange as a sign of the uniquely British freedom to innovate, which they then made available and even familiar to a wide audience, indexing and translating this language for wider exchange. The vernacular, one's own "vulgar tongue," as it were, might turn out to be a language of novelty, of pleasing surprise, of the unfamiliar—the place where generative "living" aspects of the tongue found a home. In claiming to mediate a rapidly transforming language for their readers and celebrating the political capacity of British speakers to be linguistically inventive, Grose and Parker wrote out the customary qualities of vulgar and cant language as these become instead the language of the new.

Gendering Obscurity: The Male Trade in Slang

Language wandering from itself in a process of constant innovation and the generation of newly fashioned, if obscure, words also reflected the market logic that was itself overturning custom. While markets might imperceptibly consolidate social groups, as Adam Smith was to argue, relentless change, as opposed to a rhetoric of custom, would challenge Britons' ability to imagine bases of national affiliation. The print production of a "vulgar tongue" was one means of promoting new forms of social attachment, through both mimetic representation of a social whole and the reproduction of witty, ludicrous innovations that might be learned and traded between readers. Sharing such words and their "poetic" effects offered a diverting, consolidating pleasure, creating a sense of the vernacular as a medium through which the surprisingly unfamiliar could become familiar and exchanged between English-speakers.

In Grose's and Parker's accounts, the source of this stock of ever new burlesque witticisms was, as we have seen, the "common people." The *Lexicon Balatronicum*, an 1811 expanded edition of Grose's *Classical Dictionary*, lamented that, while the merit of Grose's collection of vulgar words had been universally acknowledged, still, cant and vulgar languages' "circulation was confined almost exclusively to the lower orders."[70] This text aimed to expand vulgar language's circulation further, to "initiate" its readers "into all peculiarities of language"; its subtitle *Buckish Slang, University Wit, and Pickpocket*

Eloquence lumps together different classes, all secret sharers of naughty new terms. This is perhaps why labor and property relations once designated by particular words, words now deemed vulgar or flash, disappeared from Grose's and Parker's lexicons. Such inequities needed to become invisible or be transformed in order to allow for a perceived commonality between Britons of different classes. *Lexicon Balatronicum*, like the earlier works of Grose and Parker, displays and explains the novelty and obscurity of the "vulgar tongue," making good on the promise of representations of cant to, in Certeau's words, "restore vocal delinquency to an order of signifieds," where cant becomes part of the fold of English as obscure yet knowable, as separate and yet somehow the reader's own, but on specific de-classed terms.[71]

Grose's connection of these verbal witticisms to a rhetoric of British freedom helped to "English" such terms and make them the reader's own language, in a sense. But that rhetoric also always assumed exclusions along racial (as we saw in Chapter Two) and gender lines. Thus, while these works revealed the secret meanings of new vulgar words, they also operated on the unspoken but open secret that the vernacular language of which they were a part was not actually everyone's. Grose and Parker strongly asserted that the words they collected were not those of women. These publications, as they celebrated a language indebted to "English freedom" and inviting cross-class affiliations, explicitly gendered that language as male, thus enabling the urbane gentleman's appropriation of that "vulgar tongue." The "money laden and the cultivated" of this period, as Vic Gatrell notes, "hobnobbed in licensed venues with publicans, pugilists, and sporting swells," in what might have been perceived as a shared moment of Britishness.[72] In adopting a mischievously humorous and sexualized tone, Grose and Parker ushered in a series of other works of linguistic hobnobbing, such as Pierce Egan's *Life in London*, works that simply assumed that "fashionable" male readers would want to mimic "pickpocket eloquence" as part of a modishly ribald repertoire.[73] Better-off readers, exposed to and adopting slang, could now become social rovers, those verbal wanderers free to exercise linguistic liberties by adopting the new coinages of a volatile vulgar tongue. The masculine culture they supposedly shared with the lower orders, including vulgar languages, would come to offer one of the last possibilities for national unity in a British nation that by the nineteenth century was becoming "two nations," in Benjamin Disraeli's famous assessment.[74]

Imitation of the lower social rank of men by the higher is an early modern phenomenon discussed by a number of critics, including Judith Frank, who has written about the eighteenth-century "imitation of the poor by gentlemen, an imitation ritualized in . . . social practices."[75] In print representations of the vulgar tongue, we find that language practices, specifically the mastery and trade in unfamiliar, if somehow also indigenous, cant or slang words, was one key means by which men might imagine collective affiliation through imitation.[76] The resolutely masculine "vulgar tongue" that Grose made available to upper-class male compatriots created a "common ground" between classes, as Frank calls it, crucially between men. Grose's language of novelty, as an explicitly gendered banter, was filled with epithets for women. The exchange of these words, like the exchange of women, could solidify relations between men. Many of Grose's entries dramatize this exchange: "COFFEE HOUSE. A Necessary House. To make a coffee-house of a woman's ****; to go in and out and spend nothing," or "DIRTY PUZZLE, a nasty slut," or "ROOMS, she let's out her fore room and lies backwards, saying of a woman suspected of prostitution." Grose's terms "BROTHER STARLING. One who lies with the same woman, that is, builds in the same nest" and "BUTTERED BUN. One lying with a woman that has just lain with another man, is said to have a buttered bun" put this unifying homosocial exchange in unequivocal terms.

These heterosexual dynamics, by which women were the object of sexual exchange, might also have aimed to ward off the dangers of too close an association to the sodomitical. Grose's *Classical Dictionary* also included some of the first printed terms from a male same-sex sexual subculture, including, "BACK GAMMON PLAYER, a sodomite" and "MOLLY, a miss Molly, an effeminate fellow, a sodomite."[77] The trade in the "vulgar tongue" became a means of affiliating men across classes on comical, safe terms: a heterosexual, homosocial affiliation sometimes overtly imaged in the very terms that composed it.

This gendering of "vulgar" language represents a shift. While B. E.'s earlier *New Dictionary* had contained coarse terms for sex as well as other bodily functions, it also included domestic terms such as "*homine*, Indian Corn. *To beat Homine*, to pound that in a Mortar." Grose excluded such domestic terms, separating those words and worlds and focusing on terms of a sexual nature. He also expanded his list of sexual terms to a vast range, including terms such as "BEST, to the best in Christendom, i.e. the best **** in Christendom, a health formerly much in vogue" (that toast, one might argue, the ultimate celebration of male homosociality) and "A BITE, a cheat, also a woman's privities." The insistence that trade in these words was a male prerogative that should be kept from polite women (if not from the Billingsgate fishwives and prostitutes who supposedly spoke such language) involved some tortuous dynamics regarding who could know and how.

In her discussion of what can be known and what remains unknown in texts, Eve Kosofsky Sedgwick advocates that we "attend to what are often blandly called [the texts'] 'reader relations,' as sites of definitional creation, violence, and rupture in relation to particular readers."[78] In representations of cant and vulgar languages, particularly the gendered and sexualized print lexicons of the later part of the century, such moments of violence and rupture were particularly acute, and were a crucial aspect of the formation of the illusion of British cross-class male sociality. Grose's and Parker's celebration of vulgar linguistic culture, even—or perhaps especially—as it heralded a lexicon of bawdy terms as a sign of British freedom, shut out women readers on explicitly sexual terms. These texts insisted that their contents were obscure, unknown, and improper for ladies to know. Of course, women might well have known this language, and even read the books, but the publications positioned the verbal world contained within them as exclusively male.

Lexicon Balatronicum, which bears the revealing subtitle "A Dictionary of Buckish Slang," points directly to this gendered obscurity, assuring readers that "improper topics can with our assistance be discussed even before the ladies, without raising a blush on the cheek of modesty. It is impossible that a woman should understand the meaning of twiddle diddles (testicles), or rise at the table at the mention of Buckinger's boot (P—k, the virile member)."[79] Parker, too, warns women readers off his chapter of "low life dramatically introduced," admonishing, "I do beseech my fair readers to shun it, lest, in the primrose path, they meet a snake in the grass," and again, "I once more conjecture the fair reader will pass over the following pages, for the man who could be capable of instilling poison into the chaste recesses of a female breath, deserves not the name of man, nor the happiness a virtuous and fond woman can bestow."[80]

The understanding of these innovative, vulgar languages as exclusively male demanded a fair amount of rewriting of textual and social history. Sixteenth- and seventeenth-century works had described a canting world that was disproportionately male but nonetheless shared by men and women; the lines between who knew and who did not were not explicitly gendered. The full title of *The Fraternitye of Vacabondes* (1575) includes "*beggerly men and women, boys and gyrles.*"[81] In Thomas Dekker's and Thomas Middleton's *Roaring Girl*, Moll Cutpurse is a criminal who translates cant for wealthy gentlemen.[82] Richard Head's later *A Canting Academy* (1673) includes plenty of women canters, as in his description of "Palliards or Clapperdogeons" as "jades [who] know how to screw their faces into what pitiful posture they please, and have melting words at their fingers [sic] ends; as for gods sake bestow your charity on these poor fatherless children."[83] Perhaps more important, these works do not divide male from female readers but cater to, as B. E.'s title page put it, "all sorts of people . . . to secure their Money and preserve their lives; besides very Diverting and Entertaining, being wholly New."[84] In this appeal, the division between who knows and who does not is based not on gender but on class lines.

In the eighteenth century, the figure of the flash-talking Moll King, owner of the notorious King's Coffee House, gives lie to the notion that the trade in cant and vulgar language was exclusively male. Images of Moll King and her coffee house circulated in a Hogarth print, a Fielding play, a mock-heroic poem, and several pamphlets, including *The Life and Character of Moll King*.[85] A late-night haunt of the young and fashionable, King's Coffee House in seedy Covent Garden was nightly packed with people engaging in or seeking illicit sexual relations. Both the establishment and its proprietor were famed for the flash speech they generated, and *The Life and Character of Moll King* even reproduces a dialogue between Moll and a client, including a short glossary explaining the terms of their conversation, such as "*A Buttock*, A whore," "*Porpus*, an ignorant swaggering fellow," and "*to puff*, to impeach." Helen Berry has observed that such evidence suggests that flash or cant, "unlike Latin or Greek . . . was a form of obscure speech which was accessible to female 'wits' and women of the town, and it could thus not be used safely by men as a means of excluding women from understanding their conversation."[86] Obscurity, it turns out, can be as contested as meaning, its terms of social alignment, who knows and who does not, shifting and unstable.

We might recall, as well, the facility in cant language shared by both men and women in Gay's *Beggar's Opera*. Betty Doxy taught Filch the tricks—and language—of the canting trades. Even the naïf Polly is well-versed in cant. *The Beggar's Opera* is deeply interested in gender relations, repeatedly exposing the hypocrisy of sentimentalism and its expectations of male and female behavior and values, and in making the cant wedding/hanging comparison, it depicts marriage not as the scene of conclusive domestic virtue but as a kind of noose. The truisms of the play adumbrate an antisentimental world in which men and women alike are out for their own interests, sexual and otherwise, and both genders know a bawdy or cant term when they hear one, giving as well as they get. This staggeringly popular play neither genders the underworld it reveals nor suggests that male and female audience members and readers would be differentially privy to its obscurities.

These earlier representations of cant and the "vulgar tongue," with their rudeness open to all comers, are part of a larger body of comic literature that openly resists what Simon Dickie has described as the "politeness and sentimentality that enabled the newly prosperous trading class to differentiate itself at once from the mob below and the corrupt aristocracy above."[87] The masculine, crude, licentious, and comic nature of this language sneered at the middle-class aspirations that involved "improved" language as part of a larger emphasis on politeness in what has been called a feminization of culture.[88] The dynamic of imitation found in Grose and Parker hearkened back to that older alliance between "aristocracy" and "mob below." In insisting on a new gendered basis of a masculine national popular culture, they might be said to counter the mores of a "prosperous trading class" whose language had been gendered female. What might be considered vernacular English comprises, necessarily, a big tent. We will turn in the following parts of this book to representations of regional and maritime language to see how those strange languages were made vernacular on different, and differently gendered, terms. The low, urban, vulgar language being made vernacular, however, was gendered male and decidedly unsentimental.

Those gendered "reader relations" began as early as the 1725 *New Canting Dictionary*, which characterizes the canters' world as masculine, pruning away various earlier representations of women co-conspirators.[89] Even Defoe's *Moll Flanders*, despite Moll's interludes of cant speaking, opens with a note from the editor indicating that he has had to clean up her language. Some women might have known and understood this language, but, *Moll Flanders*'s preface suggests, the full representation of those women and their fluency was inappropriate for print accounts.[90] No such notice of bowdlerizing precedes *Colonel Jack*. Even as early as Defoe's work, the representation of a male criminal figure and his use of cant—and the possibility of men's reading and imitating him—is different from the figure of the female criminal and her use of disgraceful language.

Grose's and Parker's representations of "vulgar" language, then, were the most explicit in a series of texts slowly making it the exclusive and excluding domain of men. They also transformed the understanding of cant from a language of criminals into a subset of the "vulgar tongue," making the vernacular residually criminal. Their work was part of the history behind the now-conventional association of "popular speech" with "tough guys" and the "underworld," as Pierre Bourdieu has put it.[91] As their writings grapple with the strangeness, instability, deep internal divisions, and dislocations encountered in any attempt to name and institute a vernacular, they both reveal but also obscure language, tentatively establishing distinct knowing and unknowing publics. In making space for the vulgar within the vernacular, they attempted to fix it in place, locating it in the mouths of the "low," jokingly imitated by their male betters, bestowing upon it a wayward, sniggering masculinity, so that vulgar, slang language found a home, in those terms, in English.

PART TWO

The Language of Place

FROM "LIVING" PROVINCIAL LANGUAGES TO THE LANGUAGE OF THE DEAD

THE NEW APPRECIATION for cant and "vulgar" language as part of an English vernacular spotlighted a male urban population and their novel inventiveness in language use. In associating these languages with the town and in-the-know (white) men, late eighteenth-century dictionaries of the "vulgar tongue" effaced the intricate and changing relations between country and city, women and men, African and European laborers, and laborers and the destitute poor that would make for a considerably more complex understanding of language. Insisting on their novelty and mobility, collections of cant and what was coming to be called slang occluded the linguistic histories that might help elucidate those relations. As important as urban male "vulgar" languages were to developing conceptualizations of an English vernacular, however, in many ways even more crucial were the very different representations of provincial languages—languages (supposedly) remote from London, often rural, associated with the "common people," sometimes with women, and increasingly prized for what was seen as their deep connection to national history and place. While representations of cant depicted it as a wandering language, provincial languages appeared fixed, grounded in and grounding space over time. And, unlike cant and vulgar languages, which were, after all, criminal, or haunted by a sense of criminality, provincial languages were often represented as more squarely of the law-abiding "common people," even if sometimes low and vulgar.[1]

Thus, in eighteenth-century Britain, even as dictionaries, grammars, and elocution lectures warned readers off provincial terms and pronunciations, collecting these became something of a rage, even among polite women. In a 1789 letter, George Nicol, a successful bookseller, wrote to a lady, "Madam— Happening lately to be in company where the provincial dictionaries were the subject of conversation, and knowing your very laudable pursuit in collecting them, it occurred to me to ask the favor of a Norfolk lady, who's conversant on the subject, to set down what words she could recollect."[2] Those provincial terms could appear and sound every bit as strange as cant, their printing an illumination of—and another attempt to negotiate—the alien components that were unavoidable in any Briton's encounter with the languages of their nation.[3] One's own and not, at once naming intimate particulars yet also appearing as strange-sounding and -looking ciphers, these terms oscillated between familiar and alien, an ongoing movement, as we are coming to see, in the instituting of a vernacular more generally. In phrases such as those one finds, for instance, in the dialogues of *View of the Lancashire Dialect* (for example, "ogreath tilly welly coom"), most contemporary readers would encounter a disorienting wall of words, reduced to black letters on a page and, when sounded out, voice without meaning, at least initially.[4] Like representations of cant, print depictions of provincial languages posed an otherness, that "stranger relationality" Michael Warner has identified as inevitable in imagining a national public, particularly, as I have been arguing, the "common people" of that national public.[5] Such languages have something of a secret sense, known to some and not to others, often accessed and assimilated through a sort of riddle-solving, which is part of their allure. Learning and collecting provincial terms, as did the lady addressed by the gentleman of Pall Mall, or reading print representations of them, might help make these languages and the places they evoked feel like a reader's own.

The very strangeness of print representations of provincialisms offers a means of affiliation not simply through that repeated process of familiarization, with its sense of entry into membership. Their strangeness is also a means of locating a specific "there and not elsewhere" against the generally abstracting force of print (even though print genres such as glossaries were the very media that produced and circulated such specificities), with terms such as "Cragge. A small beer vessel used in the South of England" or "Elvers," a term from Bath for young eels.[6] Penny Fielding describes this dichotomy between strangeness and affiliation, noting that "in one sense, the nature of dialects is to be different each from the other. But . . . all dialects are alike in their warmth, affective quality and expressiveness."[7] Some of that affective quality derives from the naming of the local, and some from the distinct sound of provincial languages, the strangeness that reminds readers of voice and perhaps proximity in phonemic spellings, such as "measter" for "master" and "whot" for "what."[8] As well, some of the strangeness of provincial languages derived from their reputed pastness, with writers claiming them to be the language of national ancestors. In those writings, the strange look and sound of provincial languages might provide a poignant if uncanny link to those ancestral others who were also compatriots, of sorts.

This section of the book, discussing representations of provincial languages, divides their strangeness, perhaps counterintuitively, into two respective sources—remoteness in space and remoteness in time. While the two are, of course, deeply connected, the rhetoric surrounding the obscurity produced by provincial spatial distance in the present is distinct from that of the obscurity of temporal remoteness. Emphasizing the oddness of spatially distant provincial languages makes strangers of contemporaries. Representing the piebald quality of its languages over space, however, was essential, one part of the imperative of representing an inclusive Britishness itself. If, as Benedict Anderson has argued, nations are "horizontal," some representation of the "many" who compose it is requisite.[9] Furthermore, in Britain in particular the composite quality of the nation was part of its national cultural and political rhetoric.[10] Like the diverse practices that made up its common law or the mixed genealogy of its people, which Defoe had both mocked and celebrated in his poem "The True-Born Englishman," the composite quality of its language, too, was seen as uniquely British. That composite character, however, made for troubling obscurities that rendered the vernacular itself strange. Drawing on the glossaries, poems, print dialogues and novels that attempted to place provincial languages, Chapter Five explores their relation to the vernacular in complex terms of embodiment and disembodiment and of transparency and obscurity. Provincial writers, I go on to argue in Chapter Six, strategically deployed the obscurity that arose in representations of supposedly sentimental and familiar, yet also spatially remote, tongues. Sometimes invoking the language of English liberty, they critiqued what they saw as metropolitan incursions into provincial virtue. Ultimately, however, these writers reconstructed neither national nor provincial language communities but provisional and ephemeral social connections, reminding readers that languages create social bodies only intermittently and in part through opacity itself.[11]

The imputed temporal strangeness of provincial languages, their supposed inherent pastness, alternatively, reckons with the strangeness of national ancestors, a troubling alienness that is, however, inevitable in a nation that at times legitimates its status through claims of continuity in customs—including the linguistic. If, as many writers argued, provincial languages retained the earliest forms of English, this early English had become strange over time. Chapter Seven explores how provincial languages posed not only the strangeness of one's spatially remote compatriots in the present day but also the strangeness of English-speaking generations of the past—or of the vulgar, as emblem of the past writ large.[12] In tracking the turn to history, we find complex temporal terms of anachronism and related images of spectrality, images that saturated the accounts of "popular antiquities," which often included discussions of provincial languages. Provincial writers, aware of the anachronizing characterizations of their tongues, often responded with surprising parodies, pointing to the absurdity of notions of fixed, unchanging provincial languages and highlighting the eerie terms of such models of national connection.

CHAPTER FIVE

Provincial Languages out of Place

Strange Neighbors and Homey Dialects

In early modern accounts, one did not need to travel far to encounter the strangeness of one's compatriots' language.[1] Adam Fox cites John Hart, who in 1551 observed that if people "heare their neyghbour borne of their next citie, or d[w]elling not past one or two dais [j]ourny from theim, speaking some other word then is (in that place) emongest theim used, yt so litell contenteth their eare, that . . . they seem the stranger were therefore worthie to be derided, and scorned."[2] Emphasizing the alien nature of England's own provincial languages, Alexander Gil, in his 1619 *Logonomia Anglica*, had written that in Somersetshire, "you could easily wonder whether they are speaking English or some foreign idiom."[3] In his 1616 *English Expositor*, a collection of "hard words," John Bullokar remarks on the "great store of strange words not only from Greek and Latin but also from forrain vulgar languages round about us."[4] This work lists, alongside exotic terms from faraway places (such as "acatia, a little thorn growing in Egypt") and many Latinate terms, English dialect terms such as "Badger, He that buyeth corn in one place in order to carry it to another" and "Deft, little and pretty." (Both terms appear over a century later in Francis Grose's *Provincial Dictionary*.) Strange words and sounds saturated English, but it is not to actual languages and speakers but to representations and accounts of them that I turn my attention, examining how they highlighted the alien status of provincial languages, as when Gil distances Somersetshire pronunciation by using the third person—"For *S* they substitute *Z* as zing for sing"—while also making provincial languages essentially English.[5]

In some accounts, a kind of ongoing linguistic fall produced these now-alien tongues, corrupting a once-unified English and reducing it to a series of mere sounds or "jargon." Hugh Jones, in a pronunciation guide for uneducated men, boys, and women, asserts that "for want of right instruction and correction of error in the sound of our letters arise the various disagreeable tones of common English and the distinguishing tangs or brogues of strangers . . . carelessness or ignorance proceeds [sic] a wrong pronunciation."[6] For Jones, "want of care" (11) has led to the fact that "almost every county in England has gotten a distinct dialect . . . perfectly ridiculous to persons unaccustomed to hear such jargon"; speakers of those dialects are "almost unintelligible to each other" (12). This "want of care" has somehow also produced "terms peculiar to place," as "some say *thick* and *thuck* for *this* and *that*; *bodder* used in one Place, and *dunny* in another, instead of *deaf*" (12). These terms might be the result of a fall, but they are also discrete strange terms in need of and even worthy of explanation. The print glosses of such languages resonate with David Simpson's assertion that the "recognition of the need for intralingual translation, to use Roman Jakobson's term, suggests that the stranger is already within and that the process of foreignization is by no means restricted to sources outside the British Isles."[7] In a curious, but at this point in our study not entirely unpredictable formulation, the "Mother-Tongue" itself becomes an alien thing: in Jones's words, "it must require some Enquiry, and Remarks, before we can be masters of our *Mother-Tongue*" (13). It is so alienated that for Jones, contra depictions of the "African" creole in Defoe's novels, not only Londoners and "Gentile People everywhere" but also "the inhabitants of the plantations (even the Native Negroes) may be esteemed the only people that speak *true English*" (14). "True English" is the language that polished cosmopolitans and foreigners speak—the "Mother-Tongue" needs translating for everyone else.

In these depictions, the "disagreeable tones of Common English" and the "tangs and brogues of strangers," the languages of most Britons, differed each from the other, bereft of meaning for many compatriots and displeasing in sound. In Richard Dawes's *The Origin of the Newcastle Burr*, the voice of provincial Northerners is vaguely threatening, the "mark / by which you know them in the dark."[8] For Dawes, their regional pronunciation reduces them to something animal-like: "in their Throat a Burr is plac'd, / By which the Savage Crew is trac'd; / And which, when they wou'd speak, betrays, / A gutt'ral Noise, like Crows and Jays . . . / A rattling Ear-tormenting Yell, / Much us'd 'mong low-liv'd Fiends in Hell."[9] Like cant, the starkest symbol of post-Babel fallen language, the Newcastle Burr signifies a fall; long ago these speakers chose the devil's path, and the burr is the reminder of their subsequent curse.[10]

In John Hart's above account of linguistic strangers, language difference, even at the level of one word, wrought hostility: "the stranger were [sic] therefore worthie to be derided, and scorned."[11] Like early representations of cant, imbued with fear and enmity, his description of the strange tongues of other regions is filled with suspicion and animosity. In 1563, Thomas Wilson echoed this wariness when he included within a list of "evil voices" that of "the man

[who] barks out his words Northernlike, with I say and thou ladde," a voice akin, he argues, to those who "grunt like a hog" or "cackle like a hen."[12] Moreover, the threatening foreignness of provincial languages is a moving target, different provincial languages nefariously alien at distinct moments, in an always-changing linguistic landscape. N. F. Blake notes that in medieval mystery plays, a Southeast dialect "tended to be used for wicked characters," while in a 1581 play an evil priest was given a Northern dialect.

Like depictions of cant, representations of provincial languages were multivalent and underwent particular changes, even revaluations, in the eighteenth century. Print depictions of the language of regional rustics had appeared as early as the mid-fifteenth century. Fox has catalogued what he calls the "dialect literature" of this earlier period, but his research has also shown most of this to be "merely the stylized parody of an outsider written for comic effect" for "genteel audiences."[13] While a good number of representations of provincial languages continued to view it as merely comic and debased, some eighteenth-century works, alternatively, treat provincial terms as valuable English artifacts, worthy objects of modern learning. In some early discussions, attention to what Richard Bentley called "coarse, rustic" language or "vernacular idiom" had the imprimatur of classical learning.[14] Rustic language, the "vernacular idiom," as Bentley showed, could function as evidence in authenticating debates about philology. Bentley offered an extensive discussion of ancient Doric dialect, what would have been the "vernacular idiom" of the tyrant Phalaris, as a means of determining the authorship and authenticity of epistles attributed to him.[15] Phalaris's supposed use of official Attic dialect instead of his native Doric, especially for correspondence regarding private household affairs, made visible their status as forgeries, Bentley argued. Because Phalaris wanted to be popular, wanted to be ruler, he would not have made himself a "stranger of his language" by using Attic. The Doric he thinks Phalaris would have used, however, would itself be a language "clouded with obscurity," an enduring characterization of authenticity associated with even the most humble and domestic provincial languages.

For Bentley, Doric is obscure, but it is not foreign. Rather, it is the language of the home, of the familiar. This tension between the opacity of provincial languages and their homey Englishness comes to the fore in the eighteenth century. In tours and glossaries, writers aimed to capture the languages of the whole of Great Britain in an inclusive vision of the nation, but this meant confronting the strangeness of the English of various regions, particularly that of their "common people." In his *Tour thro' the Whole Island of Great Britain* Defoe comments on the language of Somersetshire: "[W]hen we are come this length from London . . . the country way of expressing themselves is not easily understood. This way of boorish country speech, as in Ireland, it is called the brogue upon the tongue; so here 'tis called *jouring* and 'tis certain, that though the tongue be all mere natural English, yet those that are but a little acquainted with them cannot understand one half of what they say."[16] Here is a "boorish country speech," English "strangely altered" over space, nearly incomprehensible, but still "natural English." It is the movement between rendering such language strange and obscure and also, on those terms, reclaiming it as English, as a kind of common knowledge worth knowing, by virtue of its appearance in printed works, that we shall track in this chapter.[17]

The reclamation of such languages as domestic English is in evidence toward the end of the seventeenth century, when provincial terms began to migrate from lexicons of "foreign" or "hard" words to print genres instituting a national vernacular, such as John Ray's 1674 *Collection of English Words, Not Generally Used*, which alphabetizes provincial terms and their definitions and adds a collection of "local proverbs."[18] Ray reflects the oscillation between familiar and strange within the vernacular not only in his title—the collected words are "English," but not "generally used" English—but also in his observation that "in many places, especially of the North, the Language of the common people, is to strangers very difficult to be understood."[19] Such descriptions position speakers of "general English" as strangers to their spatially remote compatriots, while the glossary describes "the Language of the common people" of those regions as alien, as an object of study, further estranging it in its alphabetical columns, but also announcing it as something worth knowing. In Ray's work, the "dialect" and "local words" encountered in his travels while accumulating scientific knowledge through extensive observation are curiosities on par with those "other things, which I principally minded and pursued" (1), namely regional flora and fauna. For Ray and his readers, the vernacular is an enticingly diverse set of objects to be learned and collated. His wealthy patron, Peter Courthope, encouraged him from the start, and the *Collection* "found favourable acceptance among the Ingenious," sold out, and "a new one was desired by the Bookseller" (1).

A good number of colleagues shared Ray's interest in strange but English words. His circle of well-educated friends—ministers, scholars—forwarded more words for inclusion in the new edition. Their lexicographic nominees, however, revealed the complex porousness between "provincial" and "general" English, exposing the relative nature of stranger relationality. If it is already difficult to answer the question all national languages pose—as David Simpson puts it, "What is one's own language, after all? Does it include regional dialect?"—the question of what is regional and what is not is itself often unclear.[20] To the proposed provincial contributions of one Mr. William Nicholson, "an ingenious Minister, living in Cumberland," Ray responded, "some Words I observe therein of common and general use in most Counties of England, at least where I have lived or conversed, which I . . . omitted."[21] Although he did not include new contributions that some considered provincial and he considered "common," Ray went on to include a long list of these indeterminate words—are they provincial? Are they standard English?—in the preface to the second edition, underscoring the uneasy and ever-shifting quality of the border between them, moving in relation to one's location and experiences.[22] Ray describes this dilemma: "These gentlemen being, I suppose, North Countrymen, and, during their Abode in the Universities, or elsewhere, not happening to hear those words used in the South, might suppose them to be proper to the North. The same Error I committed myself in many Words that I put down for Southern, which afterwards I was advised were of use also in the North, viz. Arders, Auward, to Brimme, Bucksome, Chizzle."[23] Who the strangers were or what might constitute strange language remained tenebrous—not simply a matter of provincial speakers who knew and urban-dwellers who did not. Instituting the vernacular could not be simply a matter of readers mastering the language of clearly designated others.

Over and over again, as we shall see, the boundaries between spaces, the languages attributed to them, readers who "know" and those who do not, the division between strange and familiar, turn out to be troublingly fluid (in ways provincial writers would come to pursue suggestively in their own writing). At the other end of the century, Grose, in his *Provincial Glossary*, complained of "it being difficult to find any word used in one county, that is not at least adopted in the adjoining border of the next," and so his collection of provincial words are not "attributed or fixed to a particular county."[24] Even as he designates the words in his collection with some regional mark—"Exm" for Exmore or "N" for Northern—the connection of those printed words to particular places and speakers seems more projection than recording of fact, the words he attempts to codify themselves unstable. His collection includes "*Fruggan*, the pole with which the ashes of the oven are stirred. N," "*Fukes*, locks of hair. N" and "*Rawming*, reaching any thing aukwardly. N." But even the Northern speakers Grose identifies as using these terms might not have recognized them. Nathan Bailey's *Dictionarium Britannicum* lists not "Fruggan" but "Fruggin" (the spelling also used in George Meriton's earlier *The Praise of York-Shire Ale*, discussed below), and the other terms had not appeared in print in other places.[25] It is critical to remind ourselves that everyone, not simply "outsider" readers, encountered something strange on the page in representations of provincial languages.

Despite what Richard Carew had celebrated as early as 1595—"the copiousness of our language that appeareth in the diversity of our dialects"—and the flux of that diversity, eighteenth-century works often sought to place provincial terms, attempting to stabilize them and assign them a fixed locale, usually a particular rural and domestic one.[26] Ray's glossary thus includes "A *Reward*, or a good *Reward*, a good Colour or ruddiness in the Face" and specifies that it is used "about Sheffield in Yorkshire." Throughout the eighteenth century, what might best be designated a "pseudoethnography" of provincial languages aimed to introduce Britons not to languages and cultures from afar but to diverse provincial languages of Britain, managing and codifying them and attempting to settle them.²⁷ Antiquarian studies of particular regions—Oxford, Yorkshire, Westmorland, and Cumberland—included lists of provincial terms proprietarily claimed for those respective places.²⁸ As George Starr has documented, Defoe populated his *Tour Thro' the Whole Island of Great Britain* with provincialisms he found in the respective regions through which he ranged, linking them to specific places.²⁹ Later tours of specific areas, such as Thomas West's *A Guide to the Lakes*, often included glossaries and discussions of the provincial words found there.³⁰ Freestanding glossaries assembled and indexed provincial terms; often these named phenomena specific to particular places, such as Norfolk's and Suffolk's "Galls. Sand-galls, spots of sand through which the water oozes."³¹ Discussions of provincial languages grew increasingly detailed and quasi-scientific, accommodated by the disciplinary formation of historical philology in the nineteenth century, as seen in Thomas Batchelor's *An Orthoëpical Analysis of the English Language*, which includes a painstaking "Minute and Copious Analysis of the Dialect of Bedfordshire."³² All attempted to situate provincial languages, both geographically and socially, as part of making them familiarly British, even as they also had the effect of making what was English strange.

Provincial Languages and the "Common People"

It is one thing to claim that representing the helter-skelter assortment of languages from across the space of Britain helped to constitute a full understanding of the English language. It is another to claim that eighteenth-century print representations also helped to institute these languages as part of an English vernacular. That is, however, what I am arguing, and I turn again to the works of Francis Grose to help make that case. The ever-enterprising Grose, acutely aware of the day's obsessions with language—and helping to create them—was a crucial participant in the gleaning, ordering, and publication of strange languages, presenting them as part of the language of the British "common people," not only with his cant and vulgar words collection but also with a compendium of provincial terms and lore. He popularized these digests, appealing respectively to city-dwellers and those observing the city from a distance. While his 1785 *A Classical Dictionary of the Vulgar Tongue* had aimed in part to familiarize provincial readers with new metropolitan words said to be constantly emerging from the mouths of the mobile urban subjects he called "common people," the 1787 *Provincial Glossary* reversed direction, introducing back to metropolitan readers the supposedly unchanged English of a different kind of common people, seemingly rooted provincials throughout Great Britain, including not only those "local words" that had evaded "modern refinements" but "local proverbs" and "popular superstitions."

Grose's vision of provincials was influenced by writers such as Shaftesbury, who saw them as eluding the "vice" that stemmed from "the growth of luxury in capital cities."³³ Conflating provincial space and the lower orders, he believed "the hardy remote provincials, the inhabitants of smaller towns, and the industrious sort of common people" avoided the "irregularities" of "wanton plenty."³⁴ Despite such claims, provincial languages were, of course, necessarily varied and divided within themselves; members of different classes within a region might well speak differently, even speak distinct languages, and were, as we shall explore, on the move.³⁵ William Marshall observed that in Yorkshire there are "two distinct provincial languages . . . one spoken by the lower class, . . . the other by the superior class of *provincialists*."³⁶ William Chetwood's 1746 *A Tour of Ireland* distinguishes between the provincial yokel and the provincial theater audience who laugh at him. The narrator explains how travellers, stopping in Coventry, view a play in which an "Enactor" began a prologue to one of Farquhar's Comedies, thus:

> *Powets ned nowthing mour to chick thire Faury,*
> *Then Wytes, Kites, Beveocks, and Womin for ther Joury*

That is in Good English

> *Poets need nothing more to check their fury,*
> *Than Witts, Cits, Beaux, and women for their jury.*³⁷

The "superior" class of this provincial audience laughs uproariously at the enactor's pronunciation, to which "the prolector cries out with a voice elevated with passion: *Wauns! Maybe Ise not so good an Enactor as other Fowkes; Yet for aw that Ise tag a lace with the best o' you let the tuther be whoa he will.*"³⁸ The vulgar provincial cannot transcend his peculiar pronunciation—"nothing" become "nowthing"—and cannot see beyond the particularity of his social status and laboring talents—he fails to realize that few would care that he could "tag a lace" better than they, as he proudly asserts. Something similar is going on in Tobias Smollett's depictions of provincials, some of whom speak in a comic provincial manner, and some of whom do not. Ignoring such class distinctions, Grose and others associate provincial languages with both a particular place and a particular lower-class "common people."

Provincial languages, of course, need not be conflated with the common people. Chaucer's "The Reeve's Tale" had made not its rural miller but Cambridge scholars the speakers of provincial Northern language. Much later, in John Vanbrugh's play *A Journey to London*, completed by Colley Cibber in 1728 as *The Provok'd Husband*, it is a knight who speaks Northern language.³⁹ Increasingly in the eighteenth century, however, writers equated provincial languages with the language of the vulgar and common. Ray appealed to like-minded colleagues "to communicate to me what they had observed each of their own Countrey words, or should afterwards gather up out of the mouths of the people" (2). For educated provincials themselves, provincial words of "the people" might "afford some diversion to the curious, and give them occasion of making many considerable remarks" (3). Notably, it was the "language of the common people" and "what were in use among the vulgar" that Ray aimed to record. Collections of provincial languages place them not only in terms of region but, perhaps more important, in terms of a "common people" fixed in place. For Ray, as later for Grose, the "vulgar," the "common people," maintained the regional differences that an elite, supposedly, was forsaking in geographic social movement in their bid for politeness and refinement. This must have meant a strange doubling for Ray himself, who hailed from Essex and whose father was a blacksmith, but who received a Cambridge education and became an accomplished scholar.

Equating provincial language exclusively with the "common people" or the "vulgar" has several important effects. It reduces class difference to a less-threatening spatial/regional difference. That reduction turns the "common" and "vulgar" languages into the stuff of geo-ethnography. It also literally distances the "common people" as it fastens them in provincial place. This "placing" of the people offers something like what Jacques Rancière critiques in the "image of another world. Just across the straits, away from the river, off the beaten path . . . there lives another people (unless it is, quite simply, the people)."[40] Often, "another people" called up in representations of provincials are indeed "simply, the people," making provincial "vulgar" language a kind of language of the "common people" of the nation.

One of the earliest extended literary representations of a provincial language suggests that movement between Yorkshire language, for instance, and the common people posed "in its very foreignness . . . the proletariat in person," in Rancière's words, the anachronism notwithstanding.[41] George Meriton's 1685 *The Praise of York-Shire Ale*, less interesting for the anacreontic title poem in standard English than for its "York-shire Dialogue in its pure Natural Dialect as it is now commonly spoken in the North parts of Yorkshire," includes as well a compilation of local proverbs, that recognizable genre of the vernacular.[42] Written in rhyming couplets, Meriton's extensive reproduction of the dialect conversations of a farming family regarding their daily life—a calf being born, a freeze setting in, jibes about the wife's cooking—presents common and low-comic elements of rural provincial life. The father jokes about a burnt dinner: "Thur Cael tasts strang of Reeke, they're nut for me; / God sends meat and 'th Deevil sends Ceauks [cooks] I see." Here, the provenance of the provincial speaker is the homely cabbage ("cael") tasting of smoke ("reeke"). The farmer's language grounds him in particular place, his place irredeemably low and "common." He speaks in proverbs, part of the lexicon of the vernacular, as we have seen, and this is a vernacular firmly situated in Yorkshire and with common people.

In Meriton's work, as in so many of the eighteenth century, that provincial vernacular world is also an obscure one, at least at the level of language. One passage reads:

> F[ather]: Ise not farr, ist Cow Cawv'd that's a Goodin,
> Now *Tibb* weese git some Beestling Pudding:
> Letts spang our geates for it is var Snithe,
> And Ise flaid Wife it will be Frost Belive;[43]

The gist of the passage is that the father, joining up with his wife and daughter, explains he wasn't far away ("Ise not farr") and then, having overheard their conversation, looks forward to the dish made with a cow's first milk, "beestling pudding," and telling them to hurry up, "letts spang our geates," explaining he is afraid, "flaid," it will frost that evening. It is a scene of humble rural life in a strange language, however, which readers must piece together to access. Those less familiar with the language must use familiar English and rhyme patterns ("Pudding") to figure out pronunciation of unfamiliar terms ("Goodin"). In the second and later editions, a glossary is provided, but reading the work is still tough going. Meriton's is an early moment in the poetry of glossary and footnote annotations to which readers became accustomed in eighteenth-century Britain. His provincial language draws attention to, while bringing home the stranger, acknowledging that the nation is filled with strangers and their languages. Even for Yorkshire readers who might pronounce "believe" "belive," as the glossary translates, there is puzzle work involved in sounding the term and hearing the meaning—as printed, "belive" might be strange for them too.

Such language answers to the estrangement that, for Viktor Shklovsky, defines poetry itself as "impeded, distorted speech"—and Shklovsky cites dialect language as a crucial device of poetic estrangement.[44] In presenting a strange language for all, if strange in different ways for different readers, the statement "Cael tasts strang of Reeke" alienates in order to force readers to attend to the materiality of humble familiarities of vulgar domestic life. Paradoxically, it is strange language that invites readers to see, to experience the quotidian, the stinking cabbage and bad cookery, by emphasizing the materiality of language itself, its graphic representations, its sounds. Strange words "make us feel objects... make a stone feel stony," as Shklovsky puts it, in their very strangeness.[45] In Meriton's and other representations of provincial language, this estrangement and the attention it demands feeds back into a material sense of the particularity of provincial place and, ultimately, in complex terms, into a sense of the common as a series of such places and the "common people" of those places that make up the nation. In these depictions of provincial language, it is the "common people" who are mysterious strangers. Their mysteriousness is linked to a language of place that is always slipping into a language of class, just as class slips into a notion of "common people" in the intricate and moving dynamics of provincial vernaculars.

These movements—between familiar and strange, place and class, low and common, "foreign" and national—and the process of solving a remarkable puzzle that turns out to be an unremarkable and yet representative moment (burnt cabbage)—also inform the reappraisal of provincial languages that was taking place in the pages of new forms of prose fiction, as we began to see in Chapter Two. Daniel Defoe's *Moll Flanders* and *Colonel Jack* include a good number of provincial terms revealed and explained by his polyglot protagonists. Even an early emergent instance of prose fiction writing, Thomas Deloney's *The Pleasant History of John Winchcomb, in His Younger Years Called Jack of Newberry*, offers among its variety of characters Jack's father-in-law, who states, in Southwest dialect, "I cham but a poore man."[46] While Jack marries well and soars to improbable class heights, the odd-sounding tongue, with its provincial form of "I am," in "cham," is the language of the statically vulgar, common man.

In the mid-eighteenth century, Richardson's Pamela and her language are recognizably common and British, perhaps most powerfully and oddly when she uses the unusual Bedfordshire terms on which both Margaret Doody and Thomas Keymer have commented.[47] This interesting dynamic, whereby readers might see a Moll or Pamela as most pointedly British in the moments in which they speak provincial terms—when, for instance, Moll (mistakenly) explains to readers that she was in "a place call'd *Stone* in Cheshire" or Pamela refers to a "corse" (for corpse)—neatly encapsulates the suggestive movement between alien and familiar, particular and common, common and nation, in representations of provincial languages. Defoe's, Richardson's—and certainly Smollett's—consciously British works invite readers to imagine the nation and the common people who populate it, in part, through depictions of language, but they often invoke the "common people" of that nation through unfamiliar provincial terms or pronunciations.

Getting at Britishness in this way is, however, a dicey affair, and not only because characters sometimes get it wrong or because language can remain untranslated and unclear. We noted in Chapter Two that in *Pamela* the Britishness of the heroine indicated through her language was in some ways a put-on, a kind of performance.[48] In this novel that performative quality of the provincial is erotically charged. It is the moment of the familiar knowingly made strange, Pamela outfitted as rustic, that decisively compels Mr. B's desire to have her, and later, when he finally comes to possess her, it is in this guise that he thinks of her, as he refers to her repeatedly as "my pretty rustic" (284). Pamela describes her country dress and the imagined return to her provincial village that provides the occasion for her wearing it, as a "pleasure of descending" that includes provincial and low common language. Pamela colloquially exclaims "Hey day!" (55) and "Good sirs!" (56) when in her most rustic of guises, the one that has made her an attractive "stranger" (55) to Mr. B.[49] And it is when Pamela imagines herself as an other, a rural laborer—more pleasurable in the imagining than in the actuality, which never materializes—that she deploys the provincial phrase "beechen trencher" to figure the hardness of her hands as the result of such labor. The representations of "simple" provincial languages as part of the national vernacular were similarly complex, the humble posed, riddlelike, to be pleasurably discovered, a gratifying dance between tantalizingly unfamiliar and intimately familiar, between low and high, between particular local and "general" national, between embodied and disembodied. In the following sections I investigate some of the dynamics that made it so.

"Debased... by Flesh and Blood": Provincialisms and Disembodiment in Language Theory and Practice

To situate unusual provincial languages within consolidating notions of a national vernacular is to depart from some of the dominant critical narratives of the relationship between print language and nation in eighteenth-century Britain. These have tended to emphasize standardization and the general, depersonalized, transparent language of a modern national public.[50] It is true that disapproval of provincial languages in the establishment of a standard English was often unsparing. Thomas Sheridan's 1762 *Lectures on Elocution* describes not just Irish and Scots but all provincial languages as "vicious" and explains that "all dialects... have some degree of disgrace annexed to them."[51] Batchelor describes provincial pronunciation as "depraved."[52] James Harris goes further when he argues that the particular terms of provincial speech are "hardly a part of Language."[53]

We might, however, regard these exclusions of provincial languages from a different position, one informed by what Rancière identifies as "one of the master logics of modernity, exclusion by homage."[54] Moreover, if one story of linguistic nationalism in the eighteenth century highlights the need to set aside the particular for the general (creating the fiction of a "standard language"), attending to print representations of provincial languages tells a different story. That story reveals the valuation of the material particulars from diverse remote areas that help create the fiction of rooted, regional languages and situate them as part of the language of the people.[55] This reclamation is partly behind the printing of opaque words naming specific regional things, such as terms found in Ray's *Collection*: "*Braughwham*; A dish made of Cheese Egges, Clap-bread and Butter boyled together, *Lancash*." Or "A *Capo*; a working horse. *Chesh*."[56] Print exclusions and collections of provincial languages are, however, interrelated stories, and putting them together might account for the odd way in which the provincial—and to many unfamiliar—terms of a character such as Pamela could also be recognized, nonetheless, as signs of Britishness. Key to this relationship is the status of the particular, the sense-based, the carnal. Downgraded in the institutionalization of a standard English, those particular and physical elements, elements actually quite important to the rhetoric of cultural nationalism, were relegated to the odd terms of provincial language, the familiar made intriguingly foreign. It is, however, specifically the ongoing movement between familiar and foreign, provincial and standard, and what Eric Gidal calls the "subjective navigation of readers" between them that generates the affective charge of provincial language representations in instituting vernacular English.[57]

To understand this charge, we might begin by examining the the standardization of print English and an emerging public sphere logic that demoted much language of specific places and particular things, and, at times, the body itself.[58] That demotion is familiar to students of eighteenth-century Britain, in which the capacity for abstract, rational exchange, an ability believed to be facilitated by a standard language and the powers of print, provided the basis for imagining the nation and readers' relationship to it.[59] In excluding regional particulars, standard English and the consequent abstracting powers attributuded to it allowed for—or, better, enabled the fiction of—a model of the national polity composed of equal, disinterested participants in a free, rational exchange of ideas. This understanding of language dovetailed neatly with conceptualizations of print technology as promising a distancing, neutral medium of communication, capable of transcending local differences and even the human bodies that were unavoidably evident in the spoken or handwritten word.[60] Ideal participants in a national print-based republic of letters assume, in Michael Warner's words, a "principle of negativity," which demands a "negation of persons" as a "condition of legitimacy"—made possible by a seemingly uninflected national language and print's supposed powers of abstraction.[61] Kathleen Wilson notes as well that the press, in particular, "recasts politics as spectatorial, critical activities," and that this position of observation "bestows the authority of disinterest" on the then-national observer.[62] The ability to transcend one's interests through technologies of language, print media, and a related instrumental reason becomes a condition of participation in the national public sphere. As Jerome Christensen has put it, throughout the eighteenth century, for the ideal man of letters "the language of the general remain[ed] . . . proper."[63]

James Harris's authoritative *Hermes* (1751) suggests the theoretical underpinnings of this conception of "the language of the general." For Harris, a language's "*general* terms are by far its most excellent and essential part."[64] Particular terms, by contrast, are the symbols of ideas only "secondarily, accidentally, and mediately" (348), for the ideas they represent are not general but lesser and particular ones unique to a specific place.[65] To illustrate what he means by these lesser, particular terms, Harris turns explicitly to regional terms, explaining that they are the names for the "new particular objects that would appear on every side" if "the inhabitants of Salisbury were transferred to York" (373). Adam Smith poses the limiting particularism of the rustic provincial in even stronger terms, describing a "'clown' who knows the river which runs by his house simply as 'the river,'" his perspective so partial that he does not even know of other rivers.[66] In a crucial slippage, akin to that in Ray's and Grose's collections, the particular terms of provincials, terms that connote their inability to think at the level of the general, shift from their status as the language of distinct regional places to the language of "the vulgar" as a whole. Harris reluctantly acknowledges, "Life we know is merged in a multitude of Particulars, where an explanation by Language is ... requisite" but quickly goes on to saddle the vulgar with the language of particulars, stating, "The vulgar indeed want it [language] to no other end" (344).

Working in tandem with the estrangement of provincial terms from the language and an estrangement of the language of the vulgar more generally was a longstanding devaluation of "sense" and of the sensing—and therefore troublingly interested—body. Steven Shapin summarizes early modern discussions of this hierarchy: "The philosopher might be distinguished from the vulgar man precisely because the latter was a slave to his senses while the former was at liberty to disbelieve the immediate impressions of eyes and ears when his rational knowledge of the nature of things informed him of sensory error."[67] Harris thus condemns speakers of particular sense-based languages—provincials, the vulgar—as benighted by their wallowing in sense. He writes, "The vulgar merged in Sense from their earliest Infancy, and never once dreaming any thing to be worthy of pursuit but what either pampers their Appetite, or fills their Purse, imagine nothing to be real, but what may be tasted or touched" (350). Such characterizations resemble Richard Dawes's reduction of provincial speakers to a debased—animal—state, "like crows and jays ... croaking frog ... hog," brutes incapable of reason.[68] Unable to transcend their sensing bodies to contemplate more worthy general ideas (a failure, too, of empirical scientists, he believes), they remain, in Harris's lyrical phrasing, "lost in a labyrinth of infinite particulars" (351). Harris, in his disparagement of misleading sense, finds an ally in Lord Monboddo, who bluntly insists that the mind is "degraded and debased by its necessary connection with flesh and blood."[69]

Suggestively, the physical, in the sensed particulars attributed to provincial and vulgar languages, was considered especially alien. Susan Manly describes how Monboddo characterizes terms naming specific material experiences and perceptions as "foreigners." For Monboddo, she writes, "it is the evidence of the senses that is the foreigner in the nation-state we call the mind" (45). Monboddo argues that ideas formed not from the universal operations of the mind but from the senses are not "*natural-born* subjects of the state" but are "*naturalized* only," and that "the *sensations* are altogether *foreigners*" (45). Monboddo's trope positions the thinking and language of the provincial and vulgar—so often construed as merely sensible and particular—as that of an "outsider," inscrutable even to the abstract "natural-born" language of an elite able to transcend sense-based thinking and language.

This exclusionary logic regarding sense parallels that directed at provincial languages, which, as we have been seeing, could also be derided as foreign. In a suggestive and common conflation of the externality of the provincial with the low, Johnson's 1755 *Dictionary* registers high suspicion of the provincial, defining it as "Not of the mother country; rude; unpolished."[70] Samuel Pegge later characterized Johnson's attitude toward "dialectical words": "He seems not to consider them as *free-born*, or even as *denizens*; but rather treats them as *out-laws*, who have lost the protection of the commonwealth."[71] For Thomas Sheridan, provincials are like foreigners at the level of their pronunciation of the spoken word—both find it impossible to pronounce the "English tongue" with "exactness," despite "all the pains they can take."[72] Even radical Thomas Spence, in his *Grand Repository of the English Language*—a pronouncing guide—aimed, once and for all, to eliminate differences in pronunciation that marked class hierarchies. Spence recast pronunciation variations as provincial, and it was the provincial that had to go. He writes, "By provincials is here meant all British subjects whether inhabitants of Scotland, Ireland, Wales, the several counties of England, or the city of London, who speak a corrupt dialect of the English tongue."[73] Increasing numbers of Britons would have found themselves provincialized, as it were, aliens within the nation.[74] Johnson himself "had to guard against lapsing into the pure Staffordshire" of his native Lichfield, even as his became the final word (for some) on English usage.[75]

In the glacial move away from a strictly vertical, monarchic model of power, a move underwritten in part by the challenge of public sphere critique, the legitimacy of that national public depended on something like a parallel and related disappearance of the sensory and embodied, which, as we are beginning to see, were deeply associated with provincial languages.[76] As Pamela enters a new order that elevates the literate middle-class subject, her language is drained of its witty banter and provincialisms, becoming more the bland global English David Simpson associates with an emerging "single world system."[77] As Peter Stallybrass and Allon White have put it, the public sphere aimed for, if it was far from fully realizing, "the creation of a sublimated public body without smells and coarse laughter, separate from both the court and church and the fair and alehouse."[78] To know anything about eighteenth-century British writing and culture is to know just how much the unruly body and rude laughter, however, remained a part of that world. Such corporeality, however, was increasingly displaced onto provincials, the vulgar, and their language. As Pamela ascends, her provincialisms disappear. As well, she loses much of her provincial language in succeeding editions of the novel.[79] At the same time, the other rural, provincial characters who inhabit the book—farmers, superannuated servants—continue to use and use more of those terms and phrases. For those characters, as Doody has noted, the regionalisms are even "amplified . . . the farmer is now given direct (instead of reported) speech, in country language: 'he will not come NERST her', 'a quite otherguess light.'"[80]

The period's myriad dictionaries, grammars, and elocution guides reveal the extent to which to speak and write in an emerging standard English, that new medium of horizontal social structure, indeed to participate in what one writer has called "the formation of Modern England as a stable socio-linguistic entity," was to leave behind those particular linguistic practices associated with the provincial and common.[81] Convinced that rational principles of analogy formed the basis, even, of pronunciation, John Walker, as late as 1791, argued that knowledge of those principles would eliminate difference, producing a uniform pronunciation in all of Britain's speakers. "If the analogies of the language were better understood," he optimistically asserted, "it is scarcely conceivable that so many words in polite usage would have a diversity of pronunciation, which is so ridiculous and embarrassing."[82] For Walker, homogeneity was achievable—and desirable—not only in a shared lexicon but also at the level of the spoken word, as the rational understanding of the language's analogical principles would come to triumph over the piecemeal, embodied practices developed over time.

Scots writers' efforts to "improve" their language, forsaking the "vulgar" and "provincial" for a standard English, are only the most extreme version of this estrangement, an alienation that produced what some saw as lifeless language. Nigel Leask cites Burke's estimation of the resulting prose of Scottish historian William Robertson, who "writes like a man who composes in a dead language, which he understands but cannot speak."[83] The figuration of this estrangement as a deadening and an "often remarked 'disembodiment' of eighteenth-century Scottish prose," as Leask has noted, is telling. As Scots provincials (and indeed, most Britons) aimed to teach themselves and others to speak a standard English, they themselves sometimes invoked the rhetoric of the corrupting body, insisting that speakers turn to the abstractions of grammar if they wanted to speak and write English well. Provincial grammarian Anne Fisher, Newcastle author of the best-selling *A New Grammar*, had insisted, "A person who understands English grammatically, must be allowed to have good notions of grammar in general, i.e., that of every other nation.... On the other hand, the man who speaks or writes English ... through custom, from being his Mother Tongue, cannot be supposed to have any ... reasonable assurance that he does it either with propriety or elegance."[84] Here, in fairly explicit terms, we find the provincial asserting that to speak or write the national language "with propriety" meant moving beyond those habits of the living body, the "mother tongue," the unthinking practices of custom, and instead deploying purely mental and universal operations of "grammar in general."[85]

Given the movement we have been tracking between outside and inside, alien and familiar, it is significant that provincial writers produced English guides to grammar and pronunciation. (Newcastle published the second highest number after London.[86]) An expanding system of print and letter distribution, including the postal system, deepened the perception of bodiless, anonymous communication, easily enabling provincial writers and readers to imagine themselves as part of a national public sphere, in part by formalizing their language. Not at all marginal to the process of standardizing English, provincial towns and residents were often central to it. Wilson writes, "London's status and growth as a major publishing center depended upon the flourishing of provincial trade. The London tri-weekly newspapers, for example, were produced specifically with the provincial audience in mind (printed on Tuesdays, Thursdays, and Saturdays, the days on which the post left the capital)" (30). And she notes, "the success of Cave's *Gentlemen's Magazine* stemmed from [Edward] Cave's exploitation of well-placed provincial printers to create a national market" (30). Even provincial women writers, such as Anne Seward, whom John Brewer discusses at length in his *Pleasures of the Imagination*, could participate in a print public sphere, publishing in the *Gentleman's Magazine* without ever setting foot in London.[87]

Provincial Clowns and Comic Corporeality

As Andrew Elfenbein has comprehensively documented, imaginative literature of the early eighteenth century played a key role in this institutionalization of a standard English. In the neoclassical poetics of the first part of the century, poets eschewed markers of provincial linguistic difference in verse. Even as Augustan poetry, as Doody has noted, often displays a range of languages, including a "'low' language of short words and proverbs," these dabblings helped to establish, by contrast, an authoritative polished English. And when these poems did include the "low," they tended to stop short of representing explicitly provincial terms.[88] While the writings, and sometimes persons, of provincial rustic subjects, from Stephen Duck to Mary Leapor, made their way into the fashionable world of eighteenth-century letters, for the most part their language, even in the georgic verse that took labor as its subject, obeyed the stipulations of a poetics of polish and refinement that rejected the particular terms, let alone pronunciations, of provincial language.[89]

Literary criticism of the period also disavowed provincial terms. Addison dismissively referred to provincial labor terms as "the low phrases and turns of art that are adapted to husbandry."[90] Johnson even accused Shakespeare—"one of the original masters of our language," in part, one might argue, for exactly his inclusion of provincial terms—of using "corrupted language."[91] At least as far back as the sixteenth century Edmund Spenser (whose *Shepheardes Calendar* [1579], we should note, included the first glossary of English provincial words) had deployed these terms to convey a sense of Englishness, of a specifically vernacular English culture. It was to that very provincial language that many early eighteenth-century writers objected, in part on the basis of its lowness. Alexander Pope wrote, "the old English and country phrases of

Spenser were either entirely obsolete, or spoken only by people of the lowest condition. As there is a difference betwixt simplicity and rusticity, so the expression of simple thoughts should be plain but not clownish."[92] "Clownish" here means, as Nathan Bailey had defined it, "unmannerly, rude," associated with "rusticity"—he defines "clown" as "a country fellow"—and the provincial. The provincial, rural, and low, in early eighteenth-century criticism, collapsed into a single category of language to be avoided.[93]

Thus, the language of "clowns"—rustic, low, common—is frequently represented as comic. Pope satirized the "simplicity" of provincial language as mere simple-mindedness in the "Pastoral Ballad" that he facetiously claimed to have found amongst some old manuscripts. In his pastiche, bodies—with their mispronouncing voices and demands for gratification—are part of the humor. The "passion of jealousy" becomes merely humorous in the rustic names and provincial language of his spoof, as a resentful Cicily protests "Ah Rager, Rager ches was zore avraid, / When in yon Vield you kiss'd tha parson's maid; / Is this the love that once to me you zed, / When from the Wake thou brought'st me gingerbread?"[94] Provincial language here is trivializing, a sign of the illiterate who confuses the petty and physical—a gingerbread treat—with genuine passions.

Cambridge-educated poet Christopher Anstey portrays a Gloucestershire provincial describing his daughter's preparations for a ball at Bath in similar comic terms in a poem that foregrounds its depiction of provincial language in its title, "Zomerzetshire Dialect":

> You must know too that Madge has a wonderful passion
> To appear like a Lady of very high Vashion,
> Then with Presence of Mind flying up to the Garret,
> Brought down my old Wig, that's as red as a Carrot,
> And to it she went, dear, ingenious, zweet zoul, . . .
> Then with Dripping and Flour did so baste it and frizzle,
> The Hairs all became of a beautiful Grizzle.[95]

One notes here the connection of mildly accented provincial language with the absurd, as the poem makes provincials ludicrous not only through the young woman's pretenses to "appear like a lady of very high Vashion," but also through the speaker's (her father) unselfconscious use of provincial pronunciations. This passage, like so many representations of provincial languages, imputes an indecorous physicality to the provincial, whether in Madge's unladylike "flying up to the garret" or her basting of her father's wig with fat drippings. To speak a differently pronounced dialect is to embody oneself in unseemly ways, an invocation of the (wrongly) speaking body. And while all fashionable people take strange and sometimes grotesque measures for their appearances, it is only in the provincial-speaking figure that such crude physicality is represented. For the provincial, however fashionably gray ("grizzle") their wig might be, its base physical origins cannot be transcended, just as their provincial (mis)pronunciation cannot be overcome.

A good number of representations of provincial languages in the period were of the comedic strain Simon Dickie has identified, emphasizing the crude body and pointedly antisentimental.[96] Such humor is a part of Grose's *Glossary*, as when he points out when provincial words themselves morph from terms for objects to terms of laboring, humorous bodies, as in "HOPPET. A little basket, chiefly for holding seedcorn, worn by the husbandmen, in sowing, at their back, whence a man with protuberant buttocks is compared to a man accoutered with a hopper, and stiled hoppet-arsed, vulgarly hopper-arsed. N[orth]." His *Provincial Glossary* gathers terms ranging from the benignly physical "BEVERING. Trembling. N[orth]" and "BOOSTERING. Labouring busily so as to sweat. Ex[more]" to "QUOP. To throb. Glouc.," "FEAT. Nasty tasted. Berks[hire]," "LAND or LANT. Urine. To lant or leint ale, to put urine into it to make it strong. N[orth]," and "SLEAK. To sleak out the tongue, to put it out by way of scorn. N[orth]." In Meriton's Yorkshire glossary, a third of the entries under the letter K are about boisterous physicality: "A KEAUSTRIL, is *a great bon'd course Creature* . . . To KEDGE, is *to fill one very full* . . . KNARL'D, is *eaten and torn with the teeth*; To KITTLE, is *to tickle* . . . KELK, signifies *to groan*."[97] Increasingly visible in the glossaries of cant and vulgar language, the disorderly, crass body features, too, in representations of provincial languages, both common and comically displaced.

Early jest books offered occasional provincial-speaking characters in their variety of comic personae, these embodied in their distinct speech and incapability of much thought at all. One early edition of *Mery Talys and Quicke Answeres* includes a "Welcheman" who exclaims "by cottes plut" for "by God's blood."[98] In the jest, comic pronunciation helps mark the Welsh servant as a simpleton and the butt of the joke, which turns on his mistaking "male" (in this case a stag, which he is supposed to capture) for "mail," which he instead captures, in the form of a bag of mail, much to the chagrin of his master. As N. F. Blake notes, early jest books often depend on such outsider figures, marked by their provincial misunderstandings of English, for their comedy. Those outsiders could be from the North, from the Southwest, from Wales, or from an altogether foreign country in a suggestive parallel between provincial and actually foreign figures.

If I am correct in seeing depictions of provincial languages as part of the institutionalization of a national vernacular, however, they must represent provincial languages and their speakers not simply as outsiders but also in complex terms of affiliation with English readers. As Katie Wales has argued, by the end of the century provincial laborers such as Newcastle coal-pit workers appear "as a jolly, patriotic set of fellows, bringing home their pay to their families once a week, enjoying dancing and drinking."[99] Such appearances are not those of the outsider. The attachment of readers to provincial language speakers takes place in part through comic representations of provincial languages that invoke embodiment and the senses. One of the first poems in print to use Northeast dialect, Edward Chicken's *The Collier's Wedding* of the 1720s, serves as an example. Comic in its parody of a pastoral epithalamion, describing in frank and bawdy detail the courtship and wedding of a coal miner, the poem might seem initially to poke fun at and isolate provincial-language speakers as outsiders.[100] Rhymes such as "teeth" and "breath" or "begun" and "tune" betray distinct pronunciation, and provincial terms such as "Cods" (13), meaning cushions, appear. Moreover, the provincial terms are spoken primarily by the bride's foulmouthed mother, who exclaims at one point, "Hout lad, get Hame, ye're nought but Fash" (13). This provincial is depicted as a disgusting woman who "would funk, smoke, fart, and drink, / and sometimes raise a hellish stink" (12). The poem itself, however, also provides a quasi-ethnographic description of the customs and ceremonies of rural life—stripping a bride of her garter, paying fees to the minister for a marriage service, the fare served at a wedding dinner.

This catalogue of customs provides a sort of verse equivalent of Ray's or Grose's assembly of provincial terms. At one point the poem itself highlights and explains provincial language, as in its phrase "what Country call the Kail" (22). As the poem presents these provincial terms, however, it elicits a sentimental relation to them unavailable in glossaries and dictionaries. It places them in the past and characterizes their speakers as virtuous: they "were honest servants, virtuous wives / led harmless, inoffensive lives" (4). With provincial characters at once virtuous and bawdy, representing both difference and "universal" sentiment, *The Collier's Wedding* is one of a number of texts representing provincial languages that offer possible terms of connection.

The embodiment and coarse humor of provincial languages are, not surprisingly, often gendered, and in this, too, we might find various ways in which readers are invited to relate to these languages, even in their otherness, their embodiment, and their low and common status. In describing the bride's mother as "spew[ing] her liquor as she went" (14), *The Collier's Wedding* invokes the longstanding figure of the grotesque and incontinent female body (think Ben Jonson's Ursula in *Bartholomew Fair*) and attaches to it the sounds of provincial language. Her language is a compromised, while literal, "mother" tongue. *The Origin of the Newcastle Burr*, cited above, similarly places the fallen Northern tongue in the throat of a female—in this case figured as a peacock. (Never mind that the peacock is male by definition.) "Just so, tricked out, the Tyne-sprung Fair / Affects the consequential Air, / But when you hear her Peacock scream, / She wakes you from your short-liv'd Dream."[101] Smollett's provincial women sometimes speak (and certainly write) a scandalous and unmistakably outrageous and humorous language. In these cases, the profane is displaced to the provincial and the abusive comic speech Bakhtin located in the marketplace moves to the feminized space of the domestic.[102]

Not all gendered representations of provincial languages, however, were comic and easily dismissed. Earlier, in Richard Brome's play *The Northerne Lass*, first published in 1632 but republished throughout the early eighteenth century, the language of the fully fledged provincial heroine "yielded a delightful sound; which gain'd her many lovers and friends."[103] She is described as "honest, and modest." Aptly named Constance, she speaks virtuous sentiments in what is called, in the play, "broad" language: "I wot not what he means. But I is weeil sure, Ise nerebee sure to ony Man but hee. And if hee love mee not as well, God pardon him." And later, again in Smollett's fiction, Jery Melford praises the virtuous young ladies of Scotland and moons, "my ear is perfectly reconciled to the Scotch accent, which I find even agreeable in the mouth of a pretty woman. It is a sort of Doric dialect, which gives an idea of amiable simplicity."[104] By the end of the century, of course, the singing mouth of the provincial woman would become the site of the recovery and preservation of age-old language and ballads, the vital antiquarian source of a melancholically fading "oral tradition," quite safe for polite consumption.

These two opposed conceptualizations of female provincial-language speakers, as either custodians of ancient language and song (perhaps faintly in evidence in that virtuous speaker of provincialisms, Pamela) or loud, horrid, incontinent creatures, suggest different terms of relation between readers and provincial languages, corresponding to the two fantasies of the maternal voice, one positive, one negative, that Kaja Silverman has described.[105] These fantasies attempt to recompense the loss entailed in the subject's entry into the symbolic order of language. In an "age of refinement" that saw demands for ever-tighter control of one's manners, including a hyperconsciousness about language use, this coercion into symbolic order entailed a barbed sense of loss. One compensatory fantasy offered a "return" to the "sonorous envelope" (87) of the maternal voice (as Silverman points out, itself an after-the-fact symbolic structure), which might help explain the projects that aimed to recover and recuperate provincial oral lore, language, and songs, evidenced by, for example, the obsessive search for female singers of provincial ballads later in the century.

Consider, too, how Pamela's smattering of provincial terms appears in a sentimental linguistic economy filled with "lumpish" hearts (244) and "hearts turn'd to butter and running away at my eye" (75), in one bizarre and bizarrely physical turn of phrase. In these instances, the feeling body becomes the means of creating an intimate sense of familiarity with a dialect-speaking heroine. "You might have beat me down with a feather," she proclaims in a well-known but not particularly high-spoken phrase, and when she writes that "my heart was up at my mouth" (46) or that she "colour'd up the ears," her language invokes the strongly sensing body, both familiar and evocative for readers at the same time as it locates her amongst the provincial unpolished and their supposed language.

Alternatively, the negative fantasy Silverman describes, one of entrapment within a grotesque physicality, seems to be at work in other female figures, like the mother in *The Collier's Wedding*, or, as we shall see in a moment, the termagants of Andrew Brice's *An Exmoor Scolding*. The female speakers in these works reject the symbolic order of conventional linguistic structure, transparent meaning-making, and decorous talk. They are about as remote from the refined, rational, disembodied public sphere as one could find in a subject capable of speaking. Their unconventional oral pronunciation (as in "hame" for "home" in *The Collier's Wedding*), the use of raw provincialisms, and the occlusion of meaning are tied to an extravagant, sometimes nauseating physicality. These provincialism/vulgarism-streaming lowly women might answer to Silverman's description of a projection of "lack onto female characters in the guise of ... discursive inadequacy" (1).

Such dynamics inform *An Exmoor Scolding, in the Propriety and Decency of Exmoor Language* (1727, 1746) and Tim Bobbin's *A View of the Lancashire Dialect* (1746), comedic dialogues between agricultural laborers overloaded with provincial terms and phonetic spellings nearly incomprehensible to the nonnative, running roughshod over the strictures against representing the particular and bodily.[106] These print dialogues, which loll in dirty, violent, sexual, and nearly indecipherable imagery and language, sold remarkably well, both in their provinces of origin and beyond. *An Exmoor Scolding* first appeared anonymously in the Devon-based *Brice's Weekly Journal* in 1727 and then, coupled with "Exmoor Courtship," as a stand-alone publication sometime before 1746, appearing in *The Gentleman's Magazine* in 1746, and going through three editions in its first year alone, with new editions produced through the 1790s.

Under the pseudonym Tim Bobbin ("bobbin" being a weaving term for the spindle that holds yarn), Lancashire native John Collier published *A View of the Lancashire Dialect* in Manchester in 1746. *The British Magazine* also published it in 1746, while *The Gentlemen's Magazine* rejected the dialogues of "A View" but printed its glossary in the same year, describing the excluded *View* dialogue as consisting of "corrupt pronunciation of known words" (which is not actually true) and "dry and unentertaining," surely a counterintuitive way to describe a narrative in relation to a glossary.[107] In Manchester, *A View* went through multiple editions before its initial, undated publication in London. (The second London edition appeared in 1770.) Reprinted in over sixty editions well into the nineteenth century in a variety of formats, it was one of the most popular provincial-language texts of its age and beyond. As Collier's occasional patron, Richard Townley, put it, the book "took very much with the middle and lower classes of the people in the northern counties"—its appeal to poor laborers evidenced in the many inexpensive illustrated editions.[108] Circulating in both London and the provinces, these works had a national sweep over decades, making them important in positioning provincial languages within an English vernacular, even as that might look different to different readers.

Both Brice and Collier represented provincial language as the language of the "lowest classes" and as peculiar and puzzling. Collier's patron Townley notes that Collier recorded "all the awkward vulgar obsolete words and local expressions which ever occurred to him in conversation amongst the lower classes."[109] The results are often-bewildering strings of words, the appeal of which might easily escape a present-day reader. In Brice's *An Exmoor Scolding*, two sisters verbally attack each other with accusations of rank promiscuities. In a typical passage Thomazin calls her sister "a crewnting, querking, yeavy, dugged-yess, chockling baggage." Confronted with this list of odd terms, readers are posed with a challenge: whether to struggle to find the meaning or, in later editions, turn to a provided glossary to decipher it methodically and slowly. Part of the payoff is the comic grotesqueness of the words. (Those in the previous quotation translate as "groaning like a grunting horse, tending to groan as one in pain, wet and moist, wet and with the tail of their garment dragged along in the dirt, hectoring hag.") On being so described, Thomazin's sister Wilmot replies:

> Net zo chockling, ner it zo crewnting, as thee art, a colting Hobby-horse! Nif tha dest bet go down into the Paddick, to stroke the Kee, thee wut come oll a gerred, and oll horry. (9)

The glossary tells us a "Hobby-horse is one who romps with the men," Wilmot's point being that Thomazin never goes to the barn to milk the cow without returning dirty, foul, and filthy from a roll in the hay, so to speak. Here, as in Meriton's Yorkshire verses, we find, however, not only humor but also that overlay of the provincial, the particular, the low, the embodied, and the foreign-sounding in a language that actually name the uncouth familiar— strange language that is also claimable as complexly national.

In both *An Exmoor Scolding* and *A View of the Lancashire Dialect*, part of the comic sense derives from the subject matter of low bodies, part from the association of that material with thickly accented orality, and another part from the frisson between the terms of vulgar embodiment and their placement in the genre of the glossaries appended to the works. Those word lists record and translate with academic studiousness terms from "*Allernbatch*, a kind of old sore," and "*A'xwaddle*, a dealer in ashes and one that tumbles in them," to "*Tidle mouth*, The Mouth awry, or more extended on One Side than the other" and "*Zwop*, ... the noise made by the sudden Fall of any Thing; as, 'He fell down, zwop.'" They overflow with terms for the grotesque body, the low corporeal realm imputed to rustics.[110] Readers begin in an alien place, with a weird word such as "allernbatch," yet, as they move into meaning, they find themselves in another familiar yet alienating space of dirt, violence, and wounds, with multiple entries for local expressions for urine, feces, physical beatings, and sex, including "Ballocks, *the testicles*" and "Barklt, *dirt hardened on hair.*"[111] There is a dual sense in these translating representations as they incite both curiosity and laughter.

Seventeenth- and eighteenth-century representations of provincial languages often featured humorously bloody, besmeared, bedraggled, and sometimes highly sexualized bodies depicted in peculiar, particular language. While *An Exmoor Scolding*'s women are obscenely physicalized, Tummus (an attempt to reproduce "Thomas" with a Lancashire accent) is jokily and rather mean-spiritedly embodied, as he trips into a muddy ditch, falls off a ladder, faints from the fright of a children's prank, and is beaten bloody in a barroom brawl in which he unwittingly finds himself. These comic portrayals of embodied provincials and their physically marked languages seem the logical complement to print representations of standard English, supposedly clear in meaning, its users disembodied participants in a rational public sphere, the letters on the page themselves becoming nearly transparent as they convey meaning. Alternatively, in a representative page from *A View of the Lancashire Dialect*, the alien provincial language takes on its own visible embodiment (Fig. 6). The appearance of the language on the page itself is opaque, nearly impenetrable, a drawing of attention to the physical characters.

In the passage, Tummus tells his interlocutor, Meary (Mary), how he sold his master's cow, which had died on his watch, to a butcher: "I axt the Butchur whot he'd gi' meh for th' Hoyde, on tak't grooing to th' Karcuss? Throtteen-pence ko he." The butcher buys the cow—"so ot lung-length he took hur; on I bowt two peawn'd o'Sawt for awer Fok, on went toart Whoam ogen."[112] The passage in standard English would appear "So I asked the butcher what he would give me for the hide if he takes it growing to the carcass. Thirteen pence quoted he . . . So at long length he took her; and I bought two pounds of salt and went toward home again." With talk of stripping the hide from a cow's carcass (and, later, the butcher's selling of the rancid meat for food, thus hoodwinking Tummus out of the full price for the cow), we are in the realm of the animal body at its most abject, the familiar if distasteful realm of many rural workers, here aligned with obscure provincial language. In *A View* the protagonist is a male, but he suffers multiple body-based indignities as a disgustingly feminized, disempowered figure. "Tummus" provides the acoustic mirror, becomes that inarticulate figure onto which a Briton might project a lack to compensate for his own losses upon entry into the symbolic order of "proper" English, and through which an idea of himself as one type of national subject—the rational, standard-English-speaking, disinterested citizen—might be formed. Hobbled by their language, the provincial speaker's attempt to participate in an abstracted, general national polity would be as compromised—as interested and irrational—as their provincial, orally inflected, we might say embodied, language.

Enter *Tummus* & *Mearey*.

T. Odds me, *Mearey!* whooad o' thowt o' feeing thee here, fo foyne this Moarning?

M. Beleemy *Tummus*, I as little dreeomt o' feeing yo here.

T. Odd, on I'll tell thee *Mearey*, 'twur feign Peawn'd t'a tuppunny Jannock, I bin os deod os a Dur Nele, be this awer: For laſt Oandurth, meh Meaſter had lik't o kill meh: On juſt neaw, os ſhure os thee on me ar ſtonning here, I'm aƈtilly running my Country.

M. Why, whot's bin th' matter, hanneh fawn ate withur Meaſter.

T. Whot! there's bin moor to doo thin o Gonnor to muck, I'll uphowdteh.——For whot duſt think? boh Yuſterdey huz Lads moot'n ha o bit on o Hallidey, (becofe it wur
th'

FIGURE 6: From Tim Bobbin (John Collier), *A View of the Lancashire Dialect* (Manchester, 1746). Y1255.206. Photo courtesy of the Newberry Library, Chicago.

Of Dream Holes and Muxy Drawbreeches: Particulars, Bodies, and Provincialisms

The implications of associating strange provincial languages with embodiment and sense extend, as we have noted, beyond the merely comic. As with depictions of cant and slang, there was more at stake in print representations of provincial languages than the depiction of rude outsiderness. While conceptions of the depersonalized abstraction and transparency of a printed standard English might have helped to underwrite the fiction of a national polity able to transcend the differences that threatened to divide, such notions were at a disadvantage within a rhetoric of cultural nationalism that increasingly invoked the customary particularities and embodied experiences that supposedly tied compatriots together. Thus, provincial words redolent of sense, eccentric language naming particulars, might also stock a linguistic national imagining that was based not on abstract (and uncompelling) uniformity but on concrete details. The dynamics involved in establishing a standard English associated provincial words with the body and the particular. Such an association, in turn, might add powerfully to the feelings of attachment attributed to provincial languages, making them a part of a national vernacular, both in terms of their connection to sense, to things, as I shall explore in this section, and in their appeal to voice itself.

Terms from Grose's collections—such as the evocative "*Dream Holes.* The openings left in the wall of steeples, towers, barns, &c for the admission of light. Glouc." or the tangibly specific "*Drinking.* A refreshment between meals, used by the plowmen, who eat a bit of bread and cheese and drink some beer, when they come out of the fields at ten in the morning and six in the evening. Kent." or even Pamela's particular terms, such as "mort," a large amount, which Grose links to Bedfordshire, or phrases such as "worth a power of money"—get at the very specifics, the material lived experiences of place that were becoming important to the imagining of national cultural life.[113] Such representations of language, and indeed Harris's and Smith's images of provincials whose language locks them in place, underwrite the myth of a nation in which particular experiences, specific places, provincial languages, and "the people" might be mapped onto each other.

Provincial languages, it seems, cannot help but home in on the particular, as evinced in terms from Meriton's Yorkshire glossary, most naming unprepossessing physical objects:

> An HURN, is a *hoal behind the chimney.*
> HINDERENDS, are the *Offal of corn when it is winnowed* ...
> HAMMES, are the *crooked pieces of wood that are put upon horse-collars.*
> An HOPPER, is a *seed-lip, or Basket the husband-men put their Seed-Corn in, when they sowe their land.*

> An HEMBLE, is an *Hovel or house to put Cattel under, or Wayns or Carts into.*
>
> An HAVER RIDDLE, is a *sive they use in winnowing of oates.*[114]

Similarly, Grose's *Provincial Glossary* includes such terms as "SILLS (of a wagon). The shafts, the same as thills" or "SKEELING. An Isle or bay of a barn," or "SLAKE. Very small coals." These collections seem to promise a stark and inarguable connection between language and the thingish world.[115] If some of the words found in the cant collections discussed in Chapter One (in which provincial language sometimes also appeared) named those specifics, they were always in danger of sliding into wider and wicked meanings. But in provincial language collections, suggestive words land on innocent specifics—"Hinderends" alights safely on grain hulls, and an unusual provincial term such as "hurn" is in no danger of traveling into doubled bawdy or criminal meaning. In this linguistic utopia, each word seems fixed to a specific thing in the world.

As Susan Manly has noted, in contrast to theories of language that emphasized abstraction, the language theory of John Locke had not seen particular sensible words as inferior.[116] Such words named a sensible thing—or more accurately, its concomitant idea, the origin of linguistic signification. Locke argues that, even with the most general terms, "I doubt not, but if we could trace them to their sources, we should find in all Languages, the names, which stand for Things that fall not under our Senses, have had their first rise from sensible *Ideas*."[117] In this account, words recognizably naming sensible ideas were closer to their source. Indeed, if the senses were at times viewed as untrustworthy routes to knowledge, at others they were the basis of true knowledge. As Steven Shapin observes, "In one mood, early modern commentators vigorously endorsed direct sensory experience over preconception and theoretical prepossession."[118] From this perspective, provincial terms, in their explicit physicality, point directly to the sensible things and ideas of the physical world. Not a qualitatively different and lesser form of verbal expression for their particularity, as James Harris would have it, they in fact offer a clearer instance of the connection between word and particular object or the sensible idea the object produces.

What is more, as Manly also notes, for Locke, such plain, sense-based words, in offering a less mediated grasp of the relation between word and sensible thing, provided an easily shared understanding, which contributed to "social affection" between language users.[119] There might not be much social affection when Wilmot calls her sister a "gurt, thonging, banging, muxy drawbreech" in Brice's *An Exmoor Scolding*.[120] However, the specifics in the body and its description—a great, large, filthy, lazy jade, as the glossary explains—make for an understanding hard to mistake, more compelling for its appeal to sense. The bizarre, almost thingish quality of the words themselves, adds surprisingly to the power of the "social affection," because to people using these strange terms, the meaning, grounded in things, is unmistakable. When the particular and embodied have been displaced to the provincial, readers might perceive such powers in their strange words. Those odd provincial terms might bespeak a community of language users somewhere else sharing speech of unmistakable and powerful meaning.

"Unrestrained Freedom of Tones": Hearing the Provincial Voice

We have noted how print representations of provincial languages suggest that they have some connection to the nation's vernacular and to readers of English, that they are more than the language of somewhere and someone else. One of the most powerful means of establishing them as part of an English vernacular was through the invocation of the sounded voice and its associations with embodiment. To understand the significance of the voiced quality of provincial language that print representations attempted to reproduce (and indeed, made possible) requires a brief rehearsal of the cultural meaning of voice in national rhetoric in this period. The idea of orality and its rhetorical power expanded throughout the eighteenth century, increasingly connected to a body-based conceptualization of language that might work more effectively—and affectively—than an abstract standard English to build a sense of national attachment.[121] Christopher Looby has described these forms of vocal linguistic national affiliation in the early American republic.[122] For him, orality offers a "countercurrent" to the print public sphere, one that "valorizes the grain of the voice in addition to, or instead of, the silence of print" (3), a differentiation between "the abstract, alienated, rational polis of print culture and the more passionately attached, quasi-somatically experienced nation" (5). How might we use this insight to understand the work of provincial languages, with their pointed dramatization of the "grain of the voice," back across the Atlantic, within British national discourse?

In Britain, one place where we find evidence of the power of the "passionately attached, quasi-somatic" sense of the *sound* of language is in Edmund Burke's *Enquiry*. Burke notes that

> The eye is not the only organ of sensation, by which a sublime passion may be produced. Sounds have a great power in these as in most other passions. I do not mean words, because words do not affect simply by their sounds, but by means altogether different... The noise of vast cataracts, raging storms, thunder, or artillery, awakes a great and awful sensation in the mind.... The shouting of multitudes has a similar effect; and by the sole strength of the sound, so amazes and confounds the imagination, that in this staggering and hurry of the mind, the best

established tempers can scarcely forbear being borne down, and joining in the common cry, and common resolution of the croud [*sic*].[123]

The sound of shouting, collective voices, outside of the actual meanings of any of their words, awakens a sensation—"sublime passion." In Burke's assessment, the crowd's vocalization is naturalized, akin (like artillery) to waterfalls and thunder. Those voices "confound the imagination" and "hurry the mind," thereby impelling the body to partake in "the common cry" and to adopt the same thinking, the "common resolution" of the crowd. For Burke, these are stronger passions than those raised by any written document, or distinct words, as sound skips reason and verbal mediation to act directly on the body, producing feelings that force the hearer into group associations and actions.

Burke's assessment of the connections between collective "cry" and group affiliation is less than sanguine—it is, after all, something to which "the best established tempers" unwillingly succumb. The powers of the multitude's shouting pose danger, the threat of irascible mobs and revolutions. The Scots-authored *Encyclopædia Britannica*, which also articulates the connection of voice and group affiliation, does so in much more confident and serene terms:

> [A]s the people of great Britain are a bold, daring, and impetuous race of men; subject to strong passions, and from the absolute freedom and independence which reigns among all ranks of people throughout this happy isle . . . our language takes its strongest characteristic distinction from the genius of the people . . . Peculiarly happy too in the full and open sound of the vowels . . . and in the strong use of the aspirate H in almost all those words which are used as exclamations . . . interjections have, in our language, more of that fullness and unrestrained freedom of tones . . . and are pushed forth from the inmost recesses of the soul in a more forcible and unrestrained manner, than any other language whatsoever.[124]

In this description, sound is again linked to social affiliation. Pronunciation, "our" voiced language, in "the full and open sound of the vowels" or "the strong use of the aspirate H . . . in exclamations," speaks to the very "genius" of "the people of great Britain," their boldness, daring, and "strong passions." But here, sound does not produce so much as reflect social affiliation, and to speak is not to succumb to an incontestable force but to announce one's shared "freedom and independence." Moreover, the article ties the genius of "our" pronounced language to a political rhetoric of freedom that we have seen in other discussions of particular Englishes, such as cant. The "absolute freedom and independence . . . among all ranks" is evidenced in the "full and open sound of the words" and the "unrestrained freedom of tones" of interjections. It is in the voiced moment, both produced and heard through the body, that the "inmost recesses" of those unrestrained souls become public.

This passage, however, reveals the inevitable complexities surrounding claims about the body, the voice, and just whose language might be "ours." The "aspirate H," a distinctive national pronunciation not found in, say, French, is an especially loaded example to choose. Although the *Encyclopædia* writer attributes the breathed H to "all ranks of people among this happy isle," many Londoners dropped the H in most pronunciations, while the Scots still preserved it—even pronouncing "it," which had long ago lost its aspirated H south of the Tweed, as "hit." Here is a moment in which provincial language—in this case Scots, both a provincial and national language—might be said to have preserved a once-common feature of English pronunciation now lost to the nation's center, making Scots a kind of foreign but also originary language within Britain in the present.[125] We shall explore this spatial anachronization in the following chapter. Conversely, however, given the restrictions many Scots provincials placed on their written and spoken English, it is difficult to square the notion of freedom with pronunciation in Britain. Scots at this time were emphatically not free to pronounce without fear of social repercussions—pronouncing "it" as "hit" would be a dead giveaway of provincial and, to bigots, inferior status.

The elevated classes of the metropolitan center often already spoke English without "error," the telltale sounds of provincial pronunciation, and could further refine their language technique. Lectures and books on elocution offered, in increasingly minute detail, guidance for "proper" pronunciation of English for gentlefolk and aspirants within both England and Scotland; Thomas Sheridan's *A Course of Lectures on Elocution* is one of the best-known, all the more interesting for its author being an Irish actor.[126] Thomas Batchelor and Thomas Spence, among others, developed increasingly intricate notation system for ever more exact and polished pronunciation of English words, Batchelor even detailing "the manner of their formation by the vocal organs."[127] Within this context, however, some believed the vulgar best preserved national character and feelings at the level of sound. This belief in the power of the common people's vocal sounds extended to their supposed oral transmission of national fables. As Adam Ferguson wrote, "when traditionary fables are rehearsed by the vulgar, they bear the marks of a national character ... raise the imagination and move the heart."[128] As the common folk "rehearse" (another term for oral recitation) traditionary (meaning spoken) fables, their speech works on the imagination and heart, the realm, for Ferguson, of national affiliation. Similarly, the author of "Dissertation on the Oral Tradition of Poetry" writes that the dialect of "Scotish" [*sic*] Ballads "gives them a great advantage in point of touching the passions. Their language is rough and unpolished and seems to flow immediately from the heart.... They possess the pathetic power in the highest degree, because they do not affect it; and are striking, because they do not mediate to strike."[129] In an inverse relation, the sounds of provincial languages of the lowest degree "possess pathetic power in the highest degree."[130]

This appeal to simple oral language and its reputed production of strong feeling could be found in Thomas Blackwell's writing on Homer, Hugh Blair's on the Ossian poems, or Robert Lowth's on the sacred poetry of the Hebrews, but what I am interested in here is the displacement of vulgar orality and its striking powers specifically to printed provincial languages.[131] For readers, provincial phrases such as "dugged-yess, chockling" function much like the child's prattle Ann Wierda Rowland discusses in her investigation of eighteenth-century theories of the origins of language. In those theories, "prattle," in detaching "the meaning of words from their sounds," reiterates the origins of language and poetry, in which sound and feeling preceded signification.[132] It is that pronounced, "embodied" quality of language that print representations of provincial languages aim to visualize and call up, in strings of printed letters that initially help produce sounds, if not yet meaning, for their readers. Alternatively, adopting a standard English, as Burke claimed above, turned the Scot William Robertson's language into something "dead." It is little wonder that provincial languages suggested, by contrast, the lively and intimate, even as they were depicted as outlandishly physical—languages of "thick" accents and odd-sounding, opaque provincialisms. If standard print English was seen as effacing the powerful voiced qualities of language, it was left to representations of provincial languages, with their marked peculiarities on the page, to draw attention to pronunciation and the power of voice. In the intermediality of sound represented on the printed page, voice appears in its most resounding fashion not in a standard form whose point was to efface the pronounced sense of language altogether but in representations of dialect, such as "cuil" for "cool" or "zewnteen or zoewnteen" for "seventeen."[133] Significantly, it is the very intermediality, the movement between visual and aural, the use of standard phonetic system to depict peculiar dialect, that produces the power of such representations.

Thus, while we have become used to thinking about print as a disembodying, virtual technology, it could also produce a sense of embodiment, an invocation of the voiced word, perhaps most strongly when attempting to replicate provincial languages in all of their vocal strangeness.[134] When these print representations invite their sounding, we find support for Leigh Eric Schmidt's argument against the idea that the Enlightenment was responsible for "profound hearing loss in which an objectifying ocularcentrism triumphs over the conversational intimacies of orality."[135] The word on the page, particularly the provincial word, might also conjure sound, evoking—and producing—a version of these intimacies.[136] Interestingly, it is the gradual development of a standard print English that enabled increasingly "deviant" incarnations of the language, with odd pronunciations such as "vashion" for fashion and unusual terms such as "crewnting," to read, in their pointed veering from the standard, as essentially "oral." In moments of unmeaning, readers can at least or at best sound it out.

Even when provincials are reading and writing, they are using a language that refuses to be reined in by a uniform script—they pronounce differently from the standard form, and reproducing that pronunciation means writing differently. Defoe records his bemusement at the wild difference in "tone and diction" of a boy reading from the Bible in Somersetshire:

> I observed the boy read a little oddly in the tone of the country, which made me the more attentive, because on enquiry, I found that the words were the same . . . as in all our Bibles. . . . "I have washed my coat, how shall I put it on, I have washed my feet, how shall I defile them?" The boy read thus, with his eyes, as I say, full on the text. "Chava doffed my coat, how shall I don't, chav a washed my veet, how shall I moil'em?" How the dexterous dunce could form his mouth to express so readily the words . . . in his country jargon, I could not but admire.[137]

Against the printed text in front of him, the boy "form[s] his mouth" to a specific tone, which Defoe also calls a distinct "country speech" of Somersetshire. It is both a kind of accomplishment, "dexterity," and a sign of stupidity—in the translation, the "dunce" is not even consistent in his expression of "I have"—it is "chava" in one instance, "chav a" in the next. Suggestively, Defoe's transcription of the boy's oral reading creates a new print language, a strange double of the English he is reading.

One finds similarly mutating language in the lowly provincial's stab at letter-writing often depicted in collections of otherwise model examples of polite correspondence; the humor of the letter stems in part from the fact that the provincial can't or won't shut up. *A New Academy of Compliments* includes, amongst its mainly love-letter samples for elegant men and women, a note from illiterate Hodge the Plowman, who must hire a scribe to write to his sweetheart, Joan. This cannot, alas, remain writerly—it becomes a record of Hodge's imagined spoken effusions. In his letter, he conjures a scene and his retort to those who would tease him for buying a small gift for Joan ("but, thought I, hoot and be hang'd and you will") and verbalizes his exclamation at his future, projected marriage celebration: "then hey away to the Alehouse," all of which the scribe records for him phonemically.[138] The contrast of his transcribed letter ("hoot" and "hey away" are also expressions Pamela "voices") to the polite language of the collection's gentle speakers and correspondents is based in part on sound—on imagined vocal expressions committed to paper.

Early cant glossaries had enticingly distanced their lexicons from readers, and Defoe's novels openly staged the mediating acts of translation his protagonists needed to perform, with their "as they call it"s. But something slightly different is going on in representations of provincial languages that refrain from such translation, demanding instead that readers attempt to voice the languages themselves. Smollett's *Roderick Random*, for instance, reproduces provincial language as direct speech, without translating commentary, when

"Joey . . . called with an arch sneer, 'Waunds, captain! Whay woan't yau sooffer the poor waggoneer to meake a penny—Coom, coom, young man, get oop, get oop,—never moind the coptain.'"[139] The language is a riddle solved only when readers inhabit the provincial's pronunciation. And when they do, they occupy that particular embodied and powerful place of affiliation based on voice that a standard English seemed to eschew.

As print dialogues, *A View of the Lancashire Dialect* and *An Exmoor Scolding* consciously invoke oral exchange. The latter, in particular, draws from the generic framework of the medieval flyting, with its display of traded spoken insults for relish. The provincial rustics of *An Exmoor Scolding* show off an undeniable facility with spoken language in their quick, even witty, stream of words. Here the rude, incontinent body is also a deeply oral one—"not" becomes "net," "so" becomes "zo," in their visualized accent—as the deranged female speakers communicate through an unmistakably voiced dialect. *A View*'s title page announces that the dialogue's (fictitious) author, one "Tim Bobbin," is an "opp'n Speyker o'th' Dialect."[140] "Crewnting, querking, yeavy, dugged-yess, chockling"—readers confront in these strings of unmeaning words, as they did in certain representations of cant language, Certeau's "glossolalia": "*noises of otherness* . . . different voices disrupting the organizing system of meaning."[141] "Crewnting" and "querking," sounds without meaning for many readers, which actually name nonverbal groans and grunts, resemble something like Certeau's "glossolalic utopia . . . all that is not language and comes from the speaking voice," exuberant utterance, "'torrents' of passing voices," before becoming an "actual language."[142]

Without narrators, *A View* and *An Exmoor Scolding* engulf readers in alien tongues, insisting that readers, too, voice these strange words.[143] Readers move from meaningless letters on the page to pure sound, initially nonsensical in pronunciation (e.g., "Hoyde, on tak't grooing to th' Karcuss") and then to meaning, as Tummus here describes a cow's hide still "growing to the carcass," something a reader might piece together, slowly and perhaps incompletely, with the help of the glossary. Part of the process of coming to meaning, too, is sounding out the language and, crucially, hearing pronunciation that is different from the standard. Rustics and provincial dairymaids, whether Tummus and Meary or sisters Thomazin and Wilmot, are figures of comic distance, yet readers must become proximal to them, pronounce as they would pronounce, form their mouths to the contours of theirs, to arrive at any meaning. This is another version of the process of moving between unfamiliar and familiar central to vernacularization. It is an ongoing process, and one that seduces with the desire to know, but one that can also repulse. In *An Exmoor Scolding*'s phrase "a crewnting, querking, yeavy, dugged-yess, chockling baggage," language shuttles between pure sound and semimeaningful, placeable words, particularly when the glossary is used, but not all words appear there, and those that do mean "groaning like a horse," "groaning as one in pain," "wet," "dirty"—immersing readers in the experiencing, often traumatized, body.

"Whoam Ogen": Provincial Languages and the Unhomely

The odd phrases catalogued in provincial glossaries, such as "*Muckson up to the Huckson*, dirty up to the knuckles," the printed dialogue words that invoke odd sounds, present, at least at first encounter, obscurity just as they call up the sounds and bodies of fellow Britons. It is, however, through this estranging sequence that readers are returned to their British selves. It is when the reader can sound out Tummus's odd-looking "Whoam Ogen" with provincial sonic alterity that they recognize and arrive at "home again." In the eighteenth century, one form of linguistic obscurity was tied to specifically provincial spaces, but it was also part of a circuit that might return readers to themselves. It was the very obscurity of provincial languages that helped make them part of the vernacular.

Might we think of this movement between familiar and unfamiliar as uncanny? The print catalogues of provincial words are both English and strange: of the home, as it were, and not. And they name the humble and familiar in unrecognizable terms. Ray's *Collection*, for instance, features words naming intimacies of the body, such as "*Clem'd* or *clam'd*: starved, because by famine the guts and bowels are as it were clammed or stuck together," and words naming familiar customs, such as "*Doundrins*: *Derb*: Afternoons drinkings." Despite the familiarity of the things they name, those words are also unfamiliar. Grose's provincial terms, from "THROPPLE. The windpipe. Yorksh[ire]" to "SALLIS. Hog's-lard. Glouc[ester]," set provincials apart from the reflective and abstract in naming humble objects of sensation, whether sense-producing, such as windpipes, or grossly sensed, as in hog's lard, and yet, they are obscure. The printing of and fascination with such odd language answers to Irving Ehrenpreis's notion of the "negative particularity" of many eighteenth-century writers. As he argues, "What had to be rendered in bright detail was what did not belong to the familiar things of their world."[144] We might alter that claim in relation to provincial language to say that what had to be rendered in bright detail did not belong to the familiar language of most readers' worlds, even when it named the most familiar of items and experiences.

Consider, too, the particular terms excluded from general dictionaries that name procedures of physical labor. Grose's *Provincial Glossary* includes examples such as "YOTED, or WHESED. Watered. The brewer's grains must be well yoted, or whesed for the pigs. W.," and "RIVE. To rend or tear. To rive all a dawds, to tear all to rags. N.," as well as names for specific tools, such as "JACK-

O-LEGS. A clasp knife. N."—all words naming quite specific material practices and artifacts, and all odd, largely unknown. In such moments, the uncanny shades into the gothic motifs of spectrality. For, increasingly, such terms named things and practices no longer in use in an industrializing, modernizing manufacturing landscape.[145] And in instances where such terms named things and practices still in use, they were associated with a laboring class hidden from sight in most printed texts. Bruce Robbins has shown how in nineteenth-century Britain literary images of the laboring class were limited to servants depicted, in ghostlike fashion, as amputated parts—hands, in his discussion—that exert incongruous energies.[146] In Robbins's study, the unrepresented physical labor of the servant, through the metonymy of the laboring body part, returns with eerie power. Provincial terms found in print glossaries and other writing, with their representations of unusual, doggedly particular languages naming types and objects of labor, suggest an analogous uncanny return of laboring and provincial bodies.

Finally, it is not only that the *unheimlich* quality of provincial language creates a toggle between familiar and strange, but that its excess of voice contributes to a sense of narrative obscurity. The underling's capacity for endless speech—one shared by the Pamela Mr. B initially encounters—has a long literary pedigree. Horace Walpole famously credited Shakespeare for the loquacious low characters who appear in his own *The Castle of Otranto* and contended that they bestowed realism upon his text and, by way of contrast, brought sublimity to his protagonists. In his second preface, he writes that they "should not be made to express their passions in the same dignified tone ... the contrast between the sublime of the one, and the *naiveté* of the other, sets the pathetic of the former in a stronger light."[147] Walpole's domestics, however, bring their own gothic qualities of suspense to the narrative. Exceedingly garrulous, they often produce words without meaning, words that delay the discovery of outcomes, as in the servant Bianca's failure to explain the cause of her fear, which her listeners (and readers) are anxious to hear, as she instead exclaims, "I fear my hair—I am sure I never in my life—Well!" (103). This low verbosity and linguistic nonsense, and the way they keep readers in the dark, are not unlike the temporal encounter with provincial language itself. Confronted with a line such as "Lock! Wilmot, vor why vore de'st roily z upon ma up to Challacom Rowl?," readers are likely to feel frustration, a simultaneous expectation and thwarting of understanding. An editor is tempted, Viktor Shklovsky notes, "to delete the retardations and repetitions. The creators of these tales were aware of such a possible perception and even played with it."[148] Like gothic narrators, provincial writers, too, played with obscurity, using it to unsettle too-easy alignments of place, language, and national vernacular, as we shall see in the following chapter.

CHAPTER SIX

"I Do Not Like London or Anything That Is in It"

THE PROVINCIAL OFFENSIVE

IN GLOSSARIES AND PRINT DIALOGUES of provincial languages, tours, poems, and novels, linguistic obscurity becomes the very sign of authenticity, placing languages that make up the vernacular. In these works, travel to the "foreign" worlds of the provincial vulgar and their language offers the promise of a language of the material and the real, as well as a stable relation between world and word—in part through linguistic obscurity. Explanatory mechanisms, from narrative asides to footnotes and glossaries, might seem to control that obscurity. David Simpson argues, for instance, that with glossaries, "the glossed word is indeed the image of the foreigner or stranger within, but there is a sense that the stranger can be managed, accommodated easily enough by being transposed (if not quite translated) into the textual household."[1] Provincial glossaries reassure readers that what they are reading is not truly foreign—these are, after all, English terms, however remote the location of their use, and not full-blown foreign languages in need of translation (as was supposedly necessary to produce, for instance, the printed Ossian poems). Representations of the provincial, including glossaries, however, often defy such management. For the new genres that provincial writers developed, particularly print dialogues, often left in place a frustrating opacity that haunts even the most intensely glossed texts, as we shall see throughout this chapter.[2]

The late seventeenth-century verse dialogue *The Praise of York-shire Ale*, which we examined in Chapter Five, went through three editions, yet the language is and remains a puzzle for anyone who needs the glossary. It provides only partial and sometimes confusing access to the text. For the lines

> F[ather]: Ise not farr, ist Cow Cawv'd that's a Goodin,
>   Now *Tibb* weese git some Beestling Pudding:
>   Letts spang our geates for it is var Snithe,
>   *And Ise flaid Wife it will be Frost Belive;*[3]

the glossary explains that "Ise" actually means "I shall," and "ist" means "is it," but offers no explanation for "Goodin" or "snithe." The spelling of the Yorkshire terms even changes in different editions. Is it "naught" or "nought"? "Ewer" or "ewes"?[4] Here, as elsewhere, the most ordinary of accounts of the daily life of the common people of Britain are also tantalizingly opaque and ever changing.

Provincial Pastoral and Dispossessed Readers

Provincial writers knew better than anyone that the idea of provincial languages as fixed markers of space and time was a convenient fiction. While in the previous chapter we saw the ways in which representations of provincial languages aimed to place and fix them, this chapter explores how provincial writers put those languages out of place, as it were, playing with their obscurity, bucking the idea that they might be easily managed in glossaries, unmooring them from their supposed ties to specific geographical sites, and experimenting with the genres, particularly the pastoral, that would place them. Works authored by schoolteachers, clergy, printers, radical weavers, and activist journalists offer intriguing evidence of familiarity with and, importantly, resistant responses to the dominant dynamics surrounding print provincial languages. Circulating through provincial networks, with places of publication not in London or even Edinburgh but in Exeter, Newcastle, Manchester, York, Kendal, Glasgow, and Kilmarnock, these works suggest a canny resistance to representations of provincial languages that would place them. They shatter the idea of a national vernacular that could incorporate "common people" through spatially fixed, simply embodied languages.

One rare collection of dialect poems from the first half of the century, Josiah Relph's *A Miscellany of Poems*, published posthumously in 1747, suggests such sly self-consciousness and barbed retort. Relph, a minister and schoolmaster, renders a Cumberland way of speaking on the page and, on the surface, seems to connect it to a local community held together by ages-old practices, drawing from those pastoral conventions that, as we noted in Chapter Three, attempted to represent "beautiful relations between rich and poor."[5] The opening poem, "Harvest, or The Bashful Shepherd," takes up the pastoral motif of a shepherd pining for his love. A speaker, disembodied and removed from the scene, sets the scene in standard English: "When welcome rain the weary reapers drove / Beneath the shelter of a neighboring grove." But when the reaper (alas, a laborer, not actually a shepherd) speaks, he is embodied in terms that resonate with our discussion in Chapter Five. As he longs for his virtuous maiden, he accidentally cuts himself with his sickle ("out gusht the bleud," he exclaims), which his "grandy" (grandmother) cures with a folk-remedy: "the gushen bluid wi' cockwebs staid" (she staunches the bleeding with cobwebs).[6] In the poem's representations of spoken provincial language, and indeed in the bleeding figure of the reaper, the speaking, spewing body is ushered into being on the page. Phonetic spelling marks this language as oral, its allophonic deviations from standard English registering a different—provincial—pronunciation. Printing "bluid" instead of "blood" also estranges the term, inviting the reader to pronounce the odd-looking word—and pronounce it with a difference—in order to understand it.

Unlike Anstey's "Zomerset" provincial speakers, with their absurd attempts to be fashionable, Relph's "shepherd" seems to know his place in terms of his own frank and simple embodiment, his self-conscious localism, his low class, and his generic location in pastoral. Through the figure of the lowly reaper, Relph engaged the emerging poetics of the period that embraced the rude for its seeming artlessness, promoting the idea that, as Mina Gorji has put it, a writer "would be more touching . . . because of low social rank"—that status increasingly associated with provincial language, as we noted in Chapter Five.[7] With his rude dialect, Relph's rural figure appeals to readers' feelings, depicting his own in a thickly accented immediacy, as when, after viewing his love, "a springing blush spred fast owr aither cheek" (3). The shepherd is all over-heated body, as he confesses in his first lines: "Thur drops may cuil my out-side heat; / Thur callar blasts may wear the boilen sweat / But my het bluid, my heart aw'in a bruil, / Nor callar blasts can wear, nor drops can cuil" (1–2).

It is through this language, however, that Relph also questions what it might mean for the shepherd/reaper to know his place. His language disturbs, for instance, the generic conventions of the dominant form of pastoral of the mid-eighteenth century. While Relph's poem, subtitled "A Pastoral in the Cumberland Dialect," answers to William Empson's "praise of simplicity" with its hero "in contact with nature," in its use of dialect it rejects the model of pastoral that, as Annabel Patterson notes, "promotes a magic circle of idyllic manners and aesthetic pleasure that were supposed to exclude political experience while implicitly supporting a conservative ideology."[8] Included within these "idyllic manners" was language uncompromised, so to speak, by provincial associations. As Empson explains, "the essential trick of old pastoral . . . was to make simple people express strong feelings (felt as the most universal subject, something fundamentally true about everybody) in learned and fashionable language."[9] Endorsing this approach, authorities such as Pope, as we have seen, stipulated that low, particular, and especially provincial language had no business in pastoral or even georgic poetry. Relph opted, alternatively, for the less-fashionable Theocritean pastoral, taking seriously the dialect use Pope had dismissed in his parody of the style in an "old ballad" in "Somersetshire dialect."[10] Relph's collection presents both the "shepherd" and his provincial author as deeply feeling souls—a preface describes the poet as having "a passionate fellow feeling for all the distresses of mankind."[11] It is precisely through unlearned and impolite provincial language, however, that he invokes this feeling.

In using particular contemporary provincial language, Relph seems to deploy a more recognizably vernacular language than did earlier writers of pastoral. Of course, there had been experimentation with regionally specific and archaic terms in the writings of Edmund Spenser, William Browne, and, in the eighteenth century, Ambrose Philips. Yet the pastoral of these writers had little connection to provincial speakers of their own day.[12] Alternatively, as we saw in Chapter Three, Gay pursued Theocritean pastoral's emphasis on the national demotic to absurd depths in *The Beggar's Opera*, exploding a sense of a vernacular via unseemliness and scandal. And, as we shall see, his *The Shepherd's Week* made a mockery of claims regarding provincial languages and a national vernacular. Despite compiler of "archaic and provincial words" Jonathan Boucher's approving nod that in Relph's writing, "dialect is . . . highly advantageous to pastoral poetry," a closer reading shows that, like Gay, Relph reveals estranging and displacing capacities in the present and a skepticism about the idea of a consolidating vernacular.[13]

In Relph's pastoral the reaper-shepherd foregrounds his own feeling body, showcasing the nature and simplicity attributed to the contemporary rustic, in part through the clotted language of the provincial, but his particular speech also distances the immediacy of that feeling body, with puzzling words such as "thur," "cuil," and "boilen" demanding readerly adjustment, often through pronunciation, to make sense of the transcription of provincial pronunciation. As well as oddly pronounced recognizable words—"there," "cool," and "boiling"—the poem includes regionalisms such as "powen," meaning pulling, "gliff," meaning transient view, "callar," meaning cold, and "stummer'd," meaning stumbled, terms that estrange readers, evoking not immediate feeling but rather provoking a mediating turn to the glossary at the end of the volume.[14] Even in these terms referring to the body, the odd language short-circuits any "unmediated" striking of the passions. Such diction makes the reader a sort of exile within the linguistic territory of the poem, propelled out of the seemingly familiar English countryside of the historical moment.[15] We might say that, through these linguistic moves, the poem recovers the political aspects of dispossession that critics from Patterson to Michael McKeon, Stuart Curran, and Nigel Leask have attributed to some versions of pastoral.[16]

Relph's enigmatic words and phrases and the mediations they place in some readers' ways suggest that sharing the poet's "passionate fellow feeling" must take a circuitous route, moving between possession—"here is a poem of my English countryside, in low, familiar language"—to dispossession—"here is language of my own moment that is not actually my own"—and perhaps, but not always, repossession—"here is a glossary that will make this particular English language mine." If some representations of provincial languages seemed to help construct a national vernacular, "Harvest, or The Bashful Shepherd," on a linguistic level, offers further evidence of McKeon's assertion that "patriotism complicates pastoralism."[17] For here, what is for some intimate patriotic belonging at the level of the word is, for most others, the very expulsion from belonging. The route and the terms of possession and dispossession differ for different readers—between those who know and those who do not know the Cumberland dialect, between those who can move between the phonetic representation of words on a page and understanding and those who cannot. The editorial voice of Relph's collection and its glossary remind readers that the language is clearly the provenance of some, but not of others. The latter's compiler, likely Relph's editor, underscores this division by positioning himself within the community familiar with that dialect, using the first-person plural to explain "Sweels of laughter, Swells or bursts of laughter. We likewise say the candle sweels, when it blazes or burns away."[18] There is a "we," but those for whom the language is obscure, those who need the glossary-writer's explanation, are not a part of it. Such readers, with their incomplete knowledge, are meant to experience proximity at a distance.

Making a Puzzle of Print

Relph's poem also resists the sometimes-parallel association of provincial language with rural "nature" counterposed to urban "art." Rather, it exemplifies what McKeon describes as a dialectic between them. The poet's most profound undoing of a stable binary that would confine the provincial to a timelessness universality of "nature" is his reckoning with the commercial print context of his poem's moment. His simple dialect-speaking "shepherd" inhabits a surprisingly contemporary world of commodified books and bookstores, and it is to that world that he turns in search of standard lines of love. Feeling here is conventionalized, less through the commonplaces of pastoral and more through commercially available printed lines, both lines on a page and something like pickup lines for sale (as found in works like *A New Academy of Compliments*, discussed in Chapter Five).[19] *New Academy* had represented shepherds as illiterate, but at this poem's end the rustic heads "straight to the stationers shop" to buy a "beauk / ... o' Compliments I trow they caw it" (5) to write formulaic flattery to his sweetheart.[20] In this way he recapitulates the "complex man's" own turn to conventionalized feeling in pastoral, reprising by reversing Empson's notion of the genre's "double attitude of the complex man to the simple one ('I am in one way better, in another not so good')."[21] If Relph's shepherd is in one way better—supposedly simpler, closer to nature—in another it is *he* who is not so good, turning to commercial media to parlay sentiment.

In depicting his rural laborer as a participant in a commercialized economy of print, even in his writing of love lines, Relph dissolves the obscure in a shared moment of commercial print banality. In doing so, he suggests that he, too, recognizes "native simplicity" (in Samuel Richardson's phrase) and its occasional obscurity, as something one can put on and take off. In one poem, Relph even addresses this now-you-see-it-now-you-don't power of conventionalized simplicity in Richardson's *Pamela*, writing "What is it, happy Author, say, / that steals thus unperceiv'd away; / That where but negligence appears, / Dissolve the reader into tears. / Thy pages like thy wondrous theme / Artless and undesigning seem, / Yet warmth to each beholder lend."[22] Native simplicity, Relph suggests, is a convention that merely seems undesigning. Like vernacular pastoral itself, this language and sentiment that merely appear artless are made possible not by a pristine, untainted rural culture but by mobility, urbanization, and the circulation of commercial print works. As Hugh Blair had perceptively argued, "it was not until men had begun to assemble in great cities, after the distinction of ranks and station were formed, and the bustle of Courts and large societies were known, that Pastoral Poetry assumed its present form."[23] Pastoral is a product of movement and dispossession, the unfamiliarity and distance of the provincial languages Relph and others associated with it the source of its consolidating charm.

Like Relph, provincial writers Andrew Brice and John Collier, to whom I shall now return, reveal a shrewd awareness of and response to the complex dynamics surrounding the print representation of provincial languages. This is not surprising, given that Brice and Collier were mobile figures steeped in print. Having run away from his printer's apprenticeship, Brice became a printer himself and, publishing his own newspaper and other works in Devon for decades, was part of a thriving provincial print culture. Collier apprenticed as a weaver, served as schoolmaster in the village of Milnrow (now part of Greater Manchester), painted public-house signs and caricatures, and published, along with his massively successful *A View of the Lancashire Dialect*, political verse and satire as well as extensive reviews of contemporary works on antiquarian topics. Brice's and Collier's work appeared in both London-based and provincial publications, Collier's publishing life extending from contributing to periodicals in the capital to posting his broadsheets on trees in his village.

These writers overturned notions of a simple provincial language and clownish rural speakers through the medium of print, Collier even drawing attention to his work as a commercial publisher by opening one edition with a dialogue between the author and his book. "Buk" asks the pseudonymous author Tim Bobbin, "donneh aim at sending me eawe agen on another tramp?" (wondering if he plans to send the book out again "on another tramp," i.e., publish a new edition). Tim responds "theawrt likt strowll ogen, as shure os Tup's a sherp" (he does: the book is likely to "stroll again, as sure as a tup is a sheep").[24] The dialogue is striking, bestowing upon a talking book the same Lancashire language Tim speaks, and even depicting the book defending that language. Tim asks "buk," "dust think Rime mun owlus tawk stumpt Loncasher?" (Do you think rhyme must always talk some Lancashire), to which "buk" responds "Eigh, why naw?" (Hey, why not?) (viii). Striking in its play of notions of sound and orality, literacy, publication, and language, Tim and Buk even code switch, trading rhymes in English.

The opening of the actual dialogue of Collier's *View* introduces its ill-spoken characters as if they were part of a comic stage play:

Enter Tummus & Mearey.

T. Odds me, Mearey! Whoad o' thowt o' seeing thee here, so foyne this Moarning? . . .

M. Beleemy Tummus, I as little dreeomt o' seeing yo here.

T. Odd, on I'll tell thee Mearey, 'twer seign Peawn'd t'a tuppunny Jannock, I'd bin os deeod os a Dur Nele, be this awer: For last oandurth, meh Measter had lik't o kill meh[25]

Such passages wield obscurity, whipsawing between semicomprehensible language ("who'd have thought of seeing thee here?") and confrontations with clusters of odd, initially meaningless words such as "'twer seign Peawn'd t'a tuppunny Jannock," in which "jannock" will not make sense no matter how pronounced, if a reader does not know the provincial word, meaning a twopenny loaf. English estranged, this foreign-looking line actually embeds a familiar (to some) proverb—something along the lines of "it were seven pounds to a two penny loaf that X would have happened"—a kind of humble observation such as "dollars to doughnuts." The odds are, Thomas explains to Mary, that he would have been dead as a doornail by this hour, "deeod os a Dur Nele, be this awer," for his master would have liked to kill him, "meh Measter had lik't o kill meh." Coming to this meaning through print, through unfamiliar sounds reproduced in print, or, for the Lancashire speaker, familiar sounds estranged in print, is like solving an arduous puzzle, the delight of recognition produced in part by realizing, in turn, the frank banality of the passage.

The very title of the work, *A View of the Lancashire Dialect*, gets at the reifying conversion of auditory into visual medium. Tummus, however, remains oblivious to such complexities, merely speaking the thick-accented language that comes "naturally." Apostrophes mark the incomplete pronunciations of the dialect speaker, an incompleteness speakers such as Tummus, presumably, would not even recognize, such as "o'" for "of" and "'twer" for "it were/was." Substituted letters ("o" for "a" in "os" meaning "as," "u" for "o" and "a" in "Tummus") and seemingly nonsensical words ("beleemy" for "believe me") phonetically reproduce the sound of the language, but also visibly mark its "incorrectness," even illiteracy—English as one who is barely literate might imagine it. Tummus's unwitting thing-making of language itself becomes a joke, as elsewhere he pronounces "long" to make it "lung".[26] Local terms—"seign" for seven, "Peawn'd" for pound, and "jannock" for "a kind of loaf bread made of oatmeal levened," as the glossary explains—particularize these speakers, presented as subordinates, with Tummus referring to his master's wrath in the opening sentences. There is no mistaking the fact that Tummus and Mearey are not only provincial but vulgar speakers, oblivious to their constant veerings from standard English, veerings put in "view" in the printed text.

Provincial Language and Political Offense

Collier, however, particularly with his opening conversation between Tim Bobbin and his book, makes clear that this representation is conscious of the stakes involved in such representations. While the dialogues of *A View* seem to lampoon rude, provincial language and its speakers, Collier defends it from such accusations, writing, "I do not think our country exposed at all by my view of the lancashire [*sic*] dialect."[27] Both Brice and Collier held strong lifelong attachments to their birthplaces. Collier, brandishing his provincial status, proclaimed, "I do not like London, or any thing that is in it."[28] Brice described his deep affiliation to Exeter: "Born, brought up, and having always dwelt in this City, I have a natural inclination to love her, as my Mother."[29] His monumental *Grand Gazetteer* included an "extensive and lively account of Exeter" within its 1,400-plus pages.[30] Far more than jokey sendups, Brice's and Collier's popular works are complex, self-conscious interventions into contemporary representations of provincial languages, produced, like Relph's poem, out of the estranging and dispossessing dynamics of a modernizing Britain and contesting the instituting of a national vernacular that was a part of those dynamics.

Significantly, Brice and Collier were early figures in the provinces-based national opposition politics Kathleen Wilson has described.[31] From his perch in Bristol, Brice saw himself as a defender of national liberties. He was summonsed for illegally printing proceedings of the House of Commons in his newspaper in the early eighteenth century and ran a campaign for national prison reform. His humorous *Freedom, A Poem* satirizes Prime Minister Robert Walpole while advocating on behalf of prisoners, whom he calls "slaves" and compares to the subjugated Israelites, a provocative move given the connections between the rhetoric of the freeborn Englishman and the vernacular that we traced in Chapter Two.[32] Another long poem, *The Mobiad, or the Battle of the Voice*, written in 1737 but not published until 1770, depicts the rowdy hullabaloo of an election day, displaying the actions and languages of a range of "low life" provincial figures, as the poem calls them, from joiners and smiths to servants and street vendors, often in local expressions and provincial terms, sometimes with explanatory footnotes at the bottom of the page. As suggested by the title, the poem figures the mob as an aural and oral phenomenon, a raging "throat battle" as "The Babel Clamours, varying, around" (121). In presenting their tumultuous shouting on election day, the poem serves as a reminder of the literal role of provincial voices in national government. "Low life" provincials could not vote, but they could lend their shouting voices for candidates, raucously appealing to those who were entitled to a ballot:

> Thus plainly, with confus'd Distinction, sound:
> '*Blue*!—Yellow!–Sound for HADDY!—*Sound for* HEATH!
> '*H-a-h! Sh—sack!* Sound for Yellow—*Blue to Death*!
> '*The Church for ever!*—Down with PERKIN's Crew!
> *No Courtiers!*–No Mock Patr'ots!—*Sound for Blue*!
> And not a Mouth but what, expanded large,
> Does thrice a Threescore Times its Load discharge (121)

With political differences reduced to party colors, fragments of slogans, and utter noise ("H-a-h!"), the antagonistic sounds of a confused Babel these "low" provincials produce could hardly be said to be forwarding the cause of patriotism. Instead, the poem renders the sounds of "low life" as animalistic— "A currish Growl, and a deep mastive Bark, / Bays you in light, and follow in the Dark: / H-a-a-ah! With Barbarity of Look gnarrs one," and a footnote translates even that sound: "H-a-a-ah! A rugged, harsh, grating sort of quaver, much lengthen'd, like the arring or gnarring growls of a great Dog" (25). With page after page describing the unruly racket and violence of the mob, Brice's poem seems more indictment than celebration of a participatory, extraparliamentary provincial politics and its embodied vocal subjects. However, the reason for this bad behavior, according to the poem, is the corrupting influence of their betters—"Too often they suborn th' Inferior Mob / With vassal Rage you of your Peace to rob: / With hir'd Sedition they direct the Broil, / And pay in Drink the Wages of the Toil" (27). Crooked leaders, no longer limited to London but now invading the provincial landscape, incite the mob with bribes, drawing out their worst, animalistic tendencies, exploiting while degrading the power of voice.

Significantly, when the duped provincials manage to use words, they are English words—"Down with PERKIN's Crew!" It is the speaker, removed from the scene, whose diction is filled with provincialisms, as in his description of the futility of trying to fight the mob:

> Where might just (s) *Wherrets, Scats,* and *Whisterpoops,*
> Reap Satisfaction on the *truant* Troops,
> When, (t) *Michers*, they for Nest, hedge-breaking go
> Or (u) *Oackcub*, Haw, Blackberry, Hep, or Sloe.
> ...
>
> (s) *Wherrets, Scats,* &c.] Country Words for Blows &c.
> (t) *Michers*] or *Truants*. Shakespeare uses the Word in his Hen. 4.
> (u) *Oakcub.*] *So the people of Exeter call the Chaffer, probably from that Insect's pitching on Oaks, and feeding on the leaves.* (42)

A critique of a politics in which the voice of the low can be sold to the highest (shady, Metropolitan-influenced) bidder, the poem reserves actual provincial language for the explanatory critique of that sad state of affairs. It is the very corruption of the London and London-influenced provincial powerful that underwrites a distinct—even oppositional and virtuous—sense of the provincial language here.

Collier's poetry, what one writer has called "protest verse," also observes and resists perceived infringements of powerful London ministers on traditional English ways.[33] A supporter of the parliamentary reformist John Wilkes, Collier entertained crypto-Republican sympathies, and in print he attacked everything from the imitation of French aristocratic fashion to Methodists, the superstitions of "papists," and crooked local town officials and clergy. His poem *The Cobbler's Politics* rails against those who waged war on the American colonists in class-based terms: "some sign for a war, / And want the poor slaughter'd, both soldier and tar" (324). He authored, in 1757, under his pseudonym Tim Bobbin (the same nom de plume he had used for *A View*), an allegorical defense of the Manchester food rioters, condemning as "sons of Belial" the city merchants manipulating regional grain prices.[34] Like Brice, Collier, too, turns to the rhetoric of slavery as his Biblical narrative designates the provincial farmers of the "Valley of Saddleworth" as "the people," whom city interests threaten to turn into "slaves."[35]

Like the pastorals generated out of the modernizing discourse of improvement that Nigel Leask has parsed in his analysis of the poetry of Allan Ramsay, Robert Fergusson, and Robert Burns, Brice's and Collier's writings esteem the provincial as the bastion of liberty standing in the face of, and violated by, moneyed interests.[36] For Collier, the incursions of a Whig Court elite into the provinces represented the corruption of a once-virtuous nation. An early proponent of the provincial consciousness that would lead to the Country movement later in the century, as J. A. Hilton notes, Collier persistently embraced the concept of the Anglo-Saxon "freeborn Englishman."[37] This provinces-based country politics promised to return all of England to its former honorable self by opposing the corrupt, money-driven dealings of the City spreading across Britain.[38] In this view, Lancashire's distance from

London, both geographic and linguistic, made for its superiority to the debased center.

Brice and Collier connected their representations of vulgar "offensive" language, with its complex obscurities, to a larger position of protest against a polished, fraudulent metropolitan center. Using the Virgilian dialectic Annabel Patterson has identified in pastoral, we might say the refined language of the center (and the tyrant) signals its deceptive, tainted qualities, while the unrefined language of Lancashire and Exmoor speaks to their ingenuous virtue, superiority, and continuity with an older, honorable national identity as the language of the dispossessed. The use of provincial language to wage a politics of place that was also a politics of class extended into the nineteenth century in an 1803 poem published in Newcastle that voices discontent with conservative politics through provincial figures and language. In *Advice to the Advised*, weaver William Shuttle and tailor Thomas Thimble contemplate a book: "Here, gi' me the Beuk—(reading)—'ADVICE' meets my eye ... (reading) 'address'd to the lower Ranks o Soci'ty' ...—(reading) 'Useful at all times'— they can't de without us."[39] This reading makes not provincial language but standard English multiply meaning, as William, in a provincial accent, pointedly misreads the "useful at all times" to refer to working people, not the conservative advice on offer in the book it critiques, William Burdon's *Advice, Addressed to the Lower Ranks of Society*. He reads Burdon against the grain: when the latter counsels, "The way to be happy's to trust to yourselves," invoking a regressive pull-yourself-up-by-your-bootstraps rhetoric, William declares, "Gi' me the mon ... who's bless'd with a spirit that breathes independence" (7), praising instead the defiant man willing to fight his bosses. And to Burdon's "we must not invite mouths too many to eat," he responds, "I have hard it remark'd by my grandsire of auld, / And it ought to be written in letters of gould, / Where God sendth Bellies he Vittals doth send, / And the poor mon who sarves him wull ever befriend."[40] Invoking Christian faith and virtue, he does so in a provincially accented language.

As we explored in the previous chapter, representations of provincial language often conflated it with the vulgar and low, with the "common people," by way of making provincial languages vernacular. Brice's and Collier's writings drew from that conflation, representing the most vulgar of provincial languages, which allowed them to include within the violated virtuous nation the "rabble" or "mob" against which "the people" were frequently defined in polite writing.[41] They played their representations of crude provincial language for broad laughs, but in the manner of jesters, those laughs conceal a critique. Readers distanced from these provincials might regard themselves as "not so good," remote from the uncorrupt language of that mythic figure, the freeborn Englishman. *Advice to the Advised*'s political critique is sharper, but like Brice and Collier, it pursued the same established connections between provincial place, class, and nation to oppositional ends. Rather than slipping back to a safely placed provincial/metropolitan distinction, however, some provincial writers, including Brice and Collier, as we shall see, also used provincial obscurity to undo such ready categories.

Provincial Diversity: A "Mixed" Britain at the Heart of the Nation

To allude to the concept of the "freeborn Englishman" was often to invoke notions of custom. The privileging of particular, repeated local practices was supposedly what made the Englishman unique and free. The British liberty that Edmund Burke claimed "I love" is not that of "metaphysical abstraction."[42] In this way, British liberty might be located in the very particularities of provincial practices. Alternatively, as Burke had notoriously put it, the French, in their post-revolutionary divvying up of the Republic "in the spirit of ... geometrical distribution and arithmetical arrangement ... treat France exactly like a country of conquest," making slaves of the people (7). Placing a premium on custom, however, meant an insistence on and high valuation of England's and then Britain's diversity as a nation, be it in the piebald fabric of its ancient legal customs, its mixed government, its inarguably mixed genealogy, or, indeed, its multiple regional linguistic practices.[43]

For some, the English language that included provincial tongues resembled the "mixed laws" that made up the uniquely English legal framework of customary law, valued precisely for its plethora of practices. Common Law scholars such as William Blackstone took a certain amount of pride in this patchwork of legal customs. In his *Commentaries* he cited Francis Bacon, affirming, "Our laws, saith Lord Bacon, are mixed as our Language: and as our Language is so much the richer, the laws more complete."[44] That rich profusion and heterogeneity at the linguistic level is particularly evident in provincial terms, including Scandinavian loan words found in Northern dialects, such as "steg," meaning "gander," or "lea," meaning "scythe."[45] And in this age of linguistic standardization, it is worth remembering, as we saw above, that writers could nonetheless celebrate the linguistic diversity of England. Ray's *Collection of English Words not Generally Used* revels in its verbal cornucopia. Even James Harris boasts, "we Britons in our time have been remarkable borrowers, as our multiform language may sufficiently show," adding, "in copiousness ... few languages will be found superior to our own."[46]

The flipside of such diversity, however, is obscurity. As we have seen, at the most basic of levels, obscurity, even regarding quotidian experience, is endemic to any national public, a crucial reminder of how that public is always, after all, based on a stranger relationality, especially evident in the negotiations of language. But that obscurity was especially salient in a British national culture that defined itself, more and sometimes less comfortably, through its heterogeneous genealogical origins, its complex mix of often-obscure customs and customary languages. Locating England's legal and linguistic identity in its thick cluster of separate and particular legal and linguistic customs placed a dark opacity at its heart. Indeed, Burke would come to celebrate this "dense medium," which the French revolutionaries' "metaphysical rights ... like rays of light" mistakenly attempted to pierce (54). For Burke, it was because there were "obscure" causes to prosperity or adversity "that the edifice which has answered in any tolerable degree for ages" should not be "pulled down."[47] The very diversity and resulting obscurity of customary authority, however, meant Britons necessarily encountered strangeness in the spoken and sometimes published languages of geographically dispersed compatriots.

It was, then, not simply the relative oddness of respective local practices but their overwhelming multiplicity that made for obscurity. As Matthew Adams has noted, the "sheer bulk of laws" made for uncertainty, and Jeremy Bentham would attack the "proliferation of common law" as "beyond the comprehension of one man."[48] Burke, on the other hand, was more sanguine about the fact that "the science of government requires ... more experience than any person can gain in his whole life." For him, multiplicity shaded into sublimity, as the diversity and abundance of laws and languages was incomprehensible to any one Briton. That sublimity has suggestive implications regarding models of polity, as we shall see in a moment. The limiting of incomprehensibility to lower spheres and remote provinces in printed comedic dialogues and mock pastoral poems might seem to check the dangerous implications of this peculiarly British model of a patchwork nation. But the obscurity of their language actually inverted those conventional power dynamics when it was polite readers who could not piece together meaning.

Linguistic obscurity, according to Edmund Burke, raises the passions: "The proper manner of conveying the affections of the mind from one to the other, is by words," not because words make meaning clear, but because they are often obscure—more obscure than painting. Painting might be more clear, but, Burke believed, "clearness helps but little towards affecting the passions," and again, "it is our ignorance of things that causes all our admiration, and chiefly excites our passions. Knowledge and acquaintance make the most striking causes affect but little."[49] Burke cited the poetry of the ancients and of Milton as moments of such linguistic obscurity. In doing so he attempted to stave off the threat of what Karen Swann calls the "vulgar sublime," for vulgar language, particularly the languages of the rude provincial, are certainly capable of producing obscurity as well.[50] At the very least, verbal obscurity produces a kind of leveling effect. In James Harris's assessment of those "local proper Names ... hardly a part of language," he had noted that such terms "must equally be learnt both by learned and unlearned, as often as they change the place of their abode."[51] For Burke, obscurity puts all who confront it in the position of the vulgar, for "all men are as the vulgar in what they do not understand."[52] In encounters with provincial languages—languages that, as we have seen, Harris and others conflated with "vulgar" language—metropolitan readers of standard English were confronted with what they did not understand, becoming "vulgar" at that point, as Burke would have it.

We saw in Chapter Two one danger of the authority of custom in the restriction to one particular set of customs, a threat to English liberty: just what or whose customs count, and what alternatives do they exclude? Widening the base of customary practices to an overpowering diversity, however, also undermines the legitimacy of political authority, even when, as Burke had argued, overpowering diversity, in its inevitable obscurity, produces sublime effects. For Burke, the sublime was always about absolute power: the fearful passions stirred by obscurity formed the basis of "despotic governments."[53] This, as Swann puts it, is "power that maintains itself through a hoodwinking of the credulous ... [playing on] the superstitions of the vulgar."[54] As we are seeing, however, the identities of the credulous and unknowing might shift in readers' encounters with provincial and vulgar languages, encounters forced (but also eagerly experienced by readers) in the publications of Brice and Collier and others. Inasmuch as any readers found themselves overwhelmed in the face of the dizzying obscurity of print provincial languages, it was not only the vulgar who were hoodwinked. Such encounters with the vulgar sublime posed a significant contrast to the idea that the print representations of provincial clowns only belittled them or that the digressive "coarse pleasantries" of servants, according to Horace Walpole, only underscored the sublimity of "princes and heroes."[55]

Provincial Writing and Strategic Obscurity

To put this in a slightly different way, the phenomenology of obscurity has been conventionally—and wrongly—associated exclusively with elite writing, with "the arcane, the virtuosic," as Daniel Tiffany has observed.[56] We also find obscurity, however, in provincial writing, not as a function of esoteric erudition but rather of particular colloquialisms, of specific pronunciations, of foreign-seeming provincial terms, and of what some readers considered the low unknown. Thus, as Tiffany argues, that "phenomenology of obscurity" might also or instead be "rooted in the social misunderstanding of demotic speech"—something produced, perhaps necessarily, in the very moment when language "descended." George Campbell, approvingly citing William Kenrick, describes this inverted power differential: "the case of language, or rather speech, being quite contrary to that of science; in the former, the ignorant understand the learned, better than the learned do the ignorant."[57] "Native" Lancashire, Devonshire, or Scots readers would be literate in English—enough so to read and write in English—and fluent, too, in provincial languages, masters of the *copia verborum*, as Burns called it, not simply of one provincial language but of divisions within languages as well.[58] If provincial obscurity shifted the terms of power relations, those unfamiliar with opaque provincial languages on the page could themselves become a (virtual) group sharing an affective experience, a social body seized with passion, if only briefly, in the face of the unknown, subject to the sublime.

In her discussion of the politics of linguistic obscurity, Susan Manly maintains that linguistic obscurity is a politically driven obfuscation of transparent, sensible language, a conservative darkening and occluding of what should be clear and accessible to all. Obscurity certainly can function in that way. Henry Fielding suggests as much in his skeptical responses to the characterization of provincials and their opaque languages as virtuous Britons. In his novels, provincial languages produce not the obscure sublime, but comic effects. In *Joseph Andrews*, for instance, the greedy, uncharitable farmer/parson Trulliber speaks a provincially accented language when refusing Adams's plea for aid, saying "I don't know, Friend, how you came to *caale* on me."[59] Similarly, it is in a provincial tongue that the Sussex "clowns" of Smollett's *Roderick Random* voice their selfish strategy for moving a badly injured Roderick out of their jurisdiction rather than help him: "Dick, go vetch the old wheel-barrow and puten in, and carry him to good-man Hodge's back-door, he is more eable than we to lay out money upon poor vagrants."[60] More to the point, the provincial martinet enforcing the new laws privatizing the commons (and enacting parochial misrule) writes in a provincially inflected language, recording that

> betwin the Ours of 2 and 4 in the afternoon, he zeed Joseph Andrews and Francis Goodwill walk akross a certane felde belunging to Layer Scout, and out of the Path which ledes thru the said felde, and there he zede Joseph Andrews with a Nife cut one Hassel-Twig, of the value, as he believes of 3 half pence

The Justice's provincial language is as corrupt and mistaken as the new laws and petty interests of the provincial aristocrats he serves. Such moments remind us that while some writers celebrated provincial languages as a sign of British liberty or played up the sublime effects their obscurity might elicit, others connected them to the corruption and even destruction of the privileges of the freeborn Englishman, to self-serving interests rather than virtuous parochial rule, and to comic effects. For Fielding, the linguistic obscurity of his provincial characters maps onto the obscuring rhetoric that would defy British liberty and ends up being darkly funny.

Fielding's satire attacks the claims that linked provincial language to English liberty, too, when *Tom Jones*'s Squire Western—named for the West Country and the provincialisms that go with it—legitimates his wanton language by claiming his "oaths and curses" as a "privilege . . . claimed as a freeborn Englishman."[61] As well, his provincial language is connected to the body and its most antisocial of passions. In more sober moments, the Squire is capable of a standard English without even a hint of accent, as when he calmly asserts, "to take away my girl's bird was wrong, in my opinion" (140). Yet when he discovers the liaison between Tom and his daughter Sophia, he breaks into proverbs, local accent, and provincialisms. He rails, "there is a fine kettle-of-fish made on't up at our house . . . It's well vor un I could not get at un: I'd a lick'd un" (265). His explosive provincial language is laced with images of the grotesque body. Of Sophia, he exclaims, "she shall be no better than carrion: the skin o'er is all he shall ha, and zu you may tell un" (265), and these images are not redeemed by any provincial rhetoric of liberty and the common people.

In *Tom Jones* it is a squire whose language is marked with provincialisms. With the exception of the occasional "voke" for "folk," the book's lower orders do not speak it. Western's language, along with his love of low popular songs, his assertions of country interests, and dismissal of the Hanovers as "turnep" eaters suggest a residual Tory alliance between rural folk and Cavaliers, the vestigial merging of high and low against a Puritan middle that we noted in Chapter Three. Such alliances might pose an alternative to the Whig hegemony that linked politeness, including polite language, to class mobility and a new model of the national polity. In opposition, Western crows, "I am a true Englishman" (292). But Fielding does not hold up Western's alternative, in which a shared use of low provincialisms underwrites a Cavalier alliance with the people.[62] The more virtuous Squire Allworthy (and Tom) speak a recognizable standard English and the suggestion, perhaps, is that the "provincial" should give way to the ecclesiastical domain, the best model of polity being a well-run parish.[63] Operating on a small scale, the parish does not require cultural markers or language to help imagine affiliation. The large scale of the nation, however, does.

Whether republicans endorsing clear language or writers dubious of the claims of virtue or power some would make for obscure provincial languages, there were certainly skeptics to be found regarding the strategic uses of provincial linguistic obscurity. I want to argue, however, that for some writers, the opacity and strangeness of provincial languages that necessarily appear on the national page and their reduction to readerly effects, an aestheticization that makes them riddlelike and figuratively foreign, enables a self-conscious, cagey and resistant provincial writing. Theirs is a writing that questions the identification of obscurity with place, resists the fixing of provincial place through language, and responds to the misrecognizing and defusing of the strategic potential of a class-based obscurity. Provincial writers seized the obscurity of and between these strange and estranged languages for their own use, resisting the contemporary notion that the provincial vulgar were mere "carriers," as Matthew Adams has put it, "of culture recorded and scrutinized by an elite."[64] They actively produced writing that dramatized the politically ludic dynamics of linguistic obscurity.

In a prescient meditation on these dynamics, the diction of John Gay's *The Shepherd's Week* points to strategic uses of obscurity.[65] In part a satire of Ambrose Philips's pastoral, which, as we saw in Chapter Three, had aimed to provide a particularizing British setting, Gay's poem also parodies Edmund Spenser's use of provincial and archaic language to convey Englishness, from which Philips had drawn.[66] Mockingly adopting the voice of those practitioners of a specifically nationalist pastoral, the preface dismisses the notion of a Golden Age, that universal, placeless time, as an "outrageous conceit."[67] Moving instead into the particular territory of the contemporary nation—"love of my native country Britain much pricketh me forward"—the writer promises in his pastorals instead "the manners ... meetly copied from the rustical folk therein."[68] Key among these "manners" is language use; *The Shepherd's Week* brims with the "uncouth" terms and sounds of those "rustical folk," and includes proper names that sound both provincial and archaic, such as "Lobbin Clout" (3) and terms for provincial practices such as "white pot" (9), meaning rice and milk pudding. The rustics of this Theocritean pastoral are located via their language: it is "The Western lass that tends the *Kee*," and "Kee," a footnote tells us, is "a West-Country Word for Kine or Cows" (14). Throughout the poem's armature of footnotes Gay explains that the language is national, unalloyed with foreign influence, as in the commentary for the word "Dumps." A footnote (humorously) explains, "*Some have pretended that it is derived from* Dumops *a King of* Egypt, *that built a Pyramid and dy'd of Melancholy ... but our* English *Antiquaries have conjectured that* Dumps, *which* is a grievous heaviness of Spirits, *comes from the Word* Dumplin, *the heaviest kind of Pudding that is eaten in this country, much used in* Norfolk" (21).

Moreover, in this facetious commentary and elsewhere, the vulgar materiality of the body that we have seen associated with the provincial and vernacular more generally, is returned to again and again. Whether in the term "queintly," which a footnote admits can have an "obscene sense" (8), or expressions such as "brought her cow to bull" (18), a reference to animal copulation, or characters such as turnip-loving Blouzelind or the tobacco-breathed Clumsilis, the provincials' foul bodies are part of the joke. Gay's vulgar rustics speak a language that seemingly grounds them in their bodies, their place, and their class. Or so it seemed to eighteenth-century critics. As William Ayre described it, "Here is nothing but plain and simple Nature: The flowers, the beasts, the seasons, nothing out of their sight or reach, nothing affected, but all in character."[69] *The Shepherd's Week* seems to offer a low realism in the particular provincial language capable of representing it, and for Samuel Johnson that was the basis of their appeal. He opined that "the effects of reality and truth became conspicuous ... These pastorals became popular and were read with delight, as just representations of rural manners and occupations."[70]

If, as we have seen, provincial language sometimes operated like a riddle, Gay's poem at times drains the puzzle quite out of it. A cumbersome authenticating apparatus of footnotes offers to translate opaque provincial terms into recognizable English, and the work closes with a nod to the new learning with

"An Alphabetical Catalogue of Names, Plants, Flowers, Fruits, Birds, Beasts, Insects, and other material things mentioned," recalling Ray's *Collection of English* and the catalogues of flora and fauna that accompanied it, lists that would elevate the status of humble "material things." For Gay, however, this knowledge of the moderns was no knowledge at all, but instead a simpleton's recital of things thingified in an absurd list: "Roast Beef, Ribbon, Rosemary, Riddle." When *The Shepherd's Week* poses an actual riddle (in the italics used throughout the poem to indicate rustic lore): "*What Flow'r is that which bears the* Virgin's *name, / The richest Metal joined with the same?*" (10), it immediately answers it in a footnote—"Marygold." Some potentially perplexing terms, such as "ken," are also explained in footnotes, the one for "to ken," in fact, citing Ray and his repertoire of etymological origins, including Anglo-Saxon, Gothic, and Danish. The footnotes' glosses position provincialisms alongside the foreign languages of Latin and Greek. Like those remote classical languages, these terms need explanation, and that explanation is provided immediately, in what turns out to be a critique of the notion that lists and simplistic translations produce any knowledge worth having.

Despite its seemingly comprehensive array of translations and explanations, in Gay's work a good number of the provincialisms remain unglossed, such as the following found in just two successive stanzas: "hight" (14), "Younglins" (14), "Whilom" (15), "strow" (16), "misling" (16). Moreover, some of the words, as in the name "Bumkinet" (23), are simply made up, in this case a witty diminutive of "bumpkin" and an allusion to Ambrose Philips's shepherd Colinet.[71] Crucially, Gay's evasive maneuver is often to put a *fictitious* rustic language in the mouths of his shepherds, as he explains in the opening "Proeme," "such as is neither spoken by the country maiden nor the courtly Dame; nay, not only such as in the present times is not uttered, but was never uttered in Times Past; and, if I judge aright, will never be uttered in times future."[72] Neither the language of the low country maiden nor the high courtly dame, much of the provincial language of Gay's text, seemingly fixed in provincial place and also in national, as English, is no one's.

It is the very obscurity of provincial languages that allows Gay to switch out supposedly real, rooted language for a concocted language that merely calls up notions of rootedness and particularity. This strategically deployable obscurity is at least as old as Spenser, who also invented provincial terms for inclusion in his *The Shepheardes Calendar*—Gay's language of the "rustical folk" of "my native country Britain" a cheeky fabrication of a fabrication. In fact, such concoctedness is inherent in any representation of a language as vernacular. As Tiffany writes, "all poetic formulations of vernacular speech should be viewed as synthetic vernaculars."[73] This is in part because of the impossible tensions at work in the idea of a vernacular—it is the language of compelling, familiar felt particulars, but strange, obscure, the language of particular spaces that is also, somehow, the property of all nationals. Tiffany describes this tension in terms of social class, in which the vernacular is "the jargon of an inaccessible 'commons,' both above and beneath the multitude."[74] But in many representations of provincial languages, the tension is also spun as a spatial one, the languages somehow both locally particular and transcending local particularities to speak to everyone. This could not be anything but a fictional projection, perhaps best captured through an invented language producing effects rather than meaning. At this early moment, Gay already exposes the strange impossibility of the vernacular.

The poem's resulting mix of languages, then, is not simply a superficial parody of the "wrong" kind of pastoral writing, but an astute commentary on the impossible tensions involved in representing as somehow familiar and national what would be, in many ways, alien and obscure languages. A displaced Devon native himself who, if the *Dictionary of National Biography* is to be believed, viewed himself as a "humble provincial" and never "felt at home" in London, Gay humorously points to the contradictions of a nationalist rhetoric that at once depends on the particularities (and language) of everyday, supposedly "unchanging" provincial rural life and yet also promotes a pastoral poetics—and indeed wider cultural logic—of a general national collective.[75] His shepherds and their ingenious mix of languages actually spoken by no one are mere ciphers of provinciality. They could not be otherwise. The provincial language of Gay's rustics must stand as hollow place markers, calling up the effects, but not the actuality, of a provincial, rustic language that looks like it could be placed both geographically and temporally and yet can never be, it if is also to function as part of the general vernacular of a large, diverse nation. Gay answers, then, the conundrum of evoking the general, the national, the vernacular through the particulars that vary over place and time by inventing a language that merely looks old and alien. He plays with the dynamic of an English national language, based on customs and rooted in places, that, consequently, must be obscure at many points—an impossible model of a national vernacular.

Confronting the same dilemma at the end of the century, William Wordsworth (himself enough of a provincial to claim he understood Burns's language) in his *Lyrical Ballads* chose the other side of the coin.[76] Rather than inventing a fictional language of particulars that could stand in for a national language, he used an English denuded of those particulars altogether. The language of Wordsworth's poetry, as he describes it, the "very language of men," bears resemblance to characterizations of provincial language.[77] It keeps readers "in the company of flesh and blood"; it is "plainer and more emphatic"; it is "rural" and "more durable" than standard English; it is the language of the low, marked by the "narrow circle of their intercourse," although Wordsworth uses it to represent "common life."[78] Without obscure provincial terms, this language is "purified"—and is, as a result, just as much a projection as Gay's, just as much a recognition of the impossibility of a language that is at once grounded spatially and nationally common.[79] In turning to words unmarked by provincial specifics, Wordsworth avoids both the class associations that haunted provincial language in England and the problem that any particular language poses for the idea of a national vernacular that is somehow meant to be everyone's.

Writing earlier, Andrew Brice, too, had illuminated the unresolvable tensions between provincial languages, with their claim to the particularities and intimacies of a specific locale and a national vernacular. Investing the language of the "lowest class" with "patriotism," Brice wrote, "As its [*sic*] natural and full of Honour to love one's Country, so its natural (And why not as praiseworthy?) to love its Language. Thus every Nation is big with Commendations of its own peculiar Dialect... Since, therefore, its esteem'd a kind of Patriotism to stickle for our native Speech,—I, in Honour of my matchless County Devon... shall make it my peculiar care to transmit to future Times our pure Vernacular Language."[80] The complexity of Brice's intervention becomes apparent as his "vernacular language" does not map neatly onto nation—Devon is not a nation, the language of Devon not the language of Britain, although he tries to make them synonymous, and in doing so troubles the very idea of "pure Vernacular Language" to which he refers. In oddly overlaying "Nation" and Devon, the language of nation and of province, Brice illuminates the difficulties and perhaps impossibilities of squaring the provincial vernacular, "native speech" and the nation it is meant to bespeak.

Moreover, Brice, like Gay, deploys obscurity to produce not language and meaning but linguistic effect. His is not "authentic" provincial language but often also one of his own making. Obscure words that might seem "pure vernacular" to an outsider are often Brice's own inventions: "grilliard," "unupright," "whelving," "doubty," "pounch'd."[81] He was famous in his day for inventing terms his contemporaries called "Bricisms."[82] These provincial writings suggest Mikhail Bakhtin's heteroglossia, "another's speech in another's language, serving to express authorial intentions but in a refracted way."[83] Yet they are a particularly complex version in that they are inventions, fabricated to elicit the effects of encountering another's speech, another's language, while disavowing the limitations of confining that otherness to particular places and particular, placed others.

Brice's linguistic inventiveness disturbs not only characterizations of his provincial language as "pure vernacular" but also of English as its nonobscure, transparent counterpart. As Bakhtin noted, heteroglossia "not only foregrounds the words of people normally excluded from the realm of the 'norm' and the 'standard,' it also relativizes the norm itself."[84] Brice's *Mobiad*, for instance, which is largely written in standard English, comes off, nonetheless, as just as perplexing and riddlelike as his puzzling *An Exmoor Scolding*, written almost exclusively, Brice claims, in Exmoor dialect—relativizing what Bakhtin calls "the norm." In *Mobiad*, with lines such as "O'er the pounch'd Lip boars foaming Dudgeon fumes" (78), the obscurity a reader might be tempted to attribute to the poem's Exmoor location gives way to the obscurity of poetry in English itself, for "dudgeon" could be found in Nathan Bailey's *Dictionarium Britannicum*.[85] Such moments belie the understanding of a national English as known to all—many readers would stumble over the "standard English" words, and not just the "odd" provincial ones. In making English itself noisy, Brice troubles clear lines of demarcation between communicants and Serres's third man.

Similarly loose-handed with his "Lancashire" lexicon, John Collier does not limit his language in *A View* to terms and pronunciations exclusive to Rossendale or even Lancashire but includes examples spanning a wider region, a representation that was, in fact, a composite of several local dialects, extending to Yorkshire, as Harold Whitehall has shown.[86] Such mingling of languages is truer to the mobility—which sometimes extended to a global scale—that was part of the experience of eighteenth-century British life. As one historian observes, "provincial towns were the prime beneficiaries of economic and imperial expansion and improvements in communication, building, publishing and international trade, experiencing the most dramatic upheavals in population growth and cultural refurbishment."[87] Nor, of course, was provincial urban space wholly distinct from the rural; "seasonal employment and migration meant many people would spend part of their lives working in urban settings," and rural villages shared many aspects of city life, not least of all the distribution of print, including political propaganda.[88] Collier himself traveled, spending time in Yorkshire, and noted that in Lancashire "trade in a general way has now flourished for nearly a century, the inhabitants not only travel, but encourage all sorts of useful learning."[89] The provincial was not fixed in place; provincial language was not "pure." The production of a sense of place through language in these cases was a product of mobility, the resulting language, both "rooted and transitive," as Eric Gidal has noted of another language meant to place its speakers, the place names of the Ossian poems.[90] Provincials might play with assumptions of static language in fixed place when the language said to be most familiar, most affecting—provincial language—was believed to be an obscure language spoken by someones somewhere else.

The uses of the obscurity ascribed to provincial languages came full circle in an end-of-century poem written to reproduce the sound of language spoken in Exmoor, entitled *The Royal Visit to Exeter, a Poetical Epistle by John Ploughshare*.[91] Here, Jan (the local pronunciation of John) writes to his sister regarding King George III's recent visit to Exeter in a letter mildly inflected with Exmoor accent: "Zester" is Jan's spelling for "sister," "gert." for "great." Contractions such as "corn's" for "corn is" signal the speaker's inescapable orality, and occasional provincialisms such as "appledranes" and "Currantin" appear. The king's visit occasions another mob scene, tamer than Brice's out-of-control "mobiad," but represented again by verbal exchanges, such as the crowd's speculation regarding his meeting with a town father, "The Squire and King be chattin'," or questions, "Did yow than zee the King?" (6). Citizens at the top, as in *Mobiad*, are especially venal and corrupt; the bishop offers no hospitality for those visiting to see the king, claiming, "that az vor he, poor man, / A had not got a pot nor pan . . . / And as vor beds they wudn't do—" (9) suggestively spoken in Exmoor dialect that moves between the third and first person.

In this poem, however, it is not the unruly provincial mob that is embodied but the King himself, arriving on horseback "With doust and zweat az netmeg brown" and the Squire, too, "Wipin his zweatty jaws and poull" (5). And, while during this late eighteenth-century moment, the king's speech was carefully vetted for its adherence to the emerging standard—he even took elocution lessons—he, too, is represented as speaking in an orally marked language reflecting his German accent, noting of a view, "'Tis Vine" (12) for "'tis fine."[92] The poem conforms to contemporary representations of the king's speech as idiosyncratic, as emphasizing sound over meaning, marked by repetition, rhyme, and odd meter, despite his elocution lessons. The king observes in Exeter cathedral—"Neat, neat—clean, very clean; / D'ye mop it, mop it, Measter Dean— / Mop, Mop it every week?" (13). And while the king speaks an odd, aurally oriented language, he is himself alienated from plain English, mistaking *it* for provincial speech. In an exchange between the king and one of his subjects, Farmer Tab, Tab declares, in reference to the king's recent episode of madness:

> 'I'm glad your MEDJESTY to zee,
> And hope your MEDJESTY (Quoth he)
> Wull nere be *maz'd* again.'

To which the king responds:

> '*Maz'd*! *maz'd*! what's *maz'd*?' than zed the KING;
> 'I never heer'd of zich a thing;
> 'What's maz'd?—what, what, my LORD?'
> 'Hem,' zed my LORD, and blow'd his nose;
> 'Hem, hem—Sir, 'tis I do suppose,
> 'Sir,—an old Dev'nshire word.'
>
> And than [*sic*] my LORD a scratch'd his head,
> And, coughing wance or twiss, he zed:
> 'I'll try to vend it out.' (21–22)

"Mazed" was a term routinely used to describe the King's mental state in his episodes of madness, circulating in the popular press and in the mouths of his subjects. Here, it is a lowly rural provincial who knows and speaks English—if intermingled with provincial pronunciations and markers of orality ("Medjesty" and "maz'd" rather than "mazed"). The attribution of an "old" provincial language to this speaker, however, is what allows him to speak a scandalous truth to the king in plain English, affording him certain freedoms, shall we say, under cover of obscurity.

The *Royal Visit* relativizes obscurity to the point of making a common English word—"mazed"—obscure to the king, a ruler who, significantly, had taken pains to display his commitment to the national language, insisting, for instance, that his marriage ceremony be conducted in English.[93] The poem comically positions those who misrecognize the common for the strange as outside of national linguistic culture. It also targets the assumption that obscure words might organize and fix a sense of place. The poem does not simply reverse the power dynamics of obscurity, the demotic replacing or becoming the arcane. Instead, like Gay's, Brice's, and Collier's writings, it undermines attempts to ground a sense of particular place or social relations or the idea of a vernacular itself in provincial languages. Obscurity is not the sign of a secret language that is known to and ties together some people and not others. It does not indicate a series of little platoons somewhere else that make up, in total, the nation. Such conceptions of provincial language are, it humorously displays, mistaken. By inventing terms or exposing the relative nature of obscurity, these English provincial writers showed that attempts to place the nation or institute a vernacular by incorporating obscure provincial languages reveal that there might be no there there.

These works, once well known to a wide body of readers, are now obscure to students of eighteenth-century writing. We might recognize their moves, however—their unfixing of place and language, their shuttling between comic dialogue and ethnographic explanatory apparatus, their reversals of who knows and who does not—in a work more familiar to readers, Maria Edgeworth's *Castle Rackrent* (1800). While this story, set in late eighteenth-century Ireland, offers no Gaelic-speakers (a move Marilyn Butler compares to Wordsworth's avoidance of dialect), it is, as Butler notes, "written in a 'provincial' variant of English"—what the "editor" of the volume calls the Irish narrator, Thady's, "vernacular idiom."[94] Like the depictions of provincial languages we have been examining, *Castle Rackrent*'s representation of "a 'provincial' variant of English" is primarily that of seeming illiterate naïfs, chiefly in the mouth of the narrator, "*honest* Thady" or "poor Thady," as he is referred to, and is marked as oral and embodied. In an especially apt image, Thady speaks "out of face," and the supposed transcription of his oral tale records his distinct voiced pronunciations: "shister" for "sister," "childer" for "children."[95] This provincial language is associated with the low—it is people of "Thady's [inferior] rank" (72), a footnote tells us, who speak thus. And the reported speech of those provincial poor, including Thady's kinswoman "poor Judy," is grammatically incorrect, with such phrases as "don't be being jealous" (113), while sonically rhythmic, in this case composed of a series of trochees.

Edgeworth's provincials speak an unusual language, but it is readers who are the outsiders. Like Sir Kit's "foreign" Jewish wife, whom Thady describes as, in appearance, "little better than a blackamoor" (76), readers must ask the meaning of various expressions and practices, as when Sir Kit's wife wonders, "what is a barrack-room, pray, my dear?" (77). An explanatory apparatus, so overwhelming that it threatens to outstrip the narrative itself, promises to make the strange everyday manners, beliefs, and things of Ireland familiar, with a reassuring preface, ample glossary, and extensive, if distracting, footnotes.[96] However, it is in the explanatory apparatus, the ostensible purpose of which is to clarify and stabilize meaning—to name and explain the specifics of place—that any sense of fixity begins to unravel. We might note that the shift in tone in both the gloss and the footnotes, between ridicule and respect, comic and serious (17), upon which Butler has remarked, was on full display in the dialogues of Brice and Collier—as well as Grose and Parker—all of whom appended prefaces and glosses "learned" in tone to comic vulgar material. Moreover, like the mobile and sometimes synthetic languages Brice and Collier "collated—multiple dialects categorized as a single provincial language that disrupted the sense of fixed provincial space and language—the "provincial" languages of *Castle Rackrent* are also mixed and unfixed. Butler notes how the vocabulary shifts "as Thady moves from the annals of one master to the next," sometimes made up of "Anglo-French" legalese, sometimes "native Irish," sometimes casual "provincial" conversational English (12). And like Brice and Collier, Edgeworth's "authentic" representations feature made-up words and places, such as "Allyballycarricko'shaughlin" (78). To represent the language of "provincial" place in these terms is to expose not continuity over time but disruption and change, even disturbing invention.

The different difficulties of incorporating provincial languages into a vernacular to which these writers—Brice, Collier, Edgeworth—point, whether within England or Great Britain or the United Kingdom, might be more a matter of degree than kind. Scots vernacular poets, too, made a point of attending to the minute and mean in both provincial language and subject matter (from drinking binges to sheep's-head suppers, from mouse to louse).[97] Rather than merely providing access to the particulars of local life via once-obscure provincial terms, however, they, like the English provincial writers I have been discussing, and like Edgeworth, play on, to borrow Tiffany's phrase, a "phenomenology of unknowing, of unresolvable obscurity."[98] In all of this provincial writing it is this opacity, not the illumination, of the "low," "minute," or "mean," that produces a sense of the polity called up not through revealed particulars but through incomprehension. Writers representing language in Ireland and Scotland, inasmuch as they are sometimes defining a separate nation altogether, might seem to be involved in a qualitatively distinct project from those representing provincial English. Their methods of generating and deploying obscurity, however, are similar as they respond to and resist a vernacular institutionalization, particularly one that would make them merely British. That this should be the case is not surprising, given that we have observed from the start of this book a proximity between the techniques of producing and managing "strangeness" in both national and imperial contexts.

Those techniques worked along not only spatial but temporal axes. Increasingly, instituting the vernacular meant rewriting obscurity as a function of the sheer passing of time—and reclaiming that obscurity as sign of pastness connected to the origins of Britain, and on those terms part of the vernacular. The anachronizing dynamics of that vision will be the subject of the following chapter. But we shall be just as interested in provincial writers who reject that anachronization, from the less well-known Brice, Collier, Anne Wheeler, and Mary Palmer to the far more famous Thomas Chatterton and Robert Burns. As *Castle Rackrent* casts and recasts the obscurity of the "provincial," it is as a sign not just of the spatially but also the temporally remote—"tales of other times" (63). In its tricky destabilization of what the obscurity of that "provincial" past might be or mean, however, that text had a series of more and less well-known precursors within Britain, to which we shall now turn.

CHAPTER SEVEN

Provincial Languages and a Vernacular out of Time

WE HAVE SEEN HOW PRINT REPRESENTATIONS of provincial languages sometimes reappraised them for their ability to convey a sense of place, their obscurity a mark of distinct locations and tangible particulars. Some writing also revalued them for their sense of history. In a move that at once redeemed and distanced provincial languages, glossaries, antiquarian treatises, and literary representations prized them as the perishing remnants of the nation's linguistic past. Words such as "*Gelt-gimmer*, a barren ewe" and "*Glam*, a wound" might have seemed foreign and even low, but their strangeness was often transmuted into ancientness, a means of recuperating past customs and manners. Designating such terms as antique became another means of making strange language part of an English vernacular for all Britons.[1] While the attribution of novelty to cant and slang words repressed many customary labor and property relationships in the course of the eighteenth century, a sense of history accrued to provincial languages, although not, again, a history of labor and property relations but rather a history that made provincial languages and their speakers a site of continuity with ancestral origins. In their particularity and obscurity, their projected embodiment and vocalization, then, provincial languages could be an important part of a wide-ranging vernacular as long as they knew their place not only in space but in time.

This is true in *Pamela*, with its provincialisms that, while managing to call up a sense of familiar Englishness in their strangeness, are also relegated to a rural world fixed not only in distant place but also in past time. Pamela uses provincialisms particularly when addressing her poor old rustic parents or imagining herself back in their world. It is when she speculates about returning to her old village that she speaks of "hands ... as hard as a beechen trencher" (77). It is when she is preparing to go back to their rural poverty that she describes her heart as "lumpish" (245). Of course, she does not return there, and as she moves into her future and ascends in social class, the provincialisms drop out of her language. They become fatally fastened to her parents, and Pamela's repeated remarks on their "gray hairs" link them to the past. Indeed, the earliest appearance of provincial languages in something like prose fiction, Thomas Deloney's *The Pleasant History of... Jack of Newbury*, had also put dialect in the mouth of Jack's wife's elderly father. The association of provincialisms with the past would come to make them a ready means of conveying a sense of history in Walter Scott's historical fiction and in the figure of the superannuated retainer who recounts the past in fiction from Maria Edgeworth to Emily Brontë and beyond.

The identification of provincial rural space as the site of a fast-disappearing "old England" (or old Scotland or Ireland) is, of course, a longstanding one, the country the location of a "perpetual recession into history," as Raymond Williams reminds us.[2] Yet the succession of histories, as he also points out, means different things at different times. In the late seventeenth century, one political tract depicted a series of conversations between a Northumberland landlord and his Scots tenant, their provincial language a point of connection in their shared Cavalier politics and mutual celebration of the coronation of James II.[3] Over the course of the eighteenth century, however, the languages of rural provincials became especially important in their illumination of a broader sense of the nation's history. The writing that represents provincials as "still speaking" the language of national forebears gothicizes provincial languages and their speakers as representatives of a past that will not stay past, a sense that receives little attention in Williams's analysis.

Designating the strangeness of provincial languages as historical made those languages history, so to speak, their strangeness redeemed as a function of their age. Samuel Johnson, for instance, wrote, "The northern speech is... not barbarous but obsolete."[4] Given the ongoing slippage between provincial and vulgar that we saw in the previous two chapters, this reassessment of the provincial strange had the effect of revaluing as it backdated "the vulgar" or the "common people" as well. Thus, Yorkshire native William Marshall noted that "provincial language spoken by the lower class ... the vulgar tongue, ... [is] in all probability the purer language," adding that "the process of corruption [is], as others perhaps will have it, refinement of languages," a reimagining of the polishing of vulgar speech as "corruption"—the Northern burr no longer a sign of degeneracy but of originary purity.[5] In this estimation, it is exactly because they are vulgar and avoid the refining forces of their urban "betters" that vulgar provincial languages avoid corruption, remaining closer to a pure original English. Similarly, *An Exmoor Scolding*, which, for all its comic outrageousness, also adopts this rhetoric in later editions, connects the language of "the Lowest class of the people" in contemporary times to that of the earliest progenitors of English linguistic culture, stating that "the antient Anglo-Saxon Tongue, with some Variation of its sound and orthography, chiefly prevails in the vulgar part of our present language."[6] By the end of the century, some writers even viewed provincial "vulgar" languages as dense with etymological information about connections to Anglo-Saxon, newly heralded as central to English political and linguistic origins.

This chapter will explore these gothicizing motifs as well as provincial writers' resistant experiments with them. First, however, we shall explore how antiquaries tied vulgar/provincial languages and the vernacular itself to the nation's past and the political rhetorics underwriting that move. It is, of course, not only fashionable urban language or underground cant that constantly changes. As Bishop Wilkins noted, "All languages which are vulgar are subject to so many alterations, that in tract of time they will appear to be quite another thing than they were at first."[7] Such changes must be negotiated within a national rhetoric that predicates itself on continuity with the past, whether in Johnson's call for submission to linguistic custom or Burke's appeal to political and legal custom. One such negotiation was the displacement of corrupting alterations to the metropolitan center. Grose claimed that the words included in his *Provincial Glossary* had "grown obsolete from disuse and the introduction of more fashionable terms, and, consequently, [are] only retained in countries remote from the capital, where modern refinements do not easily find their way" (iv). Provincial space, with supposedly deep connections to history, provides a reassuring, if fictional, counter to London and its fashionable innovations in everything, including language. In writing throughout the century, various London idiolects, associated not with the vulgar but with the middle and even high classes, came in for derision. Swift, for instance, attacked not vulgar language per se but the linguistic novelties of a licentious court, poets, and university men adopting the language of the coffeehouse and the gaming ordinary.[8] Swift was no celebrant of provincial tongues and was especially dismissive of what he perceived as the barbarity of the Northern tongue. Yet he blamed London-based neologisms for corruptions in language that were making impossible the preservation of the "memory of times and persons" so crucial to the greatness of the nation (40).

In fiction writing, as provincial languages, for some, ascended in status in their association with the past, London languages descended in status in their association with a fashionable present. While Defoe's fictions had offered protagonists who merely encountered (and translated) a strange-making diversity of languages in London, later-century novel protagonists confronted a chaotic assortment of odd specialized jargons in the metropolis and never explained or adopted them. Whether Frances Burney's ingénues or Tobias Smollett's travellers, these characters perceive the strange jargons of London as the languages of incomprehensible laughingstocks, whether incomprehensible merchants or hack writers. Evan Lloyd's midcentury satire *Conversation: A Poem* presents the "Babel's din" of various trendy scenes of the capital, in which not provincials but "City-Wights" speak a largely meaningless dialect of sounds:

"*Molasses* humm'd and ha'd his *so's* and *ifs*, / *Mundungus* answer'ed with protracted *Whiffs*."[9] Print graphics worked to call up a sense of degraded sound, italics signifying the cits' broken spoken language—"*It do not argufy, that there, this here*" (14).[10] Casual vulgarity had become the language not of laboring women in the dairy but of fine ladies at their routs, as in this exchange at the card table: "*Such Cards!* Well!— /... *Col'nel*, your Lead—so! Lord ha / Mercy 'pon us!—" (28). And wits, not rustic clowns, had become grotesquely embodied in their animal-like sounds: "you find a *Lov-sick Cat* outmew'd, / A *Bird* outwhistled, and outsnarl'd a *Dog*, / A *Hog* outgrunted, and outcroak'd a *Frog*, / The cooing *Turtle*, or the *Irish Howl*" (36). In such depictions, upper-class London, not the provinces, is the site of pernicious linguistic degradation—so much so that, by the century's end, Samuel Pegge defensively protested, in the subtitle of a book "Chiefly regarding the local dialect of London," that "the natives of the metropolis, and its vicinities, have not corrupted the language of their ancestors."[11]

Provincial terms might have been outmoded and unpolished, but this is also what positioned them as a pure language of the past, beyond the transformations of the corruptions of fashionable urban society. Even works such as William Marshall's multivolume study of regional farming practices across England included glossaries of provincial terms because they "indulge ... an inclination to an enquiry into the origin of the English language."[12] Provincials themselves claimed this antiquity of their languages as a source of pride. Defoe observed that Northumbrian natives "value" the "imperfection" of their speech "because, forsooth, it shews the Antiquity of their blood."[13] And John Collier, deceptively comic, as we have seen, in his treatment of the "Lancashire dialect," was invested in linguistic history: he studied "Old English and Middle English literature [and was] possessed of a good library."[14] Collier's contemporary, Manchester historian John Whitaker, maintained that Collier's work was "perpetuating words and forms of speech which had subsisted before the conquest."[15] Collier, despite his differences with Whitaker, also asserted the value of provincial languages in those same terms, defending his work, though it was so humorously low, saying "[I] ... think it commendable, rather than a defect, that Lancashire in general and Rossendale in particular retain so much of the speech of their ancestors. For why shou'd ... we in these parts [be] laugh'd at for adhereng [*sic*] to the speech of our ancestors?"[16]

Provincial writers such as Collier, however, were writing a provincial history, so to speak, based not only on written texts of the archives but also on their lived experience. His lively mix of languages resembles the mode of writing of another provincial writer, William Hutton, whom Ina Ferris has described as preserving the present for the future "not by stilling the present moment but by immersing [Birmingham] in the open temporal series," exploring "how ... those in the present live with the past's residue."[17] The emphasis on the body, on the experienced, on how the past remains in the present, with that physically charged sense of remains, lends power to the provincial word's status as historical artifact. In preserving the "speech of our ancestors," provincial languages preserved a closer connection to the senses and their more powerful terms of affiliation. Provincial words, some argued, deviated less from original terms and the "sensible ideas" they once transparently named. John Locke had asserted, "if we could trace them to their sources, we should find in all Languages, the names, which stand for Things that fall not under our Senses, have had their first rise from sensible *Ideas*," so provincial terms, adhering to the speech of ancestors, might be valued for being that much closer to their source.[18] Grose maintains in his *Provincial Glossary* that "provincial or local words" are "deducible from [a] primary source of language."[19] Antiquarian treatises on various regions typically included glossaries of the local language, linking it to ancient (and particular, sense-based) words and meanings, as in a "Vocabulary of Uncommon Words Used in Halifax," which lists "THACK, the covering of an house. From A.S. [Anglo Saxon] Daccian, Dhae, and Dhaek. The Islandic also has Thac. The original meaning of this word is straw, or Rushes; our Saxon ancestor using no other covering for their houses. Afterwards it was extended to slate and tile."[20] Embedded in the provincial word is both the particular, sensible impression (or idea of it) and the simple rustic view, as figured in Adam Smith's clown, discussed in Chapter Five, a speaker incapable of drawing a distinction between particular and general ideas. The material thing, straw, names and grounds the general concept, "the covering of an house," with a linguistic simplicity analogous to Smith's provincial clown, who took the river next to his house as the name for all rivers.

Even the distinct sounds of provincial language became evidence not of distance from but of proximity to English, its older, even originary self. As Samuel Johnson himself had put it, in a formulation not uncommon in the eighteenth century, "The language of the northern counties ... is uttered with a pronunciation which now seems harsh and rough, but was probably used by our ancestors."[21] For Pegge, provincial language promised sensible, originary meaning, too, at the level of sheer sound, for instance, in the wagoner's command of *ge* to his horse. Turning to "words from the humblest line of humble language ... when our waggoners [*sic*] and Carmen made use of the terms *ge* and *wo* to their horses," Pegge argued that *ge* "seems to be the imperative 'Geh' of the German verb 'Gehen'—'To go.'"[22] Provincial sounds were missing links, retaining within them terms directly traceable to originary sense. Pegge wrote,

> In Yorkshire, in Lancashire, and other Northern parts ... the term "*Ge*" is applied in other cases; for where things do not *suit* or *fit* each other, or where neighbours do not *accord*, the expression is–"They do not *Ge* well together." You will see the word "*Ge*" given, in this sense, in the glossary to the Lancashire dialect in the works of Tim Bobbin. (13)

Here, the provincial language of Collier's *A View* becomes fodder in the work of recovering the origins of English (although to do such work, Pegge must set aside the German connection). Pegge's choice of the sounds of wagoners is an interesting one, for by this means he could point to ostensibly vulgar London language—the language of wagoners—that had in fact come to the city via laboring provincials. Such speculation points to the ongoing movement between these spaces that, of course, ultimately disrupts visions of a pure provincial language, mobility once again both undermining and establishing connections between language and place.

Adam Fox and Paula Blank have both documented word lists and antiquarian studies of provincial dialect terms from as early as the sixteenth century, showing how at times these earlier representations made similar claims about the older status of provincial, especially northern, terms.[23] Blank writes that "several Renaissance linguists concurred that the language of the northern shires represented an older, 'purer' English, uncontaminated by foreign influence; northern words were thus identified with old words, or archaisms."[24] These, however, often tapped into religious histories. In his 1605 *Restitutions of Decayed Intelligence* (which went through six editions in the seventeenth century), Richard Verstegan argued that country people spoke something closer to "our ancient language [that] consisted most at first of words of monosyllables, each having his own proper signification, as by instinct or God and Nature they first were received and understood."[25] The Teutonic roots of the language of "country people" could be traced back to a pre-Babel universal language, Verstegan believed, and he sought to discover through his etymologies divine relations between word and thing.

The eighteenth century, however, saw a shift in which the provincial word functioned less as evidence of divine origins and more as a preserve of national linguistic and political continuity. John Horne Tooke pursued these connections to the past in political terms as he used provincial words to elaborate etymologies from contemporary English to a newly revalued Anglo-Saxon tongue. He maintained that the word "if," for instance, could be traced back to "give" or "given" in Anglo-Saxon, and pointed to the provincial word "gin . . . often used in our Northern counties and by the Scotch" and the Lincolnshire word "gif" for evidence of this claim.[26] For Tooke, it was, of course, that same Anglo-Saxon world, to which provincial languages, he argued, were more closely connected, that had also bequested liberty to Britons.[27] Using provincial terms to discover the Anglo-Saxon origins of English not only shed light on language but on the politics of English liberty itself. Not attending to Anglo-Saxon, Tooke argued, had led James Harris, for instance, astray in his analysis of both language and politics. When Harris asserted that the word "unless" means "adequate preventive," Tooke, who traced "unless" back to Anglo-Saxon for "take away," argued that Harris's misunderstanding of the derivation had menacing political consequences.[28] He offered the sentence, "England will be enslaved unless the House of Commons continues a part of the Legislature," and asked, "is this alone sufficient to preserve it? We who live in these times, know but too well that this very house may be made the instrument of a tyranny... I am afraid Mr. Harris' *adequate Preventive* will not save us" (220).

Pegge, too, drew from the rhetoric of the freeborn Englishman to revalue provincialisms:

> Dr. Johnson was scarcely at all aware of the authenticity of antient [*sic*] dialectical words, and therefore seldom gives them any place in his Dictionary. He seems not to consider them as *free-born*, or even as *denizens*; but rather treats them as *out-laws* who have lost the protection of the commonwealth: whereas they generally contain more originality than most of the spurious words of modern date.[29]

Pegge put "dialectical words" on a footing with wronged freeborn Englishmen and took the argument for including provincial words within English further than most. Even writers who argued that English custom should form the basis of English, such as George Campbell, were far from thinking that vulgar provincial languages should be part of English proper. As objects of antiquarian collection and as evidence of social and literary history, however, these languages made their way into the concept of the vernacular. As they did so, their strangeness became even more apparent.

The Strangeness of the Past

The provincial languages that would seem to point to English's origins became, across the eighteenth century, both more and less than English. Etymologies of provincial terms, for instance, revealed not a pure lineage for English but a mixed, often literally foreign, one. In the glossary to his *View*, Collier provides etymologies for Lancashire words, asserting Anglo-Saxon origins for many, as in the various terms for "Ask," such as "Ash, Ax, Axen, Ash'n," which, he claimed, all pointed back to Anglo-Saxon roots.[30] But his list of etymological sources for his glossary also included "Belgic," British, Danish, Dutch, French, Swedish, and Teutonic. Similarly, an entry for the word "Allernbatch," meaning "an old sore," included, in a later edition of *Exmoor Scolding*, an etymology: "From the Angl. Sax. Albon and Fr. Gal. Bosse, a botch.—[or perhaps from A.S> AElan, accendere, Botch ut supra], and then it may signify a Carbuncle or burning Boil."[31] French and Latin origins are a disturbing reminder of the very real foreignness of many provincial terms, a reminder that they, and English itself, had gone through (and were continuing to go through) a long, uneasy process of becoming English. If etymologies called up a verbal version of geographical deep time, they also called up a version of "geographic unconformities," what Eric Gidal describes as "breaks in

A GLOSSARY

OF

Lancashire WORDS and PHRASES:

CONTAINING,

About 800 Words more than were in any of the five former Impreſſions:

In which many of the uſeleſs Corruptions are o‑mitted, and wherein the Reader may obſerve,

That Words mark'd { A.S. / Bel. / Br. / Da. / Du. / Fr. / Sw. / Teu } *come from the* { AngloSaxon / Belgic / Britiſh / Daniſh / Dutch / French / Swediſh / Teutonic }

A

ACTILLY, *actually.*
Ackerſprit, *a Potatoe with Roots at both Ends.*
Addle, *to get; alſo unfruit‑ful.* A. S.
Afterings, *the laſt of a Cow's Milk,*

A

Agate, *on the Way.*
Agog, *ſet on, begun.*
Aighs, *an Ax.* A. S.
An { *if* / *and* }
Ancliff, *Ancle.* A. S.
Anent, *oppoſite.*

D 3   Appo,

FIGURE 7: From Tim Bobbin [John Collier], *A View of the Lancashire Dialect*, 6th edition (Manchester, 1757). The abbreviations ("A.S.," "Bel.") designate the language "the word comes from" ("Anglo-Saxon" or "Belgiac," respectively). Copyright of the University of Manchester.

the geologic record" that offer evidence of process not as continuity but as disruption.[32]

To extend the geological conceit, etymologies, like fossils, act as reminders that the present linguistic "here" was not always "here."[33] The successive waves of invaders—Celtic, Roman, Danish, Norman—and of invasions of Cornwall and Wales, as well as the recent political union with Scotland, were the open secret of the permeability and multiplicity of the British nation and its language, despite attempts to define both as continuous over time. Those conquests, in fact, endowed regions with much of the distinctiveness and opacity of their local languages. Old Norse elements influenced Northumbrian and East Anglian pronunciation and lexicons. Evidence of Old French could be heard in the pronunciations of Devon, East Cornwall, and West Somerset.[34] Those regions said to harbor the most enduringly distinct local languages might be the most linguistically foreign of all. Provincial terms were often the harbingers of that open secret.

Moreover, the early studies of provincial languages could be disconcerting reminders of a now-alien but once-central Catholicism. White Kennett's 1695 *Parochial Antiquities of Places in the Counties of Oxford with Glossary* includes phrases of "foreign influence" such as "Advouson of Churches. No church legally consecrated without an allotment of manse and glebe."[35] He necessarily turns to the Catholic Church for insight on the origins of provincial English language and its meaning, citing the Latin of church doctrine, for instance, to explain "abuttare. To abut, vid. Buttes. Abuttat sper praedictam terram, . . . in a Terrier, or description of the site of land, the sides on the breadth are said to be adjacentes." Such terms appear alongside more "native" phrases such as "A *bind* of eels is a string of eels." The influence of the Catholic Church was woven deep into local speech, another aspect of the gothic qualities emerging around representations of provincial language.

Perhaps the most ominously strange and gothic element posed by representations of provincial languages, however, in their invocations of ancientness, is death. Their promise of continuity across generations, their preservation of the "language of ancestors," answers to Benedict Anderson's assertion that "national imagining is . . . concerned" with "death and immortality," specifically in its attempts at a "secular transformation of fatality into continuity."[36] When provincial languages constitute an ongoing means of continuity with the past that looms within and legitimates a national present, they necessarily call up the dead. And even as the transcendence provincial languages promise would seem to efface time and the difference it makes, the very oddness of those languages reasserts for readers the strangeness of time's passing, of dead compatriots and their now-unfamiliar languages, and of the oblivion that accompanies death. Not only were provincial languages strange to Britons, but the links to the past, their etymologies, were necessarily speculative and obscure. Locke himself, who posited an original sensory-impression-based meaning in all words, acknowledged that such meaning is occluded over time. That original sense, known only to the now dead, would be evident "if we could trace them to their sources" (42), but he admitted that such tracing is often impossible.[37]

Susan Stewart has analyzed the British revaluation of "oral forms," such as old ballads, as a means of "address[ing] anxieties of place, desertion and the silence of the dead."[38] Vulgar provincials, relentlessly embodied and particularized in grammars and other dicta on proper language use, became nonetheless transcendent figures of transhistorical continuity on the basis, oddly enough, of those oral forms and sound itself. Unlike the American Republican rhetoric around voice that Jay Fliegelman and Christopher Looby have described, in which the American nation formed out of the "abrupt performativity of its inception" in a declaration, British national rhetoric demanded a sense of voice that activated not an injunction to act in the present but a sense of continuity with voices of the past.[39] The sounds of the places supposedly remote from a quickly changing center offered a powerful connection to those past-sounding bodies.[40] Representations of provincial pronunciation portrayed idealized continuity, however implausibly, through sound, with depictions of the distinct pronunciation of the provincial voice, in terms such as "daunger" for "danger," invoking, literally voicing, the supposed language of the past. Stewart does not include dialogues of provincial language among the oral forms she discusses, but these not only promise the continuity of voice but also draw from the authenticating apparatus around oral forms. A later eighteenth-century preface to *An Exmoor Scolding*, for instance, refers to its Exmoor language as "a genuine specimen" and elaborates on the means of its oral transmission. Its pseudonymous author, one Peter Lock, was an itinerant, blind fiddler who, the preface claims, recorded Exmoor dialect from the spoken tongue, not unlike the figure of the blind harpist Katie Trumpener discusses, a wandering, marginal musician and singer who preserves the linguistic history of the land, his blindness reiterating the oral quality of that language.[41]

In Britain in particular, such lowly itinerants and their singing were believed to have produced native culture. As Marilyn Butler notes, Joseph Ritson argued that the elite literary producers to whom Thomas Percy had drawn readers' attention would have been French-speaking. Alternatively, Anglophone minstrels were sub rosa "rogues and vagabonds," native writers and poets who were also necessarily anonymous—and, interestingly, given our discussion in Part One—wandering figures.[42] Continuity was also connected to the emerging idea of oral culture more generally, in the idea of unwritten customary practices passed down by word of mouth. Glossaries of provincial languages offer a treasure trove of customary practices and the words that name them, with terms such as: "DOOAL. money &c., given at a funeral" (in Lancashire) or "BRIDE-WAIN, a custom in Cumberland, where all the friends of a new married couple assemble together and are treated with cold pies and ale."⁴³

Although Edmund Burke's focus on authorized political institutions seems far afield from representations of "vulgar" language, he effectively articulates the tension within both political institutions and vulgar language in their shared model of transmission. Whether the institution of the Ancient Constitution or a language that is continuous with speakers from time immemorial, the passing down of both suggests a strange quality in each, at once permanent and ephemeral—as enduring as the traditional song, as fleeting as voice. Consider the oddly doubled terms in Burke's discussion of "our government" and "our liberties" as a "permanent body composed of transitory parts." The constitution, he argues, is "in a condition of unchangeable constancy, [it] moves on through the varied tenor of perpetual decay, fall, renovation, and progression," a strangely undead characterization.⁴⁴ Johnson too, in his well-known defense of linguistic custom, refers to language as both bodylike, subject to "corruption and decay," like men "who grow old and die," but also potentially transcendent, like "our constitution," capable of preservation across generations.⁴⁵

This gothic quality, as language hovers between decay and transcendence, dead and living, infuses the sense of provincial languages and their writers. J. Mitchell, one editor of Josiah Relph, that poet of "Cumberland dialect" discussed in Chapter Six, rhapsodized that "his abilities are seldom so transcendent as when his muse speaks in native dialect."⁴⁶ He also positioned Relph as dead, including in his prefatory material the poet's epitaph, taken from the monument that the editor himself had "caused to be erected" (xvi–xvii). Relph and his fellow provincials are otherworldly, specifically in their use of a provincial tongue. That same editor described Relph as addressing his "parochial charge" (he was also a clergyman) "in a language they all understood," one that, Mitchell believed, Relph derived from "his solitary contemplations and night-thoughts in the church-yard" (xii). Here, the provincial tongue morphs into the language of the dead, as the dead inspire provincial language writers and speakers from beyond the grave with a strange language nonetheless "understood" by fellow provincials.

We saw in Chapter Five the gothic qualities of provincial languages, their opacity drawing readers into wonder and suspense. In their reputed pastness and their status as *memento mori*, provincial languages take on gothic qualities in another sense, namely those Deidre Lynch and Joseph Roach have identified in English literary canon-making, a project contemporaneous with the national revaluation of provincial languages. Lynch describes "the melancholy... that freights the project of canon formation," its rendering of "the nation as a dead poets' society," while Roach argues that "canon formation serves the function that 'ancestor worship' once did" and that "the English classics help control the dead."⁴⁷ Gothic writing, canon formation, and, as we are beginning to see, reclamations of provincial languages all reckon with the dead, attempting to manage a past that is at once too distant, in frightening danger of oblivion, and too close, in danger of overwhelming meaning in the present.

Thus, while Andrew Elfenbein has associated a "metaphoric death" with the standard English of canonical literature (when "English experts" cited the works of poets for examples of good usage, "all were dead—in some cases, long dead"), provincial languages, too, are connected to death, even as they are lauded as still "alive."[48] This is true for their association not only with past languages but also with newly revered past national poets. David Fairer argues that by the 1760s a national literary history that "encouraged a living sense of continuity" promoted the once-dismissed obsolete language of recently revalued writers such as Chaucer and Spenser.[49] Even when writers critiqued the use of provincial language by earlier poets, they recharacterized it not as socially but as temporally remote. John Dryden, while praising *The Shepheardes Calendar* for being "wholly clear from the wretched affectation of learning," accused its harsher rustic language not of being low but of being "obsolete."[50] Similarly, writing to Thomas Gray, Benjamin West referred to the failings of Shakespeare's language not in terms of its being "clownish" but of being "antiquated."[51] Gray (notwithstanding his own attempts to capture the sounds of Welsh bardic poetry) and his circle saw such antiquated terms as a liability in contemporary poetry, and were critical of provincial writers such as Thomas Chatterton and their odd antique language.[52] Other writers, however, revalued "obsolete" language; although Ben Jonson had dismissed the attempts of Spenser's contemporary critic "E. K." to legitimate the language of *The Shepheardes Calendar*, Thomas Warton, a key figure in the institutionalization of English literary history, approvingly cited E. K.'s praise for Spenser's efforts, for he "hath labour'd to restore, as to their rightfull heritage, such good and naturall English words."[53] As attitudes toward the past changed, particularly in relation to the institutionalization of a canon of English literature, Spenser's "clownish" provincial language increasingly came to be seen less as irredeemably local and low and more as merely old and English, and in some circles valued as such.

For some, revaluing obsolete language meant revaluing as well local dialect terms of their own day—specifically as the provincial language of the "common people."[54] For Joseph Ritson, for instance, knowledge of vulgar regional and especially Northern languages could shed light on the true language and meaning of the works of Shakespeare, the national poet. That illuminating status reversed power relations between the provincial vulgar and the metropolitan elite, not unlike the "vulgar sublime" associated with obscurity that we examined in Chapter Six.[55] In a characteristic gloss of Shakespeare's language, Ritson ridicules one editor's correction of "Little wee" to "little whey"; "Little wee," he insists, "is certainly the right reading; it . . . is a very common vulgar idiom in the North."[56] In another instance, he disagrees with Dr. Johnson's gloss of "mess" as a "contraction of master," noting, "It is merely the Scottish pronunciation of Mass" (13). Here, knowledge of vulgar Scots even exposes the mistaken understanding of the Great Cham, the day's preeminent authority on English.

In such moments, if the literary canon is haunted by the dead, those ancient poets, oddly, share a space with speakers of provincial languages, and can even be brought to life by them. Antiquaries as well as literary critics credit spoken provincialisms of their present with the power to aid in interpreting, in a sense reviving, old literary texts, as when the contributor of an "Exmoor Vocabulary" to the *Gentleman's Magazine* hoped to "afford some help to understanding of our old books."[57] The humble provincial's authority in revealing the meaning of national literary works was oft-repeated. The antiquary and Church of England clergyman William Hutton, in his moral tract in provincial language, *A Bran New Wark*, offered copious footnotes tracing etymologies of provincial terms, often with citations to Chaucer or Shakespeare. Of "scal'd," he wrote in a footnote, "Scaled, scattered, leveled, so to scale muck, or molehills, to scale hay, and yet, this word puzzled most of the editors of Shakespeare."[58] Entries in John Watson's vocabulary of Halifax are used similarly to explicate passages of Chaucer.[59] As well, grammarian Charles Coote describes how the first preterite "tense was formerly inflected also in another form, *as I be, thou beest, he beeth, we be, ye be, they be.* Shakespeare, Ben Jonson . . . sometimes used this inflexion, but it is now obsolete, except among the provincial vulgar."[60] Even Josiah Relph's editor traced lowly contemporary Cumberland terms back to Chaucer. This revaluation of provincial languages for their reanimation of the nation's literary works extended into the nineteenth century; according to an 1829 *Gentleman's Magazine* letter, "among the common people in Staffordshire the word girl seems even now to be scarcely known . . . young women are called wenches without any offensive meaning, though . . . in the metropolis, the appellation has become one of contempt. Hence I have heard that line in Othello, 'O ill-starr'd wench, pale as thye smock!' thus softened down to suit the fastidious ears of a London audience."[61] The provincial-language-speaking vulgar stand in close proximity to the national literary culture that has been made strange by the changing linguistic practices of a polite metropolitan public.

Provincial Language and Its Speakers as Anachronism

The past formation of the language spoken in the present is always mysterious. As Samuel Pegge put it, "nobody knows why, nor how innovations have crept in, because the aggressors against the old fashions have never been detected."[62] Strange "aggressors" innovate language, just as unknowable speakers invent the adages and coin the colloquialisms that comprise the collective lore of a national vernacular. Provincial speakers, however, hover closer to those enigmatic origins. Thus, while Grose and his contemporaries confronted a thorny issue that had vexed antiquaries since at least the sixteenth century—how to reconcile the grandeur of the nation's language with its being spoken by provincial, vulgar speakers—one response to this quandary in eighteenth-century antiquarian writing was to render provincial languages and their speakers anachronistic. Native informants of the language of another time, enabling, as Francis Grose put it, an "understanding of our ancient poets," provincial "common people" (and their words) are not quite of their present world, but rather something like dead or spectral figures haunting the present.[63] In these narratives, their language and whole way of life were out of time, somehow coeval with ancient Britain and its customs, even as they walked—and talked—among the accounts' readers.

The historiography of the Scottish Enlightenment, with its plotting of nations on a chronological grid of development, helped produce such gothic figurations. In his discussion, James Chandler describes the unevenness that stadial history posited between nations when charted within distinct stages along a universal developmental schema, which made for a Romantic fascination with "comparative contemporaneities," particularly "anachronism... as a measurable form of dislocation."[64] Representations of provincial languages, which, even as they made those languages a significant part of national culture, also located them as spatially and temporally anterior, brought those developmental differences closer to home, pointing to *intra*-national uneven development in British regions closer even than, say, the Scottish Highlands. They situated within the nation a temporal unevenness generally ascribed to distinct (and often colonial) societies.

Christopher Anstey's *An Election Ball... in Zomerzetshire Dialect*, briefly noted in Chapter Five, for instance, in its depiction of Somersetshire speakers, presents them as anachronism. Written for "Mrs. Miller's Poetical Coterie at Bath," the poem took up that week's coterie's subject: "antient and modern dress and manners of the English Nation compared."[65] This slight volume links the contemporary provincial's language to "ancient manners" and contrasts them to those of the modern nation—a time and place so foreign to the provincial that he has become a stranger to it, needing explanation of modern mores and language. A similar logic is at work in Isaac Ritson's *Copy of a Letter, Wrote by a Young Shepherd*, which sketches a native of Borrowdale in Cumberland's impressions of urban life.[66] The provincial recounts how he "ast a man at I kent what wast matter wi sum oth wummon swok at tha war sea bryad leaway, an he telt me it was a fashion to weer huips; nut a badden nowther if it keep ther legs togidder, for there war sum o them varra bonny."[67] This ribald representation of the provincial speaker, as he discovers the new fashion of hooped skirts, and argues it's not a bad one if it keeps women's legs together, for some of them are very good-looking, links men together, not unlike Grose's representations of the "vulgar tongue." But the provincial is also himself a comically displaced figure, unaware of recent fashions—or economic developments. He marvels, in his own anachronistic provincial language, at both women's hooped skirts and at the goings-on in a city's exchange, like a rustic English Rip Van Winkle.

Dipesh Chakrabarty has urged a provincializing of Europe to reexamine the premises of political modernity. Paying attention to constructions of Europe's provinces in particular, however, might also assist that project, specifically in the ways representations of provincial languages "rend the seriality of historical time and make any particular moment of the historical present out of joint with itself."[68] If provincial languages are made part of the vernacular as living signs of the nation's past, uneasily coexisting with contemporary language, that vernacular, too, is out of joint with itself, strange. Consider the weighty two-volume *History and Antiquities of the Counties of Westmorland and Cumberland* and its writers' insistence that "the language of the country people hath large remains of the ancient Saxon."[69] The presentation of the language on the printed page has the effect of completely anachronizing rural speakers. "The country people" its authors describe are the only ones who supposedly still speak this provincial language, and the glossary is entitled "Antiquated Words." Crucially, the glossary fails to distinguish between terms still in use at the time and those that were obsolete. It includes words describing ancient regional legal customs and civic charters long superseded. We find "pulture, a custom claimed by keepers or other officers in forests, to take man's meat, horse meat, and dog meat of the inhabitants within the forest" and "marchet, a pecuniary payment, in lieu of the right which the lord of the manor in many places claimed and had, of lying with his tenant's wife the first night after their marriage."[70] Alongside these obsolete terms, however, are others quite contemporary in these regions, such as "skep, a measure of uncertain quantity" (akin to the term "bushel") and "speir, to enquire."[71] Arranging currently used terms next to words cataloguing local legal practices long fallen into disuse has the effect of rendering the contemporary speech of the provincial out of joint. Similarly, at the end of the century Jonathan Boucher composed a glossary of "obsolete and provincial words," the two conflated—and preserved—in the linguistic graveyard Boucher lovingly tended.[72]

While Scottish Enlightenment historiography rendered certain languages and customs anachronistic, past in present, some antiquarian writing encouraged "libidinous" connection to those objects of the past and their producers.[73] Anachronistic provincial speakers were also compatriots whom readers were encouraged not only to imagine but to be movingly connected to—if also haunted by. Almost all depictions of provincial languages at this time include terms for the frighteningly ghostly and for superstitious beliefs in powers that cannot be seen, alongside prosaic terms of customary rural life. Even Marshall's work on the rural economy of England's regions includes, alongside its descriptions of manuring techniques and cheesemaking, and terms such as "COTTS, lambs brought up by hand" and "KEDGE, to gluttonize," terms naming the unearthly, such as "BARGUEST, a hobgoblin of the highest order; terrible in aspect, and loaded with chains of tremendous rattle."[74] Similarly, Grose includes many such terms in his *Provincial Glossary*, from "AUTERS. Strange work, or strange things. N." to "PICKSEY. A Fairy. Devonsh.," plus a variation on "BAR-GUEST. A ghost, all in white with large saucer eyes, commonly appearing near gates or stiles; there called bars. Yorksh. Derived from Bar and Gheist." Many of these terms Grose, in turn, lifted from earlier provincial glossaries, such as, from Collier's *View*, "BOGGART. A specter," "AWF. An elf, a fairy. Derby and N," and "HOBBGOBLIN. An apparition, fairy, or spirit."

This sense of the provincial as otherworldly was compounded by the appearance, as provincial glossaries gained popularity, of companion collections cataloguing the customs and, most predominantly, superstitions of provincial regions. Such collections suggested that if provincials were closer to an originary English and England, they were also predisposed to the superstitions of a primitive state.[75] Grose's *Provincial Glossary* includes a "collection of local proverbs and popular superstitions" in which he elaborates on terms found in his glossary such as "FETCH. The apparition of a person living. N[orth]" or "SWARTH. 'The fetch or ghost of a dying man ... Cum[berland]." The name that published collections gave to such beliefs and customs—"popular antiquities"—gets at the relegation of the vulgar, "the popular," to the past that these works share with representations of provincial languages. That the studies of popular antiquities often accompanying provincial language collections describe ghosts and haunted spaces, then, is no accident. For this institution of the vernacular made room for the vulgar provincial within the vernacular, but only as anachronistic haunted and haunting subjects. The provincial vulgar and the languages they spoke were necessarily figured as spectral, as haunting, while absolutely essential to, the national imaginary. The rustics in collections of popular antiquities and the servants of gothic tales might speak of and believe in ghosts, but it is they and their languages that are the specters.

Out of sync with national development, provincial languages in these writings suggest a distinct articulation of what Srinivas Aravamudan has referred to as the "subject of anachronism," which is "an apparently obsolete remainder or superseded past."[76] Provincial writers, however, often exhibited a self-awareness of their status as "subject[s] of anachronism," mounting pointed responses in complex forms of self-representation, and thereby making their thematics of loss, displacement, and haunting all the more poignant. Two important examples took the form of collections of "popular antiquities" in rural Newcastle. These works, like many we have seen in this chapter, also redefine space in temporal terms, and what is geographically (and socially) peripheral becomes at the same moment temporally past and culturally central. Newcastle clergyman Henry Bourne, in his 1725 *Antiquitates Vulgares or*

The Antiquities of the Common People, wrote that "tho' some of them [customs] have been of national ... observance, yet at present they would have little or no being, if not observed among the vulgar."[77] A once-dominant national culture shared across classes and places now haunts the center from the peripheries and the "vulgar" classes. Further, this was a culture represented as being itself obsessed with the dead. The first seven chapters of Bourne's *Antiquitates Vulgares* detail death-related customs and provincial terms, from tolling the "soul bell" to strewing flowers on graves to avoiding churchyards by night.

Bourne, the son of a tailor, imagined his work not simply as a catalogue of practices of the past but as a guide for parishioners on those that should be retained and those that were no longer acceptable. His careful and sometimes approving description of these rites partially validates them. This defense had political significance. Newcastle, with "a fractious populace prone to riot and resistance," according to Kathleen Wilson, witnessed performative displays of oppositional cultural politics, including "the people['s] ceremonial effervescences."[78] In such performances, Wilson writes, "the chasm between the 'two nations' could scarcely be more neatly, or provocatively, embodied."[79] In this context, Bourne, not only in recording and preserving the ceremonies of the vulgar and the terms that named them, but also in stipulating those that should be carried on, situated those ceremonies and that language within a contested present.

John Brand's important *Observations on Popular Antiquities* (1777), alternatively, aimed to revive the "rites and ceremonies of the people" as a way of keeping vulgar provincials in their place—avoiding the polishing and corrupting forces of the urban.[80] Itself a sort of palimpsestic ghostwriting, Brand's work included the full text of Bourne's 1725 *Antiquitates Populares* interleaved with Brand's comments. Brand's text would be taken up and added to time and again by nineteenth-century folklorists, including British Museum head Henry Ellis. In his preface, Brand legitimates "the people" as an object of study, writing: "The People, of whom Society is chiefly composed ... is a respectable Subject to every one who is the Friend of Man."[81] He suggests that the North, removed as it is from the improving south, is where the nation's popular customs are yet retained, a window to the past that is also the site of the continued embodiment of national culture in the day-to-day practices of its "people." If Britain is a nation that prided itself—in some circles, anyway—on a vision of collective culture formed on the repetition of time-immemorial customs, as we have seen in Burke, for Brand (and not for Burke) the vulgar were the key site of that transmission. Brand writes that "tradition has in no instance so clearly evinced her faithfulness, as in the transmitting of vulgar rites and popular opinions" and "Things, composed of such flimsy materials as the fancies of a multitude, do not seem calculated for a long duration," but he adds, "yet have these survived the shocks, by which even empires have been overthrown, and preserved at least some form and colour of identity, during changes both in religious opinion and in the Polity of States" (iii).

As Brand makes space for "the common people" on these terms, however, they are necessarily figured as distant, as relics haunting the nation. He anachronizes the provincial vulgar in much stronger terms than Bourne had, for he figures vulgar provincial culture as ruins. Brand writes that though "vulgar rites and popular opinions ... persist ... many of these it must be confessed are mutilated ... as in the Remains of antient Statuary" (iii). The sense of ambivalent physicality—the culture of the people both "flimsy" and as solid as stone—reappears here, resembling the provincial languages that are at once stubbornly embodied, as we explored in Chapter Five, and at the same time ghostly, not fully of this world.[82] This figuration of living practices as ruins is a move related to the designation of "folk" that, Raymond Williams observes, "had the effect of backdating all elements of popular culture."[83] I am arguing, however, that this backdating took place as part of the creation of the very notion of a British vernacular culture, at least in its recuperation of the "provincial."

Brand's politics lend some credence to this reading. Unlike Collier and Brice, who had attacked corrupt provincial officials, Brand, a conservative, adamantly defended the Newcastle oligarchy under attack from the "rabble" at the century's end.[84] He, much more so than Bourne, seemed committed to a fixed teleological history that situated vulgar provincials as past. And yet, figured as ruins, popular antiquities called up a past age when all held them in common, a past in which the whole nation shared this belief system. When a modernizing Britain left behind superstitions and their folksy terminology, it also left behind a unified culture and language, in which all believed and spoke together. For some writers, Brand among them, the vulgar remained the "repository of the true history of civil society," as Carolyn Steedman has put it. But they retained that status *only* as remnants of the past. It was as past and superseded that the vulgar could conjure the idea that "once we were all on a foot, each a part of each other, in that lost realm of imagined community that the eighteenth century invented."[85]

The national public sphere, as Bruce Robbins has argued, is itself a "phantasmagoria: an agora (the public forum, assembly) that is only a phantasm."[86] It is already in a sense spectralized—not, finally, a social formation composed of mutually present physical bodies. As we saw in Chapter Five, its rhetoric of disinterest imposes its own eerie terms of disinterest and disembodiment. That troubling phantom quality, however, is projected onto the people in collections of provincial languages and popular antiquities. Either because they are past— no longer fully existing in the present—or because they are at once decaying and enduring, they are represented as phantasms, even as they come to stand in for some version of (once-unified) national culture. Grose humorously joins these complex terms of haunting to national political discourse when he describes the distinctiveness of English ghosts in his *Provincial Glossary*: "Dragging chains, is not the fashion of English Ghosts; chains . . . being chiefly the accouterments of foreign spectres, seen in arbitrary governments: dead or alive, English spirits are free" (10). Here Grose jokingly conceives the rational, national British public as both phantasm and haunted by its own particular phantasms. In the preposterous image of peculiarly English ghosts he reveals the way conceptualizations of embodiment and disembodiment, past and present, inform the incorporation of the vulgar provincial into the vernacular as spectral.

Provincial Languages and Melancholia

The 1788 *Critical Review*'s laudatory assessment of Grose's *Provincial Glossary* frames its discussion not in terms of Grose's humor, but instead rather wistfully notes that

> provincialisms are the vestiges of older English, not quite worn out by additions, or polished by refinements: we should look at them with the veneration which we feel when we survey a Saxon arch mouldering to its ruin, or a Gothic window tottering at every blast. If not caught at this moment they will be forgotten.[87]

Echoing Brand's figure of ruins, these are terms of deep and perhaps surprising sentiment for provincialisms that were both being weeded out of dictionaries and often comically conflated with all that was distastefully rural and vulgar. In this reviewer's forlorn account, provincial languages' "vestiges of older English," a material link to the past, are almost lost, but not quite, not yet. Once again, provincial languages are both associated with the dead and yet still here, touching reminders of time's passing. With a sense of urgency regarding the impending passing not only of provincial languages but the things they name, Grose wrote that "the customs and many of the places alluded to are sliding silently into oblivion" (vi).

In imagining provincial languages as still-present remnants of a national past, they can not be mourned, for there is no laborious process of introjection such mourning would require if they are still present.[88] Esther Schor has elaborated how mourning, specifically the mutual mourning of sympathy, could provide one important basis of social cohesion in an increasingly secularized Britain.[89] The mourning of provincial languages, particularly when they were also viewed as the language of childhood, both personal and national, might have functioned as one site of such binding affect. Provincial languages, however, cannot quite be mourned, because there is an ambiguity in the status of that loss—was it loss yet if, as suggested by the present participle, the "sliding into oblivion" was still taking place, and vulgar provincials were still speaking these languages? Instead, provincial languages are more often a site of melancholia. They continue to exist, haunting and supplementary figures of incorporation, of magical thinking and fantasy, in a dominant national historiography, including the literary.

Melancholic representations of provincial languages extended throughout the eighteenth century, underwriting the increasing fascination of more culturally authorized and upper-class readers as collectors and even writers of provincial languages. William Hutton legitimates writing a 1785 moral tract in Westmorland dialect precisely through the anachronizing, melancholic terms of loss and ongoing presence, saying that "thro' Woodland we communicate all our ideas in cast off terms, yet terms which monarchs formerly deign'd to use."[90] Provincial language, dying yet still present, continued to harbor traces of a national language that once bridged powerful and powerless, that "lost realm of imagined community that the eighteenth century invented" Steedman describes.[91] The melancholia is especially poignant in Hutton's description as national chronology paralleled personal chronology in his meditation on provincial languages. For Hutton and others, provincial languages were the languages of childhood. Tied up in the pleasure of long-ago memories, the provincial languages some writers left behind were connected to their personal past. Hutton, for instance, when addressing former provincials who, "like swallows and cuckoos, love to change to mare sunny hawghs, and now feed on richer pickings" (185), affectionately refers to the "cast off" local terms he used as "yours and mine, when we rambled together o'er the head of Heversham, or angled in the brook of Beetha" (186).

The Gentleman's Magazine included excerpts of provincial dialogues and glossaries sent in from male metropolitan readers who addressed provincial languages from a similar vantage, identifying themselves as "a son of the Tyne" and "a son of the Were" as they carried on public debates in metropolitan periodical pages regarding the meaning and origins of various "local" terms that continued to be used back home. "A Son of the Tyne," although familiar with the terms he listed because of "the town where [he] was born," admitted, "I could have made considerable additions to it if I had been still resident at Newcastle-upon-Tyne": like Hutton's "swallows," he has moved on.[92] These readers shared old remembrances of provincial words in letters written in the clubbable style associated with polite republic of letters. When "A Son of the Were" corrected some of his speculations, "A Son of the Tyne" responded—in an authoritative "proper" English—"As I do not think myself infallible, I shall not defend all my definitions, but only remark, that some of his corrections relate principally to errors of the press ... I may remark, farther, that there is an essential difference in the dialect between Newcastle and other parts of Northumberland."[93] Polished metropolitan men, these writers signaled their present distance from provincial languages while drawing authority from their past connections to them.

English poetry of the mid-eighteenth century and beyond offers up a number of spectral figurations of the rustic "common people" and their language. It is useful to think of them alongside the melancholic terms of provincial language representations. Thomas Gray's *Elegy Written in a Country Churchyard*, for instance, echoes with endless allusions to masterpieces of British literary print culture, but also harbors specters of rural provincials and their language, now dead and buried. Gray's poem presents its vision of humble rural labor and domesticity as scenes called up through ruminations on the grave markers of those modest rustics, their "uncouth rhymes" (79), and epitaphs "spelt by the unlettered muse" (81), distinguishing them through their language. It is through spectral images that the speaker presents rural laborers, calling up the memory of these once-embodied figures working in the field and embraced by children. Schor argues that loss is here introjected—buried in the graves of the country churchyard, which becomes, as she puts it, "a synecdoche for the nation," enabling a mutual mourning—not melancholia.[94] The poem, in her words, "forge[s] a ... sturdy link to the dead" and "we ... find that we have joined the dead" (953). But when we run Gray's depictions of rustics and their "uncouth rhymes" alongside the print representations of provincial languages of the time, we get something less final, less safely introjected. When placed alongside images of provincials still speaking their "uncouth rhymes," the spectral images called up in the poem become something like the literalization of fantasy that Nicolas Abraham and Maria Torok associate with melancholia: imagined rustics and their provincial languages, both embodied and hauntingly anachronistic, both absent but made present in the poem.[95]

Similarly spectral are the rustic people of Oliver Goldsmith's contemplations on a depopulated English countryside locale in *The Deserted Village*. The fictitious Auburn's rural scenes and "bold peasantry, their country's pride" are ghostly projections of a world that is "no more"—a phrase anaphorically beginning three lines of the poem.[96] Auburn once was an oral/aural environment, a place of "sounds," including the "woodman's ballad" (244). The speaker separates himself from provincial rustics as the learned and worldly spectator, once a part of but now distinct from that essentially oral world of the provincial and past. The printed word on the page now calls up past images that are both familiar scenes and estranged in their ghostliness. In Auburn's desolate present-day landscape, only a solitary widowed "wretched matron" (131) remains; a "sad historian" (136), she is the figure of the female provincial as site of oral traditions, although she is not speaking. She is, perhaps, an instance of the eighteenth-century notion Susan Stewart had described—that oral forms need "rescuing not so much from 'history' as from a generalized oblivion of the feminine."[97] And, as we know, dialogues of provincial languages were populated with just such female speakers, ribald and uncouth when they opened their mouths. It is the male speaker of this poem who "rescues" past provincial life through memory, through childhood connections to place that operate in a highly sentimental economy. He is like the male readers of metropolitan periodicals who took a custodial interest in provincial languages as the languages of their childhood, their mother tongue.

The period after midcentury saw widespread enthrallment with provincial languages on these sentimental and feminine terms; it even became something of a fashionable hobby for women to collect them. These more refined collectors, predictably enough, sometimes dropped terms related to sweating, fornicating, and drooling bodies from their lexicons, as did Joseph Banks' sister, Sarah, who, with her other antiquarian endeavors, dutifully alphabetized the Lincolnshire words she accumulated in her time spent at their rural estate from 1779 to 1784. Markedly tame in comparison to Brice's and Collier's, her list includes terms such as "shan," meaning "shy," "feert," meaning "pretty," and "beck," meaning "a brook."[98] Female-authored provincial dialogues appeared, such as the fragments of Devonshire dialogues by Mary Palmer, sister of Joshua Reynolds, that were printed anonymously in periodicals at midcentury. As Michael Baron has observed, Palmer's interest in the particular—whether local words, such as "vinny" for "mouldy," or particular pronunciations, e.g., "zummct" for "somewhat"—challenged the privileging of the general and abstract championed by her brother.[99] Among her dialogues were sentimental declarations of love between two country servants: a sweetheart bids "neart, neart, my sweeting" (23), meaning "night, night, my sweet one."

Provincial Writers and History out of Joint

Palmer's dialogues also, however, included the crude physicality attributed to provincial language. Servant Bet explains how her master (or "measter") "zed his bread was a-clit and pindy; the dumpling was claggy; the cheese was a-buck'd and vinned" (12)—"a clit" and "pindy" meaning "sticky" and "musty," "claggy" meaning "clammy" or "viscous," and "a-buck'd" meaning "goatish." This same grousing master is a patriarchal tyrant, berating and beating his wife viciously and heartlessly assaulting an orphan who works for him. Palmer's provincial world—local, embodied—is also one of stark violence within the home, of despotic fathers not unlike those of gothic novels.[100] The dialogues are oddly gothic, too, in their representations of the provincial superstitions we have seen accompanying other portraits of provincial language. Rab, Bet's interlocutor, relates how he has seen the parson in the woods and "watch'd en to zee iv a made any zerckles or gallytraps" (watched him to see if he made any circles or mysterious shapes to catch wrongdoers). Rab describes how this same parson released a trapped bird and incanted, "shear-a-muze, shear-a-muze, vlee over me head," transforming common English, "bat, bat, fly over my head," into a more aesthetically pleasing secretive chant. Rab believes the parson even talked to the animal: "a . . . zed a shud go an do zum o'at, I doan't knaw what t waz" ("he . . . said he should go and do something, I don't know what it was"), in an otherworldly exchange that the observing provincial himself does not understand. Neither Rab nor the reader ever find out why the parson was in the woods, throwing his hands in the air, nodding, and talking to himself and to a bat. The briefly introduced mystery suggestively turns the tables on just who the odd-sounding and superstitious provincial-language speakers might be.

In Palmer's *Dialogues*, the provincial is also otherworldly as a space and language out of time. As in Christopher Anstey's image of a provincial young woman aping new and urban hairstyles that we saw in Chapter Five, here young village women show up in church in extreme versions of the latest hair fashion, "prink'd out in the tip of the mode, way a lamming wallige of hair bevore and a vumping nug beheend, and a race of rory-tory ribbons, stuff'd out leek so many pincushions" ("decked out inclined to the mode, with a huge loose bundle of hair before and great knot behind and a great number of all sorts of flaring colors, stuffed like so many pincushions") (8). Bet and Rab criticize the absurdly up-to-date women in the language of the past, the provincial tongue that would put these fad-followers in their place (and time). Significantly, Bet invokes ancestral, quite gothic, ghosts in her disapproving commentary: if the women's mothers, who "ware their own hair," were "to peep out of their graves, they wid'n know their own children" (9). Provincial rustics are both beauties à la mode and ghosts of the past.

The vulgar provincial melancholically haunts the present, representing a past that is, uncomfortably and gothically, not fully past. Again and again, provincial writers resist and play with that anachronizing position. We saw Relph reconfigure his rustic reaper as a book-buyer. Collier put his provincial author in a dialogue about commercial print markets with his own book. Palmer, too, in the opening lines of a dialogue, depicts Bet as an avid reader, allowed to borrow books from the vicarage as long as she does not, in her words "make dog's-ear o' an'" (1). Moreover, despite contemporary suspicions regarding the immorality and idleness of laboring-class readers, this female servant persuasively defends her reading as virtuous. In order to read she "works the harder, and don't stand dodeling when there's a book to be had" (1). As well, from the seemingly subordinate, anachronistic place of the provincial-language speaker, Bet calmly, almost disinterestedly, presents the injustices of the tyrannical patriarch, pointedly questioning common assumptions about who can speak, read, and know, and where and when provincials belong. Such moments refuse the usual anachronizing terms of incorporation of provincial languages into the vernacular.

Palmer was a wealthy woman, bankrolling her famous painter brother's trip to Italy and hosting Dr. Johnson. A woman of standing, she never published her work as a stand-alone book, although she did circulate the manuscripts privately. Alternatively, Ann Wheeler, who published her *Westmorland Dialect in Three Familiar Dialogues* under her initials, had been a servant.[101]

A genteel dedication and preface position her illustration of "The Provincial Idiom," however, as safe for polite consumption. Situating herself as a self-effacing "authoress," Wheeler writes, "Novelty may recommend it to the ladies," and declares that it will "afford an agreeable amusement . . . to those who take pleasure in observing . . . the difference which exists between the dialect of the country and Town" (vii–viii). While there are stories of marital infidelities and even wife-beatings in Wheeler's work, the language is not particularly graphic. Some of its most physical language, as in "she had broken twoa oa their noases, an peyld their feaces black an blue, an pood off heal handfuls of haar" (34) is uttered by a "stranger." Alternatively, "native" characters, such as "Jennet," offer such moralizing notes as "I think if o'th lasses od keepth men at a girter distance, and nit lit em tak sic liberty as they deya, thear wod be fewer lasses brout to sham than ther is" (86).

Like her male predecessors (she aims to "share the laurels with Tim Bobbin" [vi]) and Palmer, however, Wheeler reveals a canny sense of the oscillating status of provincial languages, both past and present, national and not, and the ways in which their obscurity might invert relations of power—and thus might not easily be brought into a national vernacular. She prefaces her work with a story of two Cambridge graduates, not Chaucer's scholars using Northern dialect but speakers of standard English, who believe that their learning empowers them to understand any language of their land. They lose a bet to a local guide, however, when he declaims in words they cannot comprehend: "en udder blae el deat" (xi) for "another blow will do it," shouted at two fighting women. As in other print representations of provincial languages, the tables are turned as both Cambridge students and readers confront in the provincial speaker an opaque set of words, language known to provincials but not to them.

With the text's description of "two Wimen feighten," having "pood yan an udders Caps off, en Neckcloths" (xi), we might seem to be back in the impolite world of *An Exmoor Scolding*, with its crudely embodied women—the word "udder," here meaning both "utter" and "other," but, of course, also calling up the dairy barn, appears twice in four lines. Unlike *An Exmoor Scolding*, however, Wheeler's dialogues are not flytings, not gestures toward a Medieval poetic convention that confines provincial language speakers, no matter how egregiously incontinent, to the recognizability of a known, past literary genre. And, unlike Collier and Brice, Wheeler does not pursue an antiquarian analysis about the language of Westmorland's relationship to an ancient national tongue. Her dialogues contain fewer unusual words than her predecessors', emphasizing instead distinct pronunciation. And crucially, in attempting to transcribe the speech of her Westmorland speakers, Wheeler notes that "in the application of letters to sounds and pronunciations scarcely two people think alike" (viii). Such acknowledgment undermines the notion of provincial language as a source for finding a shared, originary English. The text does not set up "Westmorland dialect" as an anachronistic precursor of contemporary English, a stable language in which world and word map neatly onto each other.

Instead, we might say that Wheeler and her fellow writers in provincial languages were after something more novelistic, less governed by formal genres or antiquarian discourse and more interested in a novelizing depiction of part of the array of national life in her present—her aim, she writes, "to convey the Ideas of the People, in the Stations of Life she has fixed upon" (viii). Wheeler and other provincial writers flip the anachronizing dynamics surrounding so many representations of the provincial and vulgar as they experiment with genre. Refusing to relegate the present to the past, they insist on the ongoingness of provincial languages in the present. Indeed, David Hume's argument, that the experience of the past through various representations is indistinguishable from the experience of the present, made possible the notion of "an inescapable presentness," as Ruth Mack has detailed.[102] It is mobility—through spaces, through texts—that makes that experience of inescapable presentness or presentnesses possible for Wheeler and her predecessors. She writes that it was "her long residence in other parts of the kingdom," as she puts it (she lived in London for years before returning to Westmorland), that made her home dialect appear "novel" and worthy of recording (vii). Her reflection points toward a modernity that was often effaced in representations of the provincial. Whether the sanctioned travel of a Mr. Spectator or the unsanctioned wandering of cant-speakers, itinerancy was generally not depicted as part of the provenance of the provincial that modernity attempted to fix in time and space. And yet, for Wheeler, like the protagonist of many a novel, movement through space allowed her to take in the strangeness and estrange the language of Westmorland and other places as part of a polyphonic present. In a final dialogue added to the second edition (1802), she also depicts and effectively alienates the speech of London.

Wheeler, however, claimed such mobility not only for herself, but for the characters of her dialogues, who converse about topics such as bad marriages, domestic violence, and impressment, topics very much of her present-day, so much so that, as Michael Baron and Daniel Dewispelare have both noted, the use of dialect serves as a cover for a politically radical critique of gender and class relations.[103] Part of her critique—and in some ways the most interesting—is the intervention into the very terms upon which provincials and their languages had been represented. If room was being made for them within the vernacular as anachronisms, melancholically haunting the present, self-representations of provincial language such as Wheeler's took all sorts of liberties with their historiographies and implicit temporalities. They orient ongoingness toward the future, not the past. In doing so they overturn the class-effacing dynamics of pastoral and the anachronization of the provincial that were an inevitable part of the institution of a national vernacular.

We might invoke here Dipesh Chakrabarty's helpful if unlovely terminology to say that those who represented the provincial as the anachronistic past of a national vernacular's present wrote what Chakrabarty would call "History 1," which he defines as "a past posited by capital itself as its precondition" (63). These are histories that imagine a singular teleological trajectory toward capital to which all antecedents, both those of the past and those anachronistically still existing in the present, move. This was the dominant approach at the time to provincial languages, evident, for instance, in the *Monthly Review* article that values Collier's *A View* for its representation of the provincial speaker as a throwback and referring to the work as "a masterpiece of the kind," exhibiting "a clown in pure nature, such as a simple country fellow really is, who is quite unacquainted with the world."[104] Without trade and travel, this story goes, the clown and his language have remained untainted—"pure nature"—as all around him has changed. Such anachronistic figurations responded to the challenge of the unevenness of economic and social development Scots enlightenment writers were, at that same moment, theorizing. As we have seen, some representations of provincial languages reclaim that unevenness, making them one site of a cultural continuity threatened by development. "Undeveloped" provincial people and their languages became ciphers of vanishing origins, texts representing those languages possessing the modernity Ian Duncan ascribes to Scots writers from James Macpherson to Adam Smith, as they reckoned with the understanding of culture itself as spectral.[105]

For Chakrabarty, however, subaltern self-representations sometimes revealed how "historical time is not integral, it is out of joint with itself" (16). He calls "History 2" those "histories that do not belong to capital's life process" (50), ones "charged with the function of constantly interrupting the totalizing thrust of History 1" (66). This approach, I have been arguing, surfaces in the works of Parker, Wheeler, Relph, Brice, and Collier. If a provincial speaker is also depicted as an avid reader, bookstore shopper, or savvy producer for the commercial print market, she and her language cannot easily be relegated to the past. If she can call up the ghosts of ancestors to criticize fashion victims, who are themselves also provincial speakers, the provincial language she uses is shown to be of both the past and present, not safely consigned to the past. At these moments, and in examples we are about to explore, the provincial speaker functions in Derrida's sense of the specter, disrupting the lines between past, present, and future ("does not belong to that time, it does not give time") and confusing, as we saw above, the embodied and transcendent. (In Derrida's words, the specter is "neither soul nor body, and both one and the other."[106]) Yet in eighteenth-century Britain, that spectral figure signaled not, as it did for Derrida, mere epistemological uncertainty, but rather the ideological complexities and contradictions of nationalist narratives regarding the vernacular. Thus it is that provincial writers of "History 2" represent provincial languages as internally mixed, not easily confined to one space or time, both historical and preserving history but also multiple in any given moment and undergoing constant change.

We see this writing of "History 2" in Collier's move between multiple regional dialects discussed in Chapter Six even as he claims that the language of his *View* honors and is the singular "speech of our ancestors," troubling the notion of ancestral purity or at least presenting a mixed sense of who exactly those ancestors might be and what their languages were. As Collier reveals, the ancestors are spectral not only in the sense that they are past, living on in the anachronistic language of their progeny, but also in the sense of being not real, a projection; the supposedly singular "Lancashire dialect" that calls them up is an invention. Similarly, the language of *An Exmoor Scolding* includes those fabricated "Bricisms" as well as terms the author picked up while in residence in Cornwall, his "Exmoor" language wrought with a troubling mobility. As late as 1805 G. Dyer still asserted that the language of Devon was the originary language of the nation, but Brice's vocabulary had already positioned his provincial word collection and its genealogies as a kind of ruse, a suggestion that what the antiquarian etymologist sought, the original word that had its telos in a present-day term, the provincial vulgar language that undergirded culture's continuity, was nowhere.[107]

Crucially, when provincial writers write "History 2," it is often through the comic that they disrupt the "totalizing thrust" of "History 1." When the terms of superstition and ghostly presences appear in provincially authored books, for instance, it is frequently with an underpinning of knowing humor. Collier depicts Tummus explaining, "I thowt I'd seen a boggurt, boh it prooft o mon weh o piece-woo, resting him on o stoop ith' lone. As soon os eh cou'd speyk for whickering, I axt him where ther wur on Eleheawse?"[108] Tummus's boggart turns out to be nothing more than a man holding wool; Tummus's "whickering," or trembling, was for naught, and his attentions are quickly turned to the more pressing question of the nearest alehouse. In *An Exmoor Scolding*, the glossary contains such terms as "tee-heeing pixy, laughing fairy or goblin" (55), again, hardly the stuff of serious belief. In their representations of provincial languages, these writers both engage and undermine the figure of the spectral and the superstitious provincial.

Wheeler, Brice, and Collier, then, posed a challenge not simply to the spatial estrangement of provincial language discussed in Chapter Six, but also to the temporal dynamics around their representation. Responding to these dynamics as provincials, they, like John Gay before them, adopted those dynamics in order to disturb them, pointing to the complexly contradictory logic of anachronizing an otherwise emphatically present, embodied, often mobile, and even innovative contemporary rural vulgar. Half-jokingly making use of the antiquarian rhetoric of provincial linguistic ancientness to articulate the national value of their seemingly low works, they demonstrated their awareness of the dominant linguistic history, of History 1. Collier, for instance, drew from the authority of antiquity—and also undid that authority—in his facetious claim that he found the manuscript of "Truth in a Mask" (a radical poem he himself authored) being used as toilet paper in an alehouse privy, its discovery an antiquarian coup.[109] And, while the glossary included with Collier's text provides the kind of scholarly etymological information one would expect from an antiquarian treatise, tracing local terms back to national linguistic origins, it humorously deflates these grand antiquarian narratives with crudely embodied provincial terms. In providing Anglo-Saxon etymologies for words naming such unseemly things as "Aighs, *An ass* A.S." and "Beshite, *to foul or dirty*," these writers parodied antiquarianism's indiscriminate attention to the most lowly of subjects while reminding readers of bodies in the present.[110] These novelized representations of language, with their humorous innovations on genres of antiquarian writing, their mixed lexicons, and linguistic innovations, remind us, too, that Britain's provinces were not enclaves untouched by the period's many transformations; they were not, as anachronizing narratives would have it, the products of the "waiting-room of history."[111]

Poetry and the Provincial Vernacular

Print representations that folded provincial languages into a national vernacular depicted them as alien enough to incite curiosity and interest but also as familiar, British, part of the nation's past. Some provincial writers, as we have been observing, played with those anachronizing dynamics, insisting on the ongoing presentness of provincial languages and parodying the antiquarian discourse that would place them in the waiting-room of history. The poets discussed in this final section, Thomas Chatterton and Robert Burns, pressed the consequences and paradoxes of historicizing provincial languages still further. They took up the question of the *experience* of history that Ruth Mack has argued dominated eighteenth-century discussions on the subject. Neither the empirical evidence, documents, and objects amassed in the period nor the conceptual frames and analyses of government and social relations posed by Enlightenment thinkers could truly enable experience of, or "transport" back to, a past time, Mack notes.[112] Chatterton and Burns reckoned with the impossibility of that transport, in part through their depictions of provincial languages, experimenting with odd languages that readers could at once experience as strange graphic images, heard sounds, or even sensations produced in their throats, but that also functioned as metonyms for a whole past language and the world that produced it. In their synthetic, opaque representations of provincial languages, Chatterton and Burns made them a means of transporting readers not to the past, but at least to somewhere initially alien, while gesturing toward the need for fictional constructs to make that transport, or sense of experience, possible. As well, within their poems they situated the speakers within their communities and even within the antiquary networks that collected and transmitted their language. Their poems tied together obscure languages and the social relations that framed them in an effort to map the devices necessary to produce the sense of "experiencing" the past.

Chatterton deployed an obscure, antiqued language to challenge a provincial poetics of place and time as he wrote his own provincial history. He adopted what we might call a gothic mode of writing in the sense of Walpole's *The Castle of Otranto* or even James Macpherson's Ossian poems—fabricating an imagined past to produce readerly effects, a sense of experience, in the contemporary present. Through an antique-looking but often made-up language and a fictionalized persona, a Bristolian medieval scribe and collector named Thomas Rowley (whose name, suggestively, his creator found on a tombstone), Chatterton re-presented Bristol's past civic and cultural achievements while providing a mediating figure, in Rowley, to give one model of experiencing them. On the page, the language of Chatterton's Rowley poems are every bit as defamiliarizing as the language of other provincial writers. "Eclogue the Third," an "ancient" poem Rowley has collected, advises, "Goe, serche the Logges and Bordels of the Hynde . . . / Inne hem you see the blakied forme of kynde" (2–4), hovering between somewhat familiar ("goe") and unfamiliar ("bordels," meaning cottages). Some terms come into meaning through sound, the puzzle solved in pronouncing—"serche" sounds like "search"—or explanatory footnotes, the lines thus rendered: "search the huts and cottages of the peasant to find the plain form of humankind."[113] In this peasant or "hynde," we find the familiar characterization of the rustic clown, "pure nature" traceable to an originary past, an unreflective soul leading a carnal life of song, drink, sex, and fighting. The poem pitches this pastoral simplicity in the Theocritean linguistic terms we have seen associated with the vulgar provincial, promising "phrase of th'vulgar from the Hynde, / Wythoute wiseagger wordes" (7–8), counterposing the hind's plain "vulgar" language to that of the "wiseagger" (philosopher). Here, readers' experience of the past is in their confrontation with its alien, opaque language, while the poem extends an invitation to conceptualize the social order of this world through static categories of place and class, composed of rural hinds and urban philosophers.

The poem puts linguistic experience and social conceptualization at odds, however, breaking with contemporary depictions of provincial language as the provenance of the vulgar. It places its strange language not only in the hind's mouth but also that of Syr Rogerre, the worldly wise and socially elevated figure with whom he converses—and the poem's speaker himself writes in it. The laboring peasant complains of his low station, and Syr Rogerre reminds him, in an equally obscure language, that "the loverds ente, / Moovethe the Robber hym therfor to slea" (57–58) ("the lord's purse entices the robber to slay him"). Syrre Rogerre goes on to tell the peasant, "theeres none moe haile yan thee"

(60) ("there is none more happy than you"). In the past—either the fifteenth-century world Rowley occupies or the remote past of the ancient writings he collects—all people spoke the same language, now strange to contemporary readers. But these were clearly not those imagined realms where all were on an equal footing: the poem emphasizes that lords and hinds occupy quite distinct positions. It operates in a pastoral economy in its naturalization of class hierarchies but here, instead of the peasant using the "fine language" of an elite, all speak in a strange tongue, rendered obscure over time, creating a dissonance between readerly experience and social conceptualization.

In "An Excelente Balade of Charitie," it is again not a vulgar provincial but the removed speaker who uses odd-sounding and strange-looking language. The speaker describes the loaded figure of the beggar—"pore in his viewe, ungentle in his weede, / Longe bretful of the miseries of neede" (17–18)—but one who is more sympathetic than the depictions of beggars that we saw in relation to cant. Here, the beggar, a Christian pilgrim, speaks an ancient language, not the cant of rogues. The poem closes with the contemplative speaker reflecting on inequity and the scarcity of charity and praying for social justice: "Virgynne and hallie Seyncte, who sitte yn glorue, / Or give the mittee will, or give the gode man power" (90–91) ("Virgin and holy saint who sit in glory, either give the mighty will or give the good man power"). Readers must confront and decode an alien language, one that when pronounced sounds by turn familiar (sitte) and unfamiliar (gode), but when they do decode it, they arrive at recognizable scenarios and sentiments, the strangeness of the past dissolving into all-too-familiar social encounters of their own present.

Chatterton's Rowley poems situate provincial Bristol as site of a past that challenges the spatial and temporal configurations of the provincial found in some historiographies. On the one hand, seemingly old plights and divisions ring with contemporary concerns (the beggar and the rich man) while on the other, as we shall explore in a moment, enlightened civic relations, including patronage of antiquarian projects, are placed in what many had characterized as a benighted past incapable of such modern endeavors and relations. Yet perhaps the most profound undermining of anachronizing historiography is at the level of the language. The language of the Rowley poems connotes more a general ancient English than a specifically provincial language. Although we have seen how provincial and ancient were often equated in this period, in mapping his representations of an ancient language of Bristol onto an odd version of an ancient English itself, Chatterton makes the provincial national. But crucially, Chatterton had to make up a language to do so—he invented much of his Rowley poems' language. Walter Skeat speculated that only 7 percent of the terms were actually authentic.[114] His works feature not antique but antiqued language, words of his own coinage, a move that drew from the anachronization of the provincial, but also undid it in fabricating in the author's present words never spoken by anyone.[115] Chatterton's Rowley poems produced an experience of English pastness through encounters with a strange language of his own making. He thereby exposed the extent to which readers' sense of experiencing the past was the result of manufacturing effects through writing.

While the forgery aspect of Chatterton's writing has received much attention, its connection to the complex dynamics of provincial historiography and characterizations of provincial languages has been relatively neglected. These dynamics, however, are central to his writing. For when conjectural historiography mapped provincial spaces as past within a temporal grid, and antiquarian discourse valued particular provincial practices, including languages, as past—and as something like sensed objects of the past—they created a kind of placeholder at which provincial space and its local practices, ancientness, and value might meet. In inventing languages to occupy that placeholder, Chatterton—and Gay, Relph, Brice, Collier, Wheeler, and Palmer—turned that conjectural historiography into a machinery of writing place. They used this machinery to disrupt conventional historiography. In some ways, this use of language as a site of historical disruption had been in place as long as English began to take a standard form and certain nonstandard forms were, consequently, loaded with the weight of a representative pastness. Spenser's created archaisms, Gay's shrewdly inventive shepherds' languages, and Brice's "Bricisms" each present an ancient and local language that is, in fact, nobody's, is only the writer's concoction innovated, crucially, in his or her present moment, in a defiance of the anachronizing dynamics of provincial historiography.

Chatterton was less interested in discovering genuine old poems or even old languages than in conveying the experience of a sense of ancientness. His antiqued words on the page, much like Brice's and Collier's, *mean* at the sheer level of their opacity. Grevel Lindop writes that "non-classical antiquity meant essentially grotesqueness of form and obscurity of meaning, and these were the characteristics [Chatterton] reproduced."[116] Like provincial writers before (and after) him, his actual language is less important than the eliciting of effects—of strangeness *as* ancientness. Yet in the uncanny movement we have been tracing throughout this chapter, that alien and obscure language turns out to be the readers' own. In the Rowley poems, the evidence of linguistic ancientness exists not in the mouths of the contemporary vulgar but in the appearance of writing from documents of a (supposedly) more ancient past. When read aloud, however, this language sounds like familiar English.[117] Hearing its proximity not to a Bristol dialect—pronounced as it would be in Bristol past or present—but to contemporary standard English would return readers to the sanctioned language of their own present. Experience of this language is multiple-meaning, at once a visual experience of the past, as it were, and an aural experience fully of the present.

If the ancient language turns out to be oddly familiar, so does the very antiquarianism that generated interest in it. Part of Rowley's created persona is his collecting of Bristol's ancient manuscripts, a project, in Chatterton's fictive world, supported by Bristol's Mayor Canning, his patron. Like readers' relationship to the Rowley poems' language, distant and yet oddly proximal, their relationship to a society from centuries ago that shares the antiquarianism underwriting a revaluation of provincial place and language via its past is uncanny. Chatterton's representation of a fictional network of antiquarian transmission suggests that it is not the "provincial vulgar" speaker of the present who represents the past and continues to haunt the present, but antiquaries themselves. It is in conversation with this uncanny antiquarianism that we might think of Scots poet Robert Burns, provisionally provincial in his contributions to a Scots vernacular that was to be reclaimed as part of a British vernacular, as I shall explore in a moment. In his gentle ridicule of Grose and his *"Antiquarian trade,* I think they call it" (29–30) in "On the late Captain Grose's Peregrinations thro' Scotland, collecting the Antiquities of that Kingdom," Burns exposes the antiquary's own spectral and supernatural positioning, depicting Grose sequestered away in a haunted, roofless church "colleaguin / At some black art." (17–18).[118] Haunting the space of former (Roman Catholic) superstition, it is Grose and the "antiquarian trade" that are truly anachronistic, even gothic. Indeed, as Leask notes, Grose makes vulgar provincials themselves the onlookers and commentators on the antiquaries "colleaguin at some black art," an apt reversal of just who it is that deals in the supernatural (similar to Palmer's description above of a rustic observing a mysteriously incanting parson) and who may comment upon people who trade in the supernatural. In Burns's poem, it is not the "low peasantry" but "any gentleman who is professedly an Antiquarian" who is "deemed to be in colleague with SATHAN [*sic*], and to be a dealer in Magic and the Black Art."[119] Burns was aware of—and resistant to—the anachronistic location of Scots language and its speakers, its "provincial" location, as it were, within dominant historiographies, and he overturns traditional orders of metropolitan subject and provincial object in response.

Writing in an innovative language that also invokes the old and local, Burns responds powerfully and wittily to the haunting, spectral characterizations of the provincial and, by association, of Scots language. This chapter closes with a brief turn to Burns to situate his writing within the eighteenth-century representations of provincial languages and provincial responses to them that we have been tracking. Positioning him within that discourse illuminates his complex engagement with vernacularization. To start, in order to elaborate the poetry's connection to representations of provincial languages, it is worth reminding ourselves of eighteenth-century characterizations of Scots language as provincial. In pointing to the ways in which Scots was placed on par with provincial English languages, I do not wish to underestimate the complexities of eighteenth-century Scotland, a vexed geopolitical space that was seen, after the 1707 Union of England and Scotland as simultaneously a province of Great

Britain and a distinct entity that, until the bloody repression at Culloden, also threatened to become—or return to its status as—a challenging independent political state. That history itself was both a buried past, superseded in the interest of British national progress, and a past that continued to haunt the present, writ large in the gothic motif of unburied corpses found in Scottish literature that critics have explored, one that is especially resonant with our discussion of anachronistic specters.[120] In many ways, Scotland, including its distinct literary tradition, could never be considered a mere province to central England. Yet a number of writers in the eighteenth century characterized Scotland and Scots language as provincial, thus drawing from characterizations of the provincial to position Scotland and its languages, too, as anachronistic and spectral.

In this period Scots language shared with provincial languages ambivalent characterizations; it was represented as sonically powerful and yet disappearing, ancient and yet ongoing, reprehensibly vulgar and strange, yet (and often on those terms) a crucial element of the vernacular. Like provincial languages, it was said to be most evocatively powerful in its distinctive sound. Allan Ramsay, among others, celebrated Scots's distinctive and superior aural quality, "the pronunciation" of which "is liquid and sonorous, and much fuller than the English."[121] For Alexander Geddes, the sound of Scots was so important that he composed a phonetic reproduction in his translation of Virgil.[122] At the same time, Scots, like provincial languages, was described as (ideally) vanishing. Essays such as that in a 1788 *Edinburgh Review* urged Scotsmen to reject Scots in order to "purify themselves from all uncleanliness of speech and writing" (285).

Powerfully sounded, yet to be shunned, Scots, like provincial languages, was also, nonetheless, said to be an originary language, a key to Britain's linguistic and literary past. Writers ranging from Thomas Ruddiman, who had republished Gavin Douglas's sixteenth-century translation of the *Aeneid* into Scottish, to Joseph Ritson and John Sinclair shared the belief that contemporary Scots maintained vestiges of an older, purer English, the language of the nation's great writers.[123] Sinclair wrote, "that the Scots should indulge a strong partiality in favour of their own dialect, is the less to be wondered at, when we consider how many words are now condemned as Scoticisms, which were formerly admired for their strength and beauty; and may still be found in the writings of Chaucer, of Spenser, of Shakespeare, and other celebrated English authors."[124]

In referring to Lowland Scots as Doric (a rustic provincial language of Greece), writers such as Ramsay made Scots a "provincial" language. Yet this characterization did not necessarily equate Scots with vulgarity or a lower class. Scots language had instead continued to function as respectable across classes much longer than had the provincial languages of England, arguably until the mid-eighteenth century. And yet, by that time, as we are beginning to see, a slippage between what was considered Scots and what "vulgar" language was beginning to take place. Geddes emphasized the equation of the two, arguing that Scots was spoken in its "native purity" not among all Scots but "amang the uncorruptit poor."[125] Characterizing the language of the "poor" as the age-old version of Scots, closer to the pure original language, could legitimate its inclusion within a national vernacular. The language of the "common people" in Scotland, as within England, was viewed as closer to the national language than the polished and transformed language of the well-to-do of the present.

If this was a kind of estrangement of the language—in which the purest Scots, and that closest to an original English, was spoken by the poor—so too were the period's lists of Scotticisms, particular Scots terms, spellings, and grammatical formulations, if estranging from a different angle. In his lists of Scotticisms in his *Observations on the Scottish Dialect*, as Susan Rennie has noted, Sinclair "sought to expose unconscious Scots usages."[126] Once-unconscious, habitual language, Scots, in such works, was now "exposed" and displayed as peculiar. It was on these reified terms that Scots, like provincial languages, was then reattached to the national language (of England or Britain—the "original" geolinguistic borders of the British Isles remained an open question) as its precursor. As in characterizations of English provincial languages, it was the association of "Scots dialect" with the vulgar as a strange and even foreign entity that tied the vulgar intimately to the national language. By 1808, in his *Etymological Dictionary of the Scottish Language*, John Jamieson was advocating not the elimination of Scots, as Sinclair had, but its preservation, albeit with the same view of its vulgar-as-anachronistic status that existed around English provincial languages. Jamieson writes,

> Many of our nation [Scotland] . . . now affect to despise all the terms of phrases peculiar to their country, as gross vulgarisms. This childish fastidiousness is unknown not only to intelligent foreigners, but to the learned in South Britain. Well assured that the peasantry are the living depositories of the ancient language of every country, they regard their phraseology nearly in the same light in which they would view that of a foreign people.[127]

In this rather startling reclamation, it is when a mature (not childish) reader or speaker comes to view Scots, and "vulgar" languages more generally, as ancient—and like the language of "a foreign people"—that its value and national affiliation become clear. This is a stark articulation of the estrangement necessary to make the particular vernacular that we have been tracking throughout this book.

Both Scots and English provincial languages were characterized as anachronistic, even foreign, and so too were the belief systems of the Scots and English "vulgar." Thomas Heywood and Richard Brome's 1634 play *The Late Lancashire Witches* had situated supernatural phenomenon, such as uncanny "familiars"—demons assuming animal forms—in a northern provincial England where rural servants speak "Northern" language. And we have seen Bourne's and Brand's catalogues of the "popular antiquities" around Newcastle. But it was the Scots vulgar language and beliefs that had long been seen as the ne plus ultra of cultures both fading into the past and highly superstitious, a dying culture that was itself preoccupied with the dead.[128] In his depictions of rural Lowland Scotland, Burns intervened in the temporal economy that would make the vulgar provincial part of the national vernacular as past, its rural inhabitants alien and spectral. His representations of local superstitions in his linguistic tour de force "Tam o' Shanter," for instance, return us to Grose, who commissioned the piece for his entry on Alloway Church in his *Antiquities of Scotland*.[129] Burns urged Grose to include in his work this burial site of his father and, he imagined, of himself. Grose agreed, as long as Burns would furnish a "witch story" related to the ruined church. This exchange made for an inclusion into official history at the price of performance of provincial pastness, of primitive belief in superstitions. Written as it was for exactly the type of inscription of provincial culture into an anachronizing narrative that we have been examining—contemporary provincial practices and beliefs for a book on "antiquities"—Burns's poem allows us to see what it might mean to write poetry directly from and against that historiography, Chakrabarty's "History 1." It playfully dramatizes the gothicizing terms of that inscription, writing "History 2."

In the odd words that bring Burns's village, Ayre, to life—"bleezing . . . Ingles" (39) (blazing fireplaces) and "reaming swats" (40) (creamy ales)—the poem seems to reiterate familiar characterizations of vulgar provincial worlds as spaces of local particulars, of sensed experiences.[130] It troubles, however, the idea of a fixed, knowable location, as Penny Fielding has argued.[131] It does so, in part, by disturbing the idea of a fixed, knowable provincial language that might underwrite fixed, knowable space. This disturbance is in evidence, for instance, in the glossaries for the various editions of Burns's *Poems, Chiefly in the Scottish Dialect*. Unlike the first edition, published in Kilmarnock in 1786, the glossaries for the Edinburgh and London editions of 1787 are preceded with a paragraph explaining pronunciation ("The *ch* and *gh* have always the guttural sound"), drawing from English pronunciation equivalents ("the *a* in genuine Scots words . . . sounds generally like the broad English *a* in *wall*") to help readers hear and voice—to experience—its sometimes strange language.[132] Suggestively, this paragraph also turns to sounds not from English but from French ("the French *é*") and Latin ("the Latin *ei*"), inviting a sounding that remains, for English-only speakers, strange.

No such explanation appears before the glossary in the Kilmarnock first edition, its readers, such an omission suggests, being at home with the sounds of their local language. However, what was strange to the English or polite Edinburgh speaker might sometimes be strange for the Kilmarnock reader too.

That the Kilmarnock edition needed a glossary at all is already telling, giving the lie to the notion that provincial readers, Scots or Kilmarnock, already knew the strange language that is the printed "Scots dialect" of Burns's poetry collection. In fact, some of the usages of the words in that first Kilmarnock edition were Burns innovations. "Aback," for instance, while in the Scots lexicon since the sixteenth century, only came to have the meaning given in the glossary, "behind," in the late eighteenth century, at the same time as this collection appeared.[133] Similarly, Burns's use of "agley," which the glossary defines as "wide of the mark," was new at this time. The word listed in the glossary for an old horse, "aiver," first took this spelling in the eighteenth century; before that, it was spelled "aver." And "ava," meaning "at all," here made its first appearance. Even if it is the case that some of these terms were used in local conversation before Burns's volume, their relatively recent appearance in print suggests that these are not ages-old words; their publication in 1786 was instead a new graphic incarnation, an estranging novelty.

In "Tam o' Shanter," Burns consistently destabilizes language, that realm meant to call up experience with a strange look and sound but also supposedly able to reproduce the particular familiar experience of life in Ayre in minute detail. Tam escapes a band of witches just as they snatch his mare's "tail" (207) producing this "tale" (37), a ghostly legend or fictitious oral story, but also a homophone that veers into the obscene—as Robert Crawford points out, "tail" can refer to "genitals."[134] Such moments expose multiple meanings not just at the level of a single word but that of a single sound, disrupting, as we have seen in other provincial writing, the sense that dialect might offer evidence of a singular language, grounded in connection between word or sound and thing or sense idea—that fantasy of past linguistic stability sometimes pinned to provincial languages. Moreover, "tail" moves between registers associated with the provincial, from the merely agricultural, a horse's tail, to the bawdily physical, in a sexual reference akin to what we might find in *An Exmoor Scolding* (while also reminiscent of the urban slang we saw in Chapter Four), to the "tale" that is provincial cultural fodder for the antiquarian mill, one sound running the various, sometimes contradictory, registers of the provincial against each other.

It is, then, not simply the poem's much commented-upon passages of distanced neoclassical reflection, Augustan poetic language, and third-person point of view that suggest a code-switching self-consciousness. It is also the self-reflexive deployment of a variety of elements that appeared in contemporary representations of provincial language, from ribald humor to sentimental locality to spectral anachronization. And not only Burns's language but these supposed provincial elements are sometimes, like Brice's neologisms or Chatterton's fabricated ballads and language, of the writer's own making.[135] This is a cunning engagement with the "anachronistic" provincial linguistic and cultural practices antiquaries such as Grose sought out, staking its authority on the pose of insider knowledge but indulging comic invention and detachment.

Sly and often comic, "Tam o' Shanter" eschews the opportunity to mourn Burns's father, buried in the churchyard. It does, however, suggest a charged association of the provincial with disintegration and death, pursuing, I am arguing, the anachronizing, spectralizing dyanamics of representations of provincials and their languages. Amidst the vision of local culture familiar to readers of provincial dialogues (and of Burns)—the particulars of place, the low humor of tavern life and domestic quarrels—are references to drowning, murder, suicide, patricide, infanticide, and haunted kirks, the stuff of the sublime. In a poem publicizing vulgar provincial language and culture, violence saturates the local just as it is enlisted in an antiquarian rewriting of place. The local spaces the speaker describes are also where drunken Charlie broke his neck, where hunters found a murdered child, where Mungo's mother hanged herself, all noted in a strange and sometimes obscure language, such as "where in the snaw, the chapman smoor'd" (90) ("where in the snow the peddler smothered"). The provincial vulgar home and family, celebrated in Burns's earlier critically acclaimed and popular (and less linguistically difficult) "Cotter's Saturday Night," take on a harrowing character steeped in domestic violence as Tam sees "upon the haly table" at the witches' sabbath "Twa span-lang, wee, unchristen'd bairns" (or children) (132) plus "A garter, which a babe had strangled; A knife, a father's throat had mangled, whom his ain son o' life bereft" (137–39).

Critics have not known what to make of such images, introducing as they do a gruesomeness to an otherwise comic poem.[136] I want to link these haunting images of death and violence to the official rewriting of provincial languages and customs as national vernacular to which Grose invited Burns to contribute. The transformed catalogue of domestic goods, for instance, both reanimates the household and work implements often depicted in provincial collections and recasts the image of the simple folk, openly endowing them with the gothic qualities that, as we have seen, haunted dominant representations of them as anachronistic subjects. Provincial bodies, like the bodies of the people invoked in studies of popular antiquities and provincial glossaries, are associated with the dead and yet unburied. Tam's survey of the witches' Sabbath and its frightening images—"coffins stood round, like open presses, / that shaw'd the dead in their last dresses" (125–26)—is suggestive, especially in the term "presses," meaning cupboards, (domestic) places of hiding and containment, but also the act of preserving, according to the *OED*—and, of course, it is through the printing press that antiquaries aim to preserve the fading practices of the vulgar provincial.[137]

This ghastly reworking of the domestic figures of provincial life, the gothicizing of them in depictions of preserved unburied corpses, reworks, too, the gendering of provincial collecting. The local culture of dance and music of "hornpipes, jibs, strathspeys, and reels" (117) is gendered female but made horrific. The dancing Tam spies is the frenzied dancing of witches, supernatural forces grotesquely embodied. The speaker describes how "Ilka carlin swat and reekit" (148)—each old dancing woman sweats and stinks—and how, casting off their "duddies," (or clothes), they reveal their "creeshi flannen" (153), greasy underwear; the speaker voices his own experience at the view, as he "wonder[s they] didna turn thy [Tam's] stomach" (162). In these images the poem pursues the incoherence of a cultural logic that represents gendered, rural provincials as both grotesquely embodied (think of the flyting women in *An Exmoor Scolding*) and ghostly, transcendent figures, keepers of cross-generational continuity (think of Relph's editor's invocation of his dialect poet communing with the dead). Thus, this disgustingly embodied and sexualized world is also an ephemeral one: these wraithlike witches appear as a vision and vanish into darkness the moment Tam's actual body responds to them in his vocalized "Weel done, Cutty-sark!" (189).

In Brome's and Heywood's earlier depictions of a provincial language-speaking and supernatural world, topsy-turvy relations—servants become masters of the estate, witchcraft runs rampant—are set back in order by the rule of law at the play's end. In Burns's poem, the witches are put back in their place, too, unable to cross the keystone. Unlike Brome's and Heywood's work, however, the supernatural element in Burns's poem is never rationalized or brought to law. He refigures the sense of the anachronistic provincial, endowing it with both comic and frightening aspects that do not resolve. He seems fully aware of those spectral qualities in a vernacular sublime that moves between demotic humor and haunting presence. His evocation of an anachronized vulgar provincial is inflected with a sense of foreign otherness, offering a nod to Britain's commercial imperial past and present with the poem's mention of blood-encrusted scimitars and tomahawks (135–36). In its antiquarian writing, this culture becomes as alien as those foreign colonial spaces also being ethnographically represented in this era. The mobility that introduces these foreign objects and terms to British culture might ultimately have helped produce the interest in and writing of—indeed the very self-consciousness of— the particular, the regional, the local.[138] Recall the transatlantic migration to which Goldsmith's *The Deserted Village* points. Forced from their land by "trade's unfeeling train" (63), the poem's spectral rustics depart to "distant climes" (341); it is this mobility that has produced the writing of the imaginary local in a ghostly pastoral. When Chatterton, too, raised in Bristol, frenzied hub of transatlantic trade, including, notably, the slave trade, wrote of the particular and provincial, it was necessarily informed by that expansive global perspective. And, of course, Burns contemplated sailing to Jamaica to begin a new life as an overseer of slaves as he produced the volume of local life and language that would save him from that fate.[139] We shall see in the following chapter how those laborers most deeply entrenched in these globalizing processes were represented in depictions of obscure mariners' language as local and particular, too, and on those terms made strangely part of the English vernacular.

PART THREE

Wandering in Place

MARITIME LANGUAGE

EVEN AS PRINT REPRESENTATIONS of cant and slang languages depicted them as strange in their urbanity and innovation, and those of provincial languages depicted them as alien in their rural clownishness and antiquity, they were tied to the space of Britain and reclaimable as part of the vernacular for their connection to British liberty and their sense of location and history. In contrast, the language of British sailors, an internationally itinerant population in constant contact with non–English speakers, might well threaten to undo such connections between language and Britishness.[1] Maritime lingo, then, "a dialect . . . peculiar" to sailors, in the words of *The Critical Review*, would seem unlikely to make up part of an English vernacular.[2] And yet it did. For even as English emerged as the "general" maritime language at the turn of the eighteenth century, coming to dominate linguistic exchanges at sea for the next two-hundred-plus years, it was also at this time that maritime words and phrases such as "above board" or "on an even keel" made their way into an English vernacular that was itself being institutionalized. And even sea language that did not exactly become common speech—the technical language of Tobias Smollett's Tom Bowling, for instance—came to be seen as recognizably British.[3]

Print representations of cant depicted it and its speakers as wandering, while provincial languages, alternatively, were seen as so lodged in place as to be irredeemably parochial. Representations of maritime language positioned it as both. British sailors traversed the globe, yet eighteenth-century print depictions of their language portrayed it as limiting, a linguistic confinement that mirrored the sailor's supposedly insular being, trapped in the confines of the ship. Bruce Robbins has argued that all dislocation produces its own forms of situatedness. In some ways, that is a process this book has been tracking at the level of language. The changes wrought by early modern capitalism and Britons' unprecedented inter- and intra-national movement were always behind the fiction of the national vernacular being instituted in the period. This chapter considers the "different modalities of situatedness-in-displacement" that we find in representations of mariners and their language.[4] One key means of "situating" seamen in representations of their language in dictionaries, accounts of voyages, novels, poems, and songs was to depict primarily maritime *technical* language, a specialized argot naming ships' parts and aspects of the craft of sailing. The obscurity of this language of the "common people" who found themselves manning the ships of Britain's blue-water empire was by turns figured as the language of virtual witness, as comic, as sentimental, and even as sublime.

As was the case with print representations of puzzling cant, surreptitious slang, and opaque provincial dialects, those of technical sea language were surprisingly popular in the eighteenth century. By midcentury, print descriptions of voyages that included maritime jargon were top sellers, poems and novels used and explained nautical terms, and William Falconer's glossary of technical nautical terms, *A Universal Dictionary of the Marine*, appeared—and went through six editions by 1789.[5] Sea language might have been familiar not only to the increasing population of naval workers but also to large sections of the British population, especially those living near coasts or with sailor family members; in the wide range of people maritime life touched, its language might be said to be "common." However, the experience of reading this language, often appearing as dense, impenetrable jargon, would have been challenging for many. Falconer's much-read poem *The Shipwreck* daunts with such lines as "Adown the mast, the yard they low'r away, / Then jears and topping-lift secure belay . . . / The reef enwrapp'd, th' inserted nittles ty'd, / The hall-yards, thrott and peek, are next apply'd."[6] Uninitiated readers entered an alien world, one that remained in many ways murky and unintelligible, a world that rendered the speakers of this language and their actions obscure, even as it presented them in intricate verbal detail. The opacity of this language, however, seems to have made it strangely alluring, something readers wanted to learn and make their own, strange and yet increasingly more familiarly British. This alienation and reclamation is a function of the formation of vernaculars more generally that we have been tracking, a seeming closing-off of languages that is also a kind of opening-up—an estranging of certain languages, which are then, and on those particular terms, reclaimed as part of an English vernacular.

In the focus on technical jargon, the mobile figures of seamen and their language seem to be safely enclosed, not cosmopolitan but lodged in place in their ship. Ned Ward, in a popular comic work detailing the lives of mariners, described these world travelers thus: "They feed and sleep in their shell, like worms in a nut."[7] In stronger terms, sailors, those agents of Britannia's rule of the waves, ensuring that Britons never will be slaves, as James Thomson had declared, could also be viewed as inmates. Ward wrote that the seaman "is the greatest prisoner and the greatest rambler in Christendom; there is not a corner of the whole world he visits and yet he rarely makes one step out of sight of his old habitation" (9).[8] And Johnson famously compared the ship to a jail. Yet their technical language also, oddly, became a sign of British sailors' freedom, in contrast to the enslaved and their "primitive" language.

Affective attachments accrued around seamen and their technical language, in part because they represented a kind of freedom, and in part because the tar's limited language, while distancing, was also represented as resistant to the "worlding" influence of travel. Printed works made the language of globe-trotting strangers both remote but diminutively British, culminating in the figure of the jargon of the Jolly Jack Tar, an unworldly being who was nonetheless a valiant fighter for British freedoms.[9] On various terms, technical nautical language becomes a surprising source of sentiment, making odd sympathies possible. The image of the shipwreck, on which I close, however, reasserts the threat of utter difference, posing a brief, sublime encounter with the unsalvageable obscurity and loss that the institution of an English vernacular must repress.

CHAPTER EIGHT

Our Tars

MAKING MARITIME LANGUAGE ENGLISH

Strange Languages and the "Common End"

To understand the significance of eighteenth-century particularizing representations of maritime language, we might start by considering the languages of seafaring that did not much make their way into print representations at the time. When represented on the page, maritime language did *not* usually take the form, for instance, of the myriad of geographically diverse languages found on eighteenth-century ships. While by 1700 thousands of Britons were working naval and merchant ships, routinely traveling to distant ports, there is surprisingly little register of their global travel in representations of their language. It is only on rare occasions that words appear suggesting the international shipboard mix that Smollett calls a "sea ragout" in his seaborne play *The Reprisal*—foreign words such as "cacique," meaning a native chief in South and Central America, or "calabaca," meaning a gourd.[1] For the most part, the multilingual mix of eighteenth-century seafarers remains unrecorded. Olaudah Equiano's *Interesting Narrative* is typical in its erasure of the linguistic mediations of sea travel when no mention is made, for instance, of the challenge of language as he mingles in Turkish society.[2]

We know now of the polyglotism of the period's ship life from posthumously published journals, such as that of Jack Cremer, a low-level sailor who composed a retrospective journal of his experiences at sea in the mid-eighteenth century. This journal, which was not printed until the early twentieth century, records pidgin terms and represents surprisingly polyvocal tars. Reading accounts by such eighteenth-century seamen makes clear that no mariner could indulge the agoraphobia Ward assigns them. Interactions with coworkers of a variety of nations, with foreign passengers, with sailors on foreign ships encountered at sea, with enemy captives, and with local residents of various ports were inevitable. Cremer describes his negotiations with Italian coworkers and Greek passengers; his confrontations with hostile Turkish mariners who board his ship; his friendships with families in ports such as Zante, Venice, and Boston; and day trips upriver with indigenous peoples in North America.[3] He documents, too, the resulting wide-ranging linguistic commerce of sailors. He himself was, on one of his voyages, "put to an Irish-Spanish Preast [sic] at a church to get me to learn Spanish" (66), and he intersperses his writings with such terms as "cunnoue"—meaning canoe (109), "payseans"—meaning *paisans* (150), and "tattan"—a Mediterranean vessel (168). He describes how a fellow sailor "speaks tolerable Ittalian [sic]" (166); another comrade, an Italian sailor, "was linguister," or translator, on various occasions (151); and on a different voyage an Irish "run-a-guard"—meaning renegade (169)—served as "linggistor," also translator. In addition, a "negro afore the mast" led a mutiny, with all the linguistic mastery such an act would require (144). While late eighteenth-century English translating dictionaries of French, Italian, Spanish, and Portuguese marine terms maintained strict divisions between them, partitioning national languages into discrete columns, Cremer's journal reveals the multiplicity of languages aboard ship.[4]

Similarly, in the eighteenth century Welshman William Williams penned a semiautobiographical novel, *Mr. Penrose: The Journal of Penrose, Seaman*. Published in bowdlerized form after his death, the book narrates the adventures of a Crusoe-like hero who is taken prisoner of war by the Spanish, meets a Dutch sailor while stranded on an island, and lives amongst indigenous peoples on the Moskito Coast of Central America.[5] Williams suggests the multilingual environment of the ship, as his hero Penrose describes hearing Spaniards refer to English sailors as "*Peros Engleses*, English dogs" (45) and dangerous shoals as "*Quita Suenno* or Prevent Sleep" (51). Williams's fictional account resembles the global linguistic exchange glimpsed in some voyage accounts. James Bunn has shown, for instance, how in one voyage account Pascoe Thomas, "mathematician" aboard Commodore Anson's *Centurion*, recorded that the Chinese "puzzled over the identity of these exotic sailors: 'the best Name they could afford us was that of Ladrones (that is Thieves), and the Commodore himself was dignified with the title of *The Grand Ladrone Man*.'"[6]

Intercultural contact ineluctably left its mark on maritime language itself. Falconer's 1769 *A Universal Dictionary of Marine Terms* includes such entries as "banian days, a cant term among common sailors, denoting those days on which they have no flesh-meat; it seems to be derived from the practice of a nation amongst the eastern Indians, who never eat flesh" (in another instance of the use of cant to mean merely particular language) and "periagua, a sort of large canoe, used in the Leeward islands, South America, and the gulf of Mexico."[7] As well, etymologies of English sea terms suggest the indebtedness of many to foreign languages. Compiling his dictionary in an age revaluing English's good old Anglo-Saxon roots, Falconer begins with earnest notations of what he believes to be the Saxon origins of many of the sea terms he catalogues. He designates "apron" and "bilge," for instance, as Saxon, although they are actually of Old French derivation, likewise "eddy" and "neaped," although the origins of these terms were and remain unknown. The attempt to map sea language onto Anglo-Saxon origins breaks down, however, under the sheer weight of terms clearly originating elsewhere, from "anchor" (Greek and Latin), "brail" (Old French), "barricade" (Spanish), and "buoy" (French) to "garnet" (Dutch) and "mizzen" (Italian). By the letter C, Falconer ceases to note the derivation of the sea terms and instead provides French translations for some entries.

Marcus Rediker and Peter Linebaugh have described the ship of the seventeenth and eighteenth centuries as "a forcing house of internationalism," where the languages of the "African, Briton, quashee, Irish, and American (not to mention Dutch, Portuguese, and lascar)" mixed.[8] We might take as representative Pascoe Thomas's description of the ever-changing crew aboard Anson's *Centurion*: "We enter'd on board our Ship three Indian Seamen, whom they call Lascars, and I believe there enter'd in the hold, Dutch [and] Persians . . . about twenty, so that we had now, I think, two hundred and twenty-four Men and Boys in the whole of different Nations, Languages, and Religions."[9] Historians of pidgin and creole languages acknowledge also the role of mariners in developing the former, and some have documented logbooks recording those languages on ship. Ian Hancock notes a "pre-1800 English-derived pidgin . . . found in several eighteenth-century [manuscript] travel accounts, one of the most notable being a log-book written in one type of pidgin from Eastern Nigeria between 1785 and 1788."[10]

These views of common naval workers learning and translating foreign languages, the historical residue found in terms borrowed and incorporated into an English naval lexicon, and the pidgin innovated in the contact between mariners and indigenous peoples provide evidence of experience that falls outside the images of the blinkered mariner that stretched from the early to late eighteenth century and beyond.[11] Such linguistic blinkering, however, was crucial. Greg Dening describes the perception of dangerous consequences of the alternative, of linguistic mixing, for the crew of the *Bounty*:

> They had begun to intersperse Tahitian words in their speech with each other. It was a highly threatening strangeness to [Captain] Edwards, and he promised extreme punishment, even gagging, if a word of Tahitian was spoken. On the *Bounty* their pidgin would not have been to exclude others' understanding of what they were saying, but to underscore a relationship changed by their Tahitian experience. It bred familiarity. It lessened distinction between them and increased distinction between them and their former selves. It blurred the genres of their

sailors' talk.... They were touched and changed by something outside their wooden walls.[12]

The threat to identity might offer some explanation regarding why the polyglot hash of languages aboard a ship was generally not represented in print. Movement in space made ships multilingual, but movement in time, and the ongoing transformation of ships' crews—and ships themselves—posed perhaps the most profound challenges to notions of identity. Thomas made his observation regarding the composition of the crew and its many languages while docked in Macao, three years after Anson's voyage had left London. The expedition had begun, as Bunn notes, with "1,955 Englishmen," but on its return there were only 145 Europeans on its crew.[13] Britons lost to disease and accident were replaced by an assortment of nationals, just as English oak gave way to bamboo, cedar, and other exotic woods as necessary repairs transformed even the basic materials of which ships were composed. The alteration of a ship over time, Bunn reminds us, was a commonplace-enough notion enough to serve as a trope for Hume's meditations on the power of the fiction of identity. Hume wrote, "A ship, of which a considerable part has been chang'd by frequent reparations, is still consider'd as the same, nor does the difference of the materials hinder us from ascribing an identity to it. The common end, in which the parts conspire, is the same under all their variations, and affords an easy transition of the imagination from one situation of the body to another."[14] The parts (and people) of the ship—like those of the nation—become strangers over time. It is the imagination that moves from one situation to another to "ascribe identity," enabled by the "common end"—in the case of the ship, the pursuit of the voyage.

How might this idea of a "common end" ascribe identity, and a British identity at that, to the collectivity and language of a crew mixed over time, a multiethnic group who would seem to undermine the idea of a national identity? For, as Bunn argues, "the question about Anson's truncated fleet and crews poses a paradox about the common end of European cultural identity. It is certainly Hume's question about personal identity, except Hume's analogy of the ship can now be seen as a model of a larger collective identity, perhaps even a global model of diversity."[15] The typical globe-traversing ship—and Hume's use of the ship as an analogy—remind us that strangers and strangeness are central to the question of identity. If, as naval historian N. A. M. Rodger has asserted, the Royal Navy was a "microcosm" of British society, the diversity of that microcosm threatened the very notion of a national identity on a larger scale, particularly a national linguistic identity.[16] This was a particularly salient challenge for a nation for whom travels and naval battles across the high seas helped shape its very identity—Henry Fielding had even insisted that the King of Great Britain was "a maritime prince."[17] It was met, in part, by an exclusion in print of the global mix of languages on ships and an emphasis instead on the technological, the physical structures of and actions aboard the ship, and the language naming them, which promoted the "common end," in Hume's phrase.

Technical Language and Making the Distant Present

Technical language and the "common end" it facilitated might have bestowed a sense of identity on the ship and its crew, and that language, in all its obscurity, was described as British. Samuel Pegge claimed that, like provincial language, nautical terms illuminated English's origins. He explained that an ancient English term, "Ho," meaning "stop," "still exists ... in nautical language ... for when one ship hails another the words are 'What ship? Hoy!' That is '*Stop*, and tell the name of your ship.'"[18] And while the global mix of languages aboard a ship did not appear alongside representations of technical language, a mix of British languages often did. Smollett's *Roderick Random* represents regional dialects aboard a ship, such as that of the Welsh Doctor Morgan. His *Reprisal* features an Irishman, Oclabber, whose language is replete with "arrah"s, "gra"s and "honey"s, and a Scotsman, "Maclaymore," who avers, "nae gentleman wad plunder a leddy, awa, awa."[19]

Print works of the eighteenth century represented the tar's technical language as recognizably *British*—and superior. Henry Neuman, compiler of a translating dictionary of sea terms, esteems "English nautical phraseology" as "stand[ing] unrivalled by any ancient or modern language."[20] This language, however, was also distinct from standard English, for it was its very precise technicality (and, to many, obscurity) that enabled the "common end." Representations of sailors emphasized that common end, what Margaret Cohen describes as their "craft" and "effective practice and ingenuity able to beat high risk conditions against all odds."[21] In many sea narratives, Cohen argues, the focus is on "problem solving" in which "information has a privileged role" (8). "Collective rather than individual" (8), this craft and its arcane language formed the basis of identity in a scenario that, as we have seen, presented serious challenges to identity.

On what terms did readers come to value this language and even think of it as, in some way, their own, part of the English vernacular? In one way, it was by viewing mariners' technical language as an unusually stable language, one unmixed, unchanged over time, despite other transformations wrought through spatial and temporal difference. As it directed attention to and enabled a common end, it also made that end possible because it seemed to signify denotatively.[22] John Smith's 1627 *Sea Grammar*, which instructs in such things as "how to build a ship with the definitions of all the principall names of every part of her principall timbers," indexes in the margins of its pages individual terms such as "foot hookes" and "howle."[23] Short word lists of the technical parts of a ship were appended, as well, to guidelines for shipping and insurance. The lexicon of such specialist jargon, while naming intricate and complex ships' workings, also promised an unequivocal and grounding one-to-one relationship between word and thing or word and action. Mariners' supposed restriction to that unchanging technical register makes them, too, in some depictions, "plain dealers." Captain Manly of William Wycherley's *Plain Dealer* refers to himself as "an unmannerly Sea-fellow," distinguished from fawners and sycophants and their false language. He insists, "if I say or do ill to any, it should be to their faces," priding himself on his straight talk.[24] Maritime language, supposedly denotative—a bowsprit is a bowsprit—is an apposite language for such a plain dealer, a language that, like its speaker, supposedly does not wander in meaning.

This specialist language made its way into other forms of writing, some literary, with wider readerships. If, as Cannon Schmitt and Elaine Freedgood have argued, literal, denotative language only *seems* unavailable for interpretation and depth in literary texts, representations of technical sea language are an important instance of what they describe as the "thickening web of connotations, consequences, implications, and associated denotations that our experience may not supply," that can be, in fact, filled with complex meaning.[25] In other words, the technical descriptions readers often skip over might instead be a place to slow down. We are already seeing the ways in which denotative terms seem to anchor a language, the common end it enables underwriting the imagination of identity. Slowing down allows us to perceive the surprising innovations in such language and to explore its interactions with different genres for different meanings.

We might turn to John Dryden's nautical language in *Annus Mirabilis* (1667) to begin to explore the "thickening web" found around the "denotative" language of sailors. Dryden esteems his inclusion of this language as a kind of heroic labor akin to that he claims for his dignified quatrains—as opposed to "easy" couplets.[26] Of his own labor in writing in such technical terms, he boasts, "I have never yet seen the description of any naval fight in the proper terms which are used at sea" (117). And he makes a rather startling claim regarding technical terms and the vernacular: that "the terms of arts in every tongue bear more of the idiom of it than any other words." Moreover, truth itself lies in these particular "terms of art." By contrast, "Those who in a logical dispute keep in general terms would hide a fallacy," he asserts, "so those who do it in any poetical description would veil their ignorance" (117). In a shift that anticipates the reconfiguration of technical maritime terms in the eighteenth century, Dryden characterizes them as both part of the vernacular idiom and closer to the "truth"—defined empirically—in depictions of the world.

This vernacular, truthful language, however, also shares in the opacity of poetic language. When Dryden writes, "Some the galled ropes with dauby marling bind, / Or cerecloth masts with strong tarpaulin coats" (589–90), the meaning is opaque.[27] Obscure technical terms ("galled," "marling") appear alongside obscure poetic neologisms ("dauby"), putting the two forms of language on par. The scene is of sailors repairing their ship, some attending to "galled"—a technical sea term for "frayed"—ropes by binding them with "dauby marling."[28] "Marling" is another technical sea term for winding a string about a rope, securing each turn with a knot, so that if an area chafes, it will only break that section and not the entire string or rope. The sailors repair and anticipate future threat with an ingenious method of protection in complex knot-tying. The use of "dauby"—a word of Dryden's own invention, meaning "sticky," as in daubed with tar or the like—suggests that the rope or line was daubed, although this would not have been common.[29] Likewise, in the second line the sailors cover their masts with the tar-coated cloth that is tarpaulin, but there is a redundancy here in referring, too, to cerecloth, or wax-covered cloth. Is the cerecloth being coated with tar? Or is the mast being coated with tarpaulin and cerecloth? There is an ambiguity and obliquity to this technical language, even as it seems to announce a kind of unambiguous denotation, an obscurity that, as we shall see, also becomes one of the bases of value and allure for technical maritime language.

Dryden couches this passage within an extended conceit comparing sailors' labors to those of "laboring bees" (574), both naturalizing—part of a creaturely set of activities—but also invoking human artifice in its allusions to Virgil's own comparison of the industrious Carthaginians to bees. Interlacing technical terms with classical allusions, Dryden elevates his technical sea terms, repositioning them not as empirical truth or mere vernacular but as the language of poetry, shot through with allusive and symbolic meaning. When the Duke "furl"s and "strip"s (221) the sails of his ships, the speaker compares the scene to the "Elean plains" (223) of the Olympic games. In Dryden's poem, technical language, then, is associated not with particulars in time and space but with the timelessness of classical writing. In addition, ships and their technical parts seem to have their own otherworldly agency—"Folded sheets dismiss the useless air" (222) and "fin-like oars did spread from side to side" (628), as things become subjects.[30] In mapping classical and Christian images and allusions onto such empowered technical language, Dryden legitimates and elevates its use.

In overlaying the technical with the natural Dryden naturalizes England's naval efforts to secure control of the blue-water empire, but in doing so he must sacrifice any purely empirical sense of this technical language.[31] Thus, despite his paean to the Royal Society in *Annus Mirabilis*, Dryden did not imagine the particular, technical language they advocated as appropriate for poetry on its own terms. His work set a pattern for poetry of the next several decades that included the occasional nautical term while mythicizing British naval efforts, as in Edward Young's later "Imperium Pelagi. A Naval Lyric."[32] Increasingly, however, nautical language emerged in different print contexts, doing a different kind of work. It is in the popular published accounts of voyages that readers would have encountered a technical language stripped of the authorizing discourses of classicism and Christianity.[33]

One example from the most popular of early eighteenth-century voyages, William Dampier's *A New Voyage round the World*, contains such language: "I ... provided for a violent blast of wind by reefing our topsails ... the wind increasing upon it, we presently handed our topsails, furled the mainsail, and went away only with our foresail."[34] Or another, from the oft-reproduced account of Anson's *Voyage round the World*, "the wind blew so fresh that the whole fleet struck their yards and topmasts, to prevent driving ... the *Centurion* drove the next evening and brought both cables a-head."[35] Voyage narratives, in their efforts to render and to make credible their renderings of distant life at sea, stocked their language with such technical terms. They also revalued those technical terms as national and as masculine. Defending his recording of technical details, the author of Anson's *Voyage* depicts the British as behind the curve when it comes to such attention: "It is by a settled attachment to these seemingly minute particulars that our ambitious neighbors have established some part of that power with which we are now struggling."[36] "Attachment" to the technical is a national advantage missing from British writing, he claims, and he decries Britons' common characterization of such details as "effeminate."

Attitudes toward technical maritime language, then, were undergoing a change in the eighteenth century, particularly, as we are about to explore, as it became a means of making the increasing numbers of the remote speakers of this language present. The technical language found in popular print voyage narratives derives in part from the journals and logbooks that formed the basis of those narratives. Journals kept at sea, as Falconer explains in his eighteenth-century *A Universal Dictionary of the Marine*, "contain the state of the weather, the variation ... of the wind, and the suitable shifting, reducing, or enlarging the quantity of sail extended; as also the most material incidents of the voyage, and the condition of the ship and her crew; together with the discovery of other ships or fleets, land, shoals, breakers, soundings, &c."[37] They sometimes followed the stipulations set out by the Royal Society in their "Directions for Sea-Men, Bound for Far Voyages," which specifies the "particulars they desire chiefly to be informed about," including "declination of the compass" and "perpendicular distance between the highest Tide and lowest ebb during the Spring Tides and Neap-Tides," giving license, even authority, to the use of the technical terms that might best provide such information.[38]

The technical language of journals and logbooks, however, signaled more than the accrual of information. For their later readers (all naval logbooks were turned in to the naval office), technical particulars seem to underwrite the reality of the existence of those sailors who disappeared, as it were, for years. A typical logbook entry from 1688, for instance, notes, under "Remarkable Observations and Accidents" for July 4, "We had little wind we let our stream anchor in 50 fathoms Our Cable run out end for end at 9 we way [weighed anchor]" and for July 6, "At 9 we shortened sayles we lye by under our Topsayles wind a gentle gayle."[39] The literally quotidian (daily recorded beginning at noon) and technical details of these accounts were critical for the crew for estimating the ship's location. The technical details of logbooks, however, also call up in later readers' minds the particulars of remote and unseen lives proceeding diurnally. A seemingly insignificant detail—on July 6 there was a gentle "gayle" that was recorded as it happened—becomes the sign of remote life moving apace and faithfully recorded.

Printed accounts of voyages drew directly from such language, bringing a sense of concrete and believable reality to people and enterprises out of sight. Dampier used this aim to defend the technical language in his printed *A New Voyage*: "It has been Objected against me by some, that my Accounts and Descriptions of Things are dry and jejune.... If I have been exactly and strictly careful to give only ... a Plain and just Account of the True nature and State of the Things described than of a polite and Rhetorical narrative: I hope all the defects of my stile will meet with an easy and ready pardon."[40] The "dry and jejune" descriptions helped provide a sense of a transparent, true record of an empirically observed and measured—even as quite distant—world: a formal mechanism that might turn readers of these voyages, as were contemporary readers of experiment descriptions, into Steven Shapin's "virtual witnesses."[41]

Print representations of this technical language, however, create an odd, incomplete world, somewhere between actual and not. Even the most denotative of genres—dictionaries of marine terms—suggest a verbal environment that was a likeness but could never be a complete rendition of shipboard life.[42] The author of the most popular of dictionaries of "marine" terms, Falconer, notes, "To explain the track of every particular rope, through its different channels, would be equally useless and unintelligible to a land reader: to mariners it were superfluous: and even the youths who are trained to the sea would reap little advantage from it; because their situation affords them much better opportunities of making these minute discoveries."[43] The most inexperienced of sea readers would learn this information through work and oral communication on the ship, not needing the dictionary, while the land reader would never fully learn it—it would remain forever obscure. The printed technical language pitched at that reader was only ever an approximation of nautical technology, its very obscurity confirming its status as an essentially oral language and as authentic—a reality effect.

The implications of this view of technical language are most provocatively explored in its migration to fiction. Works such as William Chetwood's fictive "voyages" and the "biography" of the fictional Captain Misson in *A General History of the Pyrates* suggest the ways in which technical language becomes a place marker for the seemingly real but actually notional.[44] Interestingly, in the popular collection of pirate biographies in *A General History*, the narratives regarding pirates who actually existed, such as Captains Avery, Teach (Blackbeard), and Roberts, use far less technical language than that of the fictional Misson.[45] Of the sea battle with Teach, there is little technical description but rather the conventional language of romance and adventure: "they were now closely and warmly engaged . . . till the sea was tinctur'd with Blood round the vessel."[46] It is in the "biography" of a fictional pirate—who supposedly founds the legendary utopian democratic society of pirates on Madagascar—that one finds the most technical language. Among the events in the life of the fictive Misson, the writer describes a chase and encounter at sea: "She [the sloop] went so well to Windward, that she cou'd spare the Ship some Points in her Sheet, and yet wrong her" (396), and describes a battle engagement: "He [Misson] then mann'd his Bolt-sprit, brought his Sprit-Sail-Yard fore and aft and resolved to board" (398). It is especially important here that the particular language of the technical, and not the "universal" language of poetic imagery, is used to create believability and even sympathy for a fictional figure and a speculative world of equitably shared riches for which he advocates.

The armature of technological language becomes especially powerful in Defoe's experiments in fiction in his maritime narratives. His specialist nautical language is among the "vivid details" by which readers attach his characters "much more completely to their environments," a dynamic so crucial to early fiction, as Ian Watt argues.[47] Defoe deploys technical sea language to make present—and present as real—fictional depictions of the distant worlds of maritime life. Early on in *Robinson Crusoe*, the title character describes how "our ship rid Forecastle in, shipp'd several Seas, and we thought once or twice our Anchor had come home; upon which our Master order'd out the Sheet Anchor; so that we rode with two Anchors a-Head, and the cables veered out to the better end" ("better" or "bitter end" here being a technical phrase meaning the final end of the rope to which an anchor is attached).[48] Defoe's technical language makes his representations credible in emphasizing the thingishness of the ship and the specificity of the physical actions of its sailors. Watt surmises, in a formulation especially redolent given the physical distance of the mariner from readers, that in his fiction Defoe intended to "bring his object home to us." To do so he adapted a technical logbook language that had long been aiming to do just that.

We shall explore below how distant particulars might "bring objects home to us" in terms of sentimental feelings, but here it is worth noting that in Defoe's texts the distancing, even alien language of seafaring also raises attention and emotion, associated as it is with scenes of adventure on the high seas. His 1720 character Captain Singleton narrates the capture of a prize ship: "[W]e lay still, till we saw her almost within Gun Shot; when our Fore Mast Geers being stretched fore and aft, we first run up our Yards, and then hauled home the Top-Sail Sheets; the Rope-Yarns that ruled them giving Way of themselves, the Sails were set in a few Minutes; at the same time slipping our cable, we came upon her before she could get under Way upon 'tother Tack."[49] As Cohen has commented, the insertion of technological terms into "narration-description," the weaving of them into novelistic narration, had the effect of "naturaliz[ing] technological language, both humanizing and dramatizing it" (75). Similarly, Chetwood's 1720 *Voyages, . . . of Captain R. Falconer*, also fictional, repeatedly uses technological language in its swashbuckling battle episodes. In one dramatic clash, "we tack'd about, and with our six guns rak'd her fore and aft, but were immediately seconded with a broad side from them . . . they immediately boarded us on our Starboard-Quarter" (10). Through technical details, the scene and action are made present to the reader—both spatially and temporally, with the repeated "immediate"—also endowing the description with interest and emotion. An alien technical jargon becomes the captivating language of suspense and emotional investment.

For Hume, the idea of a "common end" enabled the imagination and its projection of identity. Defoe's *Captain Singleton* and *Robinson Crusoe*, with their improbable rags-to-riches tales, engage romance, that genre that assumes wild stretches of the imagination, as much as they do early realism. Aphra Behn's *Oroonoko* (1688), with all its romance elements, also describes Oroonoko and his comrades rambling "fore and aft" on the ship on which they will soon be enslaved, and their captors "set all Hands to work to hoise [sic] Sail; and with as treacherous and fair a wind, they made from the shore."[50] In Chetwood's *Voyages . . . of Captain Robert Boyle*, which includes, oddly, William Dampier as a character but is composed largely of romance tales, Boyle moves between narrating improbable stories of captive ladies and scheming eunuchs and noting the mundane details routinely cited in logbooks. These awkward mergings of wildly imaginative, emotional tales and specialized descriptions of conditions and labor aboard the ship might suggest one early means by which the technical language of sailors came to mean more than merely empirical description or reality effect, even if not loaded with the symbolic value of Dryden's language. They became a basis for readerly attachment. That sense of attachment, as we saw in Defoe, was crucial in enabling British readers to imagine a particular language as their own.

Sometimes the presentation of obscure technical language made for such attachment through the technique of display and assimiliation, as in the early fiction discussed in Chapter Two. Defoe's narratives of nautical adventures, too, position as unfamiliar and then translate sea language for English readers. "We saw plainly she trusted to her Heels, that is to say" Captain Singleton explains, "to her Sails" (147). While, as Paul Gilje notes, eighteenth-century readers might have been more familiar with technical sea terms than are twenty-first-century readers, Defoe here, nonetheless, marks that language as separate with his "that is to say" translation.[51] These are stories of outsiders who are, nonetheless, being made English both familiarly (the far-roving Singleton and his English friend William finally settle in London) and unfamiliarly (the settled pair dress in an extravagant combination of Armenian and Persian costume and speak a mix of those langauges!). Even the modes of publication suggest a vernacularization of this maritime language. Like those textual representations of odd provincial-language speakers who are also positioned as strangers/familiars, Singleton's saga was serialized by Andrew Brice, who had also published *An Exmoor Scolding*, in *The Post-Master or Loyal Mercury*. Brice's newspaper, then, helped usher into popular print not only provincialisms such as "paddick" and "crewnting" but also maritime jargon such as "Larboard Tacks" and "Rope-Yarns."[52]

Chetwood intersperses his fiction, too, with such presentations and translations of the peculiar language of sailors. Captain Falconer explains, "when we hog'd our ship (a Hog is an instrument of six feet square, something like a harrow, and stumps of old brooms fixed close in he middle part) this is put to the bottom of the ship with a rope before and aft . . . that cleans the vessel" (35). He refers to "booms" and then elucidates "(that is, spare masts that lie along from quarter to forecastle)" (78). Captain Boyle confesses, when realizing a prize has less cargo than he had hoped, "I began to fancy we should have but dry meat (as the sailors say)" (155). Like *Moll Flanders* and *Colonel Jack*, these texts display technical and specialized terms, but familiarize them for English readers. Their narrators too, like Defoe's Moll and Jack, sidle in and out of identification with those maritime speakers, using "we" and "they" in a fluctuating subject position that readers are invited to adopt.

Perhaps the best-known British naval novel of the eighteenth century, *Roderick Random*, also moves between estrangement and familiarity. Roderick's introduction to ship life stages the separation of existence on the sea from that on land: "I was . . . carried on board a pressing tender . . . [and] thrust down into the hold . . . I desired one of my fellow-captives . . . to take a handkerchief out of my pocket and tie it round my [bleeding] head. He . . . went to the grating of the hatchway, and with astonishing composure sold it to a bum-boat woman*"—a term that gets a rare footnote in the volume, explaining to readers that "*a bum-boat woman is one who sells bread, cheese, greens, liquor, and fresh provisions to the sailors, in a small boat that lies along-side of the ship."[53] Roderick's—and readers'—distance from the naval world into which he is pressed is marked through both spatial divides— "holds" and "gratings"—and linguistic difference, with terms such as "pressing tender" and "bum-boat woman." Roderick masters this and other sea language and comes to explain it to his readers, for example: "the cock-pit . . . is the place allotted for the habitation of the surgeon's mates" (143). He registers that maritime language as someone else's when he states, "he had shewn me their birth (as he called it)" (143), yet he himself comes to use this language, too. In a back-and-forth movement between strange and familiar, sailors are made present through representations of their peculiar and often technical language, even as their speech is also a reminder of their distance from the landbound.

"Different Languidge and Strange Expreshons of Tonge": The Strangeness of Nautical Language

This language, even as it makes remote characters and scenes credible and is embedded in narrative moments of excitement, bringing sailors and their actions home, as it were, is also estranging, continuously reminding readers of the distance and difference of these worlds. When Captain Singleton explains that "we had, with a kind of a Land Breeze, stretched over about 15 or 20 leagues ... just enough to lose our selves, we found the Wind set in a steady fresh Gale ... at West W.S.W. or S.W. by W." (36), the reader attaches him to a seemingly real environment. But it is a distant one, not simply because he is at sea but also because he speaks in a lingo uncommon among readers on land. Such distance, Defoe argued, might be crucial for enticing readers and even, counterintuitively, "touch[ing] the mind" of readers; he wrote of his other seafaring hero, Robinson Crusoe that "had I given you the conduct or Life of a Man you knew ... all I could have said would have yielded no Diversion, and perhaps scarce have obtained a reading, or at best no attention; ... Facts that are form'd to touch the Mind, must be done a great Way off."[54] As with other strange vernaculars, the texts of technical sea language oscillate between alien and oddly familiar, touching in their distance.

Those strange particulars were not, of course, always deemed worthy or touching. For some writers, particulars and the technical language that named them divided people, particularly when related to labor. For Elizabethan writer Thomas Dekker, discussed in Chapter One, for instance, the particular languages of physical labor figured a pernicious post-Babel incomprehensibility. He describes the tumultuous chaos of Babel's fall in terms of the linguistic misunderstanding between specific trades: "the Mason was ready to strike the bricklayer, the bricklayer to beate out the braines of his Labourer: the Carpenter took up his Axe to throw at the Carver."[55] For Dekker, to speak the technical language of labor was to evoke malign distance, potentially setting individuals at odds rather than bringing them closer.

Later, Samuel Johnson, famous for the demanding intellectual labor spent on his *Dictionary*, could not see the value of the physical labor—the trudging and courting—and the animosity he believed inevitable in finding and learning the meaning of the "living information" in the technical language of particular lines of work, "navigation" included. In his Preface, he describes how, when compiling his *Dictionary*, "I could not visit caverns to learn the miner's language, nor take a voyage to perfect my skill in the dialect of navigation ... to gain the names of wares, tools and operations, of which no mention is found in books; ... it had been a hopeless labour to glean up words, by courting living information, and contesting with the sullenness of one, and the roughness of another."[56] Johnson refused the labor—and anticipated hostility—of "gleaning" words, the act of gleaning itself a culling of relatively worthless leavings. He imagined himself alternately "courting" and "contesting" with "sullenness" and "roughness," as the lexicographer necessarily encounters surly laborers too deeply implanted in their own particular worlds to give others the time of day. Prohibitively arcane, its speakers only roused to truculence when asked to reckon them, technical languages of labor, including navigation, are and should remain obscure, forever relegated to inaccessible spaces such as dark caverns and forbidding oceans, worlds of spoken words outside of books. Readers of the *Dictionary*, in fact, will find several terms from "the dialect of navigation," including "rig," "block," "pendant," "tackling," "mizzen," "poop," "topmast," and "braces," yet the Preface casts those technical words into a kind of linguistic oblivion, for such words must be, as he puts it, "suffered to perish."[57] If that oblivion produces sublime effects for some, whether in the oblivion of the sailors' language, as we shall see below, or, as we saw in Chapter Seven, the perishing language of the vulgar rustic, it did not for Johnson.

Thus, even as technical maritime jargon seemed to promise a more accurate and sometimes-elevated account of remote life at sea, a fair number of writers were dismissive of this language and such claims. Jonathan Swift's satire is perhaps the most notorious. His *Gulliver's Travels* takes a jab at Dampier and technical sea language more generally. For sailors such as Dampier, of humble origins and a buccaneering background, conforming to the protocols of the Royal Society, using technical language, would have been part of a bid for credibility and legitimacy. This was true not only for their accounts but for themselves, positioning them as contributing scientific knowledge to the public good.[58] Dampier himself appealed to the Royal Society in the prefatory material to his *New Voyage*.[59] Winning their approval, he was brought to the attention of the naval administration and made captain of a ship. The state also funded a handsome quarto volume of his account of his voyages. Technical language, and its corroboration of a scientific emphasis on the empirical, could pay handsome dividends.[60]

Swift was skeptical. Gulliver refers to Dampier as his "cousin" and attacks him for not, in fact, writing his own book, but hiring a scholar to do so, thereby exposing the connection of technical writing and eyewitness account as something of a subterfuge.[61] Even a sailor writing his own account in his own language, however, would be no better. *Gulliver's Travels* opens with the "publisher" explaining his omission of the "the style of sailors":

> This volume would have been at least twice as large, if I had not made bold to strike out innumerable passages relating to the winds and tides, as well as to the variations and bearings in the several voyages, together

with the minute descriptions of the management of the ship in storms, in the style of sailors; . . . Mr. Gulliver may be a little dissatisfied. But I was resolved to fit the work as much as possible to the general capacity of readers. (30–31)

Such complaints about the limited appeal of the "style of sailors" were still being registered midcentury, as the author of *A Compendium of Authentic and Entertaining Voyages*, published anonymously, but likely by Smollett, complained of works "so stuffed with dry descriptions of bearings and . . . variations of the compass, leeway, wind, and weather, sounding, anchoring and other terms of navigation, that none but meer pilots, or seafaring people, can read them without disgust. Our aim has been to clear away this kind of rubbish."[62] Such complaints corroborated the argument, reiterated from Dekker to Johnson, that the "style" of particular laborers, namely their technical language, was inhospitable to the "general capacity of readers." Particular and opaque, these languages were suspect, reminding Britons of the strangers and strange languages in their midst, including common laborers and their jargons.

Of course, despite the publisher's claims, technical sea language does make its way into *Gulliver's Travels*. Yet as it does, the text dispenses with the notion that this language might represent the lexicon of a "common end" in its stability. Gulliver critiques the notion that mariners' jargon is unchanging, not subject to the whims and fashions of language, complaining:

I hear some of our sea *Yahoos* find fault with my sea-language, as not proper in many parts, nor now in use. I cannot help it. In my first voyages, while I was young, I was instructed by the oldest mariners, and learned to speak as they did. But I have since found that the sea *Yahoos* are apt, like the land ones, to become new-fangled in their words, which the latter change every year; insomuch, as I remember upon each return to my own country their old dialect was so altered, that I could hardly understand the new. (30)

Bowsprits, it turns out, had been called something different in the past, and might be called something different in the future.

If Gulliver can hardly understand the new "sea-language," readers are equally challenged by his own. He describes how

the sail was split, and we hauled down the yard, and got the sail into the ship, and unbound all the things clear of it. . . . We hauled off upon the laniard of the whip-staff, and helped the man at the helm. . . . we knew that the top-mast being aloft, the ship was the wholesomer, and made better way through the sea, seeing we had sea-room. When the storm was over, we set foresail and main-sail, and brought the ship to. Then we set the mizen, main-top-sail, and the fore-top-sail. Our course was east-north-east, the wind was at south-west. We got the starboard tacks aboard, we cast off our weather-braces and lifts; we set in the lee-braces, and hauled forward by the weather-bowlings, and hauled them tight, and belayed them, and hauled over the mizen tack to windward, and kept her full and by as near as she would lie. (92)

The very length of this technical passage (this is only a representative section) overloads the realism so that any sense of clarity or of proximity to what actually happened collapses in on itself. As well, the excess undoes readers' sense of closeness to the remote mariner, especially when terms meant to indicate particular location and movement—terms that should orient readers to the space of the ship and the mariner's location ("weather" and "lee" indicate the side encountering and away from the wind, respectively)—are difficult to parse. It is not quite clear why Gulliver uses both directional terms, the "weather" side and "starboard," one from the outside perspective, and one from the inside, respectively. It seemed nonsensical even to later nautical writers, but, as a later reviewer pointed out it, the passage had been lifted, pretty much word for word, from a seventeenth-century book entitled *Compleat Mariner*.[63] For Swift, mariners' technical language served to disorient rather than orient the reader, widening the gap between sailor and reader rather than closing it.

Like Fielding, Swift remained dubious of the claim that particular languages might be folded into a unifying vernacular, their opacity familiarized. He offers no explanation of his technical language, and he also positions the mariner who uses such terms as oblivious to just how clotted and confusing they would be for the nonspecialist. Gulliver's lack of self-awareness and his distance from every community he encounters are continuous elements of his character, but it is important for our analysis to note that those qualities are emphasized early on through his use of technical maritime language. The same qualities of technicality and opacity that for other writers made this jargon available for incorporation into the vernacular repulsed readerly sympathies in Swift.

Other writers, however, made the comic quality of maritime language the means of making it familiar and vernacular. Ned Ward's "journalistic" accounts of mariners in his *The Wooden World Dissected* also humorously focus on the technical language of seafaring, positioning it as outlandish, "all Heathen Greek to a cobbler" (35), his narrator claims. Ward was to become, as we have seen, a bestselling author of works depicting low languages of London—of taverns, of fish markets—bringing them into the vernacular, but only once they were positioned as strange and curious, almost foreign, the languages of outsiders within, as it were. Crucially, a similar dynamic emerged first in his representations of the maritime world. In his popular *A Trip to Jamaica* of 1699, a description of his brief emigration, he focuses on the foreignness not of the language of Jamaica but on that of the ship that carried him, writing: "As soon as we had *weigh'd Anchor*, under the doleful Cry and hard service of *Haul Cat haul*, there was nothing heard till we reach'd the Downs, but *About ship my Lads, bring your Fore Tack on board, haul Fore-Sail haul, Brace about the Main Yard*, That I was more amaz'd than a mouse at a Threshers Mill."[64] So different as to "amaze" with its outsized power and opacity, technical sea language vaguely and briefly produces sublime effects, but Ward's comparison of the listener to a mouse positions those effects as humorous too.

As Ward characterizes sailors and their difference from those on land, their narrow focus on their technical world, as reflected in their oral language (indicated through italics), makes them unable to transcend the physical, and their limiting embodiment is often the basis of the humor. Ward writes of the sailor, "he has seen in his days more than enough to have made any thinking creature wise; but his poor composition of beef and oatmeal views all things as sheep do stars—without any afterthought or reflection" (105). Such images of the carnality of the sailor extend at least as far back as Wycherley's *Plain Dealer*. Olivia, who jilts Captain Manly, complains he makes her "Alcove smell like a Cabin, my Chamber perfum'd with his Tarpaulin Brandenburgh, and ... vollies of Brandy sighs, enough to make a Fog in ones Room" (26). From such seventeenth-century representations to the "Japanned" trousers of Smollett's Tom Bowling, forever tarred with the stuff of his maritime labor, to Fielding's image of the "brutal roughness of the English Tar" and to the "bloated" purser and lieutenant of marines and the "hardened hand" of the captain in John Davis's *The Post-Captain*, print depictions of nautical language speakers, like those of cant, slang, and provincial-language speakers, make them out to be egregiously corporeal.[65] At times their names turn mariners into the very things of the ship, such as "Bowling" in *Roderick Random*, or "Mr. Gallipot," the ship's doctor in *The Post-Captain*.

Their vision limited to the sheerly technical world of the physical space of the ship, seafarers' own physicality was also, of course, depicted as notoriously crude. Authors presented the language of their naval characters as coarse dialect, marked by physicality. They peppered the speech of their naval characters with blasphemous curses such as "D—n my eyes."[66] In Ward's *Trip*, even the higher-ups, such as the lieutenants, "engage in unmanly billingsgate clashing" (27). Mariners' unavoidable embodiment even corrupts their English. Ward reports,

> I happen'd one Morning to hear two *Tar-Jackets* in a very high dispute; I went to them, and ask'd the reason of their Difference. Why Sir, says one, I'll tell you, there was my Master Whistlebooby, an old Boatswain in one of his Majesties Ships, who was *Superhanded*, and past his labour, and the *Ambaralatie* Divorc'd him from his Ship, and the King

allow'd him a *Suspension*, and this lubberly Whelp here says I talk like a Fool, and sure I have not used the Sea this Thirty Years, but I can *Argufie* any thing as proper as he can," resembling the obscure language of technical jibberish. (11)

Ward satirically relegates the "strange" language of those whose language does not obey the laws of standard English to outsiders, to sailors. But as the improprieties of Jack Cremer's own description of maritime language upon his initial encounter with it—"Different languidge and strange expreshons of tonge"—makes clear, one need not be a mariner to speak the strange expressions of incorrect English. Like cant-speakers and provincials, mariners become another site on which to project what was the strange and fractious language of most English-speakers.

Such particular language, the language of the reprehensibly embodied, equated with the substandard and error-ridden, disqualified sailors from the general rational discourse demanded by the public sphere. Texts that aimed to participate in public sphere debate, even when written from the point of view of the working sailor, advocating reforms to, say, the distribution of provisions, as in the *Remarks on the present condition of the navy, and particularly of the victuals*, use an unmarked "general" language: "[T]he abuses of the sailors . . . have been of too long a continuance to be born without resentment."[67] This political tract's conformity to standard English underscores the departicularized, "disembodied" position required of legitimate participants in the public sphere.

Contrast this to the "noise" of mariners' language in popular printed texts.[68] The narrator of Samuel Foote's *A Trip to Calais* humorously describes how "silence was savagely bawled out by the captain" (18). Indeed, distinct sound, not only in loudness but in a particular maritime dialect, was likely a fact onboard ships. In groundbreaking work, William Matthews traced distinct pronunciations in the "phonetic spellings" found in ships' logs of the late seventeenth century.[69] In the logbook of the *Royal William*'s Commander Cranby, one finds such spellings as "frash" for "fresh," "moch" for "much," "croned" for "crowned," and "thare" for "there."[70] While this manuscript evidence of a distinct mariners' dialect is fascinating, suggestive of alternative if ephemeral languages communities, it is less the actual sounds of their language and more a general sense of sounded strangeness that print representations of mariners' language convey. Like the absence of their cosmopolitan mix of languages, the invisibility of mariners' distinct pronunciations (pronunciations perhaps related to that mix) suggests that the vernacularization of sailors' language depended upon reducing it—its sounds, its physicality—to the technical.

The very popular early nineteenth-century novel *The Post-Captain* depicts the odd-sounding technical language of the ship, when the tellingly named midshipman, Mr. Echo, "vociferate[s] for several minutes . . . : 'Boatswain's mate! Boatswain's mate! I say, you boatswain's mate! Send the afterguard aft here to the main-topsail-haliards. Corporal of marines! Send the marines aft on the quarter-deck, to clap on the main-topsail-haliards. . . . doctor's mates and loblolly-boys! After-guard! I don't see the after-guard coming aft!'" (11). Repeated phrases and exclamation points, jargon and recurring sounds with different meanings (After-guard, aft), directly counter language that was believed to function as a transparent medium of rational thought but also emphasize the distinct sound of mariners' language as the product of their technical jargon. What is more, a "speaking trumpet" is used to amplify these sounds: Brilliant shouts through one, "Hoay! The ship a-hoy! . . . Square away the yards here! Haul the mainsail up!" (19). One character describes how Captain Hurricane, whose name, like Echo's, suggests sound and air, "roars so through his trumpet, that he would deafen a ballad-singer," and how another is so loud he sounds as if "has got a top-chain down his throat" (61), technical terms mingling with the thingishness of the throat and its noise, the illicit voice of the ballad singer situated alongside that of the roaring mariner. These comic representations of sailors' language, then, like depictions of other "strange vernaculars," position their speakers outside a rational public sphere, on the basis of a particularly defined embodied (oral) status.

Comic representations of the language of sailors, becoming more widespread, reinforced this image of seamen and their language as embodied and constrained, mired in a world of technical particulars they were unable to transcend. It is on these comic terms that mariners' language is also represented as part of the English vernacular. In works such as *A Trip to Calais*, snippets of conventionalized sea lingo such as "brought to with our kedge anchor; light airs and lightening. Here the captain went on shore for a second jib" appear alongside songs and jokes, part of a repertoire of comic set-pieces available for popular textual consumption (11) and positioned as vernacular. Such works situated sailors' language as lowbrow humor. The unseemly slapstick pranks of Captain Mirvan of Frances Burney's *Evelina* match the rotten English of this seaman, as chauvinistic as it is incorrect. He taunts the French Madame Duval: "that's *Monsieur Slippery*, I'n't it?—Why he's plaguy fond of sousing work; howsomever, I'll be sworn they gave him his fill of it."[71] By the time *Evelina* appeared in 1778, comic sea language was so familiar that Burney did not even need to represent it—the title character reports that Mirvan's substandard language "was interlarded with many sea-phrases, that I cannot recollect . . . he makes use of a thousand sea-terms, which are to me quite unintelligible" (181).

Part of the humor of these representations is the sense of confinement to technical language, a restriction so binding that it produces the additional comic effect of mariners needing to use technical terms to name things outside of their maritime world. In *The Wooden World Dissected*, for instance, Ward describes a sailor who "cannot have so much as a tooth drawn ashore, without carrying his interpreters. It's the aftmost grinder aloft, on the Starboard quarter, will he cry to the all wondering operator" (48), giving a sense that the sailor cannot imagine anything beyond his technical shipbound experiences or use any but the technical language that names them. Seamen, limited to the technical terms of shipboard life, must use literal, technical language as figures to describe their experiences in a larger world. The move from literal to figural was, according to some language theorists of the time, such as Adam Smith, the trajectory of language development itself—the first particular tree encountered and called "tree" comes to figure for all trees.[72] It is also, often, the trajectory of words and expressions comprising the vernacular. Words such as "fathom" or "log" migrate from the technical and thingish to the metaphorical—an actual wooden log, thrown over the ship's rail and used to measure speed, came to name the logbook and then the verb, "to log." "To the bitter end" and "dead reckoning" moved beyond technical ship's parts or activities to metaphorical, colloquial expressions. Print representations of sailors' language displaced this propensity to figuration, central to the workings of language, to the limitations of the sailor and his resultingly ludicrous language. The wild wandering of their language to figural uses is, in these representations, short-circuited by attributing it to the shortsightedness of the sailor.

The comic character of such language, however, is part of its charm, and readers' recognition of the meaning "aftmost grinder aloft" is part of the delight of reading this initially puzzling language. And as in representations of cant, it is not only through reading footnotes, dictionary entries, or narrative explanations that readers make this language their own but also through the challenge of solving this riddlelike figurative language. Wisecracks using technical terms as vehicles, like technological language itself, divide sailors from others, as seen in *Roderick Random* when Roderick makes his first appearance aboard their ship. One sailor "observing my wounds, which still remained exposed to the air, told me, my seams were uncaulked, and that I must be new payed.... A fourth asked me, if I could not keep my yards square without iron braces?" (143). While "insiders," the experienced tars, taunt the initiate, readers, when they understand the jokes, become insiders of a sort too, the sailors' figurative language becoming their own.[73]

It is through print representations of specialized maritime language, a "ship idiom" (112), as John Davis calls it in *The Post-Captain*, that seafarers are separated from but also brought home to English readers. Consider the narrative dynamics in this novel, when Cassandra, the captain's fiancée, is preparing to leave the ship and the captain offers "to get the whip ready for you." She responds, "surely you are not a Russian. What have I done to deserve the whip?" (51). At this the captain "laughed heartily," because, as a footnote explains, "Ladies are hoisted on board in a chair, fastened to a rope on the topsail-yard; which is called whip" (51). The reader begins in the place of Cassandra, wondering at the term, but, unlike the lady, is brought into the joke through editorial explanation. Like print depictions of underworlds on British land from Ward to Grose, and glossaries of odd provincial terms, representations of seafaring lingo could be captivating, generating curiosity, and sometimes humorous in their difference from general English, a site of some bewilderment but also of gradual textual familiarization. Like the later eighteenth-century depictions of "vulgar" language, such representations of mariners' language underwrite a sense of male homosocial bond.

As with other representations of figurative maritime language, readers are invited into this small, particular world through the logic of the riddle. Smollett's Tom Bowling's colorful language becomes the reader's own when he or she figures out additional meanings, as Bowling, like Ward's sailors, metaphorizes technical sea language to describe any and all experiences. When Roderick's malicious cousin's dogs attack him, Bowling indignantly observes that they attempted to "board me without provocation," and he declares to that threatening cousin, "lookee, ... if you come athwart me, [be]'ware your gingerbread-work [literally the gilded, painted carvings of a ship's stern]—I'll be foul of your quarter, damn me" (9), meaning something like "I'll be entangled with the back of your ship—or backside." When the reader solves the riddle, the language becomes a mark of linguistic camaraderie. Elizabeth DeLoughrey has argued that "the perpetual circulation of the ocean dissolved local phenomenology," but in these print encounters, maritime language, especially its figurative use, strangely recuperates a different kind of local phenomenology between those represented on ship and those readers who are in on the meaning of these terms.[74] Sometimes this is pointedly national. In the song "Jolly Jack Tar," a drunken English sailor stealing his French neighbors' dinner in a tavern is said to have "grappled the pudding, then boarded the beef"—"grapple," meaning to use a spiked anchor to dig into an enemy's ship; "board" meaning an unlawful entry onto a ship.[75] Readers imagine continuity and identity here, not through the shared endeavor of sailing but through the common end of recognizing comic meaning.

Sea Wit, Sailors, and British Freedom

While print works characterized many sailors as too narrow in their vision to move beyond technical language, they also sometimes depict them as creatively opening up seafaring language in their move from the literal to figural, resembling cant and slang speakers, who, at least in print representations, irreverently invented their own terms and witticisms. Their shipboard life, with its own distinct customs, also deployed figurative language to name them, as in "sea baptism," the phrase naming the ducking of sailors at the equator.[76] In Defoe's invocations, sea language even overlaps with the cant found in his criminal novels. His Singleton explains how from one prize "we borrowed about 20 pipes of the wine," while a prize taken with hostility is a "purchase" (15). "Borrow" and "purchase" are also used by Colonel Jack and Moll to describe their thievery. These are the terms of a pirate, but Grose lists an assortment of more general "sea wit" in his *Classical Dictionary*, as in

> BEARINGS, I'll bring him to his bearings, I'll bring him to reason. (*Sea Term*)
> BECALM'D, a piece of sea wit sported in hot weather, I am becalm'd, the sail sticks to the mast, that is my shirt sticks to my back.
> BOGY, ask bogy, i.e. ask mine a—se, (*sea wit*)
> BOWSPRIT, the nose, from its being the most projecting part of the human face, as the bowsprit is of a ship.[77]

Here, mariners' terms such as "bogy" remind us of the often-bawdy character of sea wit, a hint of the "abusive and reviling Language ... the most bitter and profane oaths and execrable curses" they directed even at their officers, according to one contemporary.[78] Fielding writes that sailors "see more of the world, and have ... a more erudite education, than is the portion of land-men of their degree," and yet they "seem to glory in the language and behavior of savages."[79] This attitude corroborates Rediker's argument that such language was "transgressive," expressing "opposition to the 'polite' ... elements of society."[80] An insolent language some readers might relish, it veers, in Fielding's "savage," toward the otherness that always threatened in maritime travel and those engaged in it.

In including these terms amongst his taxonomy of the "vulgar tongue," Grose presents mariners' jargon, like cant and slang, as a language defiantly wandering from initial and conventional meaning. Its innovations might also resemble the linguistic freedom he associated with cant and vulgar language. Cataloguing sea wit with the terms that demonstrated, as Grose had put it, "the freedom of thought and speech, arising from, and privileged by our constitution" invites readers to view it, too, as a cheeky sign of British freedom.[81] That link to a rhetoric of a specifically British liberty, however tenuous, might be necessary in the face of a seaborne life that, as we have seen, challenged the national rubric altogether. Sailors' language, exhibiting "neither elegance of diction nor purity of style," such rhetoric suggested, was also free of the restrictive laws of standard English.[82]

While the idea of freedom informed narratives about the Britishness of cant and provincial languages, helping to vernacularize those languages, the freedom of mariners' figurative language and supposedly untethered persons, however, instead posed a challenge to national boundaries. For sailors, despite characterizations of their narrow confinement and the rigid hierarchies of the ship, could also be said to enjoy freedoms that rendered any national affiliations relatively unimportant. Despite Johnson's famous retort regarding the dangerously imprisoned position of the sailor—"No man will be a sailor who has contrivance enough to get himself into jail; for being in a ship is being in a jail, with the chance of being drowned"—from another angle, linguistically and materially, sailors might be seen as threateningly free.[83] Able to travel far and wide on the high seas, they were free even to, in Fielding's words, "think themselves entirely discharged from the common bands of humanity."[84]

One popular song of the day made the well-worn assertion that the tar was "ranked 'mongst the free list of rovers."[85] Pirates, of course, represented the apex of such an existence, stateless and therefore unbounded by any state's law, and this was part of their popular appeal. Like the wandering canters discussed in Chapter One, pirates are "adrift" (3), as *General History of the Pirates* puts it, "straggling and begging" (4), and "hav[ing] the same sagacity with Robbers at Land" (5). Sailors could, at times, bear an uncanny resemblance to pirates in their homelessness, and to vagrants more generally. Indeed, demobbed sailors might often be one and the same as those dismissed and recuperated itinerants represented as speaking cant, pressing the point once again regarding the vagrant's status, as they wavered between criminal or common, stranger or not.

If sailors became as strange and threatening as unbounded pirates, they recuperated notions of a specifically British freedom when they appeared as vagrants on home soil. Chetwood's Captain Falconer encounters in Britain a begging sailor who asserts the common refrain that "every place is home to me. A sailor is never out of his way" (145). It is crucial that this indigent sailor make the claim for a home "every place" as a vagrant on British roads—for that is one way of reclaiming him as British. Tying his uninhibited mobility to the freedom to roam the countryside (despite the fact that vagrants were routinely pressed into naval service, and sailors lived under a punishing hierarchy aboard ship) taps into the claims forwarded by Locke and others, discussed in Chapter Two, that to wander British roads was to claim the status of a British subject and to enjoy a kind of national liberty. Chetwood's one-time sailor who now haunts the roads of Britain is also a figure licensed to wander. He enjoys a freedom of movement that supposedly distinguished Britons from as early as the Anglo-Saxon days. The figure appears in a more elevated literary register in Coleridge's *Rime of the Ancient Mariner*, the itinerant mariner speaking both an ancient-looking (and sounding) reprise of Anglo-Saxon and a technical nautical language. This one-time sailor wandering Britain is not surprising—many a seaman, after all, was a one-time provincial who chose or was pressed into maritime service. Coleridge's ancient mariner, however, at once wandering beggar, anachronistic provincial, and jargon-speaking seaman, pushes those intermingling obscurities toward dizzying gothic implications. And, of course, the ancient mariner's freedom is compromised. He recounts "agony" that both "left me free" and "forc'd me to begin my tale" (626–28).

Eighteenth-century writing, alternatively, pursued the relation between freedom and sea language to make contemporary mariners' jargon part of an English vernacular despite its users' traveling bodies and wandering figurative language. In some maritime writing, as in some early criminal fiction, contrasting this language with that of slaves helped shore up the sense of mariners and their language as British. Freedom and slavery emerge as frequent motifs in eighteenth-century maritime narratives, their English protagonists often oscillating between the two. Captain Avery of *King of the Pyrates*, Defoe's Robinson Crusoe and Captain Singleton, Chetwood's Captain Falconer, and Smollett's Roderick Random are all haunted by the fear of enslavement and find themselves captive at some point. In voyage narratives early in the century, "European liberty is tenuous," as Shrividhya Swaminathan puts it.[86] We have seen the recurring appeal to the supposedly unique liberty of the British in the innovations of cant and slang and the originary "before the Norman yoke" status attributed to provincial languages. The freedom of British mariners, too, was associated with their Britishness. As Swaminathan notes, "Singleton's 'manumission' could only take place through a reclaiming of English identity," and, as we shall see, his technical language.[87]

If voyage narratives represent mariners' relation to freedom as unstable—the free Briton always in danger of becoming an enslaved captive—the enslaved Briton is also always potentially a future slave-owner. A good number of once-enslaved mariner protagonists go on to this status. Their freedom, or the successful property ownership that will make them free political subjects, as in the case of Roderick Random, often depends on the possession of slaves. But what interests us here is how representations of maritime language parallel the articulation of British freedom in relation to the figure of the enslaved. Specifically, in some texts mariners' language is familiarized, we might say vernacularized, and redeemed in contrast to the imputed language of slaves. Defoe's and Chetwood's narratives, for instance, distinguish mariners from "natives" of Africa who, like mariners, traffic in figurative language, but who can, it seems, speak *only* in figures that remain irredeemably childish, based not on technical references but on a primitive understanding of the world. In *Captain Singleton*, for instance, the Africans Singleton enslaves use the phrase "where the sun sleeps" to mean "where the sun sets" (48). As well, Robinson Crusoe cannot initially comprehend the figurative language of Friday, who uses "two canoe" to mean "a great large boat as big as two canoes" (156).

Alternatively, as we have seen, the figurative language of sailors is often predicated on the technical world of the ship. In the relationship of the African and Indian languages to that of mariners we find one of many moments of "a glorification of European technology" that was part of colonial discourse in the early eighteenth century.[88] The figurative language of the sailor no longer looks quite so preposterous when the figurative language of the Africans and Indians depicts them as misapprehending the world entirely, their lack of knowledge about its workings in direct contrast to the mastery of the sailor over, at least, his technologically complex ship-bound world. Friday's language—"in the place where me was" (154)—and the English of "our negroes" in *Captain Singleton*—"much Lion, much spotted Cat (so they called the Leopard)" (78)—in their ungrammaticality resemble that of the North American slaves with their "muchee sorry" in *Colonel Jack*, as discussed in Chapter Two. The language of Defoe's African slaves helped make cant and slang, by contrast, part of an English vernacular. So too the language of Africans and Indians that seamen encountered helped to make the language of mariners part of a vernacular English. Thus, while some works represented sailors' views and vocabulary as limited, their figurative language evidence of their inability to see or think beyond the maritime, they are distinguished in these works of fiction from the more egregiously naïve and misspoken worldview and language of Africans and Indians. If the idea of a "common end" promotes the illusion of identity, so too, of course, does the notion of a linguistic "other."

As we have seen, texts often represent sea language as using the technical in puzzlingly figurative expression, positioning mariners as insular and minimizing the extent and meaning of their global movement. In some texts, however, their technical language also becomes specifically British and even representative of British freedom. It was for some writers, after all, the very technology of maritime travel that distinguished Britons from "the brutal kind" and even their former "savage" selves. As Henry Needler had written in "A Sea Piece," "The British race, 'till by the *Romans* led / They first the flutt'ring Canvas learn'd to spread, . . . / Differ'd but little from the Brutal Kind; / Uncultivated, ignorant, and rude, . . . / never durst a thought to entertain, / Of vent'ring on the Surface of the Main."[89] Here, maritime technology becomes the basis of British superiority.[90] In Thomson's famous formulation, "ruling the waves," not just commanding them but measuring and compassing them, ensured that Britons "never will be slaves."[91]

Olaudah Equiano repeatedly equated technical nautical language with Englishness, English superiority, and liberty itself.[92] And it was through that language, in part, that he affiliated with the English. In his *Interesting Narrative*, Equiano's technical language allows a kind of retroactive mastery over his most harrowing and subject scenarios. Early in his narrative, having recounted his kidnapping and forced movement toward the coast as a child, he describes his first view of a slave ship. He notes it was "riding at anchor," his use of technical language a means of detaching his former captive child self from his narrating liberated self in the present, a division more forcefully evident when he describes how on the ship he refused to eat, and "one of them [white men] held me fast by the hands, and laid me across I think the windlass, and tied my feet, while the other flogged me severely."[93] When recounting another flogging he received as a child on the ship he manages to note "a large rope near the foremast" (40). Equiano's triumph over that formerly enslaved and traumatized status is articulated through his technical knowledge and language.

Describing his first days as a captive aboard a slave ship, Equiano also contrasts his early childish language, deploying the conventional representations of African and slave speech, with the technical jargon of the sailor. He reproduces his naïve dialogue, but this language differs from the technical terms he intersperses within the same scene: "nettings" (39), "quartered" (40), "came to an anchor" (40). His young self thinks the vessel stops by "spell or magic," while the narrating self of the present states, "we soon anchored" (42). Equiano learns the workings of the ship that had been hidden from him by his initial captors and masters the technological language that names and facilitates those workings, which offer a freedom from being "one who was ignorant, a stranger" (46). To make himself less a stranger, more an Englishman, he uses the technical terms of seamen. Equiano, a self-described "stranger," is more shape-shifter than any Defoe protagonist—horn player, servant, hairdresser, naval worker, slave manager, clerk, merchant, parson, abolitionist. As well, he repeatedly reminds his readers that, despite the legal status as freeman that he earns, an increasingly racialized institution of slavery distinguishes his marked body, forever threatening to enslave him all over again. Despite that fluid and racialized identity, however, one of the ways in which he makes himself free—and familiar to his readers—is through that technical language of a "common end," that strange argot that was becoming a recognizable element of English vernacular.

"Our Tars" and Distant Sentiments

Equiano's use of technical language to make common cause with his English readers diverges from those representations of technical sea language as isolating and comic. Greg Dening argues, "The precise, terse, unequivocal language by which seamen controlled their 'wooden world' was thought to be incongruous and laughable on land" and that "sailors were managed in their distinctiveness by a satirical tolerance of their language."[94] While we have certainly seen this satire at work, some of the dynamics that make for a sense of the comic in this language—the small wooden world to which it confined seamen, its figurative and literal distance, a resulting obscurity—are also the means by which it elicits sentiment and even enables sympathetic relations between readers and sailors. In this penultimate section of the chapter we shall consider how that strange, technical language became familiar enough to signal an English vernacular, in part as its obscurity came to elicit sentiment for the common people who spoke it.

Consider the case of Tom Bowling. *Roderick Random* begins its representations of nautical language not with the technical denotative language that Roderick encounters and explains when he is pressed into service much later in the book, but through the amusingly figurative speech of Roderick's stout Uncle Tom, a mariner. Bowling is a sentimental character whose very name draws from that technical language of the ship—either "a ship 'bowling along,' or a rope used to keep the sail taut and steady."[95] It also functions on a figurative level, suggesting both his rolling gait and, perhaps, his status as a force attempting to steady the life of his nephew, Roderick, who has been left adrift by his unfeeling nearest relatives. Bowling's language, always entrenched in maritime references, makes him a comic figure, yet readers' introduction to his maritime idiom reveals a sympathetic man decrying the persecutors of a vulnerable young boy. This loyal tar, offering his nephew unstinting support, expresses himself in a maritime language that is also set up as a language of feeling, as when he consoles Roderick, upon finding his grandfather has bequeathed to him nothing of his vast estate—"Come along, Rory, I perceive how the land lies, ... let's tack about" (11).

Tom's linguistic difference from those on land, if comic, is also matched by the difference of his selfless generosity. He displays no material interest, no desire to accumulate property—a marked shift from the treasure-seeking pirates of the early century. If mariners' confinement to technical nautical language makes them otherworldly, this unpropertied, disinterested status was increasingly highlighted in popular print representations. Early on in the novel Bowling, thwarted in his attempts to help his nephew, relinquishes his hopes as he whistles the "Sailor's Ballad," with the refrain: "why whould [sic] we quarrel for riches / Or any such glittery toy? / A light heart and a thin pair of breeches / Goes through the world brave boy."[96] In other naval songs of the period, as in "Harry Howser," the speaker insists, "of all sorts of lives still a sailor's for me, sir / I'll shun all the great and their curs'd civil racket, / And change ev'ry suit for a sailor's blue jacket," presenting sea life as a rejection of the concerns of property (Naval Songster 40). These selfless qualities make Tom and mariners like him potentially sympathetic figures, for, as Catherine Gallagher has noted, citing Hume's influential model of the workings of sympathy, "property is an important break on the dynamic of sympathy."[97] The supposedly disinterested and distant status of mariners, signaled in part by their objective technological language, enables sympathy and is part of what allows others to "bring the case [of mariners] home," in Adam Smith's language.[98] The song "Poor Jack" combines this selfless disinterestedness with distancing technical sea language, as a sailor asserts: "Tho' the tempest topgallant-masts smack smooth / should smite, / and shiver each splinter of wood, / Clear the wreck, stow the yards, and bouse e- / very thing tight, / and under reef'd forsail we'll scud."[99]

Thus, if Ward's early eighteenth-century representations of nautical jargon locate naval workers in a comical, sometimes squalid subculture, later representations of them and their technical sea language began to appear in a more sympathetic light. They were part of new characterizations of the sailor as the "Jolly Jack Tar," described by Gillian Russell as having "a fondness for grog, women, and salty lingo, honest goodheartedness, a tinderbox temperament, and above all, loyalty to his ship, his country, and his king."[100] The nautical-jargon-speaking Jack Tar, who appeared initially in newspapers in the 1720s and then on stage in the 1740s, is somewhat comic but also a figure for sentimental attachment.[101] Russell rightly notes that the Jolly Jack Tar was "a way for civilian society to relieve its fears of the navy's alterity," a means, we might say, of making strangers familiar.[102]

Crucially, Tom is distinct from Roderick and other novelistic narrators who, as they come to learn and explain sea language, fold it into a number of specialized languages and continue to speak—and narrate—in standard English. While Roderick presents a model of novelistic assimilation of strange languages, in part by revealing his interiority, Bowling is himself all linguistic strangeness; no interior is revealed. It is this very restrictive strangeness that makes him a kind of sentimental object. As Paul Gilje notes, "Through repetition in song, stage, print, and politics the language of Jack Tar became standardized and stereotyped. It almost did not matter what the sailor really sounded like. What mattered was what people, even the common seaman himself, thought he sounded like."[103]

As Britain extended and strengthened its global maritime control, such representations domesticated the figure of the sailor as sentimental object in part, and oddly, through their technical language. Representations of sailors' language in operettas such as *Thomas and Sally*, songs such as Dibdin's "Tom Bowling," or novel characters such as Smollett's Tom Bowling intermingle the technical and sentimental.[104] This odd dynamic is observable, too, in *The Post-Captain*, whose Captain Brilliant uses bizarre, technologically inflected language to profess his humility to a new acquaintance, introducing himself as the "most humble-come-tumble out of the main-top into the lower-hold!," to which his new acquaintance, Lord Fiddle-Faddle, responds, "Technical!" (40). It is Fiddle-Faddle, however, who is unworthy of admiration, and not Brilliant. Brilliant's name signals that he is unmistakably admirable, his "technical" language contrasting him to the effeminate Fiddle-Faddle as a model of masculine Britishness, while his "humble-come-tumble" expression announces his unpretentiousness, his availability for sentimental attachment.

This domestication was akin to the small but to-scale models of ships built for investors, and sometimes by mariners themselves, a sentimentalizing-by-miniaturizing move captured in the reference to the ship as a "little wooden world."[105] These representations do not invite comic raillery but affection. In his *Philosophical Inquiry*, Burke observes that smallness is associated with affection, that "it is usual to add the endearing name of *little* to everything we love."[106] Smallness, he argues, contributes to "beauty," which is, as he sees it, "a social quality . . . inspir[ing] us with sentiments of tenderness and affection" (39). Beautiful in a conventional sense Bowling and his language certainly are not. In Burke's binary aesthetic economy, however, the miniature nature of Bowling's world, as suggested in part by his technical language, places him not in the category of the sublime—the great, the fear-inducing—but in that of the beautiful. A speaker of a specialist language, with its small frame of reference, oblivious to the larger world, Bowling, much like *Tristram Shandy*'s character

Uncle Toby, who also speaks a military argot (and builds small versions of his military world), becomes a sentimental character, inspiring readers with Burke's "sentiments of tenderness and affection."

The smallness of Bowling's linguistic field of reference and his obliviousness of its limits positions him, and seamen like him, as not of this world. Perhaps counterintuitively, it is, in part, that very quality, emphasized in the obscurity of their technical language, that helps establish affective connections and even relations of sympathy to those figures. Movement and distance are seamen's ontological condition. As moving, remote subjects, however, theirs might be those "facts" that, because "a great way off," are able to "touch the mind," as Defoe had put it. As we have seen throughout this book, that strangeness is crucial for the process of vernacularization. Distance is part of what is necessary for building a sense of attachment, even for developing sympathy.

Thus it was that the eighteenth-century literary representation of mariners most heavily laden with technical sea terms, Falconer's 1762 poem *The Shipwreck*, was also one of the most sentimental. With its use of technical language aimed at rendering physical presence but also, and mainly, at eliciting feeling, it eclipsed fictional attempts to render mariners in the second half of the eighteenth century. Falconer's poem would, in turn, help make possible the fictional depictions of sentimental and heroically British mariners that reappeared in the early nineteenth century, such as those of *The Post-Captain* and *Persuasion*. Unsurprisingly, given the context of the Napoleonic Wars, those later works evoke feelings of sentiment and patriotism around the figure of the mariner, yet both depictions include the technical language of seafaring. *The Post-Captain*, for instance, turns to patriotic rhetoric: "Such was the discipline, such the intrepidity of the British Tars, that resistance was of no avail" (118). The sentimental image of a mariner bravely dying after displaying such intrepidity is oddly facilitated through the maritime lingo he uses, as the officer tells a comrade, "I feel I shall have to capitulate. Death has already put his storming ladder to my soul. I die! I die! My God! My God!" (115). In *Persuasion*, Captain Wentworth indulges in the language of the tar, saying that "after taking privateers enough ... I had the good luck to fall in with the very French Frigate I wanted—I brought her into Plymouth ... a gale came on, which would have done for poor old Asp" (90). But this in no way detracts from his understated heroic character. And it is the mariner Captain Benwick of *Persuasion* who is the man of "feelings glad to burst their usual restraints" (121). Falconer's poem entwined technical language and the sentimental in ways that made such mariner characters possible.

A long poem in three cantos, sometimes called an epic, sometimes a georgic, *The Shipwreck* recollects the loss of a British ship and most of its crew at sea. Although little-known today, the poem was an immediate success in its day, wildly popular and reviewed favorably. In the wake of that success—it sold out quickly—Falconer (quite surprised) revised it, publishing a second version in 1764 and a third in 1769, elaborating, in those subsequent editions, a sentimental narrative regarding doomed love between a cherished shipmate and the Captain's daughter. (This narrative, by the by, criticizes the captain's avarice and the greed of commercial empires.) The poem went through well over one hundred editions and, moreover, was anthologized in every collection of "great English poets"—alongside works of Milton and Pope—right through the middle of the nineteenth century.[107] Influential to two generations of Romantic poets, including Burns, Coleridge, and Byron, the poem made way for the aestheticization of mariners' technical sea language, as the ship itself became a kind of harp, the wind "shrill thro the cordage howl[ing] with notes of woe."[108]

Falconer's reconfiguration of technical language, as a ship's "cordage" becomes aeolian harp and seamen's jargon the stuff of poetry, flies in the face, of course, of the recommendations of writers from Pope and Addison to Johnson, who all argued against the use of technical language. Even Dryden had asserted that Virgil would not have used such language (despite having done so himself and Falconer's later moniker as "Britain's Virgil") because he was writing "not to mariners . . . but to all in general, and in particular ladies and gentlemen of quality."[109] Johnson described the move from a "universal language" of poetry to a mariners' argot as a "descending" one.[110] But in part by reframing such language within a sentimental economy, drawing from earlier novelistic moves of displaying and explaining the strange, figuring the ship with its technical parts as a feeling being, an outsized body, "trembling," "confessing," "groaning," a little like the "nervous" sailors, Falconer makes technical sea language the provenance of poetry.[111]

He was adamant about the accuracy of his technical language and his own expertise. Like lowborn sailors before him, he authorized himself through his command of it.[112] A midshipman, he unashamedly asserted his superior knowledge of technical language from his years of labor as "a sailor"—the only authorial name appearing on the title page. He explains in one footnote, "it is necessary in this place to remark that the sheets, which are universally mistaken by the English poets and their readers, for the sails themselves, are no other than the ropes, used to extend the clues, or lower corners of the sail to which they are attached." (1769 II 163). Other writers' attempts to explain naval terms, Falconer sneers, have included "a silly inadequate performance that has lately appeared by a Sea-Officer so ignorant as to mistake the names of the most common things in a ship."[113] While he describes his poem as "entertainment . . . calculated . . . for gentlemen of the sea," he also aimed to introduce seaborne strangers and their alien language to a "general," wider readership, for in all of his brief prefaces, he apologizes for "swelling the Work with so many Notes . . . explaining the sea-phrases," information that would not be necessary, as we saw above, for "gentlemen of the sea."[114] Terms such as "bowsprits" and "for-cat-harpings" form a significant part of the poem's lexicon, and he gives them copious explanatory footnotes.

The naval language readers learn is not the sprawling variety of global travel but the abstruse lexicon of the technical. The volume gestures toward the perspective-expanding mode of seaborne travel, opening with a fold-out map of Greek waters and the ship's course through them and offering early passages describing the landscape of Crete. That expansiveness, however, is met by, or perhaps produces dialectically, an emphasis on the highly particularized world of technical sea language. The volume's other fold-out plate shrinks its world to the ship itself, with a diagram labeling in great detail all of its parts. The focus on the technical aspect of sailors' speech resituates these world travelers as a group limited by arcane language, much as the ship diagram suggests limitations in space. The ship's name—*Britannia*—and passages elaborating the grand paintings of personified England and Scotland on its side make that space British. The technical jargon of the poem's sailors makes them strangers, but they are always Britons, their strangeness at least partially mitigated in the diagrams and footnotes the poem supplies.

For some readers—"gentlemen of the sea"—the poem estranges their familiar shipboard world of oral sea language into a rarified context of print and neoclassical poetry. For those unfamiliar with this technical language, the strangeness is both distancing—reminding readers of the difference between those who know and those who do not—but also a challenge to be overcome in the creation of greater sentiment. The speaker suggests it is their distance, both physical and linguistic, that makes sailors more available for compassion:

> Might the sad numbers draw compassion's tear
> For kindred-miseries, oft beheld too near:
> For kindred-wretches, oft in ruin cast
> On Albion's strand, beneath the wintry blast:
> For all the pangs, the complicated woe,
> Her bravest sons, her faithful sailors know!
> So pity, gushing o'er each British breast,
> Might sympathise with Britain's sons distrest:
> For this, my theme thro' mazes I pursue (1769 III 47–56)

While they share kindred miseries, wretches on land might be "too near" for drawing "compassion's tear." Alternatively, the "complicated woe" of the sailor, which the poet must pursue through mazes—the intricate technology and actions he must explain in his depiction of a storm-tossed ship—might elicit sympathy. The shipwreck, perhaps in the end the image most repeatedly deployed to represent the sailors' world in eighteenth-century Britain, stands as an apposite figure, then, for the endlessly revolving relationship of distance and proximity between readers and maritime life.

Falconer's fellow Scot Adam Smith had described the process of sympathetic exchange as demanding the work of the imagination to bring distant physical objects and "interests of other people" into a true sense of scale (and not the false one in which one's own interests are disproportionately huge), "by transporting myself, at least in fancy, to a different station, from whence I can survey both at nearly equal distances, and thereby form some judgment of their real proportions."[115] That transport, he argues, demands that we view the situation "from the place and with the eyes of a third person, who has no particular connexion with either."[116] Smith compares this work to that needed to imagine relationships in physical space, to correct the misrepresentations in perspective when viewed from inside. For some, the view of a shipwreck from shore recapitulated the challenge of finding accurate physical and moral perspective.[117] We might say that Falconer's technical sea language, in its sheer referentiality, helps that transport in fancy, its denotative neutrality contributing to a sense of orientation in space and that sense of impartiality necessary to bring readers "to a different station."

His technical maritime language is a means but also an end. For the poet identifies creating a poem composed of technical language as the difficult goal of his project, asserting, "Not more advent'rous was th'attempt to move / Th'infernal Pow'rs with strains of heavenly love, / When faithful Orpheus, on the Stygian coast, / In sacred notes implr'd his consort lost; . . . / Than mine, in ornamental verse to dress / The harshest sounds mechanic Arts express" (1762 I 198–205). The aim is to make technical language's "harsh sounds" into poetry, a crossing of borders as impermeable as those between life and the afterlife. Yet it is the essential difference and inaccessibility of Hades that demands and produces Orpheus's powerful song, just as it is the distance of the ocean and the technical language of its seafarers that demands and might produce a powerful poem. For both Orpheus and, as we shall see, the poet speaker, distance and proximity are in dangerous play. The former's song is caused by and must overcome distance, its promise shattered in Orpheus's premature capitulation to his desire to dissolve that distance. Similarly, if, as its speaker hopes, *The Shipwreck* overcomes the distance between sailor and reader and between technical language and verse, it, too, ends in the impossible distance of death.

The poem sutures present and remote, technical and sentimental, in part by reserving its specialized language for the later catastrophic scenes. Absent in the initial canto describing Crete and sea marvels such as dolphins and waterspouts, the technical language appears at the moment of heightened emotional feeling. It is when the mortal threat of the storm becomes clear that passage after passage of technical language appear describing the impact of the turbulent sea on the foundering ship and the master's commands. The poem describes the sailors' actions at the beginning of the storm: "Impell'd by mighty pressure, down she lies; / 'Brail up the mizzen quick!' the Master cried: / 'Man the clue-garnetts, let the main-sheet fly!' / In thousand shiv'reng shreds it rends on high!" (1762 II 25–28). The sounded language of the mariner's voice—"Man the clue-garnetts"—is here no longer comic jargon but the language of an impassioned effort to avoid disaster, the language of both the sailors and the poem's speaker.

It is through this language that the speaker hopes to "draw compassion's tear" (1769 III 47). Part of its force is its appeal to voice and the attribution of power and immediacy to it. The technical language does often take the form of shouts heard aboard a ship, reproducing the aural turbulence that had "amazed" Ward. Associating this oral frenzy of technical language with the urgency and physical sensation of a ship confronting a storm, such passages even evoke Johnson's description of the forceful immediacy of an originary oral society "where all on the first approach of hostility come together at the call to battle."[118] If mariners' language had sometimes suggested a diminutive world, here Falconer's invocation of aurality and orality makes that world larger than life, the scale of the mouse to the thresher's mill with the comic element withheld, its frightening power instead firmly in place.

The technicality of the language, however, remains crucial to that effect. Burke observed that the nearer distress "approaches reality, the further from the idea of fiction, the greater the power" (53). Technical language might be key in making the description of the remote "approach reality," thereby increasing the power of the representation just as technical language in logbooks, voyage histories, and novels was a means of making the distant present. And it is also as the poem introduces technical verbal details and emotional turmoil that the nonsailing reader enters a truly alien linguistic world. The obscurity of the language suggests a profound divide between uninitiated reader and mariner in that oscillation between familiar and strange that we have seen throughout this book. Copious footnotes explain terms, and there is the diagram for consultation, but reading the poem would prove rough going for the nonspecialist attempting to imagine exactly what action is taking place.

The slowing down necessary to comprehend and "approach reality" might, however, enable sympathetic exchange. In one representative passage (Fig. 8), technical language articulates the most pressing common end—survival. The break in the action and the time demanded to read the explanatory footnotes shifts the temporality and level of feeling in the experience of the poem, not unlike those footnotes to provincial poetry we explored in Chapter Six. Reading becomes disjointed, the affecting narrative halted as the nonspecialist attempts to picture exactly what is taking place, looks down to the footnotes for explanation, and returns to the poem in a different frame of mind. Any intense feeling created by the "impetuous pressure" of "crashing boats," for instance, is dissipated by the break in reading and the mundaneness of the footnote that follows defining the next word—"the companion is a square wooden porch, erected over the hatchway, that goes down to the cabbin or apartment of the

(29)

The trembling hull confefs'd th' enormous ftroke ;
The crafhing boats th' impetuous preffure broke :
Companion ᵐ, binnacle ⁿ, in floating wreck,
With compaffes and glaffes ftrew'd the deck ;
The mizen rending, from the bolt-rope ᵒ flew,   245
Torn from the earing to the flutt'ring clue :
The fides convulfive fhook on groaning beams ᵖ,
And yawning wide, expand the pitchy ᑫ feams.
They found the well ʳ and, terrible to hear !
Along the line four wetted feet appear :   250
At either pump they heave the clafhing brake ˢ,
And, turn by turn, th' ungrateful office take ;
They both in clofe rotation ftill attend,
And help inceffant, nervous Seamen lend ;

ᵐ The companion is a fquare wooden porch, erected over the hatchway, that goes down to the cabbin or apartment of the chief officers.

ⁿ The binnacle is a box which ftands before the helm on deck, having three divifions, the middle one for a lamp or candle, and the other two for the compaffes which direct the Ship's courfe and the watch-glaffes.

ᵒ The bolt-rope furrounds or girts all fails, their edges being fewed to it : in fquare fails it is diftinguifhed by three names, viz. head-rope or upper part ; leeches or fides ; and foot-ropes or bottoms.

ᵖ Beams are ftrong pieces of timber ftretching acrofs the Ship, to keep the fides at their proper diftance, and fupport the decks.

ᑫ Becaufe the feams or junctions of the planks are filled with pitch, to prevent the water from penetrating the deck or fides.

ʳ The pump-well is an apartment in the Ship's hold that contains the main-maft and pumps, and is planked round, to keep the cargo clear of the pumps : it is founded by letting a meafured iron rod and line down the pump, by which they know whether the leaks increafe or diminifh.

ˢ The brake is the pump-handle, which is occafionally fixed and taken off.

But:

FIGURE 8: From William Falconer, *The Shipwreck* (London, 1762). PR3433.F3S45 1762. Courtesy of the Bancroft Library, University of California, Berkeley.

chief officers" (1762 ii, 243). Such moments, defusing strong feelings, might suggest the very dynamics Smith had identified in successful sympathetic exchange, which he said demands "lowering passion to that pitch in which the spectators are capable of going along." The sufferer must "flatten . . . the sharpness of its natural tone, in order to reduce it to harmony and concord with the emotions of those who are about him" (22). And what could be more flattering than a technical footnote?

The technical language, however, does not only delay and flatten. It also raises emotions with its disorienting obscurity. The ominous news of the failing pump, for instance, appears in the lines "Sound the well and, terrible to hear! / Along the line four wetted feet appear" (1762 II 249–50), with words connoting, for the uninitiated, misleading meanings, inviting the wrong questions: Does a well sound? Why would a well be terrible to hear? Whose wetted feet? (See Fig. 8.) The footnote redirects the reader, explaining that "to sound" means "letting an iron rod and line down the pump, by which they know whether the leaks increase." This clarifies that the water level has risen to a frightening four feet, and "sound" becomes a visual marker that no longer quite fits with "hear," or indeed the sense of "feet," in verse and its sounded quality. The footnote undoes some of what readers might have thought they knew, as the poem's language moves between meanings that periodically cast the reader in the dark.

Literary reviews of the period emphasized both the poem's appeal to pathos and its use of technical sea terms. *The Critical Review* praised its "great number of pathetic touches, which will not fail to interest the reader of sentiment," and *The Monthly Review* admiringly asked, "who, except a poetical sailor . . . educated by Neptune, would ever have thought of versifying his own sea language? What other poet would ever have dreamt of reef-tackles, halyards, cluegarnets, buntlines, lashings, lanyards, and fifty other terms equally obnoxious to the soft sing-song of modern poetasters?"[119] In this poem, the "obnoxious" language of which works against what is described as an increasingly feminine language of poetry, a masculine technical language creates scenes of sentiment but tempers the danger of feminization, always a threatening undercurrent of sentimental writing. Such reviews would redeem the feminized position into which most readers—male and female—would be put by the obscurity and multiple meanings of the poem, reclaiming technical language as the means of reassembling a cross-class male society.

This poem, however, even though adrift in an "obnoxious" technical lexicon, found avid female readers. In her journal, Frances Burney describes a dashing young man reading *The Shipwreck* aloud to her.[120] And in *The Post-Captain* women work to master technical sea terms: as the narrator tells us, "Indeed the novels which Cassandra and Flora had brought on board were neglected for Falconer's Marine Dictionary" (122). Such readerships—or even the representation of such readerships—suggest that the popularity and cultural meaning of this poem and of mariners' technical language cannot be reduced to homosocial national alliances.[121] The poem's technical language works toward establishing a model of a highly restricted affective community which outsiders, both men and women, might briefly glimpse and tentatively join through textual consumption.

Lost at Sea

The technical language and the particulars of life at sea registered in logbooks became available, then, for complex sentimental attachments. By 1799, in his melancholic poem *The Castaway*, William Cowper was drawing from Anson's voyage narratives, his phrase—"narrative sincere"—now functioning as shorthand for the technical language of the sailors' world (l. 50).[122] The technical and sentimental are here deeply entwined, as the logbook's seemingly unsentimental catalogue of the castaway's "name ... worth ... age" is "wet with Anson's tear" (ll. 51–2). The sentiment raised by the poem's account of a sailor who falls overboard in a storm and perishes is strong enough to be the basis for affiliation between sailor and speaker, who notes that "misery still delights to trace / Its 'semblance in another's case" (ll. 59–60). The poem's well-known shift in voice between first person singular, third person, and first person plural captures the sliding between the speaker's and "another's case," despite, or again, maybe because of the distance of the sailor dying at sea.

The shipwreck at the end of Falconer's poem, however, short-circuits connections between the technical and sentimental, reinstating the irredeemable distance and remoteness of the stranger in a turn to the sublime. Readers experience the sublime in Falconer's poem not only through witnessing the "tyranny of fear" experienced by the sailors but also by their own experience of obscurity in the poem's technical language. Obscurity, Burke argued, is central to the feeling of terror and to the experience of the sublime. "When we know the full extent of danger, we can accustom our eyes to it," he explains, "and apprehension vanishes" (54). It might seem that the poem's saturation with technical language prevents the sublime, providing knowledge of "the full extent" and a too-safe distance from the wreck. But do readers' eyes become fully accustomed to events described thus?: "Both stay-sail sheets to mid-ships were convey'd / And round the fore-mast on each side belay'd: / Then the Hallyard ev'ry Man applies / They hoist—the rending sail to ruins flies!" (1762 II 418–21)? If, as Burke argues, "verbal description raises a very obscure and imperfect idea" (55), that is especially the case in Falconer's passages of technical description. A long footnote about stay-sail sheets (here "sheets" are actually sails, contra Falconer's earlier complaint) does little to clarify the goings-on for a nonspecialist. The description of the terrors of a besieged ship is matched and made more terrifying by the obscurity the reader faces.

The sublime works in this poem, however, in a still more powerful register when technical items named and explained, those possible means of sentimental attachment to strange-speaking mariners, disappear back into the vast, unknowable obscurity of the ocean. Each named technical part of the ship is demolished or disappears in the face of the storm—or as the crew attempts to survive by hacking away at the parts of the ship—just as they are named in the poem. In the midst of the dramatic tempest, the captain counsels, "cut . . . the mizzen-mast away!," and the sailors "to the lannyards quickly run. / And quick the stay and weather-shrouds are gone: / The tall mast groans with their redoubled blows, / And tott'ring, crashing o'er the quarter goes" (1762 II 429–33). Here, knowing is predicated on disarticulation, the moment of naming nearly simultaneous with the named object's disappearance. The ship's parts inhabit a semiotic economy not unlike the period's antiquarianism, with its devotions to naming and cataloguing the fragments that metonymically call up an irrevocably lost past, oblivion.

The technical parts are named but are just as quickly tossed into the sea, littering the foaming ocean surface. If readers consult the footnotes or diagram to identify the part, they return to the narrative of the poem to find that part disassembled and cast into—claimed by—the ocean. Technical aspects of the ship and the work of sailing are presented in the process of their disappearance. The common end, survival, now depends on relinquishing technical parts in a kind of reverse order of fiction's display and explanation. In Falconer's poem the unfamiliar and distant become familiar only to be consigned again to a kind of oblivion. Significantly, both the ships' technical parts and the sailors themselves are simultaneously heaved into the watery throes of the raging ocean:

> Twelve sailors up the fore-cat-harpings haste;
> Desperate asylum! Charg'd with fatal woe!
> For lo! While dips immerst the plunging prow,
> Down prest by watery weight the bowsprit bends,
> And, loosen'd o'er the stem, deep-crashing rends.
> Beneath the bow the floating Ruins lie;
> The fore-mast totters unsustain'd on high,
> And, as she rises on th'up-lifting sea,
> Men, masts, yards, rigging tumble o'er the lee;
> While in the common wreck, the twisting stay
> Drags the Main-to-mast by the cap away.
> . . .
> The tumbling waters close around each head,
> And sink them helpless to an oozy bed. (1762 III 390–403)

Adam Smith had described how the sailor who escapes a drowning after a shipwreck by holding a plank will naturally "preserve it with care and affection, as a monument that was, in some measure, dear to him."[123] In Falconer's poem such sentimental charge is foreclosed, not only because the readers' connection to the technical is reworked in this destruction but also because the sailors' own connection to it is destroyed. The technical parts of the ship are named at the point at which they are sawn off or broken and submerged into the sublimely "oozing" ocean, the remaining hulk finally demolished and entirely subsumed, the sailors finding no asylum on the "fore-cat-harpings" to which they cling but rather death.

As the storm-broken ship disappears piece by intermingled piece ("masts, yards, rigging") into the turbulent black ocean, desperate, drowning sailors are among those pieces ("Men, masts"), alliteration and their status as items in a series even conflating man and thing. In a sublime encounter, the particularities of life at sea vanish into obscurity at their very moment of presentation. The poem's obscurity, in its disorienting effects derived, in part, from the technical language, might initially answer to the vulgar sublime, that phenomenon Burke attempted to avoid in attributing obscurity exclusively to high literary productions such as Milton's poetry.[124] Falconer's combination of "vulgar" technical terms with an elevated—indeed, sometimes Miltonic—poetics, however, complicates an easy distinction between vulgar and sublime in this poem, as do the pathetic deaths of the sailors, those jargon-speaking laborers. And if the sublime demands distance, the dynamics of the vernacularization of mariners' technical language that we have been tracing depend, as we have seen, on a movement between distance and proximity. This movement is at work, too, in the wavering in point of view (also seen in Cowper's *The Castaway*) of Falconer's poem's conclusion, as the perspective moves from first-person, the sailor speaker who has been narrating, to an awkward third-person, which now describes that sailor as among "the helpless few who yet surviv'd" (1769 III 909). The illusion of insiderness seems to be retracted in an attempt to reinstate a safe distance between shipwreck and spectator, between the speaker of an odd technical language and his reader.

If some print genres of the vernacular encouraged the illusion that readers might make a property of the language of others—in this case mariners—as part of their English vernacular, however, then the stakes of the loss at sea are high. They include the readers for whom the strange has been made familiar throughout the poem. In making the distant present and in creating affective connections that allow readers to view such language as "our" vernacular, the technical language of the poem has undone the division between spectator and shipwrecked. Or perhaps these familiarizing relations merely enable the recognition, in Hans Blumberg's terms, that spectators wrongly imagine a distance between shipwrecks and themselves, for they, too, "are ... always already embarked and on the high seas ... are shipwrecked."[125] The fabrication is the strange and the stranger, not the bridge between them.

The return of the technical language of sailors' terms to the obscurity of the sea suggests the ultimately limited terms of inclusion of various languages into the "vernacular" that we have been tracing throughout this book. This consignment to oblivion is a reminder of the distance, the mysterious allure, that must continue to suffuse the sense of the vernacular, as it moves between being one's own and another's, familiar and strange. That descent into the deep also evokes all that must remain unseen and unknown beyond the print representations that make up Britain's strange vernaculars. So much will remain always wandering, forever inaccessible, of others' lives, of others' languages, so much "suffered to perish," even if some version of them, some print artifact, is endlessly reproduced and consumed. In print genres of the vernacular, the Orphic moments of breaching of borders, powerful as they were, were always, like Orpheus's efforts, doomed, predicated, despite their invocations of freedom, on death and violence. And like them, they were always impossible, for their claims to represent a language that could be at once particular—the speech of inventive propertyless itinerants, of provincials fixed in place and speaking the language of national ancestors, of laborers at once mobile and confined—and general, a common national tongue, could never be realized. The idea of a national vernacular must remain forever strange.

NOTES

Introduction

1. Samuel Johnson, *Dictionary of the English Language*, 2 vols. (London: 1755). Editors and printers, navigating a huge expansion in print materials, helped to establish and publish that standard. See Roger Lass, ed., *The Cambridge History of the English Language* vol. 3 (Cambridge, UK: Cambridge UP, 1999) and David McKitterick, *Print, Manuscript, and the Search for Order, 1450-1830* (Cambridge, UK: Cambridge UP, 2003).

2. A wide range of books track shifts in status markers, from Jurgen Habermas's *The Structural Transformation of the Public Sphere*, trans. Thomas Burger (Cambridge, MA: MIT Press, 1989) to discussions related to the novel, such as Michael McKeon, *The Origins of the English Novel, 1600-1740* (Baltimore: Johns Hopkins UP, 1987) and Nancy Armstrong, *Desire and Domestic Fiction: A Political History of the Novel* (Oxford: Oxford UP, 1987). Pierre Bourdieu discusses the language component in particular in *Language and Symbolic Power*, trans. Gino Raymond (Cambridge, UK: Polity, 1992), as does Carey McIntosh, *Common and Courtly Language* (Philadelphia: U of Pennsylvania P, 1986).

3. Francis Grose, *A Classical Dictionary of the Vulgar Tongue* (London, 1785), s.v., "idiot pot" and "rantipole."

4. British Library MS Add 32640 and Brice, *An Exmoor Scolding* (Exmoor, 1746), 8, respectively.

5. William Falconer, *Universal Dictionary of the Marine* (London, 1769) and *The Shipwreck* (London, 1762), respectively.

6. Benedict Anderson, *Imagined Communities: Reflections on the Origin and Spread of Nationalism* (London: Verso, 1982); Tony Crowley, *Standard English and the Politics of Language* (Urbana: U of Illinois P, 1989); Andrew Elfenbein, *Romanticism and the Rise of English* (Stanford, CA: Stanford UP, 2009); John Guillory, *Cultural Capital: The Problem of Literary Canon Formation* (Chicago: Chicago UP, 1993); Olivia Smith, *The Politics of Language, 1791-1819* (New York: Oxford UP, 1984); Michael Warner, *Letters of the Republic* (Cambridge, MA: Harvard UP, 1990).

7. But see Elfenbein's chapter "Bad Englishes" in *Romanticism and the Rise of English* and Natalie Zemon Davis, "Proverbial Wisdom and Vulgar Errors," in *Society and Culture in Early Modern France* (Stanford, CA: Stanford UP, 1975), 227-67. For a comprehensive discussion of literary representations of regional Englishes, see N. F. Blake, *Non-Standard Language in English Literature* (London: Deutsch, 1981).

8. The focus of this study is on printed texts. For a study of performance and language, see Michael Ragussis, *Theatrical Nation: Jews and Other Outlandish Englishmen in Georgian England* (Philadelphia: U of Pennsylvania P, 2010). I refrain from the official "Standard English" moniker, as it was still in formation at this time. "Standardizing" might be the most accurate description.

9. Michael Warner, *Publics and Counterpublics* (New York: Zone, 2005), 75. Jurgen Habermas had also noted that nations are "a fairly abstract form of solidarity among strangers" in "Why Europe Needs a Constitution," *New Left Review* 11 (2001): 5-26, 16.

10. James Vernon, *Distant Strangers: How Britain Became Modern* (Berkeley: U of California P, 2014).

11. Karl Polanyi, *The Great Transformation* (1944; repr. Boston: Beacon, 2001), and

David Simpson, *Romanticism and the Question of the Stranger* (Chicago: U of Chicago P, 2013).

12. *Making England Western* (Chicago: U of Chicago P, 2014), 253.

13. John Thurmond, *Harlequin Sheppard* (London, 1724), 22, and Brice, *Exmoor Scolding*, 7.

14. And yet, as Serres also argues, and as we see in the expansion of print representations of the "static" outside the system of standard English, "noise gives rise to a new system." "Positions change," as Serres writes, and what was once "noise," and the stranger who produced that noise became "interlocutor" (53). While noise "interrupts at first glance, it consolidates when you look again" (14). Michel Serres, *The Parasite*, trans. Lawrence Schehr (Baltimore: Johns Hopkins UP, 1983), 52. Further citations noted parenthetically.

15. Anonymous, *New Canting Dictionary* (London, 1725).

16. Grose, *Classical Dictionary*, i.

17. First passage cited in *Oral and Literate Culture in England 1500–1700* (New York: Oxford UP, 2000), 73; the second in *Accidence to the English Tongue* (London, 1724), 11–12. For more on regional variations, see Manfred Gorlach, "Regional and Social Variations," in Lass, *Cambridge History of the English Language* vol. 3, and Gerry Knowles, *A Cultural History of the English Language* (London: Arnold, 1997).

18. Samuel Pegge, *Anecdotes of the English Language* (1803; repr. London, 1844), 3.

19. Ned Ward, *The Wooden World Dissected* (London, 1707), 35.

20. Daniel Tiffany, *Infidel Poetics: Riddles, Nightlife, Substance* (Chicago: U of Chicago P, 2009), 2 and 8, respectively.

21. Serres (*Parasite* 14) writes that "noise temporarily stops the system, makes it oscillate indefinitely."

22. Emily Brontë, *Wuthering Heights*, ed. Richard Dunn (New York: W. W. Norton, 1991), 4.

23. Ned Ward, *The London Spy* 2nd ed. (London, 1709), 40.

24. Srinivas Aravamudan, *Enlightenment Orientalism: Resisting the Rise of the Novel* (Chicago: U of Chicago P, 2012), 45.

25. Captain Bland, *The Northern Atalantis or York Spy*, 2nd ed. (London, 1713), 41–42.

26. George Parker, *Life's Painter of Variegated Characters* (London, 1789), 152.

27. *The London Spy*, 1st ed. (London, 1700), 5. Similarly, the York spy cannot help but hear the cries "Hot Black Puddings, hot, / Smoking hot, / Just come out of the Pot" and "In and Outs, In and Outs, who buys any In and Outs?" as he watches hawkers unconvincingly act on the stage. *York Spy*, 68.

28. *The London Spy* (1700), 5.

29. Sean Shesgreen, *Images of the Outcast: The Urban Poor in the Cries of London* (New Brunswick, NJ: Rutgers UP, 2002), 2.

30. Shesgreen cites Zacharias Conrad Von Uffenbach's observation that "one can also obtain [Cries] with notes, for the curious tones that they cry or sing can be freakishly imitated on the violin." *Images of the Outcast*, 46.

31. John Gay, *Trivia: or, the Art of Walking the Streets of London* (London, 1716), 5. Further page citations appear parenthetically.

32. The Cloacina section of the poem appears in a later edition (London, 1730), 29.

33. 1716 edition, 23.

34. Leigh Eric Schmidt, *Hearing Things: Religion, Illusion, and the American Enlightenment* (Cambridge, MA: Harvard UP, 2000), 7.

35. Dryden's translation italicized "Eurydice" to make more clear that it is Orpheus's

sounded word, and not the person, that is "return'd" (in an echo). *Works of Virgil*, vol. 1 (London, 1716), 209.

36. In a suggestive parallel, Shesgreen notes that the subjects of cries were often pictured in liminal spaces—doorways and thresholds—and occupied a socially liminal position, as apple sellers might also be disreputable midwives, flower sellers, or prostitutes. *Images of the Outcast*, 1 and 7, respectively.

37. William Falconer, *The Shipwreck* (London, 1762), Canto I, 198–201 and 204–5, respectively.

38. Relph writes, "When Celia sings, the notes inspire / A still attention round the fire: / Their threads no more the Maidens ply, / Before the Swains the spindles lye, / Just so, the truth if Poets tell, / When Orpheus struck his lyre in Hell, / Ixion's wheel was seen to stop / Ocnus omits to twist his rope." *A Miscellany of Poems* (Glasgow, 1747), 120.

39. John Barrell, *English Literature in History 1730–1780: An Equal, Wide Survey* (London: Hutchinson, 1983), 119.

40. Ibid., 121. See also Susan Manly, *Language, Custom, and Nation in the 1790s: Locke, Tooke, Wordsworth, Edgeworth* (Aldershot: Ashgate, 2007). William Keach explores the tensions between Locke's notion of language as "arbitrary" and the dangers of "arbitrary" government accentuated in early nineteenth-century writing in *Arbitrary Power: Romanticism, Language, Politics* (Princeton, NJ: Princeton UP, 2004).

41. James Howell, *Proverbs* (London, 1659), cited in Zemon Davis, "Proverbial Wisdom," 250–51.

42. As Raymond Williams has noted, "Common can be used to affirm something shared or something ordinary . . . or . . . to describe something low or vulgar." *Keywords: A Vocabulary of Culture and Society* (1976; repr. New York: Oxford UP, 1983), 71.

43. Nathan Bailey, *Dictionarium Britannicum* 2nd ed. (London, 1736). First edition 1730.

44. I use the term "vernacular" not because it was the term of choice for eighteenth-century writers—although one finds its use increasing eightfold in the second half of the century—but because it names the linguistic instance of the movement between low and common that I track in this book. (Based on a word search of the Eighteenth-Century Collections Online database.)

45. Guillory, *Cultural Capital*, 78.

46. Steve Newman discusses this association in *Ballad Collection, Lyric, and the Canon* (Philadelphia: U of Pennsylvania P, 2007).

47. *Spectator* 70 (21 May 1711). Newman provides an insightful reading of the place of the ballad in this revaluation of popular culture in *Ballad Collection, Lyric, and the Canon*.

48. *Characteristicks of Men, Manners, Opinions, Times*, vol. 3 (London, 1711), 64.

49. Horace Walpole, *The Castle of Otranto*, ed. E. J. Clery (Oxford: Oxford UP, 1996), 10.

50. *Spectator* 85 (7 June 1711).

51. *Dictionary of the English Language*, vol. 2, s.v. "vernacular."

52. Oliver Goldsmith, *The Citizen of the World*, vol. 2 (London, 1769), 121.

53. Richard Boyd, "Manners and Morals: David Hume on Civility, Commerce, and the Social Construction of Difference," in *David Hume's Political Economy*, ed. M. Schabas and C. Wennerlind (New York: Routledge, 2008), 65. Boyd attributes this belief to "figures as diverse as Locke, Montesquieu, Hume, Smith, Ferguson, and Burke" (65).

54. Goldsmith, *The Citizen of the World*, vol. 2, 121.

55. "Proverbial Wisdom and Vulgar Errors," 256. See also Ann Wierda Rowland's discussion of this connection in *Romanticism and Childhood: The Infantilization of British Literary Culture* (Cambridge, UK: Cambridge UP, 2012).

56. David Hume, "Of National Characters," in *Essays, Moral, Political and Literary*, ed. Eugene Miller (Indianapolis: Liberty Press, 1987), 207.

57. Wolfram Schmidgen, *Exquisite Mixture: The Virtues of Impurity in Early Modern England* (Philadelphia: U of Pennsylvania P, 2013), xii.

58. George Parker, *A View of Society and Manners in High and Low Life*, vol. 1 (London, 1781), vi.

59. Shaftesbury, alternatively, had argued that politeness, that polishing down of rough edges and difference,was "owing to liberty," 64. Anthony Ashley Cooper, Earl of Shaftesbury, *Characteristics of Men, Manners, Opinions, Times*, ed. Lawrence Klein (Cambridge, UK: Cambridge UP, 1999), 64.

60. Kathleen Wilson, *The Sense of the People: Politics, Culture, and Imperialism in England, 1715-1785* (Cambridge, UK: Cambridge UP, 1995), 9.

61. Barrell, *English Literature in History*, 21.

62. Margaret Anne Doody, *The Daring Muse: Augustan Poetry Reconsidered* (Cambridge, UK: Cambridge UP, 1985), 201. Crucially, it is in imaginative writing, and not in nonfiction prose, that we find representations of this low/common language. Even William Hazlitt insists on the difference between the familiar language for which he advocates and "vulgarisms," "low cant phrases," and "provincial or bye-phrases" in "On Familiar Style." See Marcus Tomalin, "Vulgarisms and Broken English," *Romanticism* 13 (2007), 28-52.

63. Parker, *A View of Society and Manners*, vol. 1, vi. Things look a little different in Scotland, where standard English was clearly a language imposed from beyond its borders. The consequent diglossia left intact some notion of a Scots vernacular shared by high and low in contrast to that English. For more on diglossia, see Charles Ferguson, "Diglossia," *Word* 15 (1959), 325-40. I discuss the idea of a Scottish vernacular in "The Debatable Borders of Scottish Song and Ballad Collections," in *Romanticism's Debatable Lands*, eds. Claire Lamont and Michael Rossington (Basingstoke: Palgrave Macmillan, 2007), 80-91.

64. *Spectator* 70 (21 May 1711).

65. *Spectator* 85 (7 June 1711). Interestingly, Mr. Spectator begins this revaluation of the songs of the "common people," by citing the "customs of the Mahometans" and describing himself as having "so much of the Mussulman in me" to cause him to regard every piece of print he encounters, no matter how "despicable" its circumstances.

66. Parker, *Life's Painter of Variegated Colours*, 155.

67. Jacques Rancière, *Short Voyages to the Land of the People*, trans. James Swenson (Stanford, CA: Stanford UP, 2003), 2. Peter Burke, too, has argued that the "discovery of the people" was also a distancing of them. *Popular Culture in Early Modern Europe* (New York: Harper and Row, 1978).

68. Goldsmith, *The Citizen of the World*, and Thomas Brown, *Amusements Serious and Comical: Calculated for the Meridian of London* (London, 1762), respectively.

69. James Vernon reprises this dialectic in *Distant Strangers: How Britain Became Modern* (Berkeley: U of California P, 2014), 14.

70. Viktor Shklovsky, *Theory of Prose*, trans. Benjamin Sher (Elmwood Park, IL: Dalkey, 1991), 5.

71. Ibid., 13. Shklovsky writes that "Russian literary language has so deeply penetrated into the heart of our people that it has lifted much of the popular speech to unheard-of heights.... literature has become enamored of dialect."

72. Guillory, *Cultural Capital*, 78; Tobias Smollett, *Roderick Random*, ed. Paul-Gabriel Boucé (Oxford: Oxford UP, 1981), 48; Samuel Richardson, *Pamela* 2nd ed., cited in T. Duncan Eaves and D. Kimpel, "Richardson's Revisions of *Pamela*," *Studies in Bibliography* 20 (1967): 61-88, 84.

73. Daniel Defoe, *Colonel Jack*, ed. Samuel Holt Monk (London: Oxford UP, 1989), 266.

74. Frances Burney, *Evelina*, ed. Kristina Straub (Boston: Bedford Books, 1997), 72 and 73, respectively.

75. Richardson, *Pamela*, ed. Thomas Keymer and Alice Wakely (Oxford: Oxford UP, 2001),18 and 53, respectively. Grose lists "mort" ("many, abundance, a multitude") in his *Provincial Glossary* (London, 1785).

76. Smollett, *Roderick Random*, 8 and 10, respectively.

77. *Selected Works of Roman Jakobson*, vol. 4 (The Hague: Mouton, 1966), 638–39. In one eighteenth-century collection of proverbs, Thomas Fuller describes the puzzling nature of sayings of "common people" and the pleasure of puzzling them out: they "have something of the obscure and surprize, which as soon as understood, renders them pretty and notable." *Gnomologia* (London, 1732), v.

78. Sarah Tindal Kareem, *Eighteenth-Century Fiction and the Reinvention of Wonder* (Oxford: Oxford UP, 2014), 3.

79. Bakhtin defines heteroglossia as "a social diversity of speech types" and "a struggle among socio-linguistic points of view." *The Dialogic Imagination*, ed. and trans. Michael Holquist (Austin: U of Texas P, 1986), 263 and 273, respectively.

80. James Buzard, *Disorienting Fiction: The Autoethnographic Work of Nineteenth-Century British Novels* (Princeton, NJ: Princeton UP, 2005), 43.

81. For a comprehensive exploration of these strategies in global and domestic contexts see Daniel J. Dewispelare, *Multilingual Subjects: On Standard English, Its Speakers, and Others in the Long Eighteenth Century* (Philadelphia: U of Pennsylvania P, 2017).

82. Tobias Smollett, *The Expedition of Humphry Clinker*, ed. Paul Gabriel Boucé (Oxford: Oxford UP, 1992), 219.

83. Ian Duncan, "The Pathos of Abstraction," in *Scotland and the Borders of Romanticism*, ed. Leith Davis, Ian Duncan, and Janet Sorensen (Cambridge, UK: Cambridge UP, 2004), 38–56, 51.

84. Henry Fielding, *The History of Tom Jones*, ed. J. Bender and S. Stern, eds. (Oxford: Oxford UP, 1998), 104.

85. Bakhtin, *The Dialogic Imagination*, 263 and 273, respectively.

86. Doody, *Daring Muse*, 227.

87. Tim Bobbin (John Collier), *A View of the Lancashire Dialect* (Manchester, 1746?), 4.

88. Edmund Burke, *A Philosophical Enquiry into the Origin of Our Idea of the Sublime and the Beautiful*, ed. Adam Phillips (Oxford: Oxford UP, 2008), 56.

89. Karen Swann, "The Sublime and the Vulgar," *College English* 52 (1990): 7–20, 14.

90. For a recent critique of the problematic conflation of the notion of "the people" with class, see Daniel Tiffany, who writes, "For Marx, there is no people, only classes." He cites Gáspár Miklós Tamás's critique of Rousseau, who "seeks to replace (stratified, hierchical, dominated) society with the people." "Cheap Signaling," *Boston Review* July 15, 2014.

91. Rowland, *Romanticism and Childhood*, 50.

92. It is perhaps for this reason that representations of mariners and their language disappear from literary works for decades, reemerging in the nineteenth century in adventure novels such as *Tom Cringle's Log* or historical novels, such as *The Pilot* or Coleridge's "Rime of the Ancient Mariner," with its own unnavigable sea.

93. Excellent linguistic studies include Joan C. Beal, *An Introduction to Regional Englishes: Dialect Variation in England* (Edinburgh: Edinburgh UP, 2010); *Insights into Late Modern English*, ed. Marina Dossena and Charles Jones (Bern: Lang, 2003); *Eighteenth-Century English: Ideology and Change*, ed. Raymond Hickey (Cambridge, UK: Cambridge UP, 2010); Ingrid Tieken-Boon Van Ostade, *Introduction to Late Modern English* (Edinburgh: Edinburgh UP, 2009); Katie Wales, *Northern English: A Cultural and Social History* (Cambridge, UK: Cambridge UP, 2006).

[278] NOTES TO PART ONE

94. Martyn Wakelin, *Discovering English Dialects* (1979; repr. Oxford: Shire Classics, 2008), 4–6. I have tried, however, to avoid the word "dialect" to describe the various languages under discussion because of the relative inferiority the term often implies.

Part One. Wandering Languages

1. B. E., *A New Dictionary of the Terms Ancient and Modern of the Canting Crew* (London, n.d., 1697–1699?), hereafter *New Dictionary*. This book is not paginated (n.p.). For an accessible reprint, see *The First English Dictionary of Slang*, ed. John Simpson (Oxford: Bodleian Library, 2010).

2. Anonymous, *A New Canting Dictionary* (London, 1725), and Francis Grose, *A Classical Dictionary of the Vulgar Tongue* (London, 1785). While such new additions appeared, print lexicons of cant remained highly derivative from generation to generation, many words and definitions appearing over and over again in subsequent volumes.

3. Thomas Dekker, *Lanthorne and Candle-Light*, 2nd ed. (London, 1608), n.p.

4. Comprehensive guides to cant include Julie Coleman, *A History of Cant and Slang Dictionaries*, 2 vols. (Oxford: Oxford UP, 2004); Maurizio Gotti, *The Language of Thieves and Vagabonds* (Tübingen: Max Niemayer, 1999); and DeWitt Starnes and Gertrude Noyes, *The English Dictionary from Cawdrey to Johnson 1604–1755* (Chapel Hill: U of North Carolina P, 1946), Appendix II.

5. Grose, *Classical Dictionary of the Vulgar Tongue*, i.

6. These are all terms found in B. E.'s *A New Dictionary*, where they are marked with a "c." for cant. The phrase "common people" appears in Grose's *Classical Dictionary*, i.

7. Julie Coleman, *The Life of Slang* (Oxford: Oxford UP, 2012).

Chapter One. Reappraising Cant: "Caterpillars" and Slaves

1. Suspicious of the attribution of a secret language to a criminal subculture, Linda Woodbridge has argued that the early modern figure of the roaming, cant-speaking-criminal band was actually a projection "fueled by anxiety over social mobility . . . linguistic innovation, sexual misconduct, sedition, and idleness" of social groups within "legitimate" society, even of the policing classes themselves. *Vagrancy, Homelessness, and English Renaissance Literature* (Urbana: U of Illinois P, 2001), 6. Woodbridge notes there is virtually no evidence of the use of this language outside of literary texts. There is also the basic observation that, far from hiding criminals' identity, the use of cant would have drawn attention to them. Woodbridge writes that "given the publicity attending thieves' cant, mentioning a 'bousing ken' [tavern] . . . would have been a dead giveaway" (10). Patricia Fumerton, too, argues that in "rogue and cony-catching pamphlets . . . the newly emerging unsettled labor market of late sixteenth- and seventeenth-century England was deliberately *mis*represented as manifold disguising." *Unsettled: The Culture of Mobility and the Working Poor in Early Modern England* (Chicago: U of Chicago P, 2006), 34. For approaches that treat cant as the secret language of an actual existing subculture, see Lee Beier, "Anti-Language or Jargon?: Canting in the English Underworld in the Sixteenth and Seventeenth Centuries," in *Languages and Jargons: Contributions to a Social History of Language*, ed. Peter Burke (Oxford: Polity, 1995); M. A. K. Halliday, "Anti-Language," in *Language as Social Semiotic* (London: Edward Arnold, 1978), 164–82; and Bryan Reynolds, *Becoming Criminal: Transversal Performance and Cultural Dissidence in Early Modern England* (Baltimore: Johns Hopkins UP, 2004).

2. Robert Greene uses the term in his *A Notable Discovery of Coosenage. Now Daily*

Practiced by Sundry Lewd Persons Called Connie-Catchers, and Crosse-Byters (London, 1592). See also his *Black Bookes Messenger* (London, 1591).

3. Samuel Rowlands, *Martin Mark-all, Beadle of Bridewell* (London, 1610) in *Musa Pedestris: Three Centuries of Canting Songs and Slang Rhymes*, ed. John Stephen Farmer (Private printing, 1896).

4. Thomas Harman, *Caveat or Warning, for Common Cursetors Vulgarely Called Vagabondes, or Notable Discovery of Coosnage* (London, 1566), n.p.

5. Robert Greene, *The Groundworke of Conny-Catching, the Manner of their Pedlers-French* (London, 1592), n.p. Greene's authorship is disputed.

6. Richard Head, *The Canting Academy, or, the Devils Cabinet Broke Open* (London, 1673), n.p.

7. Harman uses "Pedlers-French" in his *Caveat or Warning, for Common Cursetors*, as does Greene in *Groundworke of Conny-Catching, the Manner of their Pedlers-French*. The 1530 Egyptian Act made it illegal for "Egyptians," whom we would now call Roma, to live in England, imagining them as a distinct racial group. Yet as early as 1562, another statute revised the original ban to include "counterfeit gypsies," as the distinction between Roma and disenfranchised English pretending to be Roma blurred. While, as Deborah Epstein Nord notes, "unlike colonial subjects, Gypsies were a domestic or an internal other," they were positioned as ethnically other within legal discourse and literary texts, increasingly so by the end of the eighteenth century. Since the trajectory I am tracing moves in the other direction—the gradual inclusion of once-outsider cant within a national vernacular, within Britishness—actual "Gypsies" get less attention in this work than they would in a different kind of study. Resources on representations of gypsies include *Chronicling Poverty: The Voices and Strategies of the English Poor, 1640-1840*, ed. Tim Hitchcock, Peter King, and Pamela Sharpe (New York: St. Martin's Press, 1997); Katie Trumpener, "The Time of the Gypsies," *Critical Inquiry* 18 (1992): 843–84; Deborah Epstein Nord, *Gypsies and the British Imagination, 1807-1930* (New York: Columbia UP, 2006); and David Mayall, *English Gypsies and State Policies* (Hatfield: U of Hertfordshire P, 1992).

8. "Of canting," in Thomas Dekker, *Lanthorne and Candle-Light*, 2nd ed. (London, 1608).

9. Harman, *Caveat or Warning for Common Cursetors*, n.p.

10. Ibid.

11. Dekker, *Lanthorne and Candle-Light*, 3rd ed. (London, 1609), ff 5, verso.

12. Jeffrey Knapp, *Shakespeare's Tribe: Church, Nation, and Theater in Renaissance England* (Chicago: U of Chicago P, 2002), 61. Knapp analyzes the significance of representations of vagabonds and rogues to a national discourse challenged by the upheavals of the Reformation.

13. Dekker, *Lanthorne and Candle-Light*, 3rd ed., ff 3, recto.

14. Daniel Heller-Roazen, *Dark Tongues: The Art of Rogues and Riddlers* (New York: Zone Books, 2013), 15.

15. Dekker, *Lanthorne and Candle-Light*, 3rd ed., ff 4, recto, ff 4, verso, respectively.

16. Head, *The Canting Academy*, n.p.

17. For this understanding of "noise," see Michel Serres, *The Parasite*, trans. Lawrence Schehr (Baltimore: Johns Hopkins UP, 1982). See also Jacques Attali, *Noise: The Political Economy of Music*, trans. Brian Massumi (Minneapolis, U of Minnesota P, 1977).

18. Head, *The Canting Academy*, n.p.

19. Dekker, *Lanthorne and Candle-Light* 3rd ed., ff. 8.

20. Ibid., ff. 10, verso.

21. Robert Copland, *The Hye Way to the Spittal Hous* (London, 1536). Many of the lines

reproduced in Dekker's work also appear in Thomas Harman, *Caveat or Warning for Common Cursetors* (London, 1567).

22. Knapp tracks the movement between characterizations of canters as foreign and domestic in *Shakespeare's Tribe*, chapter 2.

23. Dekker, *Lanthorne and Candle-Light*, 3rd ed., ff. 8 verso, ff. 7 verso, respectively.

24. Michel de Certeau, "Vocal Utopias: Glossolalias," *Representations* 56 (1996): 29–47, 29 and 41 respectively, italics in original. Further citations noted parenthetically.

25. Interestingly, these are an exact reproduction of lines from Harman's *Caveat or Warning for Common Cursetors*, in which they had also already been translated. Translating the unknown and unfamiliar into meaning, it seems, must be staged again and again.

26. For a discussion of a similar dynamic of incomplete translation at work in Thomas Dekker and Thomas Middleton's *The Roaring Girl* (1611) see Reynolds, *Becoming Criminal*, 69–73.

27. Heller-Roazen, too, explores the relation between cant and the literary—particularly in relation to their shared hermeticism, in *Dark Tongues*, 28 and 42.

28. Dekker, *Lanthorne and Candle-Light* 3rd ed., ff. 7, recto.

29. Daniel Tiffany, *Infidel Poetics: Riddles, Nightlife, Substance* (Chicago: U of Chicago P, 2009), 2.

30. Ibid., 2, 139, and 140, respectively. His discussion is specifically about Schiller's notion of the sentimental: "the object here is referred to an idea" (as opposed to a feeling, as in the counterposed naive) and can be either "satirical" or "elegiac." This is not, then, the sentimental of moral sense philosophy.

31. Dekker, *Lanthorne and Candle-Light* 3rd ed., ff. 7, recto.

32. Thomas Dekker, *English Villainies* (London, 1638), title page.

33. Examples of other linguistic subcultures range from that of specific trades to the "female dialect" that Rictor Norton describes "gay men" developing in eighteenth-century Britain. See http://rictornorton.co.uk/eighteen/maiden.htm. Norton asserts that these men were seen as neither foreign nor parasitic.

34. *New Canting Dictionary* (London, 1725).

35. "Of canting," in Dekker, *Lanthorne and Candle-Light*.

36. Michel Serres, *Hermes: Literature, Science, Philosophy*, ed. Josué V. Harari and David F. Bell (Baltimore: Johns Hopkins UP, 1982), 67.

37. Dekker, *Lanthorne and Candle-Light*, and Head, *The Canting Academy*.

38. John McMullan, *The Canting Crew: London's Criminal Underworld 1550–1700* (New Brunswick, NJ: Rutgers UP, 1984), 96. The idea of "subculture" works here in the sense Sarah Thornton describes, a group "positioned by . . . others as deviant or debased . . . defined from above by the law." "General Introduction" in *The Subcultures Reader*, ed. Ken Gelder and Sarah Thornton (London: Routledge, 1997), 41. See also in that collection Milton Gordon, "The Concept of the Sub-Culture and its Application," 46–49. Establishing canters as a deviant subculture was one way of separating the "undeserving" from the "deserving" poor. Judith Frank documents in eighteenth-century fiction "the demarcation most characteristically made among the poor in the early modern period . . . between those who are respectable and laboring and those who are idle and profligate" in *Common Ground: Eighteenth-Century Satiric Fiction and the Poor* (Stanford, CA: Stanford UP, 1997), 2. See also Woodbridge, *Vagrancy, Homelessness, and English Renaissance Literature*, and E. P. Thompson, *Whigs and Hunters: The Origin of the Black Act* (Harmondsworth, UK: Penguin, 1977).

39. See Maria Assad, *Reading with Michel Serres: An Encounter with Time* (Albany: SUNY Press, 1999), 19.

40. See Serres, *Hermes* and *The Parasite*.

41. Douglas Hay, "England, 1562–1875: The Law and Its Uses," in *Masters, Servants, and Magistrates in Britain and the Empire*, ed. Douglas Hay and Paul Craven (Chapel Hill: U of North Carolina P, 2004), 59–116, 62. Elizabethan statutes had made illegal unlicensed movement beyond one hundred miles from one's home. For further discussion of the law and vagrancy, see Peter Linebaugh, *The London Hanged: Crime and Civil Society in the Eighteenth Century* (Cambridge, UK: Cambridge UP, 1992) and Douglas Hay and Nicholas Rogers, *Eighteenth-Century English Society: Shuttles and Swords* (Oxford: Oxford UP, 1997).

42. Statutes limited once-customary access to the commons—to firewood, game, and grazing—that had helped workers stay put. Hay describes the regulations enacted between 1720 and 1823 for the "compulsory recruitment to labor for the idle workers," noting that "the resulting body of law, as interpreted by the judges of the high courts, was considerably harsher towards workers than that of a century before." *Masters, Servants, and Magistrates*, 82. Although there has been much debate regarding the shift from an agrarian economy, here I agree with Judith Frank that "however controversial the measurement of quality of life . . . it is clear that the impetus of economic expansion uprooted many people from traditional types of community and labor." See *Common Ground*, 10.

43. Julie Coleman, *A History of Cant and Slang Dictionaries* (Oxford: Oxford UP, 2004), vol. 1, 27.

44. Ibid.

45. If, as Bryan Reynolds argues in *Becoming Criminal*, sixteenth- and seventeenth-century cant "menaced discrete subjective territor[ies]," they also shored those territories up again, dividing the "worthy" vulgar from the criminal on the basis of their imputed separate languages. Early cant depictions divided insiders from outsiders, high from low, stable from vagrant, known from unknown, precisely by circumscribing cant-speakers as separate beings and identifying them with chaos, impropriety, and immorality. To characterize cant and cant-speakers in those terms, as Reynolds does, is to assume the very language of authority.

46. Serres, *The Parasite*.

47. David Kazanjian, *The Colonizing Trick: National Culture and Imperial Citizenship in Early America* (Minneapolis: U of Minnesota P, 2003), 86–87.

48. Allon White has described how the comic quality of some early canting dictionaries, in contrast to the seriousness of dictionaries of "proper" and "hard" language, helped produce hierarchies of high and low. "The Dismal Sacred Word," in *Carnival, Hysteria, and Writing: Collected Essays and Autobiography* (Oxford: Clarendon Press, 1993), 129.

49. John Fletcher and Phillip Massinger, *Beggars Bush* (London, 1647) and Richard Brome, *The Jovial Crew* (London, 1652). See Julie Coleman's discussion of these plays, and their use of earlier cant glossaries, in *A History of Cant and Slang Dictionaries*, vol. 1, 45. See also Rosemary Gaby, "Of Vagabonds and Commonwealths: Beggars' Bush, a Jovial Crew, and the Sisters," *Studies in English Literature* 30 (1994): 401–24.

50. Brome, *The Jovial Crew*, n.p.

51. William Empson, *Some Versions of Pastoral* (1935; repr. New York: New Directions, 1974), 14.

52. Ibid., 13 and 21, respectively. Patricia Fumerton, too, describes the "unsettled 'freedom'" ascribed to beggars in John Taylor's *The Praise, Antiquity, and Commodity of Beggary* (1621). *Unsettled*, 56.

53. Knapp writes, "English audiences were increasingly urged to view the commonwealth of vagabonds as the crude image of a 'free' society." *Shakespeare's Tribes*, 77.

54. John Fletcher and Phillip Massinger, *Beggars Bush*, ed. John Dorenkamp (The Hague: Mouton, 1967), 143–44.

55. In both the literature and legal discourse of the period, gypsies, beggars, and vagrants—and cant-speakers more generally—sometimes occupy a discursively similar position, enviably free mobile figures who were nonetheless lawbreaking outsiders with their own way of life. The laws themselves suggested the ambiguity of cant-speakers—were they insiders or outsiders?—and their gradual classification as British. By 1572, Elizabethan Poor Law collapsed gypsies into the larger category of all those illegally wandering abroad. By 1741 statute law targeted not gypsies but those "pretending to be gypsies, or wandering in the habit and form of Egyptians." (The Justices Commitment Act [17 Geo. 2. C. 5].) This Act uses "gypsies" and "Egyptians" interchangeably. See William Addington, *An Abridgment of Penal Statutes* (London, 1775), 143.

56. Fumerton, *Unsettled*, xix.

57. Karl Marx, *Capital*, vol. 1, trans. Ben Fowkes (New York: Vintage, 1977), 875. Cited in Richard Halpern, *The Poetics of Primitive Accumulation* (Ithaca: Cornell UP, 1991), 71.

58. As cant-speaking criminals increasingly came to be seen as urban, innovating, and essentially British, gypsies, by contrast, remained a nomadic rural community represented as having fixed cultural practices, increasingly with ethnic overtones. Think, for instance, of the gypsies of Henry Fielding's *Tom Jones* and the foreign accent of their language, or, very popular in eighteenth-century Britain, Anonymous, *The Life and Adventures of Bampfylde-Moore Carew* (Exon, 1745).

59. Although performance contexts are beyond the scope of this book, I point to Bryan Reynolds's *Becoming Criminal*, which notes how early modern anti-theater campaigns objected to theater's new "naturalistic impersonations," with the troubling emphasis on mimicry that it shared with imposter criminals themselves (128). In a sort of hall of mirrors, canters often impersonated sick and lame people, and actors impersonated those impersonating beggars. Some feared that, because of its own powerful operations of imitation, theatrical experience might be in turn "so moving that it compelled its audience to imitate automatically what it saw on stage" (137). As well, as the songs of these plays circulated in collections, on broadsheets, and in the air itself, cant would be found in the mouths of a range of men and women.

60. Lincoln B. Faller, *Turned to Account: The Forms and Functions of Criminal Biography in Late Seventeenth- and Early Eighteenth-Century England* (Cambridge, UK: Cambridge UP, 1987) and Reynolds, *Becoming Criminal*. See also John Richetti, *Popular Fiction before Richardson* (Oxford: Clarendon, 1969).

61. Captain Alexander Smith, *A Compleat History of the Lives and Robberies . . .* (London, 1719) and Charles Johnson, *General History of the Lives and Adventures of the Most Famous Highwaymen . . .* (London, 1734). Smith's glossary does not appear until the fifth edition of 1719 (the first appeared in 1714), but it then takes center stage, opening the book. Johnson's preface speaks more directly to its subjects' British origins and foregrounds their learning of cant. His life of Arthur Chambers describes how he attempts to fool an innkeeper into thinking his language is foreign—specifically, Greek.

62. For the establishment of Shakespeare as national bard, see Michael Dobson, *The Making of the National Poet* (Oxford: Oxford UP, 1992).

63. *The Jovial Crew* became *The Jovial Crew, A Comic Opera* (London, 1731 and again in 1781) with many more songs, and even musical scores, but the cant was gone. *Beggars Bush* was adapted by Thomas Hull as *The Royal Merchant*, also a comic opera (London, 1768). Similarly, the anonymous *Harlot's Progress* (London, 1732), inspired by Hogarth's series of engravings of the same name, offers only a few cant terms, such as "crib'd" and "nib'd," 344.

64. *The Triumph of Wit* (London, 1688, with new editions 1702, 1712, 1724, 1780, and 1785).

65. I discuss cant and the novel in Chapter Two.

66. John Thurmond, *Harlequin Sheppard* (London, 1724), 22.

67. For the tightening legal restrictions, see Nicholas Rogers, "Policing the Poor in Eighteenth-Century London," *Social History* 24 (1991): 127–47.

68. The difficulties of the term "popular" appear in this claim, because while these dictionaries were clearly "hits" in the marketplace, their readership, like that of the criminal biographies Faller analyzes in *Turned to Account*, might have been limited to the relatively well-to-do.

69. Harman uses this expression to describe canting language in *Caveat or Warning for Common Cursetors*, ff. 2, recto.

70. Joan Platt, "Development of English Colloquial Idiom during the Eighteenth Century," *Review of English Studies* 2 (1926): 70–81, 79.

71. Jonathan Swift, *Letter to a Young Gentleman Lately Entered into Holy Orders*, 2nd ed. (London, 1721), 10.

72. In the odd sound of this language and in the hypocrisy of claiming familiarity with a language not at all their own, we find surprising connections to the cant associated with the false preaching of one's religious opponents. Mr. Spectator describes cant as "all sudden exclamations, whinings, and unusual tones" in *The Spectator* 147 (11 August 1711): 111–12, 147.

73. See Tony Crowley, *Standard English and the Politics of Language* (Urbana: U of Illinois P, 1989); Andrew Elfenbein, *Romanticism and the Rise of English*, (Stanford, CA: Stanford UP, 2009); Sterling Leonard, *The Doctrine of Correctness in English Usage 1700–1800* (New York: Columbia UP, 1929); Susie Tucker, *Protean Shape: A Study in Eighteenth-Century Vocabulary and Usage* (London: Athlone, 1967) and *English Examined: Two Centuries of Comment on the Mother-Tongue* (Cambridge, UK: Cambridge UP, 1961).

74. Raymond Williams, *Keywords: A Vocabulary of Culture and Society* (New York: Oxford UP, 1976), 70–71.

75. The *Oxford English Dictionary* cites this usage starting in 1746. Similarly, the OED shows that until the eighteenth century, the phrase "the vulgar" could refer to "the common language of the country," without any sense of the indicting lowness the phrase would come to have. See also William Matthews's survey of eighteenth-century English grammars and language guides and their references to "vulgarisms" in "Some Eighteenth-Century Vulgarisms," *The Review of English Studies* 13 (1937): 307–25.

76. *Critical Review* vol. 3 (1756): 386 and vol. 80 (1781): 165. Cited in Tucker, *Protean Shape*, 57.

77. *Critical Review* vol. 47 (1779): 447. Cited in Tucker, *Protean Shape*, 59.

78. Robert Lowth, *Short Introduction to Grammar* (London, 1783). iv, 141, 89, 28.

79. Ibid., 28.

80. *The Rambler* 208 (14 March 1752): 286.

81. *General Dictionary of the English Language*, vol. 1 (London, 1755).

82. *New Canting Dictionary*, n.p.

83. White, "The Dismal Sacred Word," 130.

84. *Bacchus and Venus* (London, 1737).

85. Roman Jakobson, *Selected Works of Roman Jakobson*, vol. 4 (The Hague: Mouton, 1966), 638–39.

86. These terms are marked as "cant" in B. E., *New Dictionary*.

87. John Ray, *Compleat Collection of English Proverbs* (London, 1670; repr. London, 1737), 29 and 51.

88. Ibid., 53.

89. Nathan Bailey, *An Universal Etymological Dictionary* (London, 1721).

90. Ibid.

91. Ibid.

92. Ray, *Compleat Collection*, 226.

93. For a discussion of these dynamics, see Benedict Anderson, *Imagined Communities: Reflections on the Origin and Spread of Nationalism* (London: Verso, 1983) and Elfenbein, *Romanticism and the Rise of English*.

94. Michael Warner, *Publics and Counterpublics* (New York: Zone, 2002), 75.

95. "Preface," *New Canting Dictionary*, n.p.

96. *Bacchus and Venus*.

97. B. E., *New Dictionary*, n.p., and "Preface," *New Canting Dictionary*, n.p.

98. Like books devoted to the canting crews before it, *New Canting Dictionary* includes "Songs in the Canting Dialect," most of which had appeared in Head's seventeenth-century *The Canting Academy*. The inclusion of these songs associated cant with entertainment; yet, the *New Canting Dictionary* eliminated some of its frankly entertaining aspects, silently removing the ribald phrases from Head's songs. See my "Vulgar Tongues: Canting Dictionaries and the Language of the People in Eighteenth-Century Britain," *Eighteenth-Century Studies* 37 no. 3 (2004): 435–54.

99. *New Canting Dictionary*, n.p.

100. "Preface," ibid., n.p.

101. Indeed, as Knapp notes in *Shakespeare's Tribe* (66), some writers, including John Webster, characterized cant as more stable than English because it withstood the changes that a series of conquests had brought to English.

102. "Preface," *New Canting Dictionary*, n.p.

103. This was a literal legal license, at least through the sixteenth and seventeenth centuries. See Paul Slack, *Poverty and Policy in Tudor & Stuart England* (New York: Longman, 1988), 63, 92, 118, 119.

104. *New Dictionary*, n.p.

105. B. E. also discusses gypsies in these terms. The vagrancy of both represented a freedom of mobility that became increasingly important in later-century discussion of Anglo-Saxon liberties. It is both strange and perhaps predictable that in some circles at this time gypsies, in their mobility and distinct form of governance, became the stand-ins for a once-free British people and the reputed speakers of cant. See *An Apology for the Life and Adventures of Bampfylde Moore Carew* (Sherborne, 1749).

106. Roxann Wheeler, *The Complexion of Race: Categories of Difference in Eighteenth-Century British Culture* (Philadelphia: U of Pennsylvania P, 2000), 74.

107. For a full discussion of this rhetoric—and an argument against its indebtedness to marginal or progressive groups—see Nicholas Hudson, "'Britons Never Will Be Slaves': National Myth, Conservatism, and the Beginnings of British Anti-Slavery," *Eighteenth-Century Studies* 34 (2001): 559–76, 563–64.

108. Charles Taylor, *Modern Social Imaginaries* (2004; repr. Durham, NC: Duke UP, 2007), 110.

109. John Barrell describes Coke and Blackstone's preference for "common, and as it were unwritten law . . . over statute law" in *English Literature in History 1730–1780: An Equal, Wide Survey* (London: Hutchinson, 1983), 120.

110. Taylor traces the relationship between this Anglo-Saxon political rhetoric and conceptions of popular sovereignty in *Modern Social Imaginaries*, 109–17.

111. Barrell, *English Literature in History*, 112 and 113 respectively.

112. John Locke, *An Essay Concerning Human Understanding*, ed. Peter Nidditch (Oxford: Clarendon Press, 1974), 405.

113. Samuel Johnson, *Plan of an English Dictionary* (London, 1747), n.p.

114. Implicitly it was not the vulgar, let alone speakers of criminal jargon. As Barrell notes (*English Literature in History* 119), for eighteenth-century writers "the customs of the vulgar have no authority whatsoever in determining matters of correct usage." In their exclusion from polite language, cant and vulgar language might reveal not the universal freedom but the peculiar unfreedom of a linguistic model based on "customary" use. This reading underscores the "imposition" aspect of Locke's "voluntary imposition" in *An Essay Concerning Human Understanding*, ed. Roger Woolhouse (London, Penguin, 1997), 363. For an expansion of this discussion of the voluntary imposition of language, see William Keach, *Arbitrary Power: Romanticism, Language, Politics* (Princeton, NJ: Princeton UP, 2004).

115. James Howell, *Lexicon Tetraglotton* (London, 1660), not paginated. Howell even argues, "In our Common Law there are some Proverbs that carry a kind of Authority with them.... Such as Possession is eleven points of the law."

116. Quotation from Taylor, *Modern Social Imaginaries*, 111.

117. Howell, *Lexicon Tetraglotton*, n.p.

118. B. E., *New Dictionary*.

119. Interestingly, Aesop, author of fables, which, like proverbs, were both seemingly simple and opaque, was also reputedly a slave. Annabel Patterson describes the power dynamics that would lead a slave to strategic opacity in *Fables of Power: Aesopian Writing and Political History* (Durham: Duke UP, 1991). Jayne Lewis notes the "self-conscious Englishness" of eighteenth-century fable collections in Britain in *The English Fable: Aesop and Literary Culture* (Cambridge, UK: Cambridge UP, 1996), 9 and 3, respectively.

120. Heller-Rozen, *Dark Tongues*, 32.

121. Tiffany, *Infidel Poetics*, 18.

122. Samuel Johnson, *A Dictionary of the English Language* (London, 1774), s.v. "vernacular."

123. *Oxford English Dictionary*, s.v. "vernacular."

124. See Alan Ryan, *On Politics: A History of Political Theory* (New York: W. W. Norton, 2012), 73.

125. Even earlier collections, such as Head's *The Canting Academy*, give a sense of the foreign in cant, with terms such as "bene," meaning good.

126. Coleman, *A History of Cant and Slang Dictionaries*, vol. 1, 80 and 100. As Paula Blank has shown, writers from as early as 1610 had described cant as "cosmopolitan... incorporating Dutch, Spanish, and French forms." *Broken English: Dialects and the Politics of Language in Renaissance Writings* (New York: Routledge, 1996), 54.

127. These appear in Thomas Fuller's *Gnomologia: Adageis [sic] and Proverbs, Wise Sentences and Witty Sayings, Ancient and Modern, Foreign and British* (London, 1736) as "foreign" but are not differentiated by country of origin.

128. James Bono, *The Word of God and the Languages of Man* (Madison: U of Wisconsin P, 1995), 64.

Chapter Two. Daniel Defoe's Novel Languages

1. B. E., *A New Dictionary of the Terms Ancient and Modern of the Canting Crew* (London, n.d., 1697-1699?).

2. DeWitt Starnes and Gertrude Noyes, *The English Dictionary from Cawdrey to Johnson, 1604-1725* (Chapel Hill: U of North Carolina P, 1946), and William B. Warner, *Licensing Entertainment: The Elevation of Novel Reading in Britain, 1684-1750* (Berkeley: U of California P, 1998), 19.

3. Michael Warner, *Publics and Counterpublics* (New York: Zone Books, 2005), 75.

4. Mikhail Bakhtin, *The Dialogic Imagination: Four Essays*, ed. and trans. Michael Holquist (Austin: U of Texas P, 1986), 272–73.

5. See Srinivas Aravamudan's helpful corrective to "rise of the novel" formulations in *Enlightenment Orientalism: Resisting the Rise of the Novel* (Chicago: U of Chicago P, 2012). Bakhtin ascribes a "diversity of speech" to the novel *Dialogic Imagination* (308).

6. Timothy Brennan, "The National Longing for Form," in *Nation and Narration*, ed. Homi K. Bhabha (London: Routledge, 1990), 49.

7. Bakhtin, *Dialogic Imagination*, 324.

8. Allon White, "Bakhtin, Sociolinguistics, and Deconstruction," in *The Theory of Reading*, ed. Frank Gloversmith, (Brighton: Harvester Press, 1984), 136 and 139.

9. Terms from Daniel Defoe's *The History and Remarkable Life of the Truly Honourable Col. Jacque, Commonly Call'd Col Jack*, ed. Samuel Holt Monk (Oxford: Oxford UP, 1989), 17, and Henry Fielding's *The Life of Jonathan Wild the Great*, ed. Hugh Amory (Oxford: Oxford UP, 1997), 76, respectively. Ian Watt describes Defoe's language as that of "artisans and countrymen" and notes that "it contains a higher proportion of Anglo-Saxon origin than that of any other well-known writer, [excepting] Bunyan." *The Rise of the Novel* (1957; repr. Stanford UP, 1967), 101.

10. Henry Fielding, *Joseph Andrews*, ed. Thomas Keymer (Oxford: Oxford UP, 1996), 79.

11. Tobias Smollett, *The Adventures of Roderick Random*, ed. Paul Gabriel Boucé (Oxford: Oxford UP, 1988), 26 and 31, respectively.

12. Thomas Keymer, "Introduction" in Samuel Richardson, *Pamela*, ed. Thomas Keymer and Alice Wakely (Oxford: Oxford UP, 2001), xvii.

13. Richardson, *Pamela*, 9.

14. Aravamudan, *Enlightenment Orientalism*, 39.

15. Ibid, 21. He cites Robert Miles, "Romanticism, Enlightenment, Mediation," in *This Is Enlightenment*, ed. Clifford Siskin and William Warner (Chicago: U of Chicago P, 2010), 173–88.

16. Aravamudan, *Enlightenment Orientalism*, 22.

17. Defoe, *Colonel Jack*. Further citations appear parenthetically.

18. Terry Eagleton, "Pineapples and Pork Chops," *London Review of Books* 23 October 2003: 17–19, 18.

19. John Richetti, "Mimesis/mimesis and the Eighteenth-Century British Novel," in *Defoe's Footprints*, ed. Robert M. Maniquis and Carl Fisher (Toronto: U of Toronto P, 2009), 78.

20. Although Defoe uses a wide range of languages in his fiction, his advocating for a language academy that would itself "decide custom" would seem, uncharacteristically, to discredit a popular-based linguistic sovereignty. Yet the "biggest cause" for the academy's concern would be swearing, and unlike other academy advocates, Defoe does not emphasize correcting vulgar use. *An Essay upon Projects* (London, 1697).

21. Michel de Certeau, "Vocal Utopias: Glossolalias," *Representations* 56 (1996): 34.

22. See Albert Rivero's annotations to *Moll Flanders* (New York: W. W. Norton, 2004), 62 and Douglas Hay, *Albion's Fatal Tree: Crime and Society in Eighteenth-Century England* (London: Verso, 2011).

23. See also Defoe's *A Tour Thro' the Whole Island of Great Britain* (London, 1724–27), which I discuss in Part Two. Cynthia Wall argues that a "new consciousness of space ... as fluid, shifting, unreliable" emerged after the Great Fire with the rapid rebuilding that took place. She refers to this, helpfully, as "uncanny modern space." "Grammars of Space: From Stow's Survey to Defoe's Tour," *Philological Quarterly* 76 (1997): 387–411, 389.

24. James Buzard, *Disorienting Fiction: The Autoethnographic Work of Nineteenth-Century British Novels* (Princeton, NJ: Princeton UP, 2005), 7.

25. Robert B. Shoemaker, *The London Mob: Violence and Disorder in Eighteenth-Century England* (London: Hambledon Continuum, 2004).

26. *OED* s.v. "bagnio."

27. Increasingly uncomfortable because at the same time as such social mixing was taking place, and in response to it, a greater premium was also placed on privacy.

28. Carla Mazzio, *The Inarticulate Renaissance: Language Trouble in a Time of Eloquence* (Philadelphia: U of Pennsylvania P, 2009), 9.

29. B. E., *New Dictionary*.

30. Lincoln B. Faller, *Crime and Defoe: A New Kind of Writing* (Cambridge, UK: Cambridge UP, 1993), 4.

31. Alexander Smith, *A Complete History of the Lives and Robberies . . .*, vol. 1 (London, 1719), 108.

32. Ibid., 127.

33. Ibid.

34. Hal Gladfelder argues that "the effect of [Defoe's] imitation of the speech of others is to induce us as readers to identify with alien subjectivities." "Defoe and Criminal Fiction," in *The Cambridge Companion to Daniel Defoe*, ed. John Richetti (Cambridge, UK: Cambridge UP, 2008), 65.

35. Faller, *Crime and Defoe*, 56.

36. Defoe, *Colonel Jack*, annotation, 312.

37. Ronald Paulson, *Popular and Polite Art in the Age of Hogarth and Fielding* (Notre Dame, IN: Notre Dame UP, 1979), describes the efforts of some jest book compilers to distance their material from the low and popular (70).

38. These dynamics might also help account for the gender disparity in predominantly male authorship of the realist prose fictions and their representations of language.

39. W. R. Owens and P. N. Furbank, *A KWIC Concordance to Daniel Defoe's "Moll Flanders"* (New York: Garland, 1985), 175.

40. Catherine Gallagher, "The Rise of Fictionality," in *The Novel, Volume I: History, Geography and Culture*, ed. Franco Moretti (Princeton, NJ: Princeton UP, 2006), 336–63, 356.

41. Faller provides additional evidence of the texts' insistence on their own fictionality in *Defoe and Crime*, 29–31.

42. *OED* s.v. "garble."

43. Adam Hansen, "Criminal Conversations," *Literature and History* 26 (2004): 26–84, 31.

44. Smith's history includes biographies of Moll Jones, Moll Raby, and Mary Frith, alias Moll Cutpurse. The latter's alias suggests that by the seventeenth century "Moll" had already become a conventional moniker for a female criminal or thief.

45. Deidre Lynch shows how later in the century this versatility became associated with the worldly perspective of the disinterested gentleman, tracking "the sorts of low life panache to which, paradoxically enough, impersonality could be linked," in *The Economy of Character: Novels, Market Culture, and the Business of Inner Meaning* (Chicago: U of Chicago P, 1998), 83.

46. Hansen, "Criminal Conversations," 41.

47. William Empson, *Some Versions of Pastoral* (1935; repr. New York: New Directions, 1974).

48. John J. Richetti, *Defoe's Narratives: Situations and Structures* (Oxford: Clarendon Press, 1975). Raymond Williams discusses "structures of feeling" in his *Marxism and Literature* (Oxford: Oxford UP, 1977).

49. Defoe, *An Essay upon Projects*. I do not want to overstate Defoe's embrace of in-

novations in language; he does, after all, describe word coining as reprehensible, as criminal as counterfeiting money. Yet the linguistic diversity he catalogues in his *Tour Thro' the Whole Island of Great Britain* (1724–27), his vision of the Academy evaluating the wit of new theatrical productions, and the linguistic exuberance of his novels, with the varying modes of attachment that I have been tracking, counter any strict linguistic authoritarianism we might be tempted to ascribe to his call for an Academy.

50. For a full discussion of these transformations in Defoe's novels see Dennis Todd, *Defoe's America* (Cambridge, UK: Cambridge UP, 2010), ix.

51. Deidre Lynch, "The Novel," in *The Restoration and Eighteenth Century*, ed. Cynthia Wall (Malden, MA: Blackwell, 2005), 123.

52. John Locke, *A Second Treatise on Government* (London, 1689), II, section viii.

53. Robert Steinfeld observes that "not until the nineteenth century did it [free labor] become the paradigm for normal employment." Cited in Roxann Wheeler, "Powerful Affections," in Maniquis and Fisher, *Defoe's Footprints*, 133.

54. In "Vulgar Tongues: Canting Dictionaries and the Language of the People," *Eighteenth-Century Studies* 37 (2004): 45–54, I explore how, at the same time as popular practices and customary relations of servitude were being criminalized, criminal linguistic terms became highly visible in wide-selling cant collections, representing popular and "low" culture as both criminal and existing outside of labor relations altogether. See also Peter Linebaugh, *The London Hanged: Crime and Civil Society in the Eighteenth Century* (Cambridge, UK: Cambridge UP, 1992).

55. Nathaniel Bailey, *An Universal Etymological Dictionary* (London, 1721).

56. Roxann Wheeler paraphrases Robert Steinfeld: "In the . . . eighteenth century, freedom and unfreedom . . . were not as absolute and opposite as they seem today." "Powerful Affections," 133. Consider the suggestive legal language, in which an apprentice's successful completion of a fixed number of years of servitude led to what was called "freedom of the company"—a key distinction between this form of servitude and slavery.

57. Todd, *Defoe's America*, ix.

58. Jan S. Hogendorn, "The Economics of the African Slave Trade," *Journal of American History* 70 (1984): 860.

59. Gwenda Morgan and Peter Rushton, "Visible Bodies: Power Subordination and Identity in the Eighteenth-Century Atlantic World," *Journal of Social History* 39 (2005): 39–64, 39.

60. Todd, *Defoe's America*, 92.

61. Herbert S. Klein writes that "where slavery came to be a recognized and important institution, it was the lack of ties to the family . . . that finally distinguished slaves from all other workers." *The Atlantic Slave Trade* (Cambridge, UK: Cambridge UP, 1999), 2.

62. Peter Okun, *Crime and the Nation: Prison Reform and Popular Fiction in Philadelphia, 1786–1800* (New York: Routledge, 2002), 35. He adds, "Samuel Johnson's dismissal of Americans in 1769 as 'a race of convicts' was hyperbolic, but not unfounded" (35).

63. For a description of the "middle passage" of white indentured servants, see Hilary Beckles, *White Servitude and Black Slavery in Barbados, 1627–1715* (Knoxville: U of Tennessee P, 1989).

64. George Boulukos argues that if Jack begins his time in North America in close proximity to and essentially undifferentiated from African slaves, he teaches himself to think of "'African' and 'black' as if they were synonyms for slaves." See "Daniel Defoe's Colonel Jack, Grateful Slaves, and Racial Difference," *ELH* 68 (2001): 615–31, 617. Todd, too, traces how the "freedom and mastery of Europeans were imagined against a savage Other." *Defoe's America*, 30.

65. David Kazanjian, *The Colonizing Trick: National Culture and Imperial Citizenship in Early America* (Minneapolis: U of Minnesota P, 2003), 10. Wheeler notes that contemporary readers would have understood such depictions of pidgin as debasing. She cites Friday's complaint that "Defoe makes him a blockhead through his pidgin English" in Charles Gildon's *The Life and Strange Surprizing Adventures of Mr. D— Def—, of London*, 2nd ed. (London, 1719). *The Complexion of Race: Categories of Difference in Eighteenth-Century British Culture* (Philadelphia: U of Pennsylvania P, 2000), 89.

66. At least not in Defoe's work. For a reading of the more complex significance of "West Indies dialect," see "Sounding Black-ish: West Indian Pidgin in London Performance and Print," expected publication in *Eighteenth-Century Studies* 51 (2017).

67. For Moll, as a woman, as for her mother before her, the past cannot be completely put behind her in North America. Moll's mother's early transport meant that Moll does not recognize her own brother when choosing a husband, and in the new world both mother and daughter are upbraided with the sine qua non of human taboos, incest. The shape-shifting powers of cant, underwritten in part by transatlantic movement and the institutionalization of a racialized slavery, it would appear, are available in a more unrestricted fashion to men. See my "I Talk to Everybody in Their Own Way," in *The New Economic Criticism: Studies at the Intersection of Literature and Economics*, ed. M. Woodmansee and M. Osteen (New York: Routledge, 1999), 75–94.

68. George Boulukos, *The Grateful Slave: The Emergence of Race in Eighteenth-Century British and American Culture* (Cambridge, UK: Cambridge UP, 2008), 77.

69. Francis Grose, *A Classical Dictionary of the Vulgar Tongue* (London, 1785), 5.

70. Wheeler, *The Complexion of Race*, 74.

71. He writes that "'new' particularities, such as race and nation vigorously emerge at the precise historical moment at which the value form abstracts subjects and commodities from their particularities, and at which capitalism represents this abstraction as 'freedom.'" Kazanjian, *The Colonizing Trick*, 20.

Chapter Three. John Gay's Overloaded Languages

1. See his Preface to *Miscellanies*: "the splendid Palaces of the Great are often no other than Newgate with the Mask on," vol. 2 (London, 1743), xx.

2. John Gay, *The Beggar's Opera*, ed. B. Loughrey and T. Treadwell (London: Penguin, 1986). Citations noted by act and scene: III.iii and I.vi; "lock" and "pumped" both appear in B. E., *New Dictionary* and the anonymous *New Canting Dictionary*.

3. *The Regulator: or, a Discovery of the Thieves, Thief-Takers, and Locks, Alias Receivers of Stolen Goods in and about the City of London* (London, 1718), 10.

4. *The Scoundrels Dictionary* (London, 1754), too, presents not a heterogeneous, permeable community of cant-speakers but a highly organized subculture, outlining subversive rituals of initiation and membership. Its dark portrait of this scheming society emphasizes their use of assigned code names: "the upright man demands his name; which known, he enjoyns him from that time to renounce it, and to take upon him one familiar to the canting strain, not understood by the vulgar" (11). This again sets the canting crew not within but against the common people. *The Scoundrels Dictionary* evokes a documentary quality, claiming to be "printed from a copy taken on one of their Gang, in the late scuffle between the watchmen and a party of them on Clerkenwell-Green; which copy is now in the custody of one of the constables of that parish." The word list, however, is lifted word for word from Head's much earlier *The Canting Academy*, and, like Head's work, it casts canters as ethnic outsiders, gypsies.

5. Dennis Todd describes the shift from the sentence of transport as a mercy shown to felons to a routine punishment after the Transportation Act of 1718 in *Defoe's America* (Cambridge, UK: Cambridge UP, 2010), 8, 11.

6. Robert Dryden makes this observation in "Polly: Unmasking Pirates and Fortune Hunters in the West Indies," *Eighteenth-Century Studies* 34 (2001): 537–57, 548. See also John Richardson, "John Gay and Slavery," *Modern Language Review* 97 (2002): 15–25.

7. Peter Reed, "Conquer or Die: Staging Circum-Atlantic Revolt in Polly and Three-Finger'd Jack," *Theatre Journal* 59 (2007): 241–58, 250.

8. Similarly, the narrator of Henry Fielding's *Jonathan Wild* describes the years his cant-speaking criminal hero spent on "Plantations in America" as "a blank in this history," containing "not one adventure worthy the reader's notice." *Jonathan Wild*, ed. Claude Rawson and Hugh Armory, notes by Linda Bree (Oxford: Oxford UP, 2003), 24.

9. At least overtly—Moll ceases to speak cant in the narrative, but recall the editor's preface and the admission that he had to clean up her "Newgate" language retroactively.

10. As Tod Gilman puts it, Gay was "championing traditionally British musico-dramatic conventions against foreign forms" and creating "a viable form of native music drama." "The Beggar's Opera and British Opera," *University of Toronto Quarterly* 66 (1997): 539–61, 539 and 540, respectively.

11. Peter Schulz offers a guide to the "Ballad Originals" of Gay's songs in *Gay's Beggar's Opera: Its Content, History & Influence* (New Haven, CT: Yale UP, 1923), but this tends to be limited to late seventeenth- and early eighteenth-century publications. For a more comprehensive resource, see the UCSB English Broadside Ballad Archive at http://ebba.english.ucsb.edu/.

12. Steve Newman, *Ballad Collection, Lyric, and the Canon* (Philadelphia: U of Pennsylvania P, 2007), 41.

13. James Relph, "Of Musick," in *The Touchstone . . . Essays on the Reigning Diversions of the Town* (London, 1728), 16, cited in *Contexts 1: The Beggar's Opera*, ed. J. V. Guerinot and R. D. Jilg (Hamden, CT: Archon, 1976), 102.

14. *Seven Sermons on Public Occasions. By the Most Reverend Dr. Thomas Herring*, ed. William Duncombe (London, 1763), ix, cited in Guerinot and Jilg, *Contexts 1*, 123.

15. *Thievery à la Mode: or the Fatal Encouragement* (London, 1728), 15–16, cited in Guerinot and Jilg, *Contexts 1*, 129–30. As well, a poem of the period claims that "Shakespear divine was cut to the Soul" by the popularity of the play. See "A Ballad, Call'd, A Dissertation on the Beggar's Opera" (1731), cited in Schulz, *Gay's Beggar's Opera*, 30.

16. Swift proposed in a letter of August 30, 1716 that Gay write a "Porter, Footan, or Chairman's Pastoral" and asks, "what think you of a Newgate-Pastoral, among the whores and thieves there?" *Works of Jonathan Swift*, 5th ed. Vol. 7. (Dublin, 1751).

17. William Empson, *Some Versions of Pastoral* (1935; repr. New York: New Directions, 1974), 200.

18. Ibid., 11 and 199, respectively. Further citations noted parenthetically.

19. Empson describes this phenomenon specifically in relation to *Henry IV* in *Some Versions of Pastoral*, 29.

20. Michael McKeon provides an excellent appraisal of the "plasticity" inherent in the genre even in at its inception and cites Frank Kermode's observation that "the eighteenth century excelled in mock pastoral." My point is to track the work of diction in Gay's mock pastoral and its particular ramifications for ideas of the vernacular. "The Pastoral Revolution," in *Refiguring Revolutions: Aesthetics and Politics from the English Revolution to the Romantic Revolution*, ed. Kevin Sharpe and Stephen Zwicker (Berkeley: U of California P, 1998), 267 and 274, respectively.

21. For a discussion of this political vision, see Isaac Kramnick, *Bolingbroke and His Circle: The Politics of Nostalgia in the Age of Walpole* (1968; repr. Ithaca, NY: Cornell UP, 1992).

22. *The Guardian* 30 (15 April 1713).

23. Alexander Pope, "Discourse on Pastoral Poetry," *Complete Poetic Works*, ed. H. Boynton (Boston: Houghton Mifflin, 1903), 3–10.

24. Joseph Addison, "An Essay on Virgil's Georgics," *The Works of Virgil* (London, 1697).

25. And down to provincial language, as I detailed in Chapter Five.

26. *The Flying Post or the Weekly Medley* 15 (11 January 1729).

27. There is occasional vulgarity—"what, a plague, does the woman mean?" (I.iv) Peachum asks; Mrs. Peachum calls her own daughter "baggage" and "hussy" (I.viii); and there are references to "whores" (I.iv) and "plaguey wives" (II.iv)—but far less than one might expect from a "realist" representation of criminals.

28. John B. Bender, *Imagining the Penitentiary: Fiction and the Architecture of Mind in Eighteenth-Century England* (Chicago: U of Chicago P, 1987), 95.

29. While I agree with Bender's helpful comparative review of the "novelization" of Defoe's and Gay's writing—despite Defoe's being "horrified" at the implications of *The Beggar's Opera*—I place more emphasis on the emerging realist techniques of Defoe's work. While Bender thus sees the "smattering of cant" in *The Beggar's Opera* as a mere convention of realism, I see cant working quite differently in Defoe's and Gay's respective works, as I detail below. *Imagining the Penitentiary*, 88 and 95, respectively.

30. It is true that the depiction of cant-speakers differs from earlier dramatic depictions such as *The Jovial Crew*, in which they are mere ciphers whose unfettered movement through the countryside and avoidance of the burden of labor represent pure fantasy, a mere trope. Gay's cant-speaking characters are instead the play's protagonists, which has the effect, as Diane Dugaw has explained, of "humanizing lower orders." But the narrative technique and generic cross-writing certainly limit this humanizing quality. See *Deep Play: John Gay and the Invention of Modernity* (Newark: U of Delaware P, 2001), 32. See also Steve Newman's discussion of character in *Ballad Collection, Lyric, and the Canon*, 23–25.

31. There are, of course, vestiges of Romance at work in Defoe's texts, qualifying this sense of random events of an individual life.

32. Fredric Jameson, *The Antinomies of Realism* (London: Verso, 2013), 24–25. Further citations noted parenthetically.

33. Lisa Freeman, *Character's Theater: Genre and Identity on the Eighteenth-Century English Stage* (Philadelphia: U of Pennsylvania P, 2002), 7. I refer here to the narrative structure of realist fiction, with the caveat that, as Leah Price reminds us, not all readers would necessarily have read whole books in sequence. See *The Anthology and the Rise of the Novel* (Cambridge, UK: Cambridge UP, 2000).

34. Jameson, *Antinomies of Realism*, 19. Jameson draws on Walter Benjamin in identifying death as a unifying principle of the récit.

35. Steve Newman argues that Gay's characters have both a flat and round quality, at once cartoonish but also sympathetic (*Ballad Collection, Lyric, and the Canon*, 39). These qualities might, in turn, be elicited by the respective genres from which Gay draws. Freeman insists that audiences trace "character in relation to generic conventions over the course of a play" (41).

36. Freeman, *Character's Theater*, 8.

37. Empson puts this another way: characters are only plausible if they don't mean all the play puts in their words. *Some Versions of Pastoral*, 215.

38. This definition of "doxy" is found in B. E.'s *New Dictionary*.

39. Erin Mackie, *Rakes, Highwaymen, and Pirates: The Making of the Modern Gentleman in the Eighteenth Century* (Baltimore: Johns Hopkins UP, 2009).

40. Thus, while violation is, on the one hand, a source of scandal, the play also resists that dichotomy by inviting odd and temporary alliances in its combinations of cant and colloquial languages. For Empson, this is one "final meaning" of the play's irony—"No distinction between high and low can be accepted for a minute." *Some Versions of Pastoral*, 249-50.

41. Daniel Defoe, *Moll Flanders*, ed. Albert Rivero (New York: W. W. Norton, 2004), 10.

42. Jayne Lewis, *The English Fable: Aesop and Literary Culture 1651-1740* (Cambridge, UK: Cambridge UP, 1996), 8.

43. Ibid., 2.

44. Whatever independence criminality and cant might seem to offer is framed from the play's opening as being rigorously monitored and controlled by Peachum, who is reciprocally controlled by Macheath in his hold over Peachum's daughter.

45. John Richardson, "John Gay, The Beggar's Opera, and Forms of Resistance," *Eighteenth-Century Life* 24 (2000): 19-30, 24.

46. One of the great ironies of the play's history is, of course, its own spectacular commodification, as the language and imagery of the play became the means for selling fans, screens, and playing cards. For a descriptive history of these commodities, see Schulz, *Gay's Beggar's Opera*.

47. Gay, *Beggar's Opera*, 41.

48. Steve Newman makes this point in *Ballad Collection, Lyric, and the Canon*.

49. See Rivero's annotation in Defoe, *Moll Flanders*, 66.

50. Peter Linebaugh, "The Tyburn Riot against the Surgeons," in *Albion's Fatal Tree* (New York: Pantheon, 1975), 109.

51. While seventeenth-century plays such as *The Jovial Crew* had featured canters singing cant-laden songs, *The Beggar's Opera* offers popular songs rewritten for and recontextualized in an "opera" of the criminal underworld.

52. For a discussion of the commodification of old ballads, see Dianne Dugaw, "The Popular Marketing of Old Ballads: The Ballad Revival and Eighteeth-Century Antiquarianism Reconsidered," *Eighteenth-Century Studies* 21 (1997): 71-90.

53. James Harding cites eighteenth-century English dialect connecting the gallows and eroticism, e.g., "'He's a gallus un' would be said to a girl as a warning against a rustic Lovelace." *English Dialect Dictionary*, vol. 2, ed. Joseph Wright (1898; repr. London: Oxford UP, 1970), 545. Cited in "'He's a Gallus Un': Excess, Restriction, and Narrative Reprieve at the Gallows in *Tom Jones*," *Eighteenth-Century Life* 18 (1994): 15-35, 26. Harding also describes "the sexual overtones of long-standing folk traditions concerning the hanging of an individual" (28) dating back to the sixteenth century.

54. *The Merry Musician; or, a cure for the spleen: being a collection of the most diverting songs and pleasant ballads, set to musick*, vol. 1 (London, 1716-33?), 237 and 238, respectively.

55. Thomas d'Urfey's *Pills to Purge the Melancholy* (London, 1698-1720).

56. Newman, *Ballad Collection, Lyric, and the Canon*, 20, and Empson, *Some Versions of Pastoral*, 11, 12.

57. *Merry Musician*, vol. 1.

58. See Dugaw's comprehensive discussion of the popular cultural elements of Gay's work, such as "songs familiar to the low from broad sheets" in *Deep Play*.

59. *Bacchus and Venus* (London, 1737), title page.

60. Daniel White discusses the hostility to cant and the connection of it to "common"

language in "'Slangwhangery of the Jargonists': Writing, Speech, and the Character of Romanticism," *Studies in Romanticism* (2017).

61. Fielding, *Jonathan Wild*, 20.

62. Daniel Defoe, *The History and Lives of all the Most Notorious Pirates* (London, 1729), 94.

63. Hollis Rinehart describes the influence of Bacon's biography on this section in "Fielding's Chapter 'Of Proverbs,'" *Modern Philology* 77 (1980): 291–96. See also Thomas Fuller, *Gnomologia, Adagies [sic] and Proverbs, Wise Sentences, and Witty Sayings* (London, 1730) and James Kelly, *Some Select Proverbs and Wise Sayings* (Dublin, 1722).

64. John Ray, *Compleat English Proverbs*, 3rd ed. (London, 1737).

65. Michel de Certeau, "Vocal Utopias: Glossolalias," *Representations* 56 (1996): 29–47, 33.

66. Ibid., 33.

Chapter Four. The Gendered Slang of Century's End

1. Samuel Johnson, *Dictionary of the English Language* (London, 1755) and Nathan Bailey, *Dictionarium Britannicum* (London, 1730), respectively.

2. James Beattie, "On Laughter and Ludicrous Conversation," in *Essays* (Aberdeen, 1776), 612 and 601, respectively. Much reproduced, "On Laughter" appeared in multiple editions of Beattie's collected essays in Edinburgh and London.

3. Peter Reed documents this shift in "Conquer or Die: Staging Circum-Atlantic Revolt in Polly and Three-Finger'd Jack," *Theatre Journal* 59 (2007): 241–58.

4. Francis Grose, *A Classical Dictionary of the Vulgar Tongue*, (London, 1785), ii and iii. The 1811 edition, entitled *Lexicon Balatronicum: a Dictionary of Buckish Slang, University, Wit, and Pickpocket Eloquence* (London, 1811) is still in print, and is even available on Kindle.

5. For brief speculation on Grose's methods, see Vic Gatrell, *City of Laughter: Sex and Satire in Eighteenth-Century London* (London: Atlantic Books, 2006), 135–36.

6. See also George Parker's *A View of Society in High and Low Life* (London, 1781) and the anonymous *New London Spy* (London, 1771), in which the term "slang" appears.

7. Beattie, "On Laughter," 647.

8. Pierre Bourdieu, *Language and Symbolic Power*, trans. Gino Raymond and M. Adamson (Malden, MA: Polity, 1992), 90.

9. Grose, *Classical Dictionary*, i.

10. Parker, *A View of Society in High and Low Life* and *Life's Painter of Variegated Characters* (London, 1786).

11. *Life's Painter*, 125. Maximillian Novak cites a letter by Defoe in which he talks about himself in similar terms, Daniel Defoe: Master of Fictions (Oxford UP, 2001), 302.

12. Grose, *Classical Dictionary*, v-vi.

13. Ned Ward, *The London Spy* (London, 1698), printed periodically from 1698 on; Tom Brown, *Amusements Serious and Comical* (London, 1700); anon, *New London Spy* (London, 1771), and *Complete Modern London Spy* (London, 1781). We might add to this list Addison's figure of Mr. Spectator in the *Spectator* papers.

14. Grose relates his militia position and word collecting in *A Provincial Glossary* (London, 1787).

15. Egan's biography of Grose describes him as being "as affable and jolly as the rest of the motley crew among the beggars, cadgers, thieves," xxvi. Pierce Egan, "Biographical Sketch of Francis Grose, Esq.," in *A Classical Dictionary of the Vulgar Tongue*, 3rd ed. (London, 1823), xxvi-viii.

16. Parker, *Life's Painter*. Parker's glossaries more closely resemble older canting dictionaries in their catalogues of the secret argot of thieves and con artists, yet they indicate a deep familiarity with that language, recording change within the lexicon: "Hands," for instance, are no longer "fambles," as they were in the seventeenth-century cant dictionaries, but "daddles," and people who are easily taken or robbed are no longer "culls" but instead are now called "flats."

17. *The Life and Adventures of Bampfylde-Moore Carew* (Exon, 1745).

18. Parker, *View of Society*, vol. 1, vi.

19. Ibid., ix and 23, respectively.

20. Grose, *Classical Dictionary*.

21. Parker, *View of Society*, vol. 1, 26 and 58, respectively.

22. Grose, *Classical Dictionary*.

23. Beattie, *Essays*, 661.

24. Grose, *Classical Dictionary*.

25. Beattie, *Elements of Moral Science* II. iv.i. (1793), 467.

26. Grose, *Classical Dictionary*, 1.

27. Ibid.

28. Daniel Heller-Roazen, *Dark Tongues: The Art of Rogues and Riddlers* (New York: Zone Books, 2013), 66.

29. Parker, *Life's Painter*, 112.

30. Pierce Egan citing Thomas Moore on the sentences of the "lower walks of society" in his "Biographical Sketch of Francis Grose, Esq." in Francis Grose, A Classical Dictionary of the Vulgar Tongue, ed. Pierce Egan, xxvi-viii.

31. Grose, *Classical Dictionary*, vii.

32. Parker, *Life's Painter*, 130.

33. Ibid., 67–68

34. Parker, *View of Society*, vol. 2, 144, 63, 69, 74, and 62, respectively.

35. Thomas Dekker, *Lanthorne and Candle-Light*, 3rd ed. (London, 1609), ff. 7, recto.

36. *Covent Garden Journal* 4 (14 January 1752).

37. *Spectator* 62, 11 May 1711.

38. John Locke, *An Essay Concerning Human Understanding*, ed. Roger Woolhouse (London: Penguin, 1997), 452.

39. Daniel Defoe, *Moll Flanders*, ed. Albert Rivero (New York: W. W. Norton, 2004), 47 and 137, respectively.

40. *Spectator* 62 (11 May 1711).

41. Grose, *Classical Dictionary*, 1.

42. More generally, Vic Gatrell notes how, also in the 1780s, Pastor Wendeborn argued that the English "laughed immoderately at trifles, and enjoyed harlequin plays. Even their House of Commons was sometimes convulsed in laughter . . . All this expressed England's liberty, he thought." *City of Laughter*, 9.

43. Locke, *An Essay Concerning Human Understanding*, 405.

44. B. E., *New Dictionary* (London, 1699), n.p.

45. Grose, *Classical Dictionary*, 1.

46. See Suvir Kaul's discussion of Thomson's masque and the various contradictions of this "negative definition of the national self." *Poems of Nation, Anthems of Empire: English Verse in the Long Eighteenth Century* (Charlottesville: UP of Virginia, 2000), 1–8.

47. Maria Edgeworth, *An Essay on Irish Bulls* (1802), ed. Jane Desmerais and Marilyn Butler (Dublin: University College Dublin Press, 2006), 4.

48. Ibid., 54 and 55. Edgeworth contrasts this colorful language with the "sober slang of an English blackguard," 58.

49. Ibid., 22.

50. B. E., *New Dictionary*.

51. Parker, *View of Society*, 5.

52. Peter Linebaugh, *The London Hanged: Crime and Civil Society in the Eighteenth Century* (Cambridge, UK: Cambridge UP, 1992), 290. Linebaugh also documents the "wandering," "picaresque" life of migrant Irish workers whose "desultory, sauntering habits ... were an obstacle to the work discipline required for accumulation" and subject to criminalization and punishment (294).

53. See Michel Serres, *Hermes: Literature, Science, Philosophy*, ed. Josué V. Harari and David F. Bell (Baltimore: Johns Hopkins UP, 1982).

54. Grose, *Classical Dictionary*, vi.

55. Douglas Hay and Nicholas Rogers, *Eighteenth-Century English Society* (Oxford: Oxford UP, 1997), 132, 159, 149, and 133 respectively.

56. Ibid., 123.

57. Francis Grose, *The Grumbler, Containing Sixteen Essays by the Late Francis Grose* (London, 1791), 34–35, cited in Gatrell, *City of Laughter*, 561.

58. See my "Vulgar Tongues: Canting Dictionaries and the Language of the People," *Eighteenth-Century Studies* (2004): 134–53 for a more detailed discussion of this process.

59. Grose, *Classical Dictionary*, iii, 5, and ii, respectively.

60. Samuel Johnson, "Preface," *Dictionary of the English Language* (London, 1755).

61. Ibid.

62. For a full discussion of "rough music," see E. P. Thompson, *Customs in Common* (New York: W. W. Norton, 1993).

63. Palmer, *Life's Painter*.

64. The phrase "moral economy" is Thompson's, from *Customs in Common*.

65. Palmer, *Life's Painter*.

66. Parker's terms are from *Life's Painter*, 130, and Grose's are from *Classical Dictionary*.

67. Grose, *Classical Dictionary*, ii.

68. Ibid., 2.

69. See John Barrell's discussion of the notion of shapeshifting in this period in "Afterword: Moving Stories, Still Lives," in *The Country and the City Revisited: England and the Politics of Culture 1550–1850*, ed. Gerald MacLean, Donna Landry, and Joseph P. Ward (Cambridge, UK: Cambridge UP, 1999), 231–50.

70. Grose, *Lexicon Balatronicum*, v.

71. Michel de Certeau, "Vocal Utopias: Glossolalias," *Representations* 56 (1996): 29–47, 33.

72. Gatrell, *City of Laughter*, 111.

73. Pierce Egan, *Life in London* (London, 1821). See also Egan's *Boxiana; or, Sketches of Modern Pugilism* (London, 1819). Allon White's work is again relevant here: see *Carnival, Hysteria, and Writing: Collected Essays and Autobiography* (Oxford: Clarendon Press, 1993).

74. See Simon Joyce's discussion of this increasing division in *Capital Offenses: Geographies of Class and Crime in Victorian London* (Charlottesville: UP of Virginia, 2003).

75. Judith Frank, *Common Ground: Eighteenth-Century English Satiric Fiction and the Poor* (Stanford, CA: Stanford UP, 2001), 4.

76. For a different analysis, see Gary Dyer, "Thieves, Boxers, Sodomites, Poets: Being Flash to Byron's Don Juan," *PMLA* 116 (2001): 562–78. I differ from Dyer's interpretation of cant's use "to emphasize difference; to deny that there is some 'we' that can be appealed to easily" (574). While the "we" might not be appealed to easily, the wide circulation of print

collections of cant, the attribution of cant to "common people," and the remarks observing and encouraging its imitation suggest a complex assembly of a male homosocial "we."

77. For a description of this subculture, see Rictor Norton, *Mother Clap's Molly House: The Gay Subculture in England 1700–1830* (London: GMP, 1992).

78. Eve Kosofsky Sedgwick, *Epistemology of the Closet* (Berkeley: U of California P, 1990), 3.

79. Grose, *Lexicon Balatronicum*, v.

80. Parker, *Life's Painter*, 111 and 112, respectively.

81. John Awdelay, *Fraternitye of Vacabondes* (London, 1575).

82. Thomas Dekker and Thomas Middleton, *The Roaring Girl* (London, 1611).

83. For an extended discussion of the shift in depictions of women in canting songs see my "Vulgar Tongues."

84. B. E., *New Dictionary*.

85. Anonymous, *Life and Character of Moll King* (London, n.d.).

86. Helen Berry, "Rethinking Politeness in Eighteenth-Century England," *Transactions of the Royal Historical Society* 11 (2001): 65–81. See also Gatrell's brief citation of Francis Place's description of the "cock and hen clubs," in which "apprentices and their girls passed their evenings 'drinking—smoking [*sic*]—swearing—and singing flash songs.'" *City of Laughter*, 95.

87. Simon Dickie, *Cruelty and Laughter: Forgotten Comic Literature and the Unsentimental Eighteenth Century* (Chicago: U of Chicago P, 2011), 2.

88. For the perceived role of middle-class women in enforcing "improved" language use, see Lynda Mugglestone, *"Talking Proper": The Rise of Accent as Social Symbol* (Oxford: Clarendon Press, 1995).

89. For a more extensive discussion of these revisions, see my "Vulgar Tongues."

90. See also Kristina Straub's "Feminine Sexuality: Class Identity, and Narrative Form in the Newgate Calendars," in *Eighteenth-Century Genre and Culture: Serious Reflections on Occasional Forms*, ed. Dennis Todd and Cynthia Wall (Newark: U of Delaware P, 2001), 218–35, in which she documents how criminal narratives from the 1770s and beyond aimed to separate "(moral) mistress and (hangable) servant" (221).

91. Pierre Bourdieu, *Language and Symbolic Power*, trans. Gino Raymond and M. Adamson (Malden, MA: Polity, 1992), 91.

Part Two. *The Language of Place*

1. Nathan Bailey, *Dictionarium Britannicum* (London, 1730).

2. British Library, Add. MS 32640.

3. I use "provincial language" rather than "dialect" to preserve the sense of distinct alternative languages as opposed to mere substandard variations of English that the term "dialect" sometimes suggests.

4. Tim Bobbin [John Collier], *A View of the Lancashire Dialect* (London, 1746), 4.

5. For a discussion of this "stranger relationality" see Michael Warner, *Publics and Counterpublics* (New York: Zone Books, 2005), 75.

6. Francis Grose, *A Provincial Glossary* (London, 1787), n.p.

7. Penny Fielding, *Scotland and the Fictions of Geography* (Cambridge, UK: Cambridge UP, 2008), 61.

8. Bobbin, *A View of the Lancashire Dialect*, 1.

9. Benedict Anderson, *Imagined Communities: Reflections on the Origin and Spread of Nationalism* (London: Verso, 1983), 22.

10. For a discussion of "England's Mixed Genius," see Wolfram Schmidgen, *Exquisite*

Mixture: The Virtues of Impurity in Early Modern England (Philadelphia: U of Pennsylvania P, 2013).

11. Both terms are from Grose, *Provincial Glossary*.

12. For discussions of the figure of the vulgar in constructions of national identity, see Carolyn Steedman, "Servants and Their Relationship to the Unconscious," *Journal of British Studies* 42 (2005): 316–50, and Matthew Adams's PhD dissertation, "Imagining Britain: The Formation of British National Identity in the Eighteenth Century," University of Warwickshire, 2002, 177, 242, 254.

Chapter Five. Provincial Languages out of Place

1. Some regions were literally associated with aliens. Geoffrey of Monmouth had described the "land across the Humber" as "offer[ing] a safe hiding-place for foreigners." Cited in Katie Wales, *Northern English* (Cambridge, UK: Cambridge UP, 2006), 32.

2. Cited in Adam Fox, *Oral and Literate Culture in England 1500–1700* (Oxford: Oxford UP, 2000), 73. For more on regional variations, see Manfred Gorlach, "Regional and Social Variations," in *The Cambridge History of the English Language*, vol. 3, ed. Roger Lass (Cambridge, UK: Cambridge UP, 1999) and Gerry Knowles, *A Cultural History of the English Language* (London: Arnold, 1997).

3. "Alexander Gil's *Logonomia Anglica* Edition of 1621," trans. Dorothy Dixon, PhD. dissertation, University of Southern California, 1951.

4. John Bullokar, "To the Reader," *English Expositor* (London, 1616), n.p.

5. Alexander Gil, *Logonomia Anglica* (London, 1619), 140.

6. Hugh Jones, *Accidence to the English Tongue* (London, 1724), 11. Future citations appear parenthetically.

7. David Simpson, *Romanticism and the Question of the Stranger* (Chicago: U of Chicago P, 2013), 168.

8. Richard Dawes, *The Origin of the Newcastle Burr* (London, 1767), 11. As early as 1387 John Trevisa, in a translation of Ranulph Higden's *Polychronicon*, characterized the "longage of the Northumbers" as "so scharp, slitting, and frotynge . . . that we Southerne men may that language unnethe [hardly] understonde." Cited in N. F. Blake, *Non-Standard Language in English Literature* (London: Deutsch, 1981), 27.

9. Dawes, *Origin of the Newcastle Burr*, 11.

10. For discussions of dialect and animal sounds, see Friedrich Kittler, *Discourse Networks 1800/1900*, trans. Michael Metteer (Stanford, CA: Stanford UP, 1990), 37, and Ann Wierda Rowland, *Romanticism and Childhood: The Infantilization of British Literary Culture* (Cambridge, UK: Cambridge UP, 2012), 123.

11. Cited in Fox, *Oral and Literate Culture*, 73.

12. Thomas Wilson, *The Arte of Rhetorique* (London, 1563), 118.

13. Fox, *Oral and Literate Culture*, 72 and 70. Paula Blank, too, has tracked Early Modern literary representations of provincial language, noting that while writers from provincial spaces, such as William Shakespeare and Edmund Spenser, made use of provincialisms, they combined these terms, in a consciously literary language, with a wide variety of other languages, from foreign words to archaisms, to newly invented terms. See *Broken English: Dialects and the Politics of Language in Renaissance Writings* (New York: Routledge, 1996), 3.

14. Richard Bentley, *Dissertation on the Epistles of Phalaris* (London, 1699), n.p.

15. Ibid.

16. Daniel Defoe, *A Tour thro' the Whole Island of Great Britain*, ed. Pat Rogers (Harmondsworth: Penguin, 1971), 216.

17. Eric Gidal tracks a similar movement at work in representations of language in the Ossian poems, which "establish a mode of defamiliarization through sonic and linguistic alterity.... Readers ... respond to the insistent foreignness of these names as suggestive evocations of communal knowledge." *Ossianic Unconformities: Bardic Poetry in the Industrial Age* (Charlottesville: UP of Virginia, 2015), 49.

18. John Ray, *A Collection of English Words Not Generally Used*, 1st ed. (London, 1674).

19. John Ray, "Preface," *A Collection of English Words Not Generally Used*, 2nd ed. (London, 1737), 1. Further citations appear parenthetically.

20. Simpson, *Romanticism and the Question of the Stranger*, 168.

21. Ray, "Preface," 1.

22. Penny Fielding discusses the relative nature of what constitutes provincial—and Scots—language in *Scotland and the Fictions of Geography*.

23. All excerpts from Ray's second edition of *A Collection of English Words Not Generally Used*. Later, Allan Ramsay would catalogue connections between words distinguished as northern and southern in *Poems* (Edinburgh, 1720).

24. Francis Grose, *A Provincial Glossary* (London, 1811), iv.

25. Nathan Bailey, *Dictionarium Britannicum* (London, 1730); George Meriton, *Praise of York-shire Ale* (York, 1685). For a detailed discussion of the ever-shifting linguistic borders of the North, see Katie Wales, *Northern English*.

26. Carew avers, "neither can any tongue deliver a matter with more variety," a result of borrowings from foreign languages in which "(like bees) [the English] gather the honey of their good properties and leave the dregges," but he remains uninterested in cataloguing those differences or identifying the location of various dialects. Richard Carew, "Epistle on Excellencies of the English Tongue," in *Elizabethan Critical Essays*, ed. G. Gregory Smith (London: Oxford UP, 1904).

27. I take this term from Srinivas Aravamudan, *Enlightenment Orientalism: Resisting the Rise of the Novel* (U of Chicago P, 2012), 35.

28. White Kennett, *Parochial Antiquities of Places in the Counties of Oxford with Glossary* (Oxford, 1695); William Marshall, *Rural Economy of Yorkshire*, 2 vols. (London, 1788); Joseph Nicolson and Richard Burn, *History and Antiquities of the Counties of Westmorland and Cumberland*, 2 vols. (London, 1777).

29. George Starr, "Defoe's Tour through the Dialects and Jargons of Great Britain," *Modern Philology* (2012): 74–95. I differ, however, from Starr's reading of Defoe's tone toward these languages as celebratory. As noted below, Defoe describes these terms as "boorish," the language of a "dunce."

30. West includes "Some remarks respecting the provincial words &c. used by the common people in the limits of this tour" at the end of *A Guide to the Lakes* (London, 1780).

31. Grose, *A Provincial Glossary*. s.v., "Galls."

32. Thomas Batchelor, *An Orthoëpical Analysis of the English Language* (London, 1809). Quotation from title page.

33. Anthony Ashley Cooper, Earl of Shaftesbury, *Characteristics of Men, Manners, Opinions, Times*, ed. Lawrence Klein (Cambridge, UK: Cambridge UP, 1999), 211.

34. Ibid., 214.

35. Carl Estabrook perceives this provincial divide along spatial lines, rural and urbane: "the most comprehensive and compelling distinction maintained by members of that society," but the issue is complicated. Joseph Banks's sister, living on her estate in rural Lincolnshire, found provincial terms odd enough to collect them, while rural gentry might have felt little compunction about using provincialisms, as is the case with Fielding's Squire in *Tom*

Jones, discussed later. Carl Estabrook, *Urbane and Rustic England: Cultural Ties and Social Spheres in the Provinces 1660-1780* (Stanford, CA: Stanford UP, 1998), 9.

36. Marshall, *Rural Economy of Yorkshire*, vol. 2, 311.

37. William Chetwood, *A Tour of Ireland* (Dublin, 1746), 18. Published in London in 1748.

38. Ibid., 19. Chetwood makes a similar distinction with regard to the Welsh, writing, "The vulgar Welch seem to have an Aversion to the English; but the better Sort are well bred, and very courteous," 43.

39. Vanbrugh and Cibber, cited in Blake, *Non-Standard Language*, 106.

40. Jacques Rancière, *Short Voyages to the Land of the People*, trans. James Swenson, (Stanford, CA: Stanford UP, 2003), 1.

41. Ibid., 2.

42. Meriton adds a "collection of significant and usefull proverbs" to the 1697 edition.

43. Meriton, *Praise of York-shire Ale*, 37.

44. Viktor Shklovsky, *Theory of Prose*, trans. Benjamin Sher (Elmwood Park, IL: Dalkey, 1991), 5. Shklovsky writes that "Russian literary language has so deeply penetrated into the heart of our people that it has lifted much of the popular speech to unheard-of heights ... literature has become enamored of dialect" (13).

45. Ibid., 6.

46. Thomas Deloney, *The Pleasant History of John Winchcomb, in His Younger Years Called Jack of Newbury* (London, 1619), first published 1597. Although John Winchcombe was an actual person, the text's depiction is novelistic in its detailed dialogues and relation of details.

47. Thomas Keymer, "Introduction," in Samuel Richardson, *Pamela*, ed. Thomas Keymer (Oxford: Oxford UP, 2001), xvii.

48. This conceptualization of provincial language as performance reaches back at least as far as Edgar's cloaking himself in the persona of a beggar and assuming the language of the provincial Southwest in *King Lear*. Michael Ragussis discusses provincial accents as disguise in Georgian theater in *Theatrical Nation* (Philadelphia: U of Pennsylvania P, 2010).

49. Richardson, *Pamela*, 55.

50. R. F. Jones, *The Triumph of the English Language: A Survey of Opinions Concerning the Vernacular from the Introduction of Printing to the Restoration* (Stanford, CA: Stanford UP, 1953); Carey McIntosh, *Common and Courtly Language: The Stylistics of Social Class in 18th-Century British Literature* (Philadelphia: U of Pennsylvania P, 1986); and Suzie Tucker, *Protean Shape: A Study in Eighteenth-Century Vocabulary and Usage* (London: Athlone, 1987) track the move to general terms over particular and certainly provincial ones, while Olivia Smith, *The Politics of Language 1791-1819* (Oxford: Oxford UP, 1984) and Michael Warner, *Letters of the Republic: Publication and the Public Sphere in Eighteenth-Century America* (Cambridge, MA: Harvard UP, 1990) describe the political models such language helped underwrite.

51. Thomas Sheridan, *A Course of Lectures on Elocution* (London, 1762), 30.

52. Batchelor, *Orthoëpical Analysis*, title page.

53. James Harris, *Hermes, or a Philosophical Inquiry Concerning Language* (London, 1751), 373.

54. Jacques Rancière, *The Philosopher and his Poor*, trans. J. Drury, C. Oster, and A. Parker (2004; repr. Durham, NC: Duke UP, 2007), xxvi.

55. Susan Manly, *Language, Custom and Nation in the 1790s* (Aldershot: Ashgate, 2007); George Starr, "Defoe's Tour through the Dialects."

56. Ray, *A Collection of English Words*.

57. Gidal, *Ossianic Unconformities*, 49.

58. Brian Cowan presents a helpful summary of the contours of the debate in "What Was Masculine about the Public Sphere?" *History Workshop Journal* 51 (2001): 127–57.

59. John Barrell, "The Language Properly So-Called," in *English Literature in History 1730–80: An Equal, Wide Survey* (London: Hutchinson, 1983), 110–75, and Olivia Smith, *The Politics of Language*. Benedict Anderson, of course, makes the case for print's role in imagining national community in *Imagined Communities*, while Jurgen Habermas theorizes rational exchange and the public sphere in *Structural Transformation of the Public Sphere*, trans. Thomas Burger and Frederick Lawrence (Cambridge, MA: MIT Press, 1989).

60. See Warner, *Letters of the Republic*, and Michael McKeon, *The Secret History of Domesticity* (Baltimore: Johns Hopkins UP, 2005).

61. Warner, *Letters of the Republic*, 42.

62. Kathleen Wilson, *The Sense of the People: Politics, Culture, and Imperialism in England, 1715–1785* (Cambridge, UK: Cambridge UP, 1995), 43, 44.

63. Jerome Christensen, *Practicing Enlightenment: Hume and the Formation of a Literary Career* (Madison: U of Wisconsin P, 1987), 6. Interestingly, Christensen's study identifies the Scot David Hume as the representative man of letters, reminding us of the extent to which the division between central metropolis and province is largely rhetorical.

64. Harris, *Hermes*, 345. Future citations appear parenthetically.

65. David Simpson sees in Harris's universal grammar a continuation of a democratic endorsement of universally available reason. But it is difficult to square this reading with Harris's insistence on the hierarchal nature of the capacity to use the language of universal grammar. See *Romanticism, Nationalism, and the Revolt against Theory* (U of Chicago P, 1993).

66. Adam Smith, *Lectures on Rhetoric and Belles Lettres*, ed. J. Bryce, (Indianapolis: Liberty, 1985), 204.

67. Steven Shapiro, *A Social History of Truth: Civility and Science in Seventeenth-Century England* (U of Chicago P, 1994), 206–7.

68. Dawes, *Origin of the Newcastle Burr*, 11.

69. James Burnett, Lord Monboddo, *Of the Origin and Progress of Language*, vol 1, 2nd ed. (Edinburgh, 1774), 46.

70. Samuel Johnson, *Dictionary of the English Language* (London, 1755), s.v. "provincial."

71. Samuel Pegge, *Anecdotes of the English Language* (London, 1803), 4.

72. Sheridan, *A Course of Lectures on Elocution*. Thomas Spence cites this passage in his *Grand Repository* (London, 1775), n.p.

73. Spence, "Preface" to *Grand Repository*.

74. Adam Fox summarizes standardization efforts starting as early as Chaucer's time in *Oral and Literate Culture*. For the eighteenth century, see Carey McIntosh, *The Evolution of English Prose, 1700–1800* (Cambridge, UK: Cambridge UP, 1998).

75. James Boswell, *Life of Samuel Johnson*, cited in Fox, *Oral and Literate Culture*, 61.

76. The transition from a monarchic, hierarchical understanding of the body politic to a horizontal, more inclusive understanding of the British nation—one that began long before the eighteenth century—depended in part on a changing sense of the body in relation to power and the particular in relation to the national. Once, as sixteenth-century Crown lawyers wrote, the king possessed both a "body politic" and "a body natural, adorned and invested with the Estate and Dignity royal," a legible site of power. By the same token, an unrefined, even compromised physical body did not especially jeopardize power or status. The lawyers added, "what the King does in his Body politic, cannot be invalidated or frus-

trated by any Disability in his natural body" (7). Ernst Kantorowicz, *The King's Two Bodies: A Study in Medieval Political Theology* (1957; repr. Princeton, NJ: Princeton UP, 1997), 7.

77. Simpson, *Romanticism and the Question of the Stranger*, 173.

78. Peter Stallybrass and Allon White, *The Politics and Poetics of Transgression* (Ithaca, NY: Cornell UP, 1986), 93.

79. T. Duncan Eaves and D. Kimpel track Richardson's alteration of the text's language in later editions in "Richardson's Revisions of *Pamela*" *Studies in Bibliography* 20 (1967): 61–88.

80. Samuel Richardson, *Pamela*, ed. Peter Sabor and Margaret Doody (London: Penguin, 1980), 11.

81. This helpful phrase is from Jayne Lewis, *The English Fable* (Cambridge, UK: Cambridge UP, 2006), 2.

82. John Walker, *A Critical Pronouncing Dictionary* (London, 1791), vi.

83. Nigel Leask, *Robert Burns and Pastoral: Poetry and Improvement in Late Eighteenth-Century Scotland* (Oxford UP, 2010), 53. See also Kirk McAuley, *Print Technology in Scotland, 1740–1800* (Lewisburg, PA: Bucknell UP, 2013).

84. A. Fisher, *A New Grammar*, 4th ed. (Newcastle, 1754), ii. For a comprehensive discussion of provincial publishing and grammar production, see Nuria Yáñez-Bouza, "Grammar Writing and Provincial Grammar Printing in the Eighteenth-Century British Isles," *Transactions of the Philological Society* 110 no. 1 (2012): 34–63.

85. For discussions of the Scottish context, see James Basker, "Scotticisms and the Problem of Cultural Identity in Eighteenth-Century Britain," *Eighteenth-Century Life* 15 (1991): 81–95, and Susan Manning, *Fragments of Union: Making Connections in Scottish and American Writing* (London: Palgrave Macmillan, 2004).

86. Katie Wales, in "Images of Northern-ness," provides this information, along with a brief discussion of Anne Fisher's *A New Grammar* (Newcastle, 1750), reminding us that women's interest in and authority on language did, indeed, extend beyond the provincial. "Images of Northern-ness and Northern English in the Eighteenth Century" in *Creating and Consuming Culture in North-East England, 1660–1830*, ed. Helen Berry and Jeremy Gregory (Aldershot: Ashgate, 2004), 24–36. See also Carol Percy, "Paradigms for Their Sex? Women's Grammarians in Late-Eighteenth-Century England," *Histoire Epistemologie Language* 16 (1994): 121–41.

87. John Brewer, *The Pleasures of the Imagination: English Culture in the Eighteenth Century* (Chicago: U of Chicago P, 2000).

88. Margaret Anne Doody, *The Daring Muse: Augustan Poetry Reconsidered* (Cambridge, UK: Cambridge UP, 1985), 221. Poems Doody cites, such as Jonathan Swift's "Humble Petition of Frances Harris" or William King's "The Old Cheese," feature colloquial, but not provincial, terms.

89. See Bridget Keegan, "Georgic Transformations: Stephen Duck's 'The Threshers Labour,'" *SEL Studies in English Literature 1500–1900* 41 (2001): 545–62.

90. Joseph Addison, preface, Virgil, *Georgics*, trans. John Dryden (London, 1697).

91. Samuel Johnson, "Preface," *The Plays of William Shakespeare* (London, 1765).

92. Alexander Pope, "Discourse on Pastoral Poetry" in *Pastorals* (London, 1717).

93. Nathan Bailey, *Dictionarium Britannicum* (London, 1730).

94. *Guardian* 40 (27 April 1713).

95. Christopher Anstey, *An Election Ball in Poetical Letters, in the Zomerzetshire Dialect* (Bath, 1766), 25.

96. Simon Dickie, *Cruelty and Laughter: Forgotten Comic Literature and the Unsentimental Eighteenth Century* (Chicago: U of Chicago P, 2011), 116. See also Patricia Parker, *Literary Fat Ladies: Rhetoric, Gender, Property* (London: Methuen, 1987).

97. Meriton, *Praise of York-shire Ale*, 95.

98. *Mery Talys and Quicke Answeres*. In *Shakespeare's Jest Books*, ed. W. Carew Hazlitt (London, 1844), 51.

99. Wales, "Images of Northern-ness," 24–36.

100. Written in the 1720s, the only extant edition is the second (Newcastle, 1764). Chicken was apprenticed as a weaver and became a schoolteacher. See Bill Griffiths, *Dictionary of North East Dialect* (Newcastle: Northumbria UP, 2004), xiii.

101. Dawes, *Origin of the Newcastle Burr*, 12.

102. Mikhail Bakhtin, *Rabelais and His World*, trans. H. Iswolsky (Bloomington: Indiana UP, 1984), 15–17.

103. Richard Brome, *The Northern Lass* (London, 1632). The play was first performed in 1629.

104. Tobias Smollett, *The Expedition of Humphry Clinker*, ed. Paul-Gabriel Boucé (Oxford: Oxford UP, 1992), 221.

105. Kaja Silverman, *The Acoustic Mirror: The Female Voice in Psychoanalysis and Cinema* (Bloomington: Indiana UP, 1988). Future citations appear parenthetically. See also *Embodied Voices: Representing Female Vocality in Western Culture*, ed. Leslie Dunn and Nancy Jones (Cambridge, UK: Cambridge UP, 1997), 12.

106. *An Exmoor Scolding* (Exon. [Exeter]: Printed and sold by Andrew and Sarah Brice, 1746)—this is the third edition, but the earliest copy extant. Later editions referred to "Peter Lock of North Moulton" as author, but the book is now generally attributed to Andrew Brice, its printer. Tim Bobbin, *A View of the Lancashire Dialect* (Manchester, 1746).

107. *The Gentleman's Magazine*, October, 1746, 527.

108. Richard Townley, ed. *The Miscellaneous Works of Tim Bobbin, Esq. (John Collier), containing his View of the Lancashire Dialect . . . To which is added, a life of the author* (London: T. & J. Allman, 1818), xiv.

109. Cited in J. A. Hilton, "'Tim Bobbin' and the Origins of Provincial Consciousness in Lancashire," in *Proceedings of Methods XIII: Papers from the Thirteenth International Conference on Methods in Dialectology*, ed. Barry Heselwood and Clive Upton (Bern: Lang, 2008), 3.

110. Brice, *Exmoor Scolding*.

111. The first two terms are from the anonymous *Exmoor Scolding*, the second two from *A View of the Lancashire Dialect*, reprinted under many different titles, including *Tim Bobbin's Toy-Shop Open'd or his Whimsical Amusements* (Manchester, 1763).

112. Bobbin, *A View of the Lancashire Dialect*.

113. Richardson, *Pamela*, ed. Keymer, 18 and 43, respectively. See Keymer's very helpful discussion in his "Introduction" to this volume.

114. Meriton, *Praise of York-shire Ale*, 92.

115. For additional examples, we might turn to the Newcastle collections of poems and songs edited by John Bell, which include provincial terms naming such particulars as coal-carrying boats and carts as well as work clothes. Although produced at the end or turn of the century, these texts often contain references to incidents earlier in the century, suggesting midcentury composition. See, for example, *Rhymes of the Northern Bards* (Newcastle, 1812).

116. Susan Manly, *Language, Custom, and Nation in the 1790s: Locke, Tooke, Wordsworth, Edgeworth* (Aldershot: Ashgate, 2007), 40.

117. Locke, *An Essay Concerning Human Understanding*, ed. Roger Woolhouse (London: Penguin, 1997), 361.

118. Shapiro, *A Social History of Truth*, 219.

119. Manly, *Language, Custom, and Nation*, 40.

120. *Exmoor Scolding* (1746), 1.

121. For discussions of eighteenth-century notions of orality, see Nicholas Hudson, "Oral Tradition: The Evolution of an Eighteenth-Century Concept," in *Tradition in Transition: Women Writers, Marginal Texts, and the Eighteenth-Century Canon*, ed. Alvaro Rivero and James G. Basker (Oxford: Clarendon Press, 1996), 161–76; and Paula McDowell, "Towards a Genealogy of 'Print Culture' and 'Oral Tradition'," in *This is Enlightenment*, ed. Clifford Siskin and William Warner (Chicago: U of Chicago P, 2008). To follow this trajectory into the nineteenth century, see Penny Fielding, *Writing and Orality: Nationality, Culture, and Nineteenth-Century Scottish Fiction* (Oxford: Clarendon Press, 1996) and Maureen McLane, *Balladeering, Minstrelsy, and the Making of British Romantic Poetry* (Cambridge, UK: Cambridge UP, 2008).

122. Christopher Looby, *Voicing America: Language, Literary Form, and the Origins of the United States* (Chicago: U of Chicago P, 1996). See also Jay Fliegleman, *Declaring Independence: Jefferson, Natural Language & the Culture of Performance* (Stanford, CA: Stanford UP, 1993) and Sandra Gustafson, *Eloquence is Power: Oratory & Performance in Early America* (Chapel Hill: U of North Carolina P, 2000).

123. Edmund Burke, *A Philosophical Enquiry into the Origin of Our Idea of the Sublime and the Beautiful*, ed. Adam Phillips (Oxford: Oxford UP, 1990), 76.

124. *Encyclopedia Britannica*, vol. 2 (Edinburgh: 1768–71), 877. James Adams echoed this notion in 1799 when he claimed that the peculiarity of Scots speech was "deliberately adopted by the northern moiety of this great Isle, and is invested with right and title, title unalienable, antient right and propriety . . . founded in legitimate choice, and perpetuated by uncontrollable liberty." *The Pronunciation of the English Language Vindicated from Imputed Anomaly and Caprice* (Edinburgh, 1799), 158–59, cited in Fielding, *Scotland and the Fictions of Geography*, 62.

125. Samuel Pegge would go on to argue that, conversely, it was vulgar Londoners, Cockneys, with their dropped H, who were actually preserving the purest form of English. See *Anecdotes of the English Language*, 192.

126. Sheridan, *A Course of Lectures*.

127. Batchelor, *Orthoëpical Analysis of the English Language*, title page. Batchelor refers to provincial pronunciation as an error (101).

128. Adam Ferguson, *An Essay on the History of Civil Society*, ed. Fania oz-Salzberger (1767; repr. Cambridge, UK: Cambridge UP, 2001), 76.

129. Anonymous, *Select Scotish [sic] Ballads*, vol. 1 (London, 1783), xli.

130. Ibid.

131. Thomas Blackwell, *An Enquiry into the Life and Writings of Homer* (London, 1735) and *Letters Concerning Mythology* (London, 1748); Hugh Blair, *Lectures on Rhetoric and Belles Lettres* (London 1787); Robert Lowth, *Lectures on the Sacred Poetry of the Hebrews* (London, 1753).

132. Rowland, *Romanticism and Childhood*, 21.

133. Bobbin, *A View*, and Brice, *An Exmoor Scolding* (Exon, 1746).

134. Fox provides ample evidence of the entwined nature of oral and print cultures of this and earlier periods. James Mulholland offers an excellent analysis of eighteenth-century British innovations in print designed to elicit voice in *Sounding Imperial: Poetic Voice and the Politics of Empire* (Baltimore: Johns Hopkins UP, 2013).

135. Leigh Eric Schmidt, *Hearing Things: Religion, Illusion, and the American Enlightenment* (Cambridge, MA: Harvard UP, 2000), 7.

136. From as early as Edmund Spenser's *Shepheardes Calendar* (1579) a standardizing print English created the possibility of alternative, even codified, versions of the language meant to call up a sense of sounded distinction associated with the vernacular. Suggestively, Johnson refers to Spenser's *Calendar* and Ambrose Philips's use of its model of language as

"natural" in *Lives of the English Poets* vol. 3 (1779–81), ed. George Birkbeck Hill (Oxford: Clarendon Press 1905), 312–25.

137. Defoe, *A Tour*, 216.

138. "A plain downright Country Love letter from Roger to his Sweet heart Joan," in Anonymous, *The New Academy of Complements*, 4th ed. (London, 1715), 60. Interestingly, this collection also offers models for polite oral interactions, with "Witty and Ingenious Sentences to Introduce and grace the art of Well Speaking."

139. Tobias Smollett, *The Adventures of Roderick Random*, ed. Paul-Gabriel Boucé (Oxford: Oxford UP, 1981).

140. Bobbin, *A View*.

141. Michel de Certeau, "Vocal Utopias: Glossolalia," *Representations* 56 (1996): 29–47, 30, italics in original.

142. Ibid., 31.

143. It was not until the 1773 edition that such mediating help was provided in the form of a glossary.

144. Irving Ehrenpreis, *Literary Meaning and Augustan Values* (Charlottesville: UP of Virginia, 1974), 46–8. Cynthia Wall discusses this notion in *The Prose of Things: Transformations of Description in the Eighteenth Century* (U of Chicago P, 2006), 35.

145. For an account of the disappearance of particular objects and practices, see Jon Klancher, *Transfiguring the Arts and Sciences: Knowledge and Cultural Institutions in the Romantic Age* (Cambridge, UK: Cambridge UP, 2013).

146. Bruce Robbins, *The Servant's Hand: English Fiction from Below* (New York: Columbia UP, 1986), ix–x.

147. Horace Walpole, *The Castle of Otranto*, ed. E.J. Clery (Oxford: Oxford UP, 1998), 10. Further citations appear parenthetically.

148. Shklovsky, *Theory of Prose*, 51. Similarly, Ann Radcliffe's servants, such as *The Italian*'s Paulo, remain grounded in the provincial land of their birth, knowing its lore and legend, participating in its rural ceremonies and celebrations, delaying knowing and narrative itself, and speaking a dilatory and comic language.

Chapter Six. "I Do Not Like London or Anything That Is in It": The Provincial Offensive

1. David Simpson, *Romanticism and the Question of the Stranger* (Chicago: U of Chicago P, 2013), 169.

2. These dialogues, which I discuss in detail in this chapter and the following, might be classified alongside what Ina Ferris has described as contemporary writings from marginal authors in an "experimental mode" that are doing "something close to ethnography or proto-sociology of the present.": "Taking on Authorship: William Hutton's Testy Relationship to Literary Authority," *European Romantic Review* 28 (2017).

3. George Meriton, *Praise of York-shire Ale*, 2nd ed. (York, 1685), 37. First edition published in 1684.

4. The first versions appear in Meriton, *Praise of York-shire Ale*, 83 and 87, respectively, the second, in (York, 1697) 93 and 97, respectively.

5. Josiah Relph, *A Miscellany of Poems, consisting of original poems, translations, pastorals in the Cumberland Dialect ... with preface and glossary* (Glasgow, 1747). The quotation is from William Empson, *Some Versions of Pastoral* (New York: New Directions, 1974), 11 and 13, respectively.

6. Relph, *A Miscellany of Poems*, 2. Future citations appear parenthetically.

7. Mina Gorji, *John Clare and the Place of Poetry* (Liverpool: Liverpool UP, 2005), 17.

8. Empson, *Some Versions of Pastoral*, 11. Annabel M. Patterson, *Pastoral and Ideology: Virgil to Valéry* (Oxford: Clarendon, 1988), 193. My discussion of pastoral here is much indebted to Nigel Leask's analysis in *Robert Burns and Pastoral* (Oxford: Oxford UP, 2010), 52-60.

9. Empson, *Some Versions of Pastoral*, 11.

10. *Guardian* 40 (27 April 1713).

11. Relph, *A Miscellany of Poems*, 4.

12. Spenser, *The Shepheardes Calendar* (London, 1579); William Browne, *Britannia's Pastorals* (London, 1613-15); Ambrose Philips, *Pastorals* (London, 1710).

13. *Poems by the Rev. Josiah Relph of Sebergam* (Carlisle, 1798), xix.

14. Relph, *A Miscellany of Poems*, 162, 167, and x, respectively.

15. Such moments of "foreignness" within the language precipitate the dynamics of translation Walter Benjamin describes, by which not the "translated" (provincial) language but the host language, standard English (and its readers), are alienated.

16. Patterson, *Pastoral and Ideology*; Michael McKeon, "The Pastoral Revolution," in *Refiguring Revolutions: Aesthetics and Politics from the English Revolution to the Romantic Revolution*, ed. Kevin Sharpe and Stephen Zwicker (Berkeley: U of California P, 1998), 267-90; Stuart Curran, *Poetic Form and British Romanticism* (Oxford: Oxford UP, 1986), 95-9; Nigel Leask, *Robert Burns and Pastoral: Poetry and Improvement in Late Eighteenth-Century Scotland* (Oxford UP, 2010), 52-60.

17. McKeon, "Pastoral Revolution," 270.

18. Relph, *A Miscellany of Poems*, 167.

19. *The New Academy of Complements* (London, 1669). Editions appeared throughout the eighteenth century.

20. Similarly, as Steve Newman has observed, Scots poet Allan Ramsay had presented—often with great cunning—images of oral culture as untainted and pastoral in his Scots language poetry and particularly in his play *The Gentle Shepherd* (1725), while also situating those pastoral characters in a print market economy. "The Scots Songs of Allan Ramsay," *MLQ* 63 (2002), 277-314. The fact that Ramsay's shepherd is "gentle" complicates the issue of class: the protagonists of this drama turn out not to be vulgar in any sense and are instead high-born Scots.

21. Empson, *Some Versions of Pastoral*, 14.

22. Josiah Relph, "Wrote after reading *Pamela, or Virtue Rewarded*," in *A Miscellany of Poems*, 111.

23. Hugh Blair, *Lectures on Rhetoric and Belles Lettres* (London, 1787), iii, 336. Cited in Leask, *Robert Burns and Pastoral*, 69. Frank Kermode has noted, "The first condition of pastoral is that it is an urban product." Cited in McKeon, "The Pastoral Revolution," 271.

24. Tim Bobbin, *Tim Bobbin's Toyshop Opened . . . Containing A View of the Lancashire Dialect* (Manchester, 1763), vii.

25. Tim Bobbin, *A View of the Lancashire Dialect; by way of Dialogue* (Manchester, 1746), 3.

26. Bobbin, *A View*, and Tobias Smollett, *Roderick Random*, ed. Paul Gabriel Boucé (Oxford: Oxford UP, 1981), 147, respectively.

27. Letter to Mr. R. W—r, 28 November 1757 in *Works of John Collier (Tim Bobbin)*, ed. Lieut.-Col. Henry Fishwick (Rochdale: James Clegg, Milnrow Road, 1894), 234.

28. Letter to Mr. Wm. Bowcock, 24 Feb. 1761, in *Works*, 247.

29. Andrew Brice, *Mobiad; Or, Battle of the Voice* (London, 1770). Further citations appear parenthetically.

30. Andrew Brice, *Grand Gazetteer* (London, 1755).

31. For a comprehensive discussion of these politics, see Kathleen Wilson, *The Sense of*

the People: Politics, Culture, and Imperialism in England, 1715-1785 (Cambridge, UK: Cambridge UP, 1995).

32. Andrew Brice, *Freedom, a Poem* (Exon, 1730).

33. D. M. Horgan, "Popular Protest in the Eighteenth Century: John Collier (Tim Bobbin), 1708-1786," *Review of English Studies* 48 (1997): 310-31.

34. Tim Bobbin [John Collier], *Truth in a Mask* (Amsterdam [Manchester?], 1757). He refers to these persons as "oppressing the poor" (iii).

35. Ibid., 16 and 17 respectively.

36. See the Introduction and Chapter One of Leask, *Robert Burns and Pastoral*.

37. J. A. Hilton, "'Tim Bobbin' and the Origins of Provincial Consciousness in Lancashire," *Journal of the Lancashire Dialect Society* 19 (1970): 2-7.

38. For more on the largely oppositional rhetoric of provincial politics, see Kathleen Wilson, who writes, "Provincial newspapers constructed a view of the provinces as having all of the virtue, culture and civic mindedness, but none of the vice, of the capital." Wilson, *The Sense of the People*, 40.

39. Theophilus Crispin (pseudonym), *Advice to the Advised* (Newcastle, 1803), 5.

40. Ibid., 8.

41. For a discussion of "the mob" and "the people," see Wilson, *The Sense of the People*, 20-21 and 41-42.

42. Edmund Burke, *Reflections on the Revolution in France*, ed. J. G. A. Pocock (Indianapolis: Hackett, 1987), 7.

43. Defoe frames in comedic terms his frank acknowledgement of England's heterogeneity in its mixed-blood origins in his 1701 "True Born Englishman."

44. William Blackstone, *Commentaries on the Laws of England* (Oxford, 1765).

45. Martyn Wakelin, *Discovering English Dialects* (1979; repr. Oxford: Shire Classics, 2008), 13.

46. James Harris, *Hermes* (London, 1751), 409.

47. Burke, *Reflections*, 52.

48. Matthew Adams, "Imagining Britain," PhD thesis, University of Warwick, 2002, 257 and 270, respectively.

49. Edmund Burke, *A Philosophical Enquiry into the Origin of Our Idea of the Sublime and the Beautiful*, ed. Adam Phillips (Oxford: Oxford UP, 2008), 56 and 57, respectively.

50. This is part of Karen Swann's analysis of the class dynamics in the *Enquiry* in "The Sublime and the Vulgar," *College English* 52 (1990), 7-20.

51. Harris, *Hermes*, 373.

52. Burke, *Philosophical Enquiry*, 57.

53. Ibid., 59 and 54, respectively.

54. Swann, "The Sublime and the Vulgar."

55. Horace Walpole, *The Castle of Otranto*, ed. E. J. Clery (Oxford: Oxford UP, 1996), 10.

56. Daniel Tiffany, *Infidel Poetics: Riddles, Nightlife, Substance* (Chicago: U of Chicago P, 2009), 8.

57. George Campbell, *Philosophy of Rhetoric*, vol. 2 (London, 1776), 355.

58. Leask, *Robert Burns and Pastoral*, 8.

59. Henry Fielding, *Joseph Andrews*, ed. Douglas Brooks-Davies (Oxford: Oxford UP, 1999), 143.

60. Smollett, *Roderick Random*, 213. See also T. K. Pratt, "A Study of the Language in Tobias Smollett's *Roderick Random*," PhD thesis, London University, 1975.

61. Henry Fielding, *The History of Tom Jones*, ed. J. Bender and S. Stern (Oxford: Oxford UP, 1998), 264. Future citations appear parenthetically.

62. Nor does he subscribe to the idea that a standard English might offer the transcen-

dence above local difference that enabled national public-sphere debate. The narrator, like that of *Jonathan Wild*, deploys a complexly layered, ironic language that defies such notions.

63. For Fielding's advocacy of the authority of the parish, see Scott McKenzie, *Be It Ever So Humble: Poverty, Fiction, and the Invention of the Middle Class Home* (Charlottesville: U of Virginia P, 2013).

64. Adams, "Imagining Britain," 179.

65. John Gay, *The Shepherd's Week* (London, 1714).

66. For a discussion of how Gay overplays his hand in his attack on Philips, see Lee Elioseff, *The Cultural Milieu of Addison's Literary Criticism* (Austin: U of Texas P, 2014).

67. Gay, *The Shepherd's Week*. This is from the unpaginated "Proeme" that opens the book. As some have noted, Pope's own neoclassical pastoral, with its notion of a "golden age," is also under attack in the poem.

68. Ibid.

69. William Ayre, *Memoirs of the Life and Writings of Alexander Pope* vol. 2 (London: 1745), 139.

70. Samuel Johnson, *Lives of the English Poets* vol. 8 (London, 1779), 5.

71. *Eighteenth-Century Poetry*, ed. David Fairer and Christine Gerrard (London: Blackwell, 2014), 43.

72. John Gay, *The Shepherd's Week*, "Proeme," n.p.

73. Daniel Tiffany, "Cheap Signaling," *Boston Review* 15 July 2014.

74. Ibid.

75. "John Gay," *Oxford Dictionary of National Biography*, ed. H. Matthew and B. Harrison (Oxford: Oxford UP, 2004).

76. *Robert Burns, The Critical Heritage*, ed. Donald Low (New York: Routledge, 1995), 131.

77. William Wordsworth, preface to *Lyrical Ballads*, ed. R. Brett and A. Jones (London: Routledge, 2005), 295.

78. Ibid., 290 and 289, respectively.

79. Ibid., 290. Wordsworth does use the odd provincialism now and again, such as "canty."

80. *Brice's Weekly Journal*, August 25, 1727.

81. These terms appear in *Mobiad*.

82. See "Andrew Brice," *Dictionary of National Biography*.

83. Mikhail Bakhtin, *The Dialogic Imagination: Four Essays*, ed. and trans. Michael Holquist (Austin: U of Texas P, 1986), 324.

84. Ibid., 139.

85. Nathan Bailey, *Dictionarium Britannicum* (London, 1730), s.v. "Dudgeon" (London, 1736).

86. Harold Whitehall, "'Tim Bobbin' Again," *Philological Quarterly* 8 (1929): 395–405.

87. Wilson, *The Sense of the People*, 6.

88. Carl Estabrook argues that great division existed between rural and urban in the area around Bristol until the mid-eighteenth century but does not address the shift away from that division in the period I am describing. *Urbane and Rustic England: Cultural Ties and Social Spheres in the Provinces 1660–1780* (Stanford, CA: Stanford UP, 1998).

89. Cited in Hilton, "'Tim Bobbin,'" 3.

90. Gidal uses this formulation to characterize the Gaelic names of the Ossian poems, another fiction of national space produced through movement in *Ossianic Unconformities: Bardic Poetry in the Industrial Age* (Charlottesville: UP of Virginia, 2015), 31.

91. The title page notes that the work was published by (the pseudonymous) "Peter Pindar, esq." (London, 1795). Future citations appear parenthetically.

92. For an excellent discussion of the king's complex relationship to the rising English standard—from awarding pensions to language codifiers such as Samuel Johnson and Thomas Sheridan to speaking an individualizing idiolect—see Carol Percy, "The King's Speech: Metalanguage of Nation, Man and Class in Anecdotes about George III," *English Language and Linguistics* 16 (2012): 281–99. See also Dafydd Moore's discussion of print representations of George III in "John Wolcott and the 'Anecdotic Itch': Peter Pindar, Biography and Historiography in the 1780s," *Eighteenth-Century Life* 40 (2016): 88–118.

93. As noted in Percy, "The King's Speech."

94. Marilyn Butler, "Introduction," *Castle Rackrent* by Maria Edgeworth (London: Penguin, 1992), 16. The description of Thady's idiom is from the "editor" within the text, 62.

95. Like the provincial figures of Brice's and Collier's work, Thady has no last name. The character's illiteracy—he must tell his story to the editor, as he cannot write—is, however, a tricky business, for Thady at one point explains that he is asked how to spell the name of a bog and does not reflect on the absurdity of this request to someone in his situation (78).

96. While the preface explains that the book will illustrate "the manners of a certain class of the gentry of Ireland" (62), it also makes claims to represent all of Ireland (63), while the glossary and footnotes include descriptions of beliefs and manners of the "common people of Ireland" (71) in slippages between general national and particular regions and classes that, as we have seen, characterize representations of the vernacular.

97. I am thinking here of Allan Ramsay, Robert Fergusson, and Robert Burns. For an expanded discussion of these Scots poets, see Leask, *Robert Burns and Pastoral*; Penny Fielding, *Scotland and the Fictions of Geography* (Cambridge, UK: Cambridge UP, 2008); and my "Local Languages: Obscurity and Open Secrets in Scots Vernacular Poetry," in Juliet Shields and Evan Gottlieb, eds., *Representing Place in British Literature and Culture, 1660–1830: From Local to Global* (Burlington, VT: Ashgate, 2013), 47–64.

98. Tiffany, *Infidel Poetics*, 6.

Chapter Seven. Provincial Languages and a Vernacular out of Time

1. Francis Grose, *A Provincial Glossary* (London, 1787), not paginated.

2. Raymond Williams, *The Country and the City* (1973; Repr. London: Hogarth, 1985), 12.

3. A typical exchange reads, "I leuve your Scotch-men in my heart, / 'Cause with our King ye teuk a part. / Dame, I to her, I can assure 'em / Ye did the same your sel's at Deurham." *A Joco-serious Discourse in two dialogues between a Northumberland-gentleman and his tenant, a Scotchman, both old cavaliers* (London, 1686), 14.

4. This is from the "Grammar" section of Samuel Johnson, *Dictionary of the English Language* vol. 1 (London, 1755), n.p.

5. William Marshall, *The Rural Economy of Yorkshire* vol. 2 (London, 1788), 311.

6. This appears in the preface to the 1775 edition, published after Brice's death (5).

7. John Wilkins, *An Essay towards a Real Character, and a Philosophical Language* (London, 1668), 6.

8. *Proposal for Correcting, Improving, and Ascertaining the English Tongue* (London, 1711), 20–3.

9. Evan Lloyd, *Conversation: A Poem* (London, 1767), 14.

10. The most notorious example of such speech is Sir Plume's in Alexander Pope's *The Rape of the Lock* (London, 1712).

11. Samuel Pegge, *Anecdotes of the English Language* (London, 1803), title page.

12. Marshall, *Rural Economy of Yorkshire*, vol. 2, 374.

13. Daniel Defoe, *A Tour Through the Whole Island of Great Britain*, ed. Pat Rogers (Harmondsworth: Penguin, 1986), 583.

14. J. A. Hilton, "'Tim Bobbin' and the Origins of Provincial Consciousness in Lancashire," *Journal of the Lancashire Dialect Society* 19 (1970): 2–7.

15. Whitaker was writing at the end of the eighteenth century. Cited in Stephen Clark, *New Lancashire Gazetteer* (London, 1830), 172. Collier vehemently disagreed with Whitaker's insistence that Manchester had British rather than Saxon ancestry.

16. "To Mr. R. W——," November 28, 1757, in *Works of John Collier*, ed. Henry Fishwick (Rochdale, 1894), 235.

17. Ina Ferris, "Taking on Authorship: William Hutton's Testy Relationship to Literary Authority," *European Romantic Review* 28 (2017).

18. John Locke, *An Essay Concerning Human Understanding*, ed. Roger Woolhouse (Harmondsworth: Penguin, 1997), 362.

19. Grose, *Provincial Glossary*, 1–2.

20. John Watson, *The History and Antiquities of the Parish of Halifax, in Yorkshire* (London, 1775), 547.

21. Samuel Johnson, *Dictionary* s.v. "Grammar."

22. Pegge, *Anecdotes of the English Language*, 13.

23. Adam Fox, *Oral and Literate Culture in England 1500–1700* (Oxford: Oxford UP, 2000), 51–111.

24. Paula Blank, *Broken English: Dialects and the Politics of Language in Renaissance Writings* (New York: Routledge, 1996), 100.

25. Richard Verstegan, *Restitutions of Decayed Intelligence* (London, 1605), 189.

26. John Horne Tooke, *The Diversions of Purley* (London, 1786), 199.

27. See Olivia Smith, *The Politics of Language 1791–1819* (Oxford: Oxford UP, 1984) and Susan Manly, *Language, Custom, and Nation in the 1790s: Locke, Tooke, Wordsworth, Edgeworth* (Aldershot: Ashgate, 2007). Stephen Prickett argues that the relation between his linguistic and political theory are not so clear in "Radicalism and Linguistic Theory: Horne Tooke on Samuel Pegge," *Yearbook of English Studies* 19 (1989): 1–17.

28. Tooke, *Diversions*, 219 and 214, respectively. Further citations noted parenthetically.

29. Pegge, *Anecdotes of the English Language*, 2–3, italics in original.

30. Tim Bobbin, *A View of the Lancashire Dialect* (London, 1746), 27.

31. Andrew Brice, *An Exmoor Scolding* (Exon, 1771), 39.

32. Eric Gidal, *Ossianic Unconformities: Bardic Poetry in the Industrial Age* (Charlottesville: UP of Virginia, 2015), 5.

33. See Kevis Goodman's discussion of the fossil in "Conjectures on Beachy Head" *ELH* 81 (2014): 983–1006.

34. Martyn Wakelin, *Discovering English Dialects* (Oxford: Shire Publications, 2008), 13, 17, and 24, respectively.

35. White Kennett, *Parochial Antiquities of Places in the Counties of Oxford with Glossary* (Oxford, 1695). All quotations are from the glossary that ends the volume and are not paginated.

36. Benedict Anderson, *Imagined Communities: Reflections on the Origin and Spread of Nationalism* (London: Verso, 1982), 18–19.

37. Locke, *Essay Concerning Human Understanding*, 361.

38. Susan Stewart, *Crimes of Writing: Problems of Containment in Representation* (Oxford: Oxford UP, 1991), 68–69.

39. Christopher Looby, *Voicing America: Language, Literary Form, and the Origins of the United States* (Chicago: U of Chicago P, 1996), 4. See also Jay Fliegleman, *Declaring Independence: Jefferson, Natural Language & the Culture of Performance* (Stanford, CA: Stanford UP, 1993).

40. A less-dominant view embraced change and new practices. The *Encyclopedia Britannica* authors saw language as undergoing "perpetual change" (863) and did not find this particularly troubling, for "the antiquity of a language does not imply any degree of excellence" (864)—a position unsurprising given the efforts of many an educated Scot, including *Encyclopedia* writers, to assimilate a polite standard English. *Encyclopedia Britannica* vol. 2 of 3 (Edinburgh, 1771), 863–64.

41. *Exmoor Scolding*, 8th ed. (Exeter, 1775), 3, 4. This was published after Andrew Brice's death in 1773. Katie Trumpener, *Bardic Nationalism: The Romantic Novel and the British Empire* (Princeton, NJ: Princeton UP, 1997).

42. Marilyn Butler points out Ritson's observations regarding Anglophone minstrels in "Antiquarianism (Popular)," *An Oxford Companion to the Romantic Age, 1776–1832*, ed. Ian McCalman et al. (Oxford: Oxford UP, 1999), 328–38, 332.

43. Bobbin, *A View of the Lancashire Dialect* (1746), 32, and Grose, *A Provincial Glossary*, n.p., respectively.

44. Edmund Burke, *Reflections on the Revolution in France*, ed. J. G. A. Pocock (Indianapolis: Hackett, 1987), 50.

45. Samuel Johnson, "Preface to the Dictionary," in *Selected Writings*, ed. Patrick Crutwell (Harmondsworth: Penguin, 1986), 239 and 242, respectively.

46. *Poems by the Rev. Josiah Relph of Sebergam*, ed. J. Mitchell (Carlisle, 1798), xix.

47. Deidre Lynch, "Gothic Libraries and National Subjects," *Journal of Romanticism* 40 (2002), 29–48, 30–31 and 33, respectively, and Joseph Roach, *Cities of the Dead: Circum-Atlantic Performance* (New York: Columbia UP, 1996), 77.

48. Andrew Elfenbein, *Romanticism and the Rise of English* (Stanford, CA: Stanford UP, 2009), 38. David Fairer discusses the development of the concept of "national literary history" in the 1760s and the revaluation of "a vocabulary with ancient roots" in "Creating a National Poetry: The Tradition of Spenser and Milton," in *The Cambridge Companion to Eighteenth-Century Poetry*, ed. John Sitter (Cambridge, UK: Cambridge UP, 2001), 177–202, 190.

49. Fairer, "Creating a National Poetry," 177.

50. John Dryden, "Dedication of the Pastorals to Lord Clifford" in his translation of Virgil (1695?).

51. Benjamin West to Thomas Gray, 4 April 1742. West adds that "were Shakespeare alive now, he would write a different style from what he did." *The Works of Thomas Gray*, 3rd ed., ed. William Mason (London, 1807), 298.

52. James Mulholland describes the negative reception of the language in Gray's poem "The Bard." Contemporaries dismissed it as "native gibberish" and "Spittel-fields poetry"— Spitalfields being known for the foreign speech that circulated amongst its French Huguenot silk weavers—in another of the suggestive mixes of native and foreign that we have seen throughout this book. *Sounding Imperial: Poetic Voice and the Politics of Empire* (Baltimore: Johns Hopkins UP, 2013), 59.

53. Thomas Warton, *Observations on the Faerie Queene* (London, 1754), 92.

54. See Butler, "Antiquarianism (Popular)," 331 for the division between provincials, such as Chatterton and Ritson, and "their competitors in the metropolis" represented in literary circles, such as Gray, Horace Walpole, Thomas Percy, and Thomas Warton. Elfenbein notes that Warton's *History of English Poetry* "was a history of the collective effort of poets to create 'the glowing elegancies of the English Language.'" Elfenbein, *Romanticism*

and the Rise of English, 28. While Warton reoriented literary criticism toward a long view of a national literary heritage, within that view he emphasized "the progress of our language" and the "improvement of the English phraseology." *History of English Poetry*, vol. 3 (London, 1774), 329 and vol. 2, 247, respectively. Crucially, polish and improvement began not with what Warton saw as a "barbaric" vernacular Saxon but with Norman French. See Manly, *Language, Custom, and Nation*, 69.

55. This parallels the secret knowledge said to be lodged in children's babble and its proximity to an originary language in the Romantic accounts Ann Wierda Rowland describes in *Romanticism and Childhood: The Infantilization of British Literary Culture* (Cambridge, UK: Cambridge UP, 2012), 20 and 74.

56. Joseph Ritson, *Remarks, Critical, and Illustrative, on the text and notes of the last edition of Shakespeare* (London, 1783), 13.

57. *The Gentleman's Magazine* October 1746. Cited in D. M. Horgan, "Popular Protest in the Eighteenth Century: John Collier," *Review of English Studies* 48 (1997): 310–31, 314.

58. Hutton published *A Bran New Wark* under the pseudonym William de Worfat (Kendal, 1785). Reprinted in Walter Skeat, ed., *Specimens of English Dialect* (London: English Dialect Society, 1879), 192.

59. Watson, *The History and Antiquities of the Parish of Halifax*.

60. Charles Coot, *Elements of the Grammar of the English Language* (London, 1788), 95.

61. *The Gentleman's Magazine* (1829): 315, 316. Cited in *The Gentleman's Magazine Library* vol. 2 (Boston: Houghton Mifflin, 1905), 5.

62. Pegge, *Anecdotes of the English Language*, 37.

63. Grose, *A Provincial Glossary*, "Preface," iii.

64. James Chandler, *England in 1819: The Politics of Literary Culture and the Case of Romantic Historicism* (Chicago: U of Chicago P), 107.

65. Christopher Anstey, "To the Reader," *An Election Ball in Poetical Letters, in the Zomerzetshire Dialect* (Bath, 1776), n.p.

66. This short piece was published in multiple editions: (Carlisle, n.d.), (Whitehaven, n.d.), (Cockermouth, n.d.), and (Penrith, 1788).

67. Isaac Ritson, *Copy of a Letter, Wrote by a Young Shepherd*, 11. Carl Estabrook cites a manuscript poem of the late seventeenth century featuring a similar dialect-speaking protagonist. Ned, from a Somerset village, says of London, "when z' did zeet schor a ready to spew / What with the neeze and what with the smoake / Twas Death in my ears and schor a ready to choake." *Urbane and Rustic England: Cultural Ties and Social Spheres in the Provinces 1660-1780* (Stanford, CA: Stanford UP, 1998), 1.

68. Dipesh Chakrabarty, *Provincializing Europe: Postcolonial Thought and Historical Difference* (Princeton, NJ: Princeton UP, 2000), 113. Further citations noted parenthetically.

69. Joseph Nicolson and Richard Burn, *History and Antiquities*, vol. 1 (London, 1777, repr. EP Publishing, 1976), 11.

70. Ibid., 613 and 612, respectively.

71. Bill Griffiths provides evidence of this term's use in eighteenth-century Britain in *A Dictionary of North East Dialect* (Newcastle: Northumbria UP, 2004), 148.

72. Published posthumously as *A Supplement to Dr. Johnson's Dictionary of the English Language, or, a Glossary of Obsolete and Provincial Words* (London, 1807).

73. On the libidinous relationship to the antiquarian object, see Mark Salber Phillips, *Society and Sentiment: The Genres of Historical Writing in Britain, 1740-1820* (Princeton, NJ: Princeton UP, 2000) and *Romanticism and Popular Culture in Britain and Ireland*, ed. Philip Connell and Nigel Leask (Cambridge, UK: Cambridge UP, 2009).

74. Marshall, *Rural Economy of Yorkshire*, vol. 2, 316.

75. Rowland develops this connection in *Romanticism and Childhood*, 14 and 93.

76. Srinivas Aravamudan, "The Return of Anachronism," *MLQ* 62 (2001): 331–54, 351.

77. Henry Bourne, *Antiquitates Vulgares or The Antiquities of the Common People* (Newcastle, 1725), ix.

78. Kathleen Wilson, *The Sense of the People: Politics, Culture, and Imperialism in England, 1715–1785* (Cambridge, UK: Cambridge UP, 1995), 288 and 297, respectively.

79. Ibid., 297.

80. See Leask and Connell, *Romanticism and Popular Culture*, 15.

81. John Brand, *Observations on Popular Antiquities* (Newcastle upon Tyne, 1777), ix.

82. Butler, "Antiquarianism (Popular)," 329.

83. Raymond Williams, *Keywords: A Vocabulary of Culture and Society* (1976; repr. New York: Oxford UP, 1983), 132.

84. See Rosemary Sweet, s.v. "John Brand," *Oxford Dictionary of National Biography*. This characterization differs from Butler's, who describes Brand as at times "something of a Jacobin" in "Antiquarianism (Popular)," 329. Sweet's account seems more accurate in light of the fact that Brand's version of provincial patriotism anachronized provincial vulgar language and customs in a way that Collier, for instance, did not.

85. Carolyn Steedman, "Servants and Their Relationship to the Unconscious," *Journal of British Studies* 42 (2002), 316–50: 329 and 350, respectively.

86. Bruce Robbins, ed., *The Phantom Public Sphere* (Minneapolis: U of Minnesota P, 1993), ix.

87. "Since more frequent communication with the provinces, and more easy access will soon make little variety, except in the wilds of Exmore, the barren heaths of Northumberland, or the sequestered mountains of Lancashire," *Critical Review* 66 (1788), 283.

88. For a discussion of mourning and melancholia, introjection and incorporation, see N. Abraham and M. Torok, *The Shell and the Kernel: Renewals of Psychoanalysis* (1972; repr. Chicago: U of Chicago P, 1994), 125–38.

89. Esther Schor, *Bearing the Dead: The British Culture of Mourning from the Enlightenment to Victoria* (Princeton, NJ: Princeton UP, 1994), 6.

90. Hutton, *A Bran New Wark*, 186.

91. Steedman, "Servants and Their Relationship to the Unconscious," 350. When print representations of provincial language occasionally put it in the mouths of landowners, they anachronized provincial space and peoples, their language still shared between the common people and their rulers. The Yorkshire Squire Sapscull in Henry Carey's *Honest Yorkshire-Man* (London, 1735), for instance, speaks the provincial language of his servant, while London servant and mistress speak distinct languages.

92. *The Gentleman's Magazine* (1794), part I, 13–14.

93. Ibid., 529.

94. Schor, *Bearing the Dead*, 53.

95. Abraham and Torok, *The Shell and the Kernel*, 126.

96. Oliver Goldsmith, *The Deserted Village* (London, 1770).

97. Stewart, *Crimes of Writing*, 118–19.

98. British Library MS Add 32640.

99. Palmer's grandson published the dialogues with a glossary, which I cite: J. F. Palmer, *A Dialogue of the Devonshire Dialect* (London, 1837).

100. Daniel Dewispelare makes this observation about the fathers of Wheeler's *Dialogues* in "Dissidence in Dialect: Ann Wheeler's Westmorland Dialogues," *Studies in Romanticism* 52 (2015): 101–26.

101. Ann Wheeler, *The Westmorland Dialect in Three Familiar Dialogues, in which an attempt is made to illustrate the Provincial Idiom* (Kendal: James Ashburner, 1790).

102. Ruth Mack, *Literary Historicity: Literature and Historical Experience in Eighteenth-Century Britain* (Stanford, CA: Stanford UP, 2009), 18.

103. Dewispelare, "Dissidence in Dialect," and Michael Baron, "Dialect, Gender, and the Politics of the Local," in *Romantic Masculinities*, ed. Tony Pinkney (Keele, Staffordshire: Keele UP, 1997), 41–56.

104. *The Monthly Review* Dec. 1750: 156.

105. Ian Duncan, "The Pathos of Abstraction," in *Scotland and the Borders of Romanticism*, ed. Leith Davis, Ian Duncan, and Janet Sorensen (Cambridge, UK: Cambridge UP, 2004), 50.

106. Jacques Derrida, *Specters of Marx*, trans. Peggy Kamuf (New York: Routledge, 1994), xx and 7, respectively.

107. G. Dyer, *Restoration of the Ancient Modes of Bestowing Names on the Rivers, Hills, Vallies, Plains and Settlements of Britain* (Exeter, 1805).

108. *The Works of John Collier (Tim Bobbin)*, ed. Henry Fishwick (Rochedale, 1894), 52.

109. Collier writes, "My business being soon done, I cast my eyes round, and saw in a hole or niche in the wall an old folio MS." *The Works of John Collier*, n.p.

110. Collier, *A View of the Lancashire Dialect*, 27 and 28. This also pushes to the breaking point that move in linguistic antiquarianism that revalued the "low" language of "ploughmen and working girls" as national and valuable because old. Blank, *Broken English*, 108.

111. Chakrabarty, *Provincializing Europe*, 8.

112. Mack, *Literary Historicity*, 20.

113. Thomas Chatterton, *Selected Poems*, ed. Grevel Lindop (Manchester: Carcanet, 2003).

114. As noted by Lindop in *Selected Poems*, 20. Lindop also points out that the term "alatche" from *Ælla* is "apparently invented by Chatterton," 91.

115. Recalling Gay's characterization of the language of *The Shepherd's Week* as "never uttered." (London, 1714), n.p.

116. Chatterton, *Selected Poems*, 20.

117. Elfenbein argues that "if one . . . reads the poems aloud, the actual phonemes follow the strictures of eighteenth-century orthoepists exactly; Rowley's pronunciation is arguably far more standard than Pope's." *Romanticism and the Rise of English*, 89.

118. *Poems and Songs of Robert Burns*, vol. 2, ed. James Kinsley (Oxford: Oxford UP, 1968), 494–96.

119. Nigel Leask discovered this prefatorial "proem to a Glasgow broadside" of Burns's "On the Late Captain Grose." *Robert Burns and Pastoral*, 264.

120. See Ian Duncan, "The Upright Corpse," *Studies in Hogg and His World* 5 (1994): 29–54; and James Barrell, "Putting down the Rising," in *Scotland and the Borders of Romanticism*, ed. Leith Davis, Ian Duncan, and Janet Sorensen (Cambridge, UK: Cambridge UP, 2004), 130–38.

121. Cited in Leask, *Robert Burns and Pastoral*, 58.

122. Bobbin, *A View*; Brice, *Exmoor Scolding* (Exon, 1746); and *Transactions of the Society of the Antiquaries of Scotland* I (Edinburgh, 1792), respectively.

123. Thomas Ruddiman, ed., *Aeneid* (Edinburgh, 1710), Joseph Ritson, *Scotish [sic] Songs* (London, 1794).

124. John Sinclair, *Observations on the Scottish Dialect* (London, 1782), 78.

125. Cited in Robert Freeman, *Robert Fergusson and the Scots Humanist Compromise* (Edinburgh: Edinburgh UP, 1984), 5.

126. Susan Rennie, *Jamieson's Dictionary of Scots* (Oxford: Oxford UP, 2012), 36.

127. John Jamieson, *Etymological Dictionary of the Scottish Language* (Edinburgh, 1808), iv.

128. These characterizations move ever further north, to the Highlands, as in Martin Martin's *Description of the Western Islands* (London, 1703); Anonymous, *The History of the Life and Adventures of Mr. Duncan Campbell* (London, 1720), Samuel Johnson's discussion of the Highlands and second sight in his *Journey to the Western Islands of Scotland* (London, 1775), or William Collins, "Ode on the Popular Superstitions of the Highlands of Scotland" (London, 1788), introducing a different set of issues, taken up in Penny Fielding's *Scotland and the Fictions of Geography*.

129. Francis Grose, *Antiquities of Scotland*, vol. 2 (London, 1797).

130. All citations of this poem are from Robert Burns, *Selected Poems*, ed. Carol McGuirk (London: Penguin, 1993), 160–66.

131. Fielding, *Scotland and the Fictions of Geography*, 44.

132. Robert Burns, *Poems, Chiefly in the Scottish Dialect* (Edinburgh, 1787), 345, and (London, 1787), 349.

133. All terms and definitions are from *Poems, Chiefly in the Scottish Dialect* (Kilmarnock, 1786), 236. All information about dates of circulation for terms and their meanings is taken from Mairi Robinson, ed., *The Concise Scots Dictionary* (1985; repr. Aberdeen: Aberdeen UP, 1991).

134. Robert Crawford, *Scotland's Books: A History of Scottish Literature* (Oxford: Oxford UP, 2008), 357.

135. For a summary of Burns's playful relation to provincial cultural practices, see Gerald Carruthers, "'Tongues turn'd inside out': The Reception of Tam o' Shanter," *Studies in Scottish Literature* 35–36 (2007): 455–63, cited in Leask, *Robert Burns and Pastoral*.

136. Burns, *Selected Poems*, 264.

137. *OED* s.v. "press, n" and "press, v."

138. For a discussion of the relation between globalization and local dialects, see Barbara Johnstone, "Place, Globalization, and Linguistic Variation," in *Sociolinguistic Variation*, ed. Carmen Fought (Oxford: Oxford UP, 2004), 65–83.

139. See Fielding, *Scotland and the Fictions of Geography*, for a discussion of the global in relation to the local in Burns.

Part Three. Wandering in Place

1. Marcus Rediker writes that "to be socialized anew into the ways of the deep-sea craft was to be stripped of previous attachments to local and regional cultures and ways of speaking." *Between the Devil and the Deep Blue Sea: Merchant Seamen, Pirates, and the Anglo-American Maritime World, 1700–1750* (Cambridge, UK: Cambridge UP, 1987), 162.

2. *The Critical Review* February 1757.

3. Tom Bowling was a beloved character in Smollett's *Roderick Random* (1748), but he also made appearances in songs and plays of the eighteenth century.

4. Bruce Robbins, "Comparative Cosmopolitanism," *Social Text* 10 (1992): 169–86, 173.

5. William Falconer, *A Universal Dictionary of the Marine* (London, 1769).

6. William Falconer *The Shipwreck* (London, 1762), Canto II, 190–95. Further citations list edition canto and lines parenthetically.

7. Ned Ward, *The Wooden World Dissected* (London, 1707), 5. Further citations noted parenthetically.

8. The designation of world-traveling sailors as too particular to be cosmopolitan suggests a genealogy of the class-based criteria for cosmopolitanism some continue to maintain. Bruce Robbins critiques Ulf Hannerz, for instance, for insisting that true cosmopoli-

tans "have chosen to live abroad" and Mike Featherstone for arguing that true cosmopolitans "adopt a reflexive ... and aesthetic stance to divergent cultural experiences." Robbins, "Comparative Cosmopolitanism," 176.

9. Gillian Russell, *The Theatres of War: Performance, Politics, and Society, 1793–1815* (Oxford: Clarendon Press, 1995), 99–105.

Chapter Eight. Our Tars: Making Maritime Language English

1. Tobias Smollett, *The Reprisal* (London, 1757), "Prologue," n.p. The first word appears in Alexandre Exquemelin, *History of the Bucaniers* (English translation, London, 1704, 4th ed.), 45, the second in William Chetwood, *Voyage and Adventures of Captain Robert Boyle* (London, 1726), 171.

2. *Interesting Narrative of the Life of Olaudah Equiano*, ed. Werner Sollors (1789; repr. New York: W. W. Norton, 2001), 127.

3. *Ramblin' Jack: The Journal of Captain John Cremer 1700–1774*, ed. R. Reynell Bellamy (London: Jonathan Cape, 1936). Further citations appear parenthetically.

4. See, for instance, Henry Neuman, *A Marine Pocket-Dictionary of the Italian, Spanish, Portuguese, and German Languages* (London, 1799) and A Captain of the British Navy, *A Vocabulary of Sea Phrases and Terms of Art used in Seamanship and Naval Architecture* (London, 1799).

5. William Williams, *Mr. Penrose: The Journal of Penrose, Seaman* (Bloomington: Indiana UP, 1969). Published anonymously and posthumously in 1815.

6. *A True and Impartial Journal of a Cruise to the South Seas, and Round the Globe, in His Majesty's Ship Centurion* (London, 1745), 277, cited in James Bunn, "Commodore Anson's *Centurion* as Global Model of Self Repair," *ISLE* 14 (2007): 25–49, 43.

7. William Falconer, *A Universal Dictionary of Marine Terms* (London, 1769), n.p.

8. Marcus Rediker and Peter Linebaugh, *The Many-Headed Hydra: Sailors, Slaves, Commoners, and the Hidden History of the Revolutionary Atlantic* (Boston: Beacon Press, 2000), 151.

9. Cited in Bunn, "Commodore Anson's *Centurion*," 41.

10. Ian F. Hancock, "A Provisional Comparison of the English-Based Atlantic Creoles," *African Language Review* 8 (1969): 7–72.

11. *The Naval Songster* (London, 1798), 6 repeats Ward's characterization of the sailor as prisoner verbatim.

12. Greg Dening, *Mr. Bligh's Bad Language: Passion, Power, and Theatre on the Bounty* (Cambridge: Canto, 1994), 58.

13. Bunn, "Commodore Anson's *Centurion*," 28.

14. David Hume, *A Treatise of Human Nature*, ed. L. A. Selby Bigge (Oxford: Clarendon, 1978), 257. The metaphor is a longstanding one, found in classical and early modern writing.

15. Bunn, "Commodore Anson's *Centurion*," 31.

16. N. A. M. Rodger, *The Wooden World: An Anatomy of the Georgian Navy* (London: Collins, 1986), 346.

17. Henry Fielding, *Journal of a Voyage to Lisbon* (London, 1755), 60. Fielding also describes the view of British merchant and naval ships as "highly warming to the heart of an Englishman" (62). For the centrality of Britain's maritime achievements to its national identity, see Suvir Kaul, *Poems of Nation, Anthems of Empire* (Charlotteville: UP of Virginia, 2000).

18. Samuel Pegge, *Anecdotes of the English Language*, (1803, repr. London, 1844), 12.

19. Smollett, *The Reprisal*, 8.

20. Neuman, *Marine Pocket-Dictionary*, v.

21. Margaret Cohen, *The Novel and the Sea* (Princeton, NJ: Princeton UP, 2011), 4 and 15, respectively. Further citations noted parenthetically.

22. For this denotative sense of seamen's language, see J. H. Parry, "Sailors' English," *Cambridge Journal* 2 (1948): 660–70, and Dening, *Mr. Bligh's Bad Language*, 57.

23. John Smith, *A Sea Grammar* (London, 1627), 2–3. The only two words reflecting intercultural contact are "hurricane" and "monsoon."

24. William Wycherley, *Plain Dealer* (London, 1677), 2.

25. Cannon Schmitt and Elaine Freedgood, "Denotatively, Technically, Literally," *Representations* 125 (2014): 1–14, 3.

26. John Dryden, "An Account of the Ensuing Poem," in *The Poems of John Dryden*, vol. 1 of 2, ed. Paul Hammond (London: Longman, 1995), 115. Further citations appear parenthetically. Milton had used some technical maritime terms in *Paradise Lost*, as had Virgil, although, as we shall see below, both Dryden and Pope were reluctant to use technical terms in their translations, viewing them as inappropriate for poetry.

27. Hammond, ed., *The Poems of John Dryden*, vol. 1. Future line citations cited parenthetically.

28. I take my definitions of the technical language from William Falconer's *Universal Dictionary of the Marine* (London, 1769).

29. The *OED* cites Dryden's 1697 translation of Virgil as the first use of "dauby," missing this earlier appearance.

30. See Hammond's notes, *Poems of John Dryden*, 165.

31. See Kaul's discussion of *Annus Mirabilis* in *Poems of Nation*, 75–82.

32. Edward Young, *Imperium Pelagi. A Naval Lyrick* (London, 1730).

33. Puritan accounts of voyages and shipwrecks, often loaded with Christian symbolism, did not tend to include technical maritime language. For more on this mode of writing, see Patricia Caldwell, *The Puritan Conversion Narrative: The Beginnings of American Expression* (Cambridge, UK: Cambridge UP, 1983).

34. William Dampier, *A Collection of Voyages in Four Volumes*, vol. I (London, 1729), 4. Not only sea voyages but their writing were collaborative affairs. Organizing print volumes through a single author, and often turning multiple voyages into one single narrative, as in Dampier's *New Voyage round the World* (London, 1703), would help create a notion of a proprietary individual and seamless identity that was illusory. See Philip Edwards, *The Story of the Voyage* (Cambridge, UK: Cambridge UP, 1994) and Adriana Craciun, "Oceanic Voyages, Maritime Books, and Eccentric Inscriptions," *Atlantic Studies* 10 (2013): 170–96.

35. George Anson, *Voyage round the World* (London, 1748), 10.

36. Both comments appear in the "Introduction" to Anson, *Voyage*, n.p.

37. Falconer, *Universal Dictionary of the Marine*, s.v. "log."

38. "Directions for Sea-Men, Bound for Far Voyages," *Philosophical Transactions of the Royal Society* 1 (1665), 140–42. Cohen cites similar stipulations in James Atkinson's *Epitome of the Art of Navigation* (London, 1686), 22.

39. Captain's Log, Falcon 1688 UK National Archives, ADM 51/345.

40. Dampier, *New Voyage round the World*, 9.

41. See Steven Shapin and Simon Schaffer, *Leviathan and the Air-Pump: Hobbes, Boyle, and the Experimental Life* (Princeton, NJ: Princeton UP, 1985).

42. *A Vocabulary of Sea Phrases* (London, 1799) aims to be useful not only to "the Sea Officer, the Naval Architects, the Ship-owner," but also "the reader of voyages" (7). Falconer makes a similar claim in his *Universal Dictionary of the Marine*.

43. Falconer, "Introduction," *Universal Dictionary of the Marine*, n.p.

44. William Chetwood, *Voyages ... of Captain Robert Boyle* (London, 1726) and *Voyages ... of Cap. Falconer* (London, 1720?); Charles Johnson, *General History*, ed. Manuel Schonhorn (1724, repr. Mineola, NY: Dover, 1990).

45. Space is too short for a full examination of the ambivalent relationship of the figure of the pirate, but his—and the mariner's—wavering status reminds us that the language attributed to them provided a range of modes of affiliation, from furtive identification with rule-breaking rogue to sentimental affection for the avuncular tar. See Erin Mackie, *Rakes, Highwaymen, and Pirates* (Baltimore: Johns Hopkins UP, 2009).

46. Johnson, *General History*, 82. Further citations noted parenthetically.

47. Ian Watt, *The Rise of the Novel* (1957; repr. Berkeley: U of California P, 1967), 26.

48. Daniel Defoe, *Robinson Crusoe*, ed. Michael Shinagel (New York: W. W. Norton, 1994), 9.

49. Daniel Defoe, *The Life, Adventures, and Pyracies of the Famous Captain Singleton*, ed. Shiv Kumar (Oxford: Oxford UP, 1990), 148.

50. Aphra Behn, *Oroonoko*, ed. Joanna Lipking (New York: W. W. Norton, 1997), 31.

51. Paul Gilje, *To Swear Like a Sailor: Maritime Culture in America, 1750-1850* (Cambridge, UK: Cambridge UP, 2016), 36. Similarly, as we shall explore below, the use of footnotes to explain these terms suggests they were not entirely familiar to all readers.

52. The serial version appeared in 1720 and 1721.

53. Tobias Smollett, *Roderick Random*, ed. Paul-Gabriel Boucé (Oxford: Oxford UP, 1981), 139.

54. Daniel Defoe, *Serious Reflections during the Life and Surprising Adventures of Robinson Crusoe* (London, 1720), n.p.

55. Thomas Dekker, *Lanthorne and Candle-Light*, 1st ed. (London, 1602), ff. 4, recto.

56. Samuel Johnson, *Selected Writings*, ed. Patrick Crutwell (Harmondsworth: Penguin, 1986), 238.

57. Ibid.

58. See Beth Fowkes Tobin, *Colonizing Nature: The Tropics in British Arts and Letters 1760-1820* (Philadelphia: U of Pennsylvania P, 2005), and Anna Neill, *British Discovery Literature and the Rise of Global Commerce* (New York: Palgrave, 2002).

59. Dampier, *New Voyage round the World*, in the "Epistle Dedicatory" and "Preface" (London, 1703), n.p.

60. Ned Ward, *A Trip to Jamaica* (London, 1698), 10.

61. Jonathan Swift, *Gulliver's Travels*, ed. Christopher Fox (Boston: Bedford, 1995), 28.

62. *A Compendium of Authentic and Entertaining Voyages*, vol. 1 of 7 (London, 1756), ii.

63. Nineteenth-century writer of maritime fiction W. Clark Russell dismissed this passage as full of mistakes and nonsensical, while a later reviewer pointed out that the text was an extract from Samuel Sturmy, *Compleat Mariner*, 3rd ed., 1684). See: *A Collection of Articles about Swift, and Reviews of Books by and about Him, Taken Mainly from 19th Century Periodicals*, Oxford University Libraries (Var. Pl.: 1766-1900).

64. Ward, *A Trip to Jamaica*, 10.

65. Fielding, *Journal of a Voyage to Lisbon*, 167, and John Davis, *The Post-Captain* (3rd ed., London, 1808), 4 and 23, respectively.

66. Samuel Foote, *A Trip to Calais, A Medley Maritime Sketch* (London, 1775), 11.

67. Anonymous, *Remarks on the Present Condition of the Navy, and Particularly of the Victuals* (London, 1670).

68. Chetwood refers to the "noise" of sailors in *Voyages ... of Capn. Robert Boyle*, 83.

69. William Matthews, "Sailors' Pronunciation in the Second Half of the Seventeenth

Century," *Anglia* 59 (1935): 193–251, 195. Matthews documents a subsequent shift to standard English in logbooks in "Sailors' Pronunciation, 1770–1783," *Anglia* 61 (1937): 72–80.

70. PRO Adm 52/86 10.

71. Frances Burney, *Evelina*, ed. Kristina Straub (Boston: Bedford, 1997), 180.

72. Smith writes that "the particular tree whose fruit relieved their hunger . . . would first be denominated by the word tree. . . . Afterwards, when the more enlarged experience of these savages had led them to observe, and their necessary occasions obliged them to make mention of other . . . trees . . . they would naturally bestow, upon each of those new objects, the same name." Adam Smith, "Considerations Concerning the First Formations of Languages," in *Works of Adam Smith*, vol. 5 of 5 (London, 1811).

73. Conversely, some who attempt to appropriate this figurative language mark themselves as outsiders. When Walter Elliot jokes that an admiral renting Kellynch Hall would have "rather the greatest prize of all, let him have taken over so many before," the forced laugh of his underling underscores Walter's outsiderness. Jane Austen, *Persuasion* (London: Penguin, 1985), 47.

74. Elizabeth DeLoughrey, *Routes and Roots: Navigating Caribbean and Pacific Island Literatures* (Honolulu: U of Hawai'i P, 2007), 55.

75. *Seaman's Garland* (Preston, 1790?), 1.

76. Anonymous, *New Collection of Voyages*, vol. 2 of 4 (London, 1745), 26.

77. Francis Grose, *A Classical Dictionary of the Vulgar Tongue* (London, 1785).

78. Library of Congress Manuscript Collection, Minutes of the Vice Admirality Court of Charleston, (1737), f. 103, cited in Rediker, *Between the Devil and the Deep Blue Sea*, 165. See also Jesse Lemisch, "Jack Tar in the Streets" *WMQ* 25 (1968): 371–72.

79. Fielding, *Journal of a Voyage to Lisbon*, 68.

80. Rediker, *Between the Devil*, 166.

81. Grose, *Classical Dictionary of the Vulgar Tongue*, i.

82. *Vocabulary of Sea Phrases*, ix.

83. James Boswell, *Life of Samuel Johnson*, vol. 1 of 2 (London, 1791), 189.

84. Fielding, *Journal of a Voyage to Lisbon*, 68.

85. Charles Dibdin, *A Collection of Songs*, vol. 2 of 2, 3rd ed. (London, 1792), 116. In another song, Dibdin refers to sailors as "Ye Free-born Sons."

86. Shrividhya Swaminathan, "Defoe's Captain Singleton," in Shrividhya Swaminathan and Adam Beach, eds., *Invoking Slavery in the Eighteenth-Century British Imagination* (London: Ashgate, 2013), 73. See also Roxann Wheeler, *The Complexion of Race: Categories of Difference in Eighteenth-Century British Culture* (Philadelphia: U of Pennsylvania P, 2000).

87. Swaminathan, "Defoe's Captain Singleton," 61.

88. Wheeler, *The Complexion of Race*, 107.

89. *Works of Mr. Henry Needler* (London, 1724), 16. Kaul stresses the role of commerce in differentiating Britons, and I wish to add emphasis to the mastery of maritime technology. Suvir Kaul, *Poems of Nation*, 185.

90. Despite the fact that, as Kaul points out, they needed to learn this technology from the Romans.

91. See Kaul's discussion in *Poems of Nation*.

92. Interestingly, it is "England" and not "Britain" that Equiano invokes.

93. Equiano, *Interesting Narrative*, 38 and 39, respectively.

94. Dening, *Mr. Bligh's Bad Language*, 56.

95. Paul-Gabriel Boucé in Smollett, *Roderick Random*, n. 438.

96. Boucé notes that the sung was written for *Perseus and Andromeda*, by Roger and

John Weaver, performed in 1717. Smollett, *Roderick Random*, n. 438. The song also appears in Allan Ramsay's *Tea-Table Miscellany* (Edinburgh, 1724).

97. Catherine Gallagher, *Nobody's Story: The Vanishing Acts of Women Writers in the Marketplace, 1670-1820* (Berkeley: U of California P, 1994), 168.

98. Smith, *Theory of Moral Sentiments*, 10.

99. "Poor Jack" (Stirling, 1800?), 2.

100. Russell, *Theaters of War*, 98. See also Gilje, *To Swear Like a Sailor*.

101. I take these dates from Gilje, who discusses the Jack Tar figure in *To Swear Like a Sailor*, 43.

102. Russell, *Theaters of War*, 99.

103. Gilje, *To Swear Like a Sailor*, 56.

104. Isaac Bickerstaff, *Thomas and Sally* (Dublin, 1761), and Charles Dibdin, *Tom Bowling* (London, 1790). Gilje notes the combination of languages in this material in *To Swear Like a Sailor*, 44.

105. The expression was common and found early in Aphra Behn's *Rover* (London, 1677).

106. Edmund Burke, *A Philosophical Enquiry into the Origin of Our Idea of the Sublime and the Beautiful*, ed. Adam Phillips (Oxford: Oxford UP, 2008), 103.

107. See, for instance, *Roach's Beauties of the Great Poets of England*, 6 vols. (London, 1793). William R. Jones provides a list of these titles in his *A Critical Edition of the Poetical Works of William Falconer* (Lewiston, NY: Mellen Press, 2003).

108. William Falconer, *The Shipwreck*, 3rd ed. (London, 1769), canto III, line 412. Future citations to Falconer's poem will include year of publication, canto, and line, listed parenthetically.

109. Jones, *Critical Edition of the Poetical Works*, 79.

110. Ibid., 80.

111. Byron celebrated Falconer's technical language as making for the "strength and reality of the poem," while Hazlitt critiqued Byron's emphasis on the technical language, arguing that "the faithful description of common feelings and inevitable calamity" are the merits of the poem. Cited in Jones, *A Critical Edition*, 31.

112. Falconer, born into a poor family in Edinburgh in 1732, went to sea for a three-year apprenticeship at age fourteen, working on Newcastle colliers. He was quite likely pressed into military service—the "hot press," as it was called, drew heavily from these colliers during the Seven Years War. He also worked on merchant ships in the Levant and in the Atlantic, on a route between Cork and Jamaica, and lived through a shipwreck that killed most of his shipmates—the subject of his popular poem. Falconer himself died in a shipwreck in 1769.

113. "Preface," *The Shipwreck*, 2nd ed. (London, 1764).

114. "Preface," *The Shipwreck*, 3rd ed. (London, 1769).

115. Smith, *Theory of Moral Sentiments*, 135.

116. Ibid., 135.

117. Hans Blumberg, *Shipwreck with Spectator*, trans. Steven Rendall (Cambridge, MA: MIT Press, 1997), 15.

118. Johnson, *Journey to the Western Islands of Scotland*, 98.

119. *Critical Review* 13 (1762): 440 and *Monthly Review* 27 (1762): 197-201, respectively.

120. Jones, *A Critical Edition*, 14.

121. For the complex gender dynamics of representations of mariners, see Dianne Dugaw, "Balladry's Female Warriors," *Eighteenth-Century Life* 9 (1985): 1-20.

122. William Hayley, ed., *The Life and Posthumous Writings of William Cowper*, vol. 1 of 3 (London, 1803).
123. Smith, *Theory of Moral Sentiments*, 94.
124. Karen Swann, "The Vulgar Sublime," *College English* 52 (1990): 7–20.
125. Blumberg, *Shipwreck with Spectator*, 19.

INDEX

NOTE: Page numbers followed by *f* indicate a figure.

Abraham, Nicolas, 212
Adams, James, 303n124
Adams, Matthew, 179, 181–82
Addison, Joseph: democratizing vision of, 12–15, 20; on euphemistic language, 113–14; on the pastoral, 93, 102; on provincial language, 148; on technical language, 263
Advice, Addressed to the Lower Ranks of Society (Burdon), 176
Advice to the Advised (Crispin), 176–77
Aesop, 285n119
"Air XLII" (Gay), 88
Amigoni, Jacob, 7, 8*f*
Amusements Serious and Comical Calculated for the Meridian of London (Brown), 15, 109
Anderson, Benedict, 131, 200, 300n59
Anglo-Saxon language, 184, 193–98, 199*f*, 219, 236, 256, 286n9
Annus Mirabilis (Dryden), 239–40
Anson, George, 235–37, 241, 269
Anstey, Christopher, 149–50, 169, 205
Antiquitates Vulgares or The Antiquities of the Common People (Bourne), 207–8
Antiquities of Scotland (Grose), 226
Aravamudan, Srinivas, 5–6, 17, 60, 207
Auerbach, Erich, 60
Avery, Captain, 243
Ayre, William, 183

Babel, 29, 31, 36, 67–68, 99, 102
Bacchus and Venus, 46, 50
Bacon, Francis, 178
Bailey, Nathan, 11, 13, 48–49, 77, 137, 187
Bakhtin, Mikhail: on decentralizing forces shaping the novel, 58; on novelistic heteroglossia, 17, 19, 74, 186–87, 277n79
ballad, 7, 9; in *The Beggar's Opera*, 22, 88–90, 96, 99, 102–3; provincial language of, 152, 161, 170, 201

The Ballman of London, 119–20
Banks, Joseph, 1, 213, 298n35
Banks, Sarah, 213
"The Bard" (Gray), 310n52
Baron, Michael, 213, 216
Barrell, John: on Britain as a polyglot nation, 73; on political liberty and language, 10–11, 14, 53, 284n109, 285n114
Batchelor, Thomas, 138, 143, 161
B. E. See *New Dictionary of the Terms . . . of the Canting Crew*
Beattie, James, 106, 107–8, 111, 112
beggars, 39, 50, 56, 76–77. See also cant
Beggars Bush (Fletcher), 37–38, 40, 282n63
The Beggar's Opera (Gay), 19, 86–105, 290nn10–11; canting criminals in, 40, 90–91, 94–99, 272n44; commodification of, 272n46; contemporary reviews of, 91, 93–94; contingencies of meaning of vernacular language in, 99–105, 272n51; gender relations in, 126; opaque characters of, 96, 291n35; ruse of pastoral inclusivity in, 90–94, 97–99, 170, 290n20; static temporality of, 95–96, 291n33; stereophonic mixture of languages in, 86, 96–99, 272n40; transatlantic movement in, 88–90, 290n5; wit and humor of, 111–12
Behn, Aphra, 244, 319n105
Bell, John, 302n115
Bender, John, 94, 291n29
Benjamin, Walter, 305n15
Bentham, Jeremy, 179
Bentley, Richard, 135
Blackstone, William, 53, 178, 284n109
Blackwell, Thomas, 162
Blair, Hugh, 162, 172
Blake, N. F., 135, 150
Bland, Captain, 5
Blank, Paula, 197, 285n126, 297n13

[321]

Bobbin, Tim, 153, 173–74, 176. *See also* Collier, John
Bono, James, 56
Boucher, Jonathan, 170, 206
Boulukos, George, 84, 288n64
Bourdieu, Pierre, 127
Bourne, Henry, 207–9, 226
Brand, John, 208–9, 226, 312n84
A Bran New Wark (Hutton), 204
Brewer, John, 148
Brice, Andrew, 23, 153–55, 158, 217, 302n106; commercial appeal of works of, 172–74; invented language (Bricisms) of, 186, 221, 227; maritime narratives published by, 245; political context of provincial language of, 174–78; strategic linguistic obscurity of, 186–91; temporal dynamics of provincial language of, 218–19. See also *An Exmoor Scolding*
Brice, Sarah, 302n106
Britain: access to the commons in, 35, 39, 107, 119, 181, 185; cant's articulation of freedom in, 36–39, 51–56, 75–78, 115–16, 282n55, 284n105, 285n114, 285n119, 288n56; Civil War songs of, 12; customary law of, 178–79; diverse national polity of, 13–14, 178–80, 306n43; free labor in, 288n53; indentured servitude and slavery in, 79–85, 88, 115–16, 256–57, 288–89nn64–65, 288n61, 289n67; Irish migrants in, 116–17, 295n52; laws on personal mobility in, 38, 77, 80–81, 117, 281nn41–42, 284n105; linguistic nationalism in, 143–48, 185, 300n56, 300n65, 300n76; literary images of laborers in, 166; making of liberal political subjects in, 76–78, 256; maritime identity and freedom of, 241, 254–59; nationalist rhetoric on liberty of, 14, 37; nation-making among strangers in, 49–50, 58, 130–31, 144; pastoral portrayals of inclusiveness in, 91–94, 97–99, 170–71, 290n20; penal practices of, 118–19; Roma travelers in, 28, 279n7, 282n55, 282n58, 284n105; slang's articulation of freedom in, 11, 107–8, 111, 114–19; state-sanctioned indentured servitude in, 81; threats to liberty in, 52, 92; Transportation Act of 1718 in, 290n5. *See also* realist fiction; standardizing English; vernacular English
Brome, Richard, 37–38, 152, 225–26, 229
Brontë, Emily, 5
Brown, Tom, 15, 109
Browne, William, 170
Bullokar, John, 133
Bunn, James, 235, 237
Burdon, William, 176
Burke, Edmund, 20, 147; on British diversity, 178–80; on endearing smallness, 261; on history of languages, 201; on obscurity and the sublime, 20, 178–80, 269; on the sound of language, 159–60; on standardized English, 162, 194; on technical language, 266
Burke, Peter, 84
burlesque, 22; comedy and satire of, 106–7, 111–14; definition of, 106; of Italian opera, 90, 103; ludicrous language of, 106. See also *The Beggar's Opera*; slang
Burney, Frances, 16, 194, 268
Burns, Robert, 6, 19, 21, 176, 185, 263; historical transport of readers by, 219–30; parodies of anachronisms by, 23, 191, 223; on provincial bilingualism, 180
Butler, Marilyn, 189–90, 201, 312n84
Buzard, James, 17–18, 62
Byron, George Gordon, 263

Caleb Williams (Godwin), 109
Campbell, George, 180, 198
cant, 3–4, 21–22, 25–56, 50; aesthetic impact of, 32–34; articulations of freedom and slavery in, 22, 36–39, 51–56, 75–85, 88, 115–16, 282n55, 284n105, 285n114, 285n119, 288n56, 288n61, 288–89nn64–65, 289n67; autonomy of expression in, 99–100, 282n44; burlesque humor and, 106–7; comedic portrayals of, 37–39, 281n48, 282n59; definitions of, 25; in Defoe's realist fiction, 58–85, 254–55, 286n9, 287n49, 288n64; dictionaries and glossaries of, 3, 25, 33*f*, 34, 39–41, 45–51, 57–58, 66, 78–80, 86–88, 107, 278nn1–2, 283n68, 284n98, 289n4, 294n16; in Gay's ballad operas, 86–105, 291nn29–30; as language of criminals and outsiders,

26–30, 34–36, 39–42, 49–50, 78, 86–88, 278n1(ch1), 279n7, 280n33, 280n38, 281nn41–42, 281n45, 285nn125–26, 288n54; linking of colloquialisms and proverbs with, 45–51, 66–71, 86–88, 98–105; meaninglessness of early representations of, 30–33, 246; moral impugning of, 50–51; pastoral portrayals of, 91–94, 290n20; in popular accounts of real criminals, 66–67; pre-eighteenth-century depictions of, 27–39, 125; shared male and female facility in, 125–27; in standardizing trends of the eighteenth-century, 27–28, 32, 39–56, 63–64, 86, 125–26, 282n63, 283n72, 283nn68–69; transformation to slang of, 106–8

The Canting Academy, or, the Devil's Cabinet Broke Open (Head), 28, 30, 45–46, 50, 125, 285n125

"Canting Song" (Thurmond), 40 41

Captain Singleton (Defoe), 244–46, 254–55, 257–58

Carew, Richard, 137, 298n27

Carey, Henry, 312n91

The Castaway (Cowper), 269, 271

The Castle of Otranto (Walpole), 12–13, 166, 219

Castle Rackrent (Edgeworth), 189–91, 308nn95–96

Catholicism, 200

Cave, Edward, 148

Caveat or Warning, for Common Cursetors (Harmon), 279n7, 280n25, 283n69

Certeau, Michel de: on glossolalia, 31–32, 38, 61, 105, 164; on the obligation to make recognizable meaning, 37, 123

Chakrabarty, Dipesh, 206, 217–18, 226

Chandler, James, 205

Charles II, King of England, 52

Chatterton, Thomas, 19, 191, 219–30; artificial antiquated language of, 23; invented language of, 221–23, 227; Rowley poems of, 220–23, 229, 313n117

Chaucer, Geoffrey, 23, 139, 203–4

Chetwood, William, 59, 139, 242–45, 256–57, 299n38

Chicken, Edward, 151, 302n100

Child, G., 7, 8f

Christensen, Jerome, 144, 300n63

Cibber, Colley, 139

The Citizen of the World (Goldsmith), 15

Clare, John, 21

A Classical Dictionary of the Vulgar Tongue (Grose), 1, 3, 25, 83–84, 107–8, 278n2; Grose's goals for, 108–9, 112, 138; Grose's pseudoethnographic approach with, 107–11; *Lexicon Balatronicum* expansion of, 122–23, 125; maritime language in, 255. *See also* slang

The Cobbler Politics (Collier), 176

Cohen, Margaret, 238, 244

Coke, Edward, 53, 284n109

Coleman, Julie, 26, 36, 55

Coleridge, Samuel Taylor, 256, 263

Collection of English Words, Not Generally Used (Ray), 136–40, 143, 165, 178, 184

collections of language. *See* dictionaries and glossaries

Collier, John, 21, 23, 153–55, 156f; commercial appeal of works of, 172–74, 214; critical response to, 217; on foreign etymologies of words, 198, 199f; historicizing of provincial language by, 195, 218–19, 309n15, 313n110; invented language of, 221; political context of provincial language of, 174–78; pseudonym of, 153, 173, 176; strategic linguistic obscurity of, 187–91, 197

The Collier's Wedding (Chicken), 151, 153, 302n100

colloquial (as term), 67–68

colloquialisms: Defoe's comingling with cant of, 66–71, 86; in dictionaries of cant, 45–51, 86–88; in Gay's *The Beggar's Opera*, 98–105

Colonel Jack (Defoe), 16, 60–85, 127; encounters with racialized slavery in, 79–85, 88, 258; fictional rhetorical spaces of characters of, 71–73; Frenchified full title of, 74; intermingling of low languages in, 61–66, 287n27; language of physical blackness in, 80, 84, 288n64; as liberal political subject, 75–78; maritime language in, 254–55; polyglot first-person narrators of, 67–71, 73, 90, 108, 142; provincial lan-

Colonel Jack (Defoe) (*continued*)
   guage in, 142; readers' affiliations to characters of, 73–76
Commentaries (Blackstone), 178
A Compendium of Authentic and Entertaining Voyages (anon.), 248
Compleat Collection of English Proverbs (Ray), 48–49, 104–5
Compleat Mariner, 249
Complete Modern Spy, 109
Conversation: A Poem (Lloyd), 194–95
Coote, Charles, 204
Copland, Robert, 31, 33–34
Copy of a Letter, Wrote by a Young Shepherd (I. Ritson), 205–6, 311n67
cosmopolitanism, 314n8
"Cotter's Saturday Night" (Burns), 228
Courthope, Peter, 136
The Covent Garden Journal's "Modern Glossary" (Fielding), 113
Cowper, William, 269, 271
Crawford, Robert, 227
Cremer, Jack, 234–35, 251
creole (as term), 83
"Cries of London," 6–7, 8*f*
criminal cant. *See* cant
The Critical Review, 44, 210, 231, 268
Cromwell, Oliver, 52
cultural nationalism, 13, 15, 144. *See also* Britain; standardizing English
Curran, Stuart, 170

Dampier, William, 241–42, 244, 247, 316n34
Davis, John, 250–54
Davis, Natalie Zemon, 13
Dawes, Richard, 134, 145
Defoe, Daniel, 4, 16, 58–85, 131, 138, 286n9, 298n29; advocacy of a language academy by, 286n20; on British diversity, 306n43; collection of provincialisms by, 135–36, 138; depictions of "African" creole by, 134; elevation of the common people by, 60–61; fictional rhetorical spaces of characters of, 71–73, 244; on figurative language, 114; gendered reader relations of, 126–27; liberal political subjects of, 75–78; maritime narratives of, 243–46, 254–55; Ordinary of Newgate Accounts and, 72–73; polyglot first-person narrators of, 66–71, 73, 90, 108, 142, 194, 287n34, 290n9; on provincial language, 135–36, 163, 195, 298n29; provincial language used by, 142, 194; pseudoethnographic approach of, 107; readers' to characters of, 73–76, 244, 287n45; shifting of linguistic registers by, 61–66, 254–55, 287n27, 291n29; on transatlantic movement and racialized slavery, 79–85, 88, 257–58, 262, 289n65, 289n67. *See also Captain Singleton; Colonel Jack; Moll Flanders; Tour thro' the Whole Island of Great Britain*
Dekker, Thomas, 25, 28–35, 112, 119–20, 125; canting glossary of, 31–32, 33*f*; on canting of incoherent outsiders, 28–30, 32, 34–35, 52, 55–56, 246; on euphemistic language, 113
Deloney, Thomas, 142, 193
DeLoughrey, Elizabeth, 254
Dening, Greg, 236–37, 259
Derrida, Jacques, 217
The Deserted Village (Goldsmith), 212–13, 229
Dewispelare, Daniel, 216
dialect, 296n3
Dialogues (Palmer), 213–15
Dickens, Charles, 109
Dickie, Simon, 126, 150
dictionaries and glossaries: for Burns's collections, 226–27; of cant and colloquialisms, 3, 25, 33*f*, 34, 39–41, 45–51, 57–58, 66, 78–80, 86–88, 107, 278nn1–2, 283n68, 284n98, 289n4, 294n16; of maritime language, 232, 235, 242, 255, 316n42; negotiation of stranger relationality in, 58; pronunciation guides in, 134, 146, 161–62, 226; of provincial languages, 129–30, 133, 136–38, 143, 148, 157–58, 165–68, 195, 206–7; pseudoethnographic collection practices for, 107–11, 116–17, 137–38, 246–47; of Scots, 225; of slang and vulgarisms, 107–27, 294n16; standardizing of English and, 147–48, 161–62
Dictionarium Britannicum (Bailey), 11, 137, 187
Dictionary of the English Language

(Johnson), 273n1; on cant and colloquialisms, 44; exclusions of vulgar, provincial, and technical language from, 120, 146, 246–48; serialization of, 1; on strangeness of modern English, 2
Dictionary of the Older Scottish Tongue, 36
"Directions for Sea-Men, Bound for Far Voyages" (Royal Society), 240–41, 247
Disraeli, Benjamin, 123
"Dissertation on the Oral Tradition of Poetry," 161
Doody, Margaret, 14, 19, 146, 148
Douglas, Gavin, 224
Dryden, John, 203, 239–40, 244, 263
Duck, Stephen, 148
Dugaw, Diane, 291n30
Duncan, Ian, 217
d'Urfey, Thomas, 103
Dyer, Gary, 295n76

Eagleton, Terry, 60
"Eclogue the Third" (Chatterton), 220–21
Edgeworth, Maria, 115–16, 189–91, 294n48, 308nn95–96
Egan, Pierce, 110, 123, 293n15
Ehrenpreis, Irving, 165
An Election Ball . . . in Zomerzetshire Dialect (Anstey), 149–50, 169, 205
Elegy Written in a Country Churchyard (Gray), 212
Elfenbein, Andrew, 148, 203, 310n54, 313n117
Ellis, Henry, 208
Empson, William, 38, 74; on *The Beggar's Opera*, 100; on fading of the pastoral, 94, 99, 169, 291n37, 292n40; on pastoral inclusiveness, 91–92, 171–72
Encyclopædia Britannica, 160–61, 310n40
English. *See* standardizing English; vernacular English
English Dialect Dictionary, 36
English Expositor (Bullokar), 133
English Villainies (Dekker), 119–20
Enlightenment Orientalism, 5–6
Enquiry (Burke), 159–60
Equiano, Olaudah, 234, 258–59, 318n92
An Essay Concerning Human Understanding (Locke), 285n114

Essay on Irish Bulls (Edgeworth), 115–16
Estabrook, Carl, 298n35, 307n88, 311n67
estranging. *See* strangeness and estranging
Etymological Dictionary of the Scottish Language (Jamieson), 225
euphemism (def.), 113–14
Evelina (Burney), 16
"An Excelente Balade of Charitie" (Chatterton), 221
An Exmoor Scolding (Brice), 153–55, 158, 164–65, 186–87, 218, 302n106; authenticity claims for, 201; foreign etymologies of words in, 198; on vulgar provincial language, 193–94, 308n6

Fairer, David, 203, 310n48
Falconer, William: maritime dictionary of, 1, 232, 235–36, 241, 268, 316n42; popular poetry of, 1, 10, 21, 232, 262–69, 319n107, 319nn111–12; on technical maritime language, 242
Faller, Lincoln, 39, 66–67, 69
Falstaff (character), 39–40
Featherstone, Mike, 314n8
Ferguson, Adam, 161
Fergusson, Robert, 176
Ferris, Ina, 195, 304n2
fiction. *See* realist fiction
Fielding, Henry, 18–19, 22, 282n58; on Britain's maritime identity, 237; burlesque humor of, 106–7; defining of terms by, 59; on figurative language, 114; maritime language of, 250; on maritime life, 255–56, 315n17; provincial language of, 181–82, 298n35, 306n62; satire of vernacular mash-ups by, 103–5, 108, 113–14; on transatlantic transport, 290n8. See also *Jonathan Wild*; *Tom Jones*
Fielding, Penny, 130, 226
Fisher, Anne, 147, 301n86
flash, 113, 122
Fletcher, John, 37–38
Fliegelman, Jay, 201
Foote, Samuel, 251–52
Fox, Adam, 133, 135, 197
Frank, Judith, 123–24, 280n33, 281n42
The Fraternitye of Vacabondes, 125
Freedgood, Elaine, 239

Freedom, A Poem (Brice), 174–75
Freeman, Lisa, 95–96, 291n35
French neoclassical principles, 13
Fuller, Thomas, 277n77
Fumerton, Patricia, 36, 278n1(ch1)

Gallagher, Catherine, 71, 73, 260
Gatrell, Vic, 123
Gay, John, 7–10, 19, 22–23, 86–105, 290nn10–11; burlesque humor of, 106–7; canting criminals of, 40, 90–91, 94–99, 291nn29–30; Devon origins of, 185; on independence, 100; invented language of, 221; on nationalist language, 185; satire of the pastoral by, 91–94, 97–99, 170, 182–85, 290n20, 307n67; satire of vernacular mash-ups by, 99–105; strategic uses of obscurity by, 182–85; on transatlantic movement, 88–90, 290n5. See also *The Beggar's Opera*; *Polly*; *The Shepherd's Week*
Geddes, Alexander, 224–25
gendered language, 119, 122–27, 129. *See also* slang
A General History of the Lives and Adventures of the Most Famous Highwaymen, . . . (Johnson), 39–40
General History of the Pirates, 256
A General Hystory of the Pyrates (Chetwood), 242–43
The Gentlemen's Magazine, 148, 153, 204, 211
The Gentle Shepherd (Ramsay), 305n20
Geoffrey of Monmouth, 297n1
George III, King of England, 187–89, 308n92
Georgic forms, 7, 21, 93, 148, 169
Gidal, Eric, 144, 187, 198–200, 298n17, 307n90
Gil, Alexander, 133
Gilje, Paul, 244, 261, 319n101, 319n104
Gilman, Tod, 290n10
Gladfelder, Hal, 287n34
glossaries. *See* dictionaries and glossaries
glossolalia, 31–32, 61, 105, 164
Godwin, William, 109
"Golden Pippins" (Amigoni), 7, 8f
Goldsmith, Oliver, 13, 15, 212–13, 229
Gorji, Mina, 169

Gothic writing, 23, 166; invocations of ancientness, haunting, and death in, 200–210, 213–14, 219–30, 256, 311n55; language of the Catholic Church and, 200. *See also* historicizing of provincial languages
grammar books, 1–2, 44, 147, 301n86
Grand Gazetteer (Brice), 174–78
Grand Repository of the English Language (Spence), 146
Gray, Thomas, 203, 212, 310nn51–52
Greene, Robert, 28, 279n7
Grose, Francis, 1, 3, 25, 83–84, 107–27; antique lexical authorities of, 119–20; Burns and, 223, 226, 228; comic view of vulgarity of, 111–14; Egan's biography of, 110, 293n15; explanatory apparatus of, 190; goals of *Classical Dictionary* of, 108–9, 112, 138; on innovative language and neologisms, 120–22; on maritime language, 255; on provincial languages, 133, 137–40, 150, 157–58, 165–66, 194, 196, 205, 207, 209–10, 312n87; pseudoethnographic practices of, 107–11; on slang and British freedom, 11, 107–8, 111, 114–19; sources of lexicon of, 116–17, 122–23. *See also Classical Dictionary of the Vulgar Tongue*; *Provincial Glossary*
Groundworke of Conny-Catching (Greene), 28, 279n7
A Guide to the Lakes (West), 138
Guillory, John, 11, 16
Gulliver's Travels (Swift), 247–49, 317n63
gypsies. *See* Roma travelers

Habermas, Jürgen, 273n9, 300n59
Hancock, Ian, 236
Hannerz, Ulf, 314n8
Hansen, Adam, 73, 74
Harding, James, 272n53
Harlequin Sheppard (Thurmond), 40–41
Harlot's Progress (anon.), 282n63
Harman, Thomas, 28, 30–31, 35–36, 50, 279n7, 280n25
Harris, James, 143–45, 157, 178–80, 197–98, 300n65
"Harry Howser," 260
Hart, John, 133, 134

"Harvest, or the Bashful Shepherd" (Relph), 168–71
Hay, Douglas, 118–19
Hazlitt, William, 276n62
Head, Richard, 28–30, 35, 45, 50, 125, 285n125
Heller-Roazen, Daniel, 29, 33, 112
Hermes (Harris), 144–45
heteroglossia: Bakhtin on, 17, 19, 74, 186–87, 277n79; Defoe's organization of, 59; in realist fiction, 17, 19, 58–59, 74, 277n79
Heywood, Thomas, 225–26, 229
Hilton, J. A., 176
historical philology, 138
historicizing of provincial languages, 131–32, 168–71, 191–230, 298n35, 299n44, 310n40; in Burns's representation of Scots, 219–20, 223–30; in Chatterton's Rowley poems, 219–23, 313n117; foreign sources of words and, 198–200; invented languages and, 221–23, 227–28; invocations of death and haunting in, 200–210, 227–30, 311n55; melancholia for the past and, 152, 204, 210–14; oscillating status of past and present in, 213–19; in Richardson's *Pamela*, 192–93; speakers as enigmatic anachronisms and, 204–10, 217, 225–26. *See also* provincial languages
History and Antiquities of the Counties of Westmorland and Cumberland, 206
History of English Poetry (Wharton), 310n54
The History of the Lives of the Most Noted Highway-Men, . . . (Smith), 39–40, 42, 282n61
Hobbes, Thomas, 62, 102
Hogg, James, 21
The Honest Yorkshire-Man (Carey), 312n91
Howell, James, 11, 53, 285n114
Hull, Thomas, 282n63
Hume, David, 13–14, 216, 237, 244
humor, 18, 22–23; in cant, 37, 67–68, 91–94, 106–7; in Gay's works, 91–94, 97–105, 111–15, 170, 182–85, 290n20, 307n67; in gendered slang, 123–27; of mariner's technical language, 249–52; in portrayals of provincial languages, 149–55, 163, 182–85, 189, 195, 210, 218–19, 227–29; in Swift's satire, 91, 93, 247–49, 290n16, 317n63
Hutton, William, 195–96, 204, 211
The Hye Way to the Spittal Hous (Copland), 31
"Hymn upon the Execution of Two Criminals" (Ramondon), 101, 102–3

imagined communities, 131, 200, 300n59
"Imperium Peelagi. A Naval Lyric" (Young), 240
Interesting Narrative (Equiano), 234, 258–59, 318n92
Introduction to Grammar (Lowth), 44
invented languages, 221–23, 227–28
Irish vernacular, 189–91, 308n96

Jack. *See Colonel Jack*
Jakobson, Roman, 16, 46, 48, 134
James II, King of England, 193
Jameson, Fredric, 95–96
Jamieson, John, 225
Johnson, Charles, 39–40
Johnson, Samuel, 1, 42, 273n1; on burlesque, 106; on colloquial language, 68; language collection practices of, 109, 246–47; on maritime life, 233, 255–56; on preservation of language, 120, 202; on pronunciation of provincialisms, 196, 204; on provincial language, 146, 148, 193–94, 198, 303n136; on the sovereignty of words, 53; on vulgar and technical language, 44, 120, 146, 246–48, 263
Jolly Jack Tar, 233, 260–61. *See also* maritime language
Jonathan Wild (Fielding), 103–5, 113–14, 290n8
Jones, Hugh, 134
Jonson, Ben, 203, 204
Joseph Andrews (Fielding), 59, 181
A Journey to London (Vanbrugh), 139
The Jovial Crew (Brome), 37–40, 51, 282n63, 291n30, 292n51

Kareem, Sarah, 16–17
Kaul, Suvir, 318nn89–90
Kazanjian, David, 37, 82, 85, 289n71
Keach, William, 53, 275n40

Kennett, White, 200
Kenrick, William, 180
Kermode, Frank, 290n20, 305n23
King, Moll, 125–26
King Lear (Shakespeare), 44, 299n48
Klein, Herbert S., 288n61
Knapp, Jeffrey, 28–29, 279n12, 280n22, 281n53, 284n101

laboring subcultures. *See* maritime language
language of place. *See* provincial languages
Lanthorne and Candle-Light (Dekker), 30–34
The Late Lancashire Witches (Heywood and Brome), 225–26
Leapor, Mary, 148
Leask, Nigel, 147, 170, 176, 223
Lectures on Elocution (Sheridan), 143, 161
letter-writing, 163
Lewis, Jayne, 99
Lexicon Balatronicum: Buckish Slang, University Wit, and Pickpocket Eloquence, 122–23, 125
The Life and Adventures of Bampfylde-Moore Carew (anon.), 110, 282n58
The Life and Character of Moll King, 125–26
Life in London (Egan), 123
Life's Painter of Variegated Colours (Parker), 108–9
Lindop, Grevel, 222
Linebaugh, Peter, 101, 117, 236, 295n52
Lives of the Highwaymen (Smith), 67
Lloyd, Evan, 194–95
Lock, Peter, 201
Locke, John: on euphemistic language, 113–14; on history of provincial languages, 196, 200–201; on making of liberal political subjects, 76–77, 256; on political society and language, 10–11, 53, 115, 158, 275n40, 285n114
Logonomia Anglica (Gil), 133
The London Spy (Ward), 5–7, 19, 56, 109
Looby, Christopher, 159, 201
Lowth, Robert, 44, 162
Lynch, Deidre, 76, 202, 287n45
Lyrical Ballads (Wordsworth), 185–86

Mack, Ruth, 216, 219
Mackie, Erin, 98
Macpherson, James, 217, 220
Makdisi, Saree, 2, 4–5
making strange. *See* strangeness and estranging
Manly, Susan, 145, 158, 181
maritime language, 4, 23–24, 231–72, 277n92, 314n1; Anglo-Saxon terms in, 236; articulation of British freedom and slavery in, 241, 254–59; crudeness of, 250–51; as denotative technical lexicon, 232–33, 238–46, 257–59, 316nn33–34; dictionaries and glossaries of, 232, 235, 242, 255, 316n42; estranging and comic depictions of, 246–54, 318nn72–73; explanatory footnotes for, 245, 253, 263–64, 266–70, 317n45; multilingual environment of, 234–38; obscurity and sublime impact of, 269–71; opacity of, 232, 239–40, 248–49; print representations of, 232–33, 238–46, 251–52; in published accounts of voyages, 240–42, 316nn33–34; Royal Society protocols for, 240–41, 247; vernacularization of, 245, 256–57, 259–72
Marshall, William, 139, 193, 195, 206–7
Marx, Karl, 38, 77
Matthews, William, 251
Mazzio, Carla, 65–66
McKeon, Michael, 170–71, 290n20
Meriton, George, 137, 141–42, 150, 157–58
The Merry Musician, 103
Mery Talys and Quicke Answeres, 150
Middleton, Thomas, 125
Milton, John, 179, 316n26
"Minute and Copious Analysis of the Dialect of Bedfordshire" (Batchelor), 138
A Miscellany of Poems (Relph), 168–72
Mitchell, J., 202
The Mobiad, or the Battle of the Voice (Brice), 175–76, 186–88
modern capitalism, 84–85, 289n71
Moll Flanders (Defoe), 60–85; encounters with racialized slavery in, 79–85, 88, 289n67; fictional rhetorical spaces of characters of, 71–73; gendered reader relations of, 126–27; incest taboos and, 289n67; intermingling of low languages in, 61–66, 114, 287n27; lan-

guage of physical blackness in, 80, 83;
as liberal political subject, 75–78; maritime language in, 254–55; polyglot first-person narrators of, 67–71, 73, 90, 108, 142, 290n9; provincial language in, 142; readers' affiliations to characters of, 73–76, 287n45; sexualized sense of "conversation" in, 68–69, 287n38; unknown real name of protagonist of, 74, 287n44
Monboddo, James Burnett, Lord, 145
The Monthly Review, 268
Morgan, Gwenda, 79–80
Mr. Penrose: The Journal of Penrose, Seaman (Williams), 235
Mr. Spectator (Addison), 12, 14–15, 276n65, 283n72
Mulholland, James, 303n134, 310n52
Mutiny on the Bounty (Nordhoff and Hall), 236–37

nationalism, 17–18. *See also* cultural nationalism
national vernacular. *See* vernacular English
Needler, Henry, 258
Neuman, Henry, 238
A New Academy of Compliments, 163, 171–72, 304n138
New Canting Dictionary (NCD), 3, 25, 34, 45–46, 278n2; anonymous author of, 110; familiar English terms in, 50–51; gendered reader relations of, 126; moral impugning of vulgarity of cant in, 50, 51, 87; "Songs in the Canting Dialect" in, 284n98
New Dictionary of the Terms . . . of the Canting Crew (ND) (B. E.), 25, 45–56, 100, 278n1; on beggars and vagabonds, 44, 51–56, 77; on cant's origins in slavery and linguistic freedom, 51–56, 75–85, 87, 115–16, 284n105; mysterious author of, 110; on the origins of proverbs, 54; terms for bodies in, 80
A New Grammar (Fisher), 147, 301n86
New London Spy, 109
Newman, Steve, 90, 103, 291n35, 305n20
A New Voyage round the World (Dampier), 241–42, 247, 316n34
Nicholson, William, 136–37

Nicol, George, 130
noise, 2, 6, 29–36, 55; of glossolalia, 31–32, 61, 105, 164; of mariner's language, 251–52; of provincial otherness, 164, 175; of the third man, 35, 58, 100, 117, 274n14. *See also* cant
Nord, Deborah Epstein, 279n7
The Northerne Lass (Brome), 152
Norton, Rictor, 280n33
nose, 50

Observations on Popular Antiquities (Brand), 208–9
Observations on the Scottish Dialect (Rennie), 225
occupational language, 4. *See also* maritime language
Okun, Peter, 81
Oliver Twist (Dickens), 5, 109
"On the late Captain Grose's Peregrinations thro' Scotland . . . " (Burns), 223
The Origin of the Newcastle Burr (Dawes), 134, 151
Oroonoko (Behn), 81–82, 244
Orpheus, 9–10, 265, 274n35, 275n38
An Orthoëpical Analysis of the English Language (Batchelor), 138
Oxford English Dictionary, 283n75

Palmer, Mary, 191, 213–15, 221, 223
Pamela (Richardson), 16; blandness of standardized English in, 146; plea for common language in, 59–60; provincial language of, 142–43, 146, 152–53, 172, 299n48; temporal remoteness of, 192–93
Parker, George, 6, 14, 15, 56, 108–27, 217, 294n16; on custom and innovation in language, 120–22; explanatory apparatus of, 190; on his audience, 112, 125; pseudoethnographic practices of, 109–11; on slang, 111–14; sources of lexicon of, 116–17, 122–23. *See also* slang
Parochial Antiquities of Places in the Counties of Oxford with Glossary (Kennett), 200
the pastoral: commodification in print of, 171–74; Gay's satire of, 90–94, 97–99, 170, 182–85, 290n20, 307n67; in Relph's poetry, 168–72

"Pastoral Ballad" (Pope), 149
Patterson, Annabel, 169, 170, 176, 285n119
Paulson, Ronald, 68
Pegge, Samuel, 3, 146, 195–98, 204, 238, 303n125
Percy, Thomas, 201
Persuasion (Austen), 262
Philips, Ambrose, 92–93, 170, 182–83, 303n136
Philosophical Enquiry (Burke), 20, 261
Pills to Purge the Melancholy (d'Urfey), 103
pirate narratives, 242–43, 256, 317n45
Place, Francis, 296n86
Plain Dealer (Wycherley), 239, 250
Plan of an English Dictionary (Johnson), 53
Platt, Joan, 43
Plautus, 54–56, 82
The Pleasant History of . . . Jack of Newbury (Deloney), 193
The Pleasant History of John Winchcomb (Deloney), 142, 299n46
Pleasures of the Imagination (Brewer), 148
Poems, Chiefly in the Scottish Dialect (Burns), 226–27
Polly (Gay), 88–90, 106–7
"Poor Jack," 260
Pope, Alexander, 91, 93, 148–49, 308n10; Gay's satire of, 307n67; on provincial language, 169–70; on technical language, 263
The Post-Captain (Davis), 250–54, 261–62, 268
The Praise of York-Shire Ale (Meriton), 137, 141–42, 150, 157–58, 167–68
Price, Leah, 291n33
Prickett, Stephen, 309n27
pronunciation guides, 226; for provincial languages, 134, 146, 169, 226; for standardizing of English, 147, 161–62
proverbs, 45–51, 54, 285n115, 285n119; in Defoe's works, 62–63; in Gay's *The Beggar's Opera*, 90–93, 98–105; Meriton's collection of, 141–42; Ray's collection of, 48–49, 104–5
Provincial Glossary (Grose), 133, 137, 138–40; on comedic terms, 150; critical review of, 210, 312n87; on ghostly themes, 207, 209–10; Grose's goals for, 138–40; historical sources of terms in, 194, 196; particularities in, 157–58, 165–66
"The Provincial Idiom" (Wheeler), 215
provincial languages, 3–5, 22–23, 129–32, 296n3, 297n1; association with common people of, 138–43; authenticity signified by, 167–68; comedic use and embodied bawdiness of, 148–56; commodification and commercial appeal of, 171–74, 305n20, 305n23; common hostility towards, 134–36, 169–70, 297n8, 298n17, 298n29; critical response to, 148–49; definition of, 129; dictionaries and glossaries of, 129–30, 133, 136–38, 143, 148, 157–58, 165–68, 195, 206–7, 226–27; explanatory apparatus for, 167, 175, 183–84, 189–90, 308n96; foreign words in, 198–200; historical philology and, 138; historicizing of, 131–32, 168–71, 191–230, 298n35, 299n44; intralingual translation among, 134, 305n15; as language of the home, 135–36; vs. London idiolects, 194–97, 308n10; naming of particulars in, 144–45, 157–59, 165, 170, 196, 302n115; opaque diversity of, 178–80, 306n43; as performance, 142–43, 299n48; phonetic spelling and punctuation of, 169, 170–71, 174, 215–16; political context of, 174–78, 306n38; print representations of oral voicing of, 159–66, 303n136; pronunciation guides for, 134, 169, 226; pseudoethnography in collecting of, 137–38; relationship between language and nation and, 143–48, 160–61, 300n56, 300n65, 300n76; in Relph's pastoral poetry, 168–72; Scots as, 223–26; as sentimental sites of female virtue, 152–53, 301n86; spatial remoteness of, 131–32, 140–41, 161, 180–92; strange familiarity of, 165–66; strategic linguistic obscurity of, 180–91, 306n62
The Provok'd Husband (Cibber), 139
pseudoethnography, 18–19, 60, 246–47; in collections of provincial language, 137–38; in collections of slang, 107–11, 116–17; in realist fiction, 18–19, 60, 107, 109–10

INDEX [331]

racialized slavery, 22, 79–85, 88, 115–16, 289n65; embodied status of, 80, 116, 288n64; in Gay's *The Beggar's Opera*, 89–90; in maritime narratives, 256–59; white indentured servitude and, 84–85, 288n61
Radcliffe, Ann, 304n148
Ragussis, Michael, 299n48
Ramondon, Lewis, 102–3
Ramsay, Allan, 176, 224–25, 298n23, 305n20
Rancière, Jacques, 15, 141, 143
Ray, John, 48–49, 104–5, 136–40, 143, 165, 178, 184
realist fiction, 16–20, 276nn62–63; cant-speaking characters of, 22, 57–85, 58–85, 286n9, 287n49, 291n29; male authorship of, 287n38; maritime language in, 245–46, 250, 253–55, 257, 259–62; negotiation of stranger relationality in, 58–60; provincial languages in, 142–43, 146, 152–53, 163–64, 172, 181–82, 192–94, 298n35, 299n48, 306n62; pseudoethnographic techniques of, 18–19, 60, 107, 109–10; role in shaping the nation of, 57–60, 108; slang in, 22, 106–7; temporal structure of, 95–96, 291n33. *See also* historicizing of provincial languages
Rediker, Marcus, 236, 255
Reed, Peter, 89
"The Reeve's Tale" (Chaucer), 139
regional language. *See* provincial languages
The Regulator of 1718, 87
Relph, Josiah, 10, 23, 202, 204, 214, 217; invented language of, 221; pastoral poetry of, 168–72
Rennie, Susan, 225
The Reprisal (Smollett), 234, 238
Restitutions of Decayed Intelligence (Verstegan), 197
Reynolds, Bryan, 39, 281n45, 282n59
Richardson, John, 101, 172
Richardson, Samuel, 16, 59; plea for common language by, 59–60; provincial language used by, 142–43, 146. See also *Pamela*
Richetti, John, 60

Rime of the Ancient Mariner (Coleridge), 256
Ritson, Isaac, 205–6
Ritson, Joseph, 201, 203–4, 224
Rivero, Albert, 61, 62
Roach, Joseph, 202–3
Roaring Girl (Dekker and Middleton), 125
Robbins, Bruce, 166, 209, 231, 314n8
Roberts, Captain, 243
Robertson, William, 147, 162
Robinson Crusoe (Defoe), 243–46, 257
Roderick Random (Smollett), 16, 24, 59, 238; maritime language in, 245–46, 250, 253–54, 257, 259–62; provincial languages in, 163–64, 181
Rodger, N. A. M., 237
Rogers, Nicholas, 118–19
Roma travelers, 28, 279n7, 282n55, 282n58, 284n105
Rowland, Ann Wierda, 21
The Royal Merchant (Hull), 282n63
The Royal Visit to Exeter, a Poetical Epistle by John Ploughshare, 187–89, 308n91
Ruddiman, Thomas, 224
Rushton, Peter, 79–80
Russell, Gillian, 260–61
Russell, W. Clark, 317n63

"Sailor's Ballad," 260, 318n96
sailors' language. *See* maritime language
Schiller, Friedrich, 34, 280n30
Schmidgen, Wolfram, 14
Schmidt, Leigh Eric, 162
Schmitt, Cannon, 239
Schor, Esther, 210, 212
Schulz, Peter, 290n11
Scotland: Burns's representation of language of, 223–29; commodified pastoral of, 305n20; dance and music culture of, 229; diglossia of, 147, 276n63; Enlightenment historiography of, 205–7, 217; preservation of English in, 161–62, 224, 225, 303nn124–25; spoken dialect of, 161–62, 223–24; Union with England of, 223–24; vernacular poets of, 190–91
Scottish National Dictionary, 36
The Scoundrels Dictionary, 289n4

Sea Grammar (Smith), 238–39
"A Sea Piece" (Needler), 258
Second Treatise on Government (Locke), 76–77
Sedgwick, Eve Kosofsky, 124
Segrais, Jean Regnault de, 114
Serres, Michel: on consolidation of noise, 55, 58; on outsider interlocutors, 36, 274n14; on the third man, 35, 58, 100, 117
Seward, Anne, 148
Shaftesbury, Anthony Ashley Cooper, Lord, 12, 265n59
Shakespeare, William, 12–13, 23, 44, 54; critical revaluation of, 203–4, 310n51; Falstaff character of, 39–40; provincial language use by, 148, 297n13, 299n48; Voltaire's attack on, 13
Shapin, Steven, 145, 158, 242
The Shepheardes Calendar (Spenser), 148–49, 203, 303n136
The Shepherd's Week (Gay), 170, 182–85, 307n67
Sheridan, Thomas, 143, 146, 161
Shesgreen, Sean, 7, 274n30, 275n36
The Shipwreck (Falconer), 1, 10, 21, 24, 262–69; affective technical language of, 263–69; obscurity and the sublime in, 232, 269–71; popularity and influence of, 262–63, 268–69, 319n107, 319nn111–12
Shklovsky, Viktor, 15–16, 141, 166, 265n71, 299n44
Silverman, Kaja, 152–53
Simpson, David, 2, 134, 136, 146, 167, 300n65
Sinclair, John, 224
Sir Gawain and the Green Knight, 62
slang, 2–4, 14, 21–22, 106–27; as articulation of British freedom, 11, 107–8, 111, 114–19; criminal outsiders and, 116–18; dictionaries and glossaries of, 107, 294n16; gendered and sexual nature of, 119, 122–27, 129; neologisms in, 120–22; pseudoethnography in collecting of, 107–11, 116–17; in realist fiction, 22, 106–7; transformation to from cant to, 106–8; witty euphemism and metaphor in, 111–14. *See also* Grose, Francis; Parker, George

slavery. *See* racialized slavery
Smith, Adam, 122, 217, 270; on language development, 253, 260, 318n72; on rustic particularism, 144–45, 157, 196; on sympathetic exchange, 264–65, 267–68
Smith, Alexander, 39–40, 42, 67, 282n61
Smith, John, 238–39
Smith, Olivia, 11
Smollett, Tobias, 16, 24, 59, 108, 194; defining of terms by, 59; maritime narratives of, 231, 234, 245–46, 248, 250, 253–54, 257, 259–62, 314n3; provincial characters of, 139, 151–52, 238; provincial language use of, 163–64, 181
social vernaculars, 21–22. *See also* vernacular English
sound, 2–9, 25–41, 159–60, 274n21. *See also* cant; noise
spatial remoteness of provincial languages, 131–32, 140–41, 161, 180–92, 198–200
Spence, Thomas, 134, 161
Spenser, Edmund, 23, 303n136; critical revaluation of, 203; Gay's satire of, 183; provincial language use by, 148–49, 170, 222, 297n13
Stallybrass, Peter, 146
standardizing English, 1–2, 273n1, 273n8; class implications of, 1; dictionaries, grammars, and pronunciation guides of, 147–48, 161–62, 301n86; in the eighteenth century, 42–44, 63–64, 125–26; fastidious scholarly writing and, 43–44; incorporation of outsider sounds and languages into, 2–5, 274n21; as model of national polity and liberty, 10–11, 13–15, 143–48, 157, 265n67, 276n59, 300n59, 300n65, 300n76; naming of sensible particulars in, 144–45; neutral objectivity of, 15–16; official policies on, 308n92; print technology and, 144, 147–48, 157, 159–65, 300n59, 303n136; in Scotland, 147, 276n63. *See also* dictionaries and glossaries
Starr, George, 138
Steedman, Carolyn, 209, 211
Steinfeld, Robert, 288n53, 288n56
Stewart, Susan, 201, 212

strangeness and estranging, 2–21, 269–72; Britain's nation-making among strangers and, 49–50, 58, 130–31; early cant and, 26; foreign etymologies of words and, 198–200; in invocations of death by provincial languages, 200–204, 206–10; "low" and "outsider" relationality in, 7–16, 86, 141–48, 274n30, 274–75nn35–36; of maritime language, 246–54; markers of speech of, 7; print representations of, 4–7, 274n21; of provincial languages, 165–66, 193–94, 198–204. *See also* dictionaries and glossaries; realist fiction

Street Robberies Consider'd (att. Defoe), 69–70

the sublime, 20–21, 178–80, 269–71

Swann, Karen, 20, 180

Swift, Jonathan, 194; satire of maritime language by, 247–49, 317n63; satire of the pastoral by, 91, 93, 290n16; on uses of cant, 43–44

Tam o' Shanter (Burns), 6
"Tam o' Shanter" (Burns), 6, 226–29
Teach, Captain (Blackbeard), 243
technical jargon. *See* maritime language
temporal remoteness. *See* historicizing of provincial languages
Thomas, Pascoe, 235–37
Thomas and Sally, 261
Thompson, E. P., 120–21
Thomson, James, 115, 233, 258
Thornton, Sarah, 280n33
Thurmond, John, 40–41
Tickell, Thomas, 93
Tiffany, Daniel, 4, 20; on aesthetic impact of cant, 277n90; on derivation of "vernacular," 54–55; on obscurity of demotic speech, 180, 190; on sentimental impact of cant, 33–34, 280n30; on synthetic vernaculars, 184–84
Todd, Dennis, 79, 80
Tom Bowling (character). See *Roderick Random*
"Tom Bowling" (Dibdin), 261
Tom Jones (Fielding), 18–19, 181–82, 282n58, 298n35, 306n62
Tooke, John Horne, 197
Torok, Maria, 212

A Tour of Ireland (Chetwood), 139
Tour thro' the Whole Island of Great Britain (Defoe), 135–36, 138, 298n29
Townley, Richard, 153–54
travelers. *See* Roma travelers
Trevisa, John, 297n8
A Trip to Calais (Foote), 251–52
A Trip to Jamaica (Ward), 249–51
Tristram Shandy (Sterne), 261–62
The Triumph of Wit, 40
Trivia (Gay), 7–10, 87
"True Born Englishman" (Defoe), 306n43
"The True-Born Englishman" (Defoe), 131
Trumpener, Katie, 201
"Truth in a Mask" (Collier), 219
Tucker, Susie, 44
"Two Children in the Wood," 13

the uncanny, 9, 23; antiquarianism and ancient hauntings in, 131, 166, 222–26; slavery and, 67
A Universal Dictionary of the Marine (Falconer), 232, 268, 316n42; foreign language terms in, 235–36; on maritime journals, 241
An Universal Etymological Dictionary (Bailey), 48–49, 77

Vanbrugh, John, 139
venereal disease, 111–12
vernacular (as term), 11–13, 275n44; Addison's use of, 13; Bailey's definition of, 11, 13; links to slavery of, 54–55
vernacular English, 1–21; common origins of, 2–5, 274–75nn35–36, 274n21, 274n30; dictionaries of, 57; double duty of, 11–12, 26; embodied voice of, 159–66, 201; estranging distance in, 7–16, 86, 141–48, 269–72, 274n30, 274–75nn35–36; foreign language sources of, 133; opacity of meaning in, 49–50; print representations of, 2, 4–7, 159–65, 274n14, 274n21, 303n136; proximity to slavery of, 22, 54–56, 101, 256–57; sublime effects of, 20–21, 178–80, 269–70; written markers of, 7, 19. *See also* cant; maritime language; provincial languages; slang
Vernon, James, 2
Verstegan, Richard, 197

A View of Society and Manners in High and Low Life (Parker), 56, 108–9
A View of the Lancashire Dialect (Collier), 130, 153–55, 156*f*, 164–65, 172–78, 187, 197; on commercial print markets, 214; critical response to, 217; foreign etymologies of words in, 198, 199*f*
A Vocabulary of Sea Phrases, 316n42
voice, 159–66, 201
Voltaire, 13
Von Uffenbach, Zacharias Conrad, 274n30
Voyage round the World (Anson), 241
Voyages . . . of Captain R. Falconer (Chetwood), 244–45, 256
Voyages . . . of Captain Robert Boyle (Chetwood), 244–45
vulgar tongue. *See* slang

Wakelin, Martyn, 21–22
Wales, Katie, 150
Walker, John, 147
Wall, Cynthia, 286n23
Walpole, Horace, 12–13, 166, 180, 219
Walpole, Robert, 52, 92, 174–75
Ward, Ned, 5–7, 19, 109, 232–34, 249–54, 260
Warner, Michael, 2, 49–50, 58, 130, 144
Warner, William, 57
Watson, John, 204
Watt, Ian, 243, 286n9

West, Benjamin, 203, 310n51
West, Thomas, 138
Westmoreland Dialect in Three Familiar Dialogues (Wheeler), 214–19
Wharton, Thomas, 203, 310n54
Wheeler, Ann, 23, 191, 214–19, 217, 221
Wheeler, Roxann, 52, 84, 288n56, 289n65
Whitaker, John, 195, 309n15
White, Allon, 45, 58–59, 146, 281n48
Wilkes, John, 176
Wilkins, Bishop, 194
Williams, Raymond, 43, 193, 209, 275n42, 283n75
Williams, William, 235
Wilson, Kathleen, 14, 144, 148, 174–78, 208, 306n38
Wilson, Thomas, 134–35
Winchcombe, John, 299n46
wit. *See* humor
Woodbridge, Linda, 278n1(ch1)
The Wooden World Dissected (Ward), 249–50, 252–53
Wordsworth, William, 185–86
Wuthering Heights (Brontë), 5
Wycherley, William, 239, 250

York Spy (Bland), 5, 274n27
Young, Edward, 240. *See also* maritime language

"Zomerzetshire Dialect" (Anstey), 149–50, 169, 205

A NOTE ON THE TYPE

THIS BOOK has been composed in Miller, a Scotch Roman typeface designed by Matthew Carter and first released by Font Bureau in 1997. It resembles Monticello, the typeface developed for The Papers of Thomas Jefferson in the 1940s by C. H. Griffith and P. J. Conkwright and reinterpreted in digital form by Carter in 2003.

Pleasant Jefferson ("P. J.") Conkwright (1905–86) was Typographer at Princeton University Press from 1939 to 1970. He was an acclaimed book designer and AIGA Medalist.

The ornament used throughout this book was designed by Pierre Simon Fournier (1712–68) and was a favorite of Conkwright's, used in his design of the Princeton University Library Chronicle.

GPSR Authorized Representative: Easy Access System Europe - Mustamäe tee
50, 10621 Tallinn, Estonia, gpsr.requests@easproject.com

www.ingramcontent.com/pod-product-compliance
Lightning Source LLC
Chambersburg PA
CBHW030605230426
43661CB00053B/1856